C000246291

— *Korea* —

KOREA

A History

EUGENE Y. PARK

STANFORD UNIVERSITY PRESS
Stanford, California

STANFORD UNIVERSITY PRESS
Stanford, California

© 2022 by Eugene Youngjin Park. All rights reserved.

No part of this book may be reproduced or transmitted in any form or by any means, electronic or mechanical, including photocopying and recording, or in any information storage or retrieval system without the prior written permission of Stanford University Press.

Printed and bound by CPI Group (UK) Ltd, Croydon, CR0 4YY

Library of Congress Cataloging-in-Publication Data
Names: Park, Eugene Y., author.
Title: Korea : a history / Eugene Y. Park.
Description: Stanford, California : Stanford University Press, 2022. |
    Includes bibliographical references and index.
Identifiers: LCCN 2021050028 (print) | LCCN 2021050029 (ebook) |
    ISBN 9781503629462 (cloth) | ISBN 9781503629844 (paperback) |
    ISBN 9781503629851 (epub)
Subjects: LCSH: Korea--History.
Classification: LCC DS907.18 .P465 2022 (print) | LCC DS907.18 (ebook) |
    DDC 951.9--dc23/eng/20211013
LC record available at https://lccn.loc.gov/2021050028
LC ebook record available at https://lccn.loc.gov/2021050029

Cover art. Untitled Korean landscape painting by Jo Jung Ae (1936–2017), September 2002. Source: Possession of Lyu Myung Seok. Photo © Lyu Myung Seok 2021.

Text design: Kevin Barrett Kane

Typeset at Stanford University Press in Centaur MT Pro

To J*OHN* B. D*UNCAN*

CONTENTS

FIGURES, TABLE, AND MAPS

FIGURES

PREFACE

This is a history of Korean civilization from early times to December 2020. For many English speakers, "Korea" evokes North Korea's nuclear weapon and ballistic missile programs. Unable to locate Korea readily on a world map, many look for it in Southeast Asia, understanding (East) "Asia" as China and Japan. Lost in the middle of the binary of North Korea and China versus America and its ally Japan is South Korea. Its global brands such as Hyundai, Samsung, and LG have gained a presence in many people's daily lives—though only a minority are aware of their provenance, and corporate South Korea prefers this over trumpeting "Made in Korea." What else a reader may know depends on age and background. For some, the Korean War (1950–53), the Third World, poverty, and communism come to mind, whereas a growing number of teenagers and young adults are fans of K-pop; and more people in general seem to be discovering Korean cuisine, although it lags behind Chinese, Japanese, Thai, and Vietnamese food in popular appeal. Regardless, most would profess ignorance about Korea's recorded history of some two millennia.

This book engages readers who seek a balanced, comprehensive overview of Korean history. Above all, the book conforms with successful surveys of China or Japan that pay due respect to the premodern period, rather than highlighting East Asia's relevance to America. In addition, the chapters are grouped according to a four-part periodization that puts Korean history in a global context: classical (ancient, antiquity), post-classical (medieval), early modern, and "late" modern periods. This scheme reflects the fact that in sedentary, literate societies of Afro-Eurasia, where writing systems historically facilitated political legitimation and identity formation, the beginnings of continuous, reliable patrilineal genealogies of the aristocracy, the middle class, and the rest of the population (as of 1900) mark the beginnings of the post-classical, the early modern, and the late modern eras, respectively. The ongoing Descent from Antiquity project among genealogists seeks to trace individual living persons' genealogy to antiquity. Finally, this book attempts to give more attention to Korea's less-known historical groups, its ethnic minorities, its LGBT groups, and its citizens' daily lives than has been the practice in the past. My effort will nonetheless surely fall short, and I look forward to readers' feedback.

I owe thanks to numerous individuals, too many to mention, cite, or quote in a textbook such as this. Still, I wish to call out Jong Chol An, Chris Atwood, Don Baker, Remco Breuker, Mark Byington, Mark Caprio, Jacques deLisle, Martina Deuchler, Alexis Dudden, Seunghyun Han, Femida Handy, Kim Hyeon, Nan Kim, Ross King, Peter Kwon, Seung Kye, Ilhyung Lee, Jay Lewis, Yung Hian Ng, Oh Soo-Chang, Sangjin Park, Mike Pettid, Nikki Pumphrey, Ned Shultz, Song Ki-Ho, Nancy Steinhardt, Holly Stephens, Etsuro Totsuka, Sem Vermeersch, Boudewijn Walraven, Anne Walthall, Sixiang Wang, Yang Jin-Suk, and Yi Tae-Jin, and also my mentor John Duncan, to whom I dedicate this book. Nonetheless, the Further Readings section acknowledges English-language books that are suitable for general readers who wish to explore Korean history in more depth. I also want to thank Marcela Maxfield for giving full consideration to my book proposal. And as ever, I am indebted to my wife, Seri, and our children, Lauren and Harry, as we continue to learn from one another and grow (old) together.

Eugene Y. Park
Reno, Nevada

CONVENTIONS

This book generally employs the Pinyin, Revised Hepburn, and McCune-Reischauer systems to romanize Chinese, Japanese, and Korean, respectively. Exceptions include such alternative spellings as "Seoul" that have become widely known and contemporary South Korean proper nouns, especially those mentioned in the final chapter. Likewise, for the sake of better recognition, colonial Korea's local place names are given in Korean pronunciation, even though the official language at the time was Japanese. Whenever a Korean term in an alternative spelling appears for the first time, the McCune-Reischauer version follows in parentheses. It may be helpful for readers to know that for the most part, English-language Wikipedia automatically converts the McCune-Reischauer spelling of a search term—with or without diacritical marks and apostrophes—to the Revised Romanization of Korean spelling used in South Korea (for example, Inch'ŏn is converted to Incheon), unless the word has to do with North Korea. North Korea generally uses McCune-Reischauer spellings, without diacritical marks or apostrophes (for example, Pyongyang instead of P'yŏngyang). Regardless, all personal names, except Western ones, have the family name first, if known. And while keeping romanized East Asian terms to a minimum, existing English translations are used as much as possible.

To the extent that these dates are readily searchable on the World Wide Web, the text provides the birth and death years of an individual and the beginning and ending dates of an entity when first mentioned. Unless noted otherwise, all East Asian dates before the late nineteenth century follow the lunar calendar, which was the standard in Korea until the government adopted the Gregorian solar calendar on the seventeenth day of the eleventh moon of 1895, or New Year's Day of 1896, according to the solar calendar.

Traditional East Asian custom regards a newborn to be one *se* (Ch. *sui*; Ja. *sai*) in age, subsequently gaining a year on each lunar new year. Accordingly, one's age in *se* is always one or two years greater than one's solar calendar age.

Aside from acronyms explained in the text or well-known, the following abbreviations are used:

b.	born
BCE	before the Common Era
c.	circa
CE	Common Era
Ch.	Chinese
d.	died
fl.	*floruit*, flourished
Ja.	Japanese
Ko.	Korean
r.	*rexit*, reigned
trad.	traditional date
YBP	years before present
+	or later

— Korea —

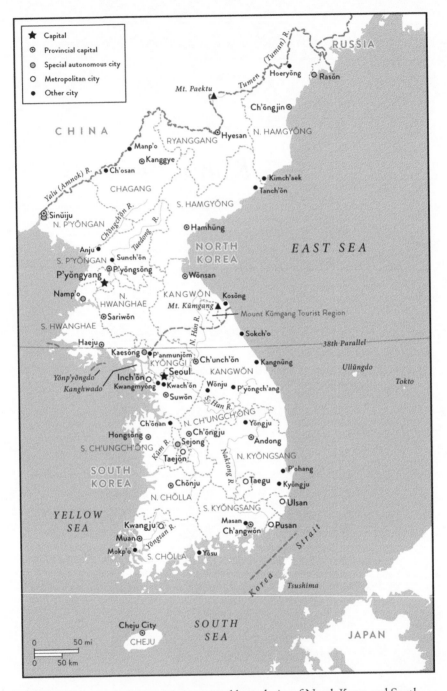

MAP I.1   Major administrative centers and boundaries of North Korea and South Korea as of 2020.

Introduction

The Korean Peninsula is an average-sized historical region in the world. On a landmass about as large as Britain, the recorded history of a distinct civilization, its languages, and the ancestors of some 85 million modern-day Koreans has unfolded for some 2,300 years. Already in the tenth century, a united monarchy had arisen, which, for the most part, enjoyed autonomy for a millennium. Only in the late modern era did Korea suffer prolonged foreign domination and political division. Japan occupied Korea from 1910 to 1945; thereafter, the United States and the Soviet Union divided and occupied Korea for three years. Since 1948, two rival states have coexisted: the Republic of Korea and the Democratic People's Republic of Korea, better known as South Korea and North Korea (Map I.1). Since the devastating Korean War, North Korea has become an isolated totalitarian state. By contrast, South Korea has emerged as a vibrant democracy that is a significant player in the global political economy.

Thinking of (East) "Asia" as just China and Japan is a legacy of turn-of-the-twentieth-century colonialism. Before the impact of Western imperialism in the nineteenth century, China had been eastern Eurasia's most influential civilization for some three millennia. Such neighboring lands as Japan, Korea, and Vietnam were participants in a distinct civilization whose epicenter was in historical China proper, which was far smaller than today's People's Republic of China (PRC), roughly the size of Europe or the United

States. As the world's longest continuing literate civilization, China has far outlived Rome, its western Eurasian contemporary during the classical period. By contrast, Japan's prominence is a relatively recent phenomenon in global history, thanks to that archipelago nation's reinvention of itself a century ago as a colonial power. Distinct from Northeast Asia, comprising China, Japan, Korea, and Taiwan, Southeast Asia is a region where, culturally and historically, Chinese influence was strong in Vietnam, and, farther west in the area, Indian influence from South Asia was stronger. To the north is Central Asia, or Inner Asia, an area from which various Turko-Mongolian groups shaped developments elsewhere in Eurasia throughout history. And predominantly Muslim Southwest Asia and, in Africa, Egypt constitute the Middle East, where South Korea has played a significant role since the 1970s in the region's infrastructure development. And among these Middle Eastern counties, Iran also maintains close relations with North Korea.

Considering Korea's importance in the global political economy, its past and present remain poorly understood, even among highly educated Westerners. For most native Anglophones, whose world view still reflects colonialism, the mainstream news media—interested mostly in the West, Russia, the Middle East, China, and Japan—offer only narrow, unbalanced coverage of Korea. One example of this is that North Korea's nuclear weapons development has received much attention while South Korea remains ignored. Even within South Korea, historians overcame the Japanese colonial historiography of Korea only a generation or so ago, and the colonizer's distortions remain pervasive among ordinary South Koreans. Accordingly, a logical place to begin exploring Korea's past is the history of understanding that past.

HISTORIOGRAPHY

Most surviving pre-twentieth-century works on Korean history reflect the Confucian perspective. Confucius (551–479 BCE) and the later thinkers who regarded themselves as followers of his tradition shared a set of convictions: (1) humans possess the innate capacity to develop morally; (2) moral development begins with moral self-cultivation; (3) through self-perfection, one helps to perfect the world; and (4) in antiquity, sages, who had perfected themselves, governed a harmonious society. Originating in early China and written in Literary Sinitic ("classical Chinese"), Confucian historiography regards history as a mirror for reflecting on the past to draw lessons for the present. Such respect for history committed the early states of East Asia to diligent record keeping. Official accounts of Korea and China in particular show the cyclical patterns of the past. A new dynasty's early phase features effective governance, military victories, social harmony, secure livelihoods among the people, and cultural efflorescence. Eventually, the dynasty suffers from moral decay within its leadership, inviting natural disasters, foreign invasions, and internal rebellions. Confucian historiography regards the resulting dynastic change as a transfer of the Mandate of Heaven from one ruling family to another. State-centered Confucian historiography was standard in both Korea and China before the impact of imperialism.

Japanese colonial historiography then supplanted Confucian historiography as the dominant style of writing about Korea's past. Propagated by apologists for Imperial Japan (1868–1945), Japanese historiography of Asia treated Japan as distinct from the rest of the continent and on an equal footing with the West while adopting the West's negative, orientalist portrayals of Asia. Japanese colonial historiography of Korea used three main lines of argument to rationalize Japan's takeover of Korea. First, "common ancestry theory" argued that Japan and Korea shared common origins. Accordingly, a natural bond existed between their peoples. Second, "stagnation theory" argued that Korea had not even entered the feudal or medieval phase of the normal societal development that the modern West and Japan had supposedly undergone. This meant that Korea needed Japan's brotherly protection and tutelage. Third, according to "dependency theory," Korea lacked independence and distinctiveness, as Japan and continental Asiatic forces had shaped its history.

In response, Korean nationalist historians wrote a Korean history centered around the *minjok*, the Korean nation ethnically or racially defined. In the early twentieth century, some intellectuals sought to promote national consciousness to resist Japanese domination. They declared that Korea's history is the history of the Korean *minjok*, a distinct people descended from the mythical Tan'gun (Sandalwood King): a demigod and the founder of Korea's first state, Kojosŏn ("Old Chosŏn"; fourth century?–108 BCE). Nationalist historians emphasized the large territories of Kojosŏn and other ancient Korean states, by which they judged the present state of the Korean nation. In doing so, they rejected Japanese colonial historiography, and also Confucian historiography, which they saw as advocating Korea's subservience to China.

By contrast, positivist historiography, produced in the 1930s by the first generation of Korean scholars trained in modern research methodology, attempted to study history more objectively. Stressing empiricism, positivism regards certain, or "positive," knowledge as that based on natural phenomena—their properties and relations—interpreted through logic and reason. Thus information acquired through sensory experience constitutes the source of true knowledge, and verified data, or "positive facts," constitute empirical evidence. Trained at Japanese universities, the early group of Korean positivist historians produced detailed studies on various subjects, especially ancient Korea. Along with like-minded Japanese colleagues, they laid the foundations for the scholarship of subsequent generations of academic Korea historians, especially in South Korea, Japan, and the West.

Another important group of Korean scholars who received training in modern historical methodology in the 1930s in Japan produced Marxist historiography. Still influential, Marxist historians focus on social classes and economic factors in analyzing causality over time. This approach views the resolution of class conflict as producing social progress through distinct developmental stages: communal society, slave society, feudalism, capitalism, socialism, and communism, the end state of history wherein the society is classless. Countering the Japanese colonial historians' claim that precolonial Korea was stuck in the slave society phase, Marxist Korean historians sought to demonstrate that Korea had attained feudalism. While debating the extent to which capitalism developed in Korea before Western imperialism, such historians also desired to show paths toward national liberation from the Japanese. Subsequently, Marxist scholarship became the orthodox historiography in North Korea in a form that highlights Kim Il-sung (Kim Ilsŏng; 1912–94), the country's founding leader, as the revolutionary who effected national triumph over both feudalism and colonialism.

In South Korea, modified Marxist historiography, "internal development theory," has been influential since the 1960s. Countering colonial historiography, the internal development theory highlights a watershed in Korean history with the rise and triumph of a new socioeconomic force. Also, it sees the socioeconomic base for political participation becoming broader in the course of history. Although influenced by Marxism, the internal development theory initially shunned overt references to the concept of class conflict as South Korea's authoritarian regimes abused the National Security Act of 1948 to prosecute anti-government activities, communist or not, until the nation's democratization in 1988.

In the 1970s and 1980s, many progressive scholars in South Korea sought to understand and narrate history from the point of view of *minjung* ("popular mass"). As emphasized by scholars in history and such other disciplines as literature and theology, the *minjung* consists of those who are politically oppressed, socially marginalized, culturally despised, or economically exploited. In the South Korean context at the time, the *minjung* comprised victims of the country's authoritarian regime, of its subservient position vis-à-vis the United States as a colonial power, or of economic injustice stemming from industrialization.

Since the 1980s in South Korea, some populist writers outside the academy have produced *chaeya* ("outsider") historiography. They propagated the earlier nationalist interpretation of Tan'gun, redefining him as the Korean people's historical ancestor and the founder of Korea's first state rather than just a mythical figure. In doing so, the *chaeya* accused academic historians not only of denying Tan'gun's alleged historicity but, more fundamentally, of perpetuating Japanese colonial historiography. Amateur historians at best, the *chaeya* date the beginning of Korean history farther back than evidence would warrant. Many even stake out a Korean historical racial space as expansive as the eastern half of Eurasia. In the 1980s, South Korea's authoritarian regime and its supporters fanned the *chaeya* flame to check generally anti-government tendencies of intellectuals, including academic historians. Even since the country's democratization, organized lobbying by the *chaeya* has affected the government's funding decisions regarding various history-related projects.

By the 1970s, a small but growing number of scholars in Europe and North America were producing more purely empirical studies in Korean history. Careful, relatively microscopic analyses have challenged various claims made by the internal development theory and Marxist historiographies. In particular, Western scholars have presented strong evidence for the continuity of Korea's ruling elite throughout much of the post-classical and early modern periods—as is true in other regions of Afro-Eurasia with a documented history and thus in no way suggesting Korea's stagnation as stressed by Japanese colonial historiography. The Western scholarship tends to view modernity as a byproduct of particularities of Western European historical experience. Until recently, most Western-language works on Korea shunned such terms as "medieval" and "early modern," regarding them as straight-jacketing non-Western history into a Eurocentric mold.

By the end of the 1980s, among Koreanists, skeptics of the empirical approach were pursuing postmodernist historiography. In critiquing more purely empirical scholarship, postmodernists have problematized such notions as truth, objectivity, teleology, determinism, grand narratives, universality, and essentialism. Seeing subjectivity as inherent in any purportedly objective scholarship, postmodernists utilize various critical theories in cultural studies. In doing so, their works devote more attention to groups deemed relatively neglected by older scholarship, including gender, racial, and ethnic minorities and popular culture.

Varieties of Korean historiography, as discussed here, are neither mutually exclusive nor unique to Korean historiography. More than ever before, scholars look at Korea's past from an interdisciplinary perspective by combining multiple methodologies. Such long-established disciplines as archaeology, cultural anthropology, historical sociology, and historical linguistics indeed remain important. Still, an ever-expanding list of newer research areas, including deep history, LGBT studies, and haplogroup genetics, has introduced new perspectives on Korean history, if not the meaning of "Korea." The following discussion uses findings from archaeology, linguistics, and genetics as ways of tracing Korean civilization's origins.

ARCHAEOLOGY

During the Paleolithic era ("Old Stone Age"), environmental changes associated with alternating colder-climate glacial and warmer-climate interglacial periods affected human life. During a colder epoch, when a glacial layer covered parts of the northern hemisphere, the sea level was lower than at the present. By about 750,000 YBP, bands of *Homo erectus* were inhabiting eastern Eurasia where China, the Korean Peninsula, and the Japanese Archipelago were all connected. Capable of using fire, *Homo erectus* hunters and gatherers were omnivores, eating products from land and sea alike. After initially using rocks as found, the Paleolithic humans devised chopped or chipped stone tools. At first, the use of fire was more critical for warmth than for cooking. Consuming raw animals and plants continued to the extent feasible in terms of chewing and digestion, but cutting edibles into smaller pieces or grinding them before cooking became common. Then by about 50,000 YBP, anatomically modern humans originating in Africa, *Homo sapiens*, arrived in East Asia, overall replacing but likely also interbreeding with indigenous *Homo erectus* populations.

The sea level rose with the end of the last glacial epoch, about 15,000 YBP, and by about 10,000 YBP, the Korean Peninsula's geography had assumed its present conditions. Geologically stable, with no active volcanism and comparatively few earthquakes, Korea remained connected to the rest of Afro-Eurasia to the north while now surrounded by water to the west, south, and east—the Yellow Sea, the South Sea, and the East Sea (Sea of Japan), respectively. To the southeast, the Korea Strait became the narrowest body of water separating the Japanese Archipelago from the peninsula. Korea's eastern coast continued to rise while the southern and western shores sank. Erosion wore down mountain surfaces, filling in valleys to create the western lowlands, adding sediment to the shallow Yellow Sea, and producing tidal flats.

From about 13,000 to 8,000 YBP, global warming flooded coastal regions and impacted the biosphere. By 13,000 YBP or so, Korea's large terrestrial creatures, such as woolly mammoths, giant deer, and bison, became extinct, forcing humans to hunt smaller, faster land animals such as deer and boar, and to resort further to marine products and plants. The change spurred innovations in hunting, plant gathering, and storage for the region's Paleolithic inhabitants. Then by roughly 10,000 YBP, the peninsula became a temperate zone, with a summer monsoon season and year-round "Asian dust," a phenomenon affecting much of East Asia, mainly in the spring. The dust comes from the deserts of Kazakhstan, Mongolia, and North China, where strong surface winds and dust storms stir up thick clouds of fine soil particles, and prevailing winds carry them eastward.

About 10,000 YBP, that is, around 8000 BCE, Korea entered the Neolithic era ("New Stone Age"), a period featuring the use of more sophisticated, polished stone tools. The more traditional view understands the transition from a hunter-gatherer economy to an agricultural economy as the beginning of the Neolithic, characterized by agricultural production, sedentary communities, pottery production, and the emergence of more complex social structures. Scholars now recognize that these changes are neither synchronous nor irreversible. As the region's transition from a hunter-gatherer society to a sedentary one based significantly on agriculture still needs more research, many archeologists prefer to use a more meaningful periodization term: the Chŭlmun Period (c. 6000–c. 1500 BCE), so named after Chŭlmun ("raised pattern") pottery vessels, which feature geometric patterns created by comb-like tools (Figure I.1). Excavated in Korea and its vicinity, this pottery, ground

FIGURE I.1   Chŭlmun pottery vessel excavated in Amsa-dong, Kangdong-gu, Seoul, c. 2610 BCE. Source: National Museum of Korea.

stone implements, and bones used as fishing and weaving tools suggest that initially, the region's inhabitants dwelt in dugout huts along the rivers and shore, hunted land animals with polished stone–tipped spears and arrows, and obtained marine products by line fishing or casting nets. Excavated shell mounds in the coastal areas of southern, central-western, and northeastern Korea reflect the importance of seafood in the diet.

Agriculture began in Korea and its vicinity around 3500 BCE, and was not fully developed until approximately 1500 BCE. Excavated artifacts include stone spades, stone scythes, sickles devised from animal teeth, hoes fashioned from reindeer horns, and burnt, unhusked millet seeds; initially, though, cultivated grain as such merely supplemented the existing diet. Late Neolithic shell mounds contain more than thirty types of shells and also the bones of snappers, chub mackerel, sharks, whales, and seals. Land animals and plants too remained significant in the diet, as shell mounds also contain deer, boar, wild dog, and hare bones, as well as acorns, chestnuts, and various edible roots. A dwelling or storage dugout hut features a hearth in the middle with remains of grain, and grinding stones and other food preparation tools excavated nearby suggest porridge consumption. For storage and preservation, Neolithic people used various techniques: burying fruits and grains underground; allowing natural fermentation of wild fruits, which eventually developed into brewing; drying fruits, marine products, and animal meat; and storing seafood in ice pits in the winter. Excavations of stone tools on one side and pottery vessels on the opposite side of a dugout hut within a dugout hut suggests a separation of enclosed space according to function and gender.

Korea's agriculture began when the amount of asteroid debris entering the earth's atmosphere increased. Lasting until about 600 BCE, the phenomenon further motivated food production and more complex religious activities. The mid-air explosion of falling celestial objects produced further large amounts of debris, among which frozen water particles in the air caused a halo effect around the sun and even an appearance of multiple sun-like objects in the sky, enough to awe if not terrorize humans. This debris also reduced the amount of sunlight reaching the earth's surface and lowered the planet's temperature—making securing enough food more challenging. This not only encouraged a better organized sedentary and agrarian way of life but also produced organized religions. Believing that the sun, the moon, mountains, rivers, and large trees all housed deities or spirits, Neolithic humans worshiped them and some animals as tribal or ancestral deities. Shamanistic rituals and artistic production assumed importance as Neolithic Korea's inhabitants pondered their ancestral journeys in time and space.

GENETICS

Now including Y-DNA and mitochondrial DNA, genome research since the 1990s is shedding more light on the deep history of humans. The DNA of a human male's Y chromosome and the DNA of any human's cellular mitochondria usually replicate the father's Y chromosome and the mother's mitochondrial DNA, respectively. In the transmission from one generation to the next, a mutation, or "copying error," is rare but common enough that researchers can estimate the date of a particular mutation shared among living individuals—who, as patrilineal or matrilineal descendants of the common ancestor who first had the mutation, constitute a haplogroup—and can construct a massive family tree of haplogroups. According to this tree, all living humans descend patrilineally and matrilineally from "Y-chromosome Adam" and "mitochondrial Eve," respectively, who lived roughly 160,000 YBP in Africa.

Among the descendants, *Homo sapiens* outcompeted other hominids and competed among themselves while populating all continents. Between 80,000 and 50,000 YBP, some began to leave Africa, driving the Neanderthals (*Homo neanderthalensis*) encountered in Eurasia to extinction by 39,000 YBP, although the two species also mated. Competition among anatomically modern humans themselves produced a disproportionately large representation of specific haplogroups over time—a pattern more pronounced for Y-DNA than mitochondrial DNA. The maximum number of biological children a person can produce varies much less among females than among males. In prehistoric times and throughout history, a male was more likely to father offspring by multiple females than a female was to give birth to numerous males' offspring. Furthermore, when one population group subjugated another, the weaker group's females were far more likely to pass down their mitochondrial DNA than their brothers were to pass down their Y-DNA, and globally, the disparity was most pronounced about 5,000 YBP, the dawn of the Bronze Age, when social stratification accelerated. Genome-wide data suggest that just three ancestral clusters account for the great majority of East Asians today in terms of their geographical origins: the Amur River basin on the boundary between Northeast China and Russia; the Tibetan Plateau; and Southeast Asia.

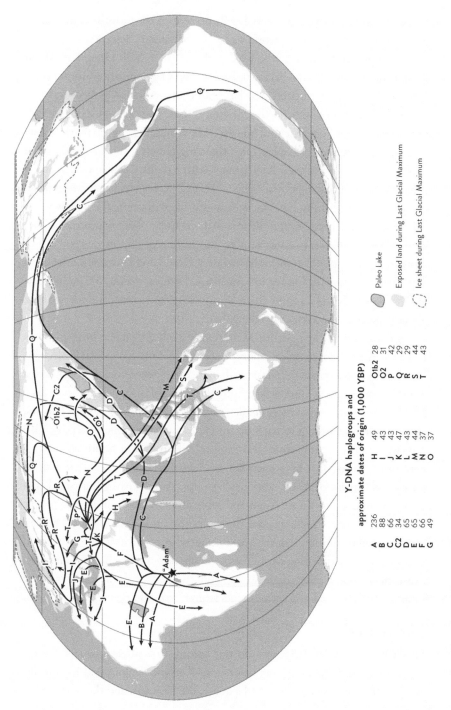

Y-DNA haplogroups and
approximate dates of origin (1,000 YBP)

A	236	H	49	O1b2	28
B	88	I	43	O2	31
C	66	J	43	P	42
C2	34	K	47	Q	29
D	65	L	43	R	29
E	65	M	44	S	44
F	66	N	37	T	43
G	49	O	37		

Paleo Lake

Exposed land during Last Glacial Maximum

Ice sheet during Last Glacial Maximum

MAP I.2   Patrilineal descent of Koreans.

Reflecting these patterns, roughly 85 percent of the 83 million or so eth-nic Koreans throughout the world today are patrilineal descendants of three haplogroup-ancestor males, who lived perhaps 30,000 YBP (Map I.2). About 40 percent of Korean males belong to haplogroup O2 (originating around 31,500 YBP in Southwest China or mainland Southeast Asia), 30 percent to O1b2 (28,300 YBP in Korea or its northern vicinity), and 15 percent to C2 (11,900 YBP in Central Asia or South Central Siberia). The remaining Korean males belong to a large assortment of haplogroups that originated in various parts of the world. Equating any of these haplogroups with a particular historical group is premature. A working hypothesis suggests that O2 Korean males are descendants of waves of arrivals from East Asia's early seat of civilization, the Yellow River valley, during the last several millennia BCE, as today about 55 percent of Han Chinese males are O2. In contrast, Korean O1b2s probably are descendants of more indigenous populations of Manchuria, Korea, and Japan, since the O1b2 haplogroup is generally limited to Korean and Japanese males. And perhaps the ancestors of Korean C2s came from Mongolia or its vicinity, considering that about 51 percent of present-day Mongolians are C2.

In comparison, the matrilineal origins of such a sizable ethnic group as Koreans are far more complex. The representation of mitochondrial DNA hap-logroups among Koreans reflects a much more diverse gene pool than that of the Y-DNA counterpart. Thus, determining the origin of each such mitochondrial DNA haplogroup is even more challenging (Map I.3). Among Korean females, about 29 percent belong to haplogroup D4 (originating roughly 24,500 YBP somewhere in Asia); 15 percent to B (50,000 YBP in East or Southeast Asia); 8 percent to A (40,000 YBP somewhere in Asia); and slightly less than half to a large assortment of many other haplogroups. Among living humans, D4 is common among Northeast Asian and Siberian populations; B among people of Southeast Asia, Polynesia, and the Americas; and A among the Chukchi of northeastern Siberia, Eskimos, and indigenous populations of North and Central America. Equating any of these mitochondrial DNA haplogroups with a historical group requires more research, but the haplogroup data take on more meaning when considered with insights from historical linguistics.

LINGUISTICS

Surviving East Asian languages do not belong to a single language family. Most are Sino-Tibetan, Altaic, Japonic, or Koreanic languages. Historically, not just the Chinese but also the Japanese, the Koreans, and the Vietnamese

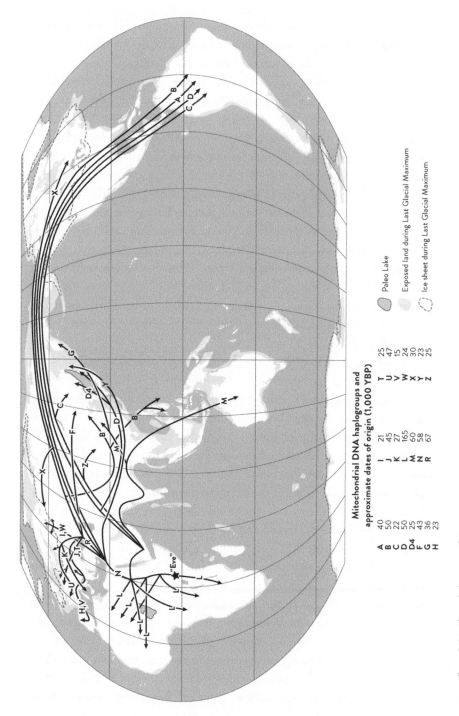

Mitochondrial DNA haplogroups and approximate dates of origin (1,000 YBP)

A	40	I	21
B	50	J	45
C	22	K	27
D	50	L	165
D4	25	M	60
F	43	N	58
G	36	R	67
H	23		
		T	25
		U	47
		V	15
		W	24
		X	30
		Y	23
		Z	25

Paleo Lake

Exposed land during Last Glacial Maximum

Ice sheet during Last Glacial Maximum

MAP I.3 Matrilineal descent of Koreans.

have all used a set of tens of thousands of Sinographs ("Chinese characters"), but this was due to the privileged status of Literary Sinitic as eastern Eurasia's oldest surviving writing system and as the region's lingua franca, generally among elites. As speakers of languages unrelated to Chinese, the Japanese and the Koreans also devised localized vernacular scripts, *kana* and *han'gŭl*, respectively.

One of the four major language groups represented in East Asia, the Sino-Tibetan language family includes some 250 living languages of Northeast Asia, Southeast Asia, and South Asia, with 1.3 billion speakers. Outnumbered only by the Indo-European language family in its population of native speakers globally, Sino-Tibetan includes various Sinitic (Chinese), Tibetan, and Burmese languages. Including Mandarin and Cantonese, Sinitic languages account for over 94 percent of Sino-Tibetan language speakers. This preponderance reflects the historical expansion of the Chinese political and cultural spheres for some 3,500 years and other groups' integration. Although Korean is not a Sino-Tibetan language, haplogroup data, as discussed, suggest that the Neolithic inhabitants of the Yellow River valley contributed significantly to the Korean gene pool.

Classification of non-Sino-Tibetan languages of East Asia, including Korean, has eluded any consensus among linguists. East Asia's second-most populous language family, Altaic, boasts about 200 million native speakers, encompassing sixty-six living languages of East Asia, Central Asia, and Turkey. Among its members are various Turkic languages such as Turkish, Uzbek, and Uyghur; Mongolic languages such as Mongolian; and Tungusic languages such as Manchu. Some linguists also view Japanese (about 128 million native speakers) and Korean (about 78 million) as Altaic languages, while others regard them as dominant surviving representatives of two distinct language families, Japonic and Koreanic, respectively. Besides Korean, Koreanic also includes the Cheju language, which has survived among its native speakers on the southern Korean island of Chejudo, and the Yukchin dialect (or language, according to some linguists), spoken not only among those who currently live in the Tumen River basin in northeastern North Korea but also in diaspora communities in North China and Central Asia. A continuing debate centers around the fact that although Koreanic and Japonic languages are morphologically similar to one another and to Altaic languages, the body of cognates—the words that descend from a common ancestor rather than being borrowed from another language—is too small

to persuade the skeptics. The problem is somewhat like comparing two animal species that share functional similarities as far as their respective body
parts are concerned. Still, the features that convincingly reflect an evolution
from the common ancestor are not many. Regardless, haplogroup data, as
discussed, suggest that prehistoric populations of Central Asia contributed
significantly to Korea's present gene pool, as speakers of ancestral Koreanic
and Japonic languages were in contact with early Altaic language speakers.
By the dawn of Korean civilization in the Bronze Age (c. 2000–c. 300 BCE),
the dominant languages of the Korean Peninsula and vicinity were ancestral
to or related to Modern Korean, Cheju, and Yukchin languages, possibly as
well as Japonic languages.

PART I

The Classical Period

CHAPTER 1

The Dawn of Korean Civilization to 391 CE

B ronze Age state formation laid the foundation for Korean civilization. Hereditary social hierarchy and a degree of private ownership
emerged with a surplus of agricultural production and the use of
bronze in place of stone. Tribal leaders with material wealth and political authority became more powerful, a trend that accelerated in the fifth
century BCE with the spreading use of iron weapons and tools. By the
fourth century, Kojosŏn, the first known among the early polities, controlled Northeast China's Liaoning and northwestern Korea. Elsewhere,
Puyŏ (second century BCE–494 CE), Koguryŏ (37 BCE, trad.–668 CE),
Chin (third century–late second century BCE), and other polities arose.
All further developed agriculture while maintaining harsh laws and distinct customs. Some became larger confederacies, each with the most powerful tribal leader as the nominal king contending with aristocratic power.
Koguryŏ and Paekche (18 BCE, trad.–660 CE) became more centralized
kingdoms by the first and the third century CE, respectively. The adoption of Buddhism and various Confucian institutions in the fourth century
enhanced royal power.

THE BRONZE AGE AND THE EARLY CIVILIZATION

In the last two millennia BCE, new technologies spread in Korea and its
northern vicinity. Toward the end of the Neolithic, around 2000 BCE, the

use of bronze began, with craftspeople initially relying on meteorite ores. The new technology accompanied continuing use of Chǔlmun pottery until about 1500 BCE when Mumun ("patternless") pottery appeared, hence marking the beginning of the Mumun Period (c. 1500–c. 300 BCE; Figure 1.1). The following millennium or so saw more intensive agricultural production of rice and other grain types, a full shift to a sedentary life, a population increase sustained in part by agricultural surplus, and increased social complexity. These trends accelerated with the introduction of bronze production technology around 700 BCE. Besides Mumun pottery, excavated artifacts from habitation sites and burials include semilunar harvest knives, disk-shaped axes, grooved stone axes, lute-shaped bronze daggers, and mirrors with coarse, linear designs. The distribution of lute-shaped daggers, which were not so much weapons as ritual objects, and Mumun pottery in Liaoning and northwestern Korea suggests that the two regions constituted a shared cultural sphere. In the latter half of the Bronze Age, the culture more confined to Korea underwent further change. In the fourth century BCE, lute-shaped bronze daggers and the mirrors with coarse, linear designs gave way to more weapon-like polished bronze daggers and mirrors with geometric designs, as the use of molds for casting bronze artifacts became more common (Figure 1.2).

The region's Bronze Age people dwelt in lots that were concentrated as settlements in the open, in contrast to Neolithic abodes near the seashore or rivers. Dwellings ranging in number from several to more than 100 were clustered around a well and formed a village that faced a stream in the front, shielded from northwesterly winds by a low-lying hill. This layout would remain typical for traditional Korea's natural farming villages. Larger than earlier dugout huts, above-the-ground dwellings constructed on roughly square sites used foundation stones, interior partitions, and a storage depot, either attached or separate. Also, not only did the location of the hearth shift from the middle of the dwelling to a wall farther inside, but larger homes had two hearths. As agriculture spread, both the overall population and the settlement size increased, and a typical dwelling was large enough for four to eight persons. Varying lot sizes within a settlement suggest that, besides homes, the inhabitants also maintained communal storage depots, worksites, assembly grounds, and worship sites.

The economy of such communities in Korea and the northern vicinity both expanded and diversified. As the climate turned milder, with the drastic

FIGURE I.I   Mumun pottery vessels excavated in Ch'angwŏn, South Kyŏngsang Province. Source: City of Changwon (Ch'angwŏn). Photo credit: Cultural Heritage Administration.

FIGURE I.2   Bronze artifacts excavated in Hwasun, South Chŏlla Province. (*Clockwise from top*) Bells, mirrors, cutting tool blades, and dagger blades. Source: Gwangju National Museum. Photo credit: Cultural Heritage Administration.

decrease in the amount of falling asteroid debris around 600 BCE, food production technology improved more rapidly. In particular, polished stone implements increased in variety, with enhanced functions. In the spring, farmers cleared the land for cultivation with stone axes, adzes, hoes, and wooden farming tools; in the fall, stone sickles were used to harvest grain ears. Most farmers pursued dry-field farming for millet, barley, beans, and sorghum, but some cultivated rice in wetland areas. Hunting and fishing remained common, but horticulture and raising such domesticated animals as pigs, cows, and horses assumed greater importance. Various types of Chinese metal currency dated to the late Bronze Age reflect economic exchanges with China and local movements of goods and humans.

The Bronze Age economy accelerated social stratification. As private possession of surplus by the powerful became the norm, conflict over control and distribution of produced goods also increased. Suggestive archeological evidence includes large-scale settlements, megalithic dolmens, shaft stone chambers, and burial goods. Distributed throughout Korea and southern Manchuria, dolmens, in particular, reflect the power of elites. A typical northern-style dolmen consists of four slab-like stones erected above the ground to form a chamber, which houses the dead and supports a large cover stone on the top (Figure 1.3). By contrast, a southern-style dolmen comprises a large rock sitting on top of smaller rocks, allowing just enough interior space for the dead. Not only did quarrying, transporting, and installing a cover stone weighing tens of tons require an enormous workforce, burial goods from dolmens reflect the social status of the buried.

Bronze ritual artifacts offer a glimpse into early Korean spirituality. They depict horses, tigers, deer, human hands, and geometric patterns—reflecting notions of charms, incantations, or magic. As the amount of asteroid debris falling from the sky greatly decreased around 600 BCE, spirituality shifted from seeking the mercy of angry gods to looking for bountiful harvests, catches, and hunts, as suggested by excavated clay figurines shaped like humans and beasts. Also, some rock carvings show deer, tigers, birds, turtles, and whales. Some are shown with harpoons embedded, or caught in nets, or inside pens. Other rock carvings employ geometric patterns such as concentric circles, crosses, and triangles. Symbolizing the sun, concentric circles suggest sun worship, common in early agricultural societies as the people performed sacrificial rituals to pray for bountiful harvests. The growing importance of religious activities and social stratification spurred

FIGURE 1.3   Northern-style dolmens in Kanghwa, Kyŏnggi Province. The largest capstone is 3.35 meters long. Photo credit: Cultural Heritage Administration.

the separation of religious and political leadership, but political leaders buried under dolmens might be thought to have supernatural power or divine descent.

Toward the end of the Bronze Age, stronger tribes headed by such political leaders subordinated weaker groups and extracted tribute from them. The frequency and scale of battles increased with the spreading use of metal, including iron, and warfare produced rulers and the ruled. As tribes merged through war and alliances, larger polities arose, first in Liaoning and northwestern Korea. The earliest known and the most powerful was Kojosŏn.

KOJOSŎN AND OTHER EARLY POLITIES

The origins of Korea's first historical state are lost in the mists of time. The distribution of lute-shaped bronze daggers and megalithic dolmens suggests that Kojosŏn's domain or sphere of influence at its peak spanned Liaoning and northwestern Korea. Documents on early Korea are sparse, and the events before the fourth century CE that are recorded in Korea's oldest extant historical work, *History of the Three Kingdoms* (*Samguk sagi*; 1145), range from semihistorical to legendary, and they do not include the founding of Kojosŏn. The oldest extant works that do discuss that event, *Memorabilia of the Three Kingdoms* (*Samguk yusa*; 1281) and *Poetic Record of Emperors and Kings* (*Chewang un'gi*; 1287), narrate the Tan'gun legend, according to which Tan'gun founded Kojosŏn in 2333 BCE, an improbable date. Older, more reliable Chinese sources do not substantiate the existence of Kojosŏn any earlier than the fourth century BCE.

The Tan'gun legend, nonetheless, sheds some light on the origins of Kojosŏn, as the story retains traces of ancient Indian cosmology as interpreted by the Buddhist author of the *Memorabilia of the Three Kingdoms*. According to that work, Tan'gun's father, Hwanung, was the son of Hwanin, an abbreviation of "Sŏkkaje hwanin t'ara," the etymology of which traces back to the early Indian god of thunder and lightning. Hwanung descended from heaven, with 3,000 followers, upon Mount T'aebaek, where he founded the City of God (Sinsi). According to the legend, assisted by his ministers of clouds, rain, and wind, Hwanung instituted laws and taught various arts, medicine, and agriculture. Hwanung may personify an emerging, agrarian elite that claimed divine origins and ruled a stratified society, especially through overseeing farming activities and criminal justice. Perhaps the story reflects a new social hierarchy being established during the transition from the late Neolithic to the Bronze Age. Justifying its authority in the name of benefiting humans as a whole, the Hwanung group presumably incorporated others through alliances and wars. According to the legend, Tan'gun was an offspring of Hwanung and Ungnyŏ, a female bear transformed into a woman by following Hwanung's instructions. The union may symbolize the alliance of a heaven-worshipping tribe and a bear-worshipping tribe in the formation of Kojosŏn. As an embodiment of religious and political authority, whomever Tan'gun represents and his successors likely asserted their descent from heaven as Kojosŏn expanded and integrated other groups.

In contrast, another legend recognizes a Chinese prince, Kija (Ch. Jizi; r. c. 1126, trad.–c. 1082 BCE, trad.), as the founder of Chosŏn (Kojosŏn). In existence by the second century BCE in China, as China's interest in Korea grew with territorial expansion under the Han dynasty (202 BCE–220 CE), the legend relates that Kija, a wise uncle of the wicked last ruler of the Shang dynasty (c. 1600–c. 1046 BCE), exiled himself in the east when the Zhou dynasty (c. 1046–256 BCE) conquered Shang. Subsequently, the Zhou founder enfeoffed Kija as the Marquis of Chosŏn, and his descendants ruled the land for almost a millennium, according to the story. Archeologists and historians deny its historicity, as distinct bronze artifacts excavated in Liaoning and northwestern Korea suggest no connection to or transmission of those found in the Yellow River valley. Interestingly, though, as discussed in the Introduction, accumulating Y-DNA haplogroup data suggest waves of population movement from the Yellow River basin to Korea during the Neolithic and the Bronze Age, accounting for about 55 percent of present Korean males. Regardless, for two millennia, until the advent of modern historical scholarship, Korean states and elites revered Kija as a sage who brought civilization from its heartland in China's Central Plain to Korea.

By the fourth century BCE, historical Kojosŏn was a state both near and powerful enough to earn mentions in Chinese records. Based in Liaoning and northwestern Korea, Kojosŏn shared its western border with one of China's Warring States, Yan (eleventh century–222 BCE). Likely spurred by the Yan ruler's adoption of the title of king (*wang*) in 323, sometime soon afterward, the Kojosŏn ruler did likewise as the two states competed. In either the late fourth or the early third century, Yan defeated Kojosŏn and took Liaoning. Although its domain was now confined to northwestern Korea, Kojosŏn continued to prosper as a significant power in Northeast Asia. Such officials as ministers (*sang*), other high officials (*taebu*), and generals (*changgun*) served the king.

China's political transition at the turn of the second century BCE produced a regime change in Kojosŏn. Refugees fleeing turmoil in China arrived in Kojosŏn, which allowed them to settle in its western domain. By 221 BCE, one of the Warring States, the Qin dynasty (ninth century–207 BCE), conquered the others and inaugurated a unified Chinese empire, but renewed warfare, during which the Qin rule ended and the Han dynasty emerged victorious, sent another wave of refugees to Kojosŏn. Wiman (Ch. Weiman; r. early second century BCE–?) arrived with some 1,000 followers. King Chun (r. ?–early second century BCE) entrusted them with western frontier defense, where Wiman created a power base. Sometime between 194 and 180 BCE, Wiman attacked the Kojosŏn capital, Wanggŏm, and made himself king. Chun and his followers fled to southern Korea.

Under Wiman and his successors, Kojosŏn became a more centralized kingdom, with more powerful armies and an expanded socioeconomic base, before succumbing to the expanding Han Chinese empire. The spreading use of iron implements stimulated Kojosŏn's agriculture and handicraft manufacturing centered around weapon production. These developments spurred commerce and trade, which facilitated the spread of new technology, especially from China. While subjugating neighboring groups to the east and south, Kojosŏn sought to monopolize profit as the middleman by preventing Chin in the south and others from trading directly with Han China (Map 1.1). The resulting tension sparked the Kojosŏn-Han War (109–108 BCE), when Han land and naval forces attacked Kojosŏn. The war continued for about a year before internal strife at the Kojosŏn court culminated in the assassination of King Ugŏ (r. ?–108 BCE) and the instigators' surrender of Wanggŏm to Han. In the former territory of Kojosŏn, the victorious Han established four commanderies, each a military colony, by the following year.

By then, other polities were thriving in the vicinity, including Puyŏ, which was in existence by the second century BCE. Founded by a certain Tongmyŏng ("Eastern Light") who arrived with his followers from somewhere farther north, Puyŏ was based near present-day Jilin, in the Songhua River basin, and then expanded across central Manchuria. By the early first century CE, the ruler was styling himself king, but he was first among equals. The king directly controlled only the central district among the five administrative districts (*pu*) that constituted Puyŏ as a tribal confederacy. Four tribal leaders, namely *maga* ("horse governor"), *uga* ("ox governor"), *chŏga* ("pig governor"), and *kuga* ("dog governor"), controlled the rest as the four outer regions (*sach'ulto*). Each served by household retainers, the four governors (*ka*) were powerful enough to hold the king responsible for a bad harvest. Nonetheless, the king's own tribe was the most powerful, maintaining a palace, city wall, prisons, and storage houses. Upon his death, the funeral entailed sacrificial burial of not only artifacts but also other individuals as attendants. Bordering two warlike peoples, the Turko-Mongolian Xianbei to the west and Koguryŏ (formerly Yemaek) to the south, Puyŏ maintained good relations with Chinese dynasties for military protection and trade. In 285, when the Xianbei attacked, the Puyŏ population took refuge in northeastern Korea. Even after recovering their homeland with the military aid of China's Jin dynasty (265–420), a group remained in Korea as the Eastern Puyŏ (285–410), as distinct from the homeland's Northern Puyŏ (285–494). After the Jin court fled south upon losing northern China proper to the Xianbei and other Turko-Mongolian groups, in 346, the isolated Northern Puyŏ suffered another Xianbei attack. Subsequently, Northern Puyŏ became a dependency of expanding Koguryŏ.

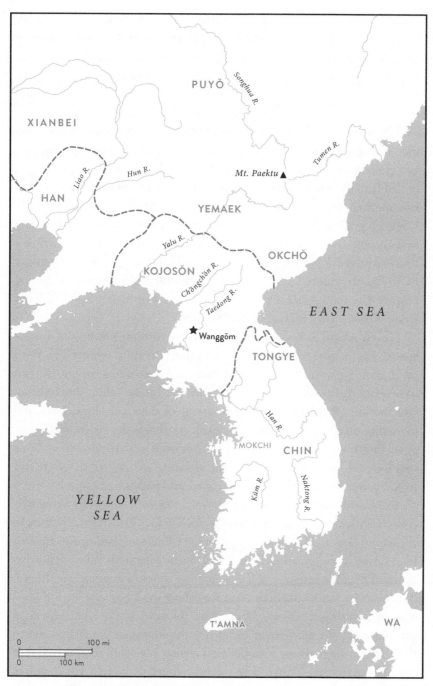

MAP I.I   Kojosŏn and other early states, 110 BCE.

In existence at least since the second century BCE, Koguryŏ's history unfolded in stark contrast to Puyŏ's, despite their shared origins. According to legend, a group led by Chumong (r. 37, trad.–19 BCE, trad.) fled southward from Puyŏ and founded Koguryŏ in Cholbon (present-day Huanren), in the basin of the Hun River, an estuary of the Yalu (Ko. Amnok) River. Mostly mountainous with deep valleys, the region offered limited arable land, which could not support all the inhabitants. Members of the Koguryŏ elite were mounted warriors who raided Puyŏ and other neighboring groups. Koguryŏ, as a confederacy of five tribes, expanded into the surrounding plains and, probably in the late first century, moved its capital from Cholbon to Kungnae (modern-day Ji'an). Attacking the Chinese commanderies in its path, Koguryŏ gradually expanded into Liaodong as well as northeastern and eastern central Korea, where it subjugated Okchŏ (second century BCE– third century CE) in the northeast in 56 CE and Tongye (second century BCE–fourth century CE?) in the eastern central area sometime in the first century CE and extracted tribute from them. The name "Korea" derives from "Koryŏ," an abbreviation for "Koguryŏ."

Closely related to Koguryŏ in language and customs, Okchŏ and Tongye survived as distinct tribal polities at least until the third century CE. With much more powerful Koguryŏ in the way and demanding tribute, the two were relatively insulated from more advanced Chinese culture and technology. In both Okchŏ and Tongye, consisting of some 5,000 households and more than 20,000 households, respectively, a tribal leader (ŭpkun, samno) governed each town or village. Each tribe maintained its territory and resources that were off limits to others. Anyone violating another tribe's sphere had to compensate that tribe with slaves, oxen, and horses.

In western central and southern Korea, dozens of polities of varying size, collectively known first as Chin and then as Samhan, existed for centuries. In the second century BCE, Kojosŏn prevented Chin from trading directly with Han China, as noted earlier. Political turmoil arising from Wiman's usurpation and the Han conquest of Kojosŏn drove waves of migrants southward. The ultimate fate of the dethroned Kojosŏn King Chun and his followers who fled south is unknown. Regardless, the new culture and technology introduced by the northerners blended with indigenous practices. Later in the century, the resulting sociopolitical change saw Chin reorganized into three confederacies: Mahan (late second century BCE–538 CE?), Pyŏnhan (late second century BCE–third century CE), and Chinhan (late second century BCE–fourth century CE), collectively known as Samhan ("Three Han"; even after their demise, "Samhan" or "Han" would remain a favored Korean name for Korea, as in "Taehan cheguk" for the Empire of Korea and "Taehan min'guk" for the Republic of Korea). Mahan comprised fifty-four states located in the Kyŏnggi, Ch'ungch'ŏng, and Chŏlla regions, centered around present-day Ch'ŏnan, South Ch'ungch'ŏng; Iksan, North Chŏlla; and Naju, South Chŏlla. The inhabitants lived in some 100,000 households, and each state's population ranged from several thousand to more than 10,000 households. To the east of Mahan was Chinhan (centered around modern-day Taegu and Kyŏngju, North Kyŏngsang). Located in the south between Chinhan and Mahan was Pyŏnhan (centered around present-day Kimhae and Masan, in South Kyŏngsang). Pyŏnhan and Chinhan each consisted of twelve states and had 40,000 to 50,000 households. A large state had 4,000 to 5,000 households, a small state just 600 to 700. Among Samhan rulers, more powerful ones were known as *sinji*, lesser ones as *ŭpch'a*.

At that time, on the island Chejudo, to the south of Samhan, T'amna (second century BCE?–1402 CE) emerged as an organized polity. Dated between 200 BCE and 200 CE, one of the largest archeological sites containing an early Korean village is in the present Cheju City, featuring dwellings of varying size, storage depots, boundary-marker stone constructions, and drainage channels. According to a local legend, the founders of three indigenous surname groups, Yang Ŭlna, Ko Ŭlna, and Pu Ŭlna, emerged from three holes close to one another, or Samsŏnghyŏl ("holes of three surnames"). The three men are said to have married three princesses from an island state farther north, Pyŏngnang (modern-day Wando, South Chŏlla), and to have pursued agriculture and animal husbandry.

On mainland Korea, Samhan gradually gave way to Paekche, the Kaya confederacy (third century–562), and Silla (57 BCE, trad.–935 CE; known as Saro until 503). In Samhan, Mahan was the most powerful confederacy, and among its member polities was Mokchi (?–sixth century CE), which was probably located around present-day Sŏnghwan, Chiksan, and Ch'ŏnan, all in South Ch'ungch'ŏng, and the ruler of Mokchi styled himself as the king of the entire Samhan or at least Mahan. In the late fourth century, expanding Paekche, a Mahan state (located near modern-day Seoul), likely drove the entire polity of Mokchi southward to present-day Iksan, from which Mokchi continued to lead shrinking Mahan. Elsewhere, Pyŏnhan turned into the Kaya confederacy, probably in the third century. To the east, the

Chinhan state of Saro, in present-day Kyŏngju, expanded and incorporated other Chinhan polities by the end of the fourth century.

EXPANSION OF THE THREE KINGDOMS:
KOGURYŎ, PAEKCHE, AND SILLA

In full contact with advanced Chinese culture and technology early on, Koguryŏ was the first among the early Korean states that came to be known as the Three Kingdoms to evolve into a more centralized aristocratic kingdom. Upon the accession of Koguryŏ's first historical ruler, King T'aejo (r. 53?–121?), one of the five tribes began to monopolize the royal succession and to turn the tribes into five tribal districts (*pu*)—with the capital moved from Cholbon to Kungnae. In the late first century, Koguryŏ also began to subjugate or incorporate neighboring groups, and with territorial expansion, the kingship became stronger, with increased military power and a stronger economic base at the ruler's disposal. Decades later, King Kogukch'ŏn (r. 179–97) reorganized the five tribal districts into five administrative districts. Their leaders constituted the capital's aristocracy, whose members served as officials. The central government was well enough endowed to institute the Relief Loan Law (194), which offered grain loans from state storehouses to the needy during the spring famine season. Then in the third century, father-to-son royal succession became the norm. After concluding the Koguryŏ-Wei War (242–59), by routing an army of China proper's Wei dynasty (220–65), Koguryŏ capitalized on chaos in China and, in the early fourth century, resumed its territorial expansion. Taking over a Chinese commandery, Lelang (108 BCE–313 CE), King Mich'ŏn (r. 300–31) positioned Koguryŏ for an eventual clash with Paekche.

Probably founded in the first century BCE, Paekche was initially an alliance of indigenous forces of the Han River valley and northern migrants of Koguryŏ stock, until the latter prevailed with superior iron technology. According to legend, a group led by the Paekche founder, Onjo (r. 18 BCE, trad.–28 CE, trad.), a son of Chumong, fled Koguryŏ and settled in Wirye (modern-day eastern Seoul and Hanam, Kyŏnggi). As one of some fifty Mahan states, Paekche expanded while fighting off military pressure from Daifang (204–314), a Chinese commandery to the north. Paekche's first historical ruler, King Koi (r. 234–86), gained full control of the Han River valley, adopted various Chinese institutions and ideas, and laid the basis for a central administrative system with a hierarchy of sixteen official ranks, each with a distinctive dress color (240–41). The new system signaled the incorporation of tribal leaders into officialdom as aristocrats.

Compared to Paekche and Koguryŏ, Silla's transformation into a more centralized aristocratic kingdom came considerably later. Originally Saro, a Chinhan state, Silla too began as an alliance of indigenous forces and migrants from the north. According to legend, six Saro village leaders elevated to the throne a boy born from an egg, Pak Hyŏkkŏse (r. 57 BCE, trad.–4 CE, trad.); hence he was considered the founder of Silla. Later, a maritime group, the Sŏks from the eastern shore, personified by the legendary Sŏk T'arhae (r. 57, trad.–80, trad.), joined the ruling elite, replacing the Paks as the royal house. Excavated ironwork sites suggest that the region produced iron goods for exchange with other groups in Korea and Japan. Local leaders likely used iron production to their advantage, subjugating neighboring polities.

In the meantime, in the lower and middle Naktong River valley, the Kaya confederacy replaced Pyŏnhan. According to legend, King Suro (r. 42, trad.–199, trad.) and five other boys born from eggs that descended from the sky became the founders of six Kaya states. In the second century, many new polities arose with the spreading use of iron, increasing agricultural productivity, and gradual coalescence of social collectives into larger entities. In the third century or so, Pyŏnhan turned into the Kaya confederacy, which comprised ten to thirteen member states. The confederacy prospered as a collaborative cluster of farming-fishing-maritime trading communities centered around Kŭmgwan Kaya (42, trad.–532) (in modern-day Kimhae). Not only was rice farming well developed in the confederacy, but an abundance of locally produced iron and booming maritime trade also enabled Kaya to become a significant middleman in a trade relationship that connected the Lelang Commandery and the Wa people of Kyushu, Japan. In the early fourth century, however, pressures from expanding Silla and Paekche severely weakened Kaya.

At that time, Paekche's power reached its zenith. Cornering Mahan in the Chŏlla region, King Kŭnch'ogo (r. 346–75) ruled a realm spanning Ch'ungch'ŏng, Kyŏnggi, and a part of Hwanghae, where Paekche came to share a border with Koguryŏ. Kŭnch'ogo not only defeated Koguryŏ and killed its king, Kogugwŏn (r. 331–71), but also extended Paekche power to the Naktong River valley and wielded influence over Kaya (Map 1.2). Internally, as Kŭnch'ogo and his immediate successors enhanced royal power, father-to-son royal succession became the norm. The adoption of Buddhism as the official religion (384) by the court of King Ch'imnyu (r. 384–85) began to lay the ideological foundation for a more centralized political system headed by the monarch.

In the north, Koguryŏ fought against powerful external foes before focusing on internal consolidation. Less than a generation after a prolonged Koguryŏ-Xianbei War (339–43), King Kogugwŏn suffered defeat by Paekche and died in a battle. His brother and successor, King Sosurim (r. 371–84), took measures to strengthen a more centralized political system. Accordingly, he adopted Buddhism as the official religion (372), established the State Confucian Academy (372) to offer Confucian education to aristocrats, and promulgated a law code (373). Most likely around this time, the central government integrated the five districts' bureaucracies and instituted a system of more than ten official ranks.

Far slower than Koguryŏ and Paekche, Silla was at this time only beginning to acquire the characteristics of a more centralized aristocratic state. The first historical ruler, Naemul (r. 356–402), completed Silla's takeover of the region east of the Naktong. Reflecting an indigenous custom less influenced by China, Naemul adopted a new royal title, *maripkan* ("supreme leader"), which stressed the ruler's secular power more than his predecessors' tribal or religious titles had but was still not the same as the Koguryŏ and Paekche rulers' title of king. Naemul's effort to enhance royal power was successful. After Naemul's death, his direct descendants, the Kims, would monopolize the throne for five centuries. Nonetheless, Silla was still weaker than either Koguryŏ or Paekche and suffered from frequent raids by the Wa of Japan, though the archipelago's emerging civilization was becoming attuned to social transformation underway in Korea.

SOCIAL STRATIFICATION, PRODUCTION, AND CUSTOMS

Early Korean states instituted laws, among which Kojosŏn's code of eight articles offers glimpses of Kojosŏn economy, society, and culture. Three of the articles are extant: (1) he who kills another shall immediately be put to death; (2) he who injures another shall pay compensation in grain; and (3) he who steals another's possession shall be made the slave of his victim; however, exemption from the penalty may be obtained by payment of 500,000 copper coins (*yang*). Capital punishment for a murderer shows that the Kojosŏn society did not tolerate senseless killing. Also, the form of the compensation due to an injured person indicates that grain functioned as a de facto currency.

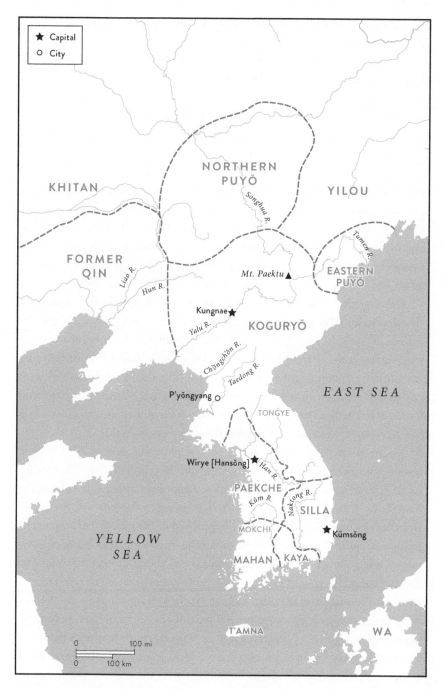

Legend on map:

★ Capital
○ City

Map labels:

KHITAN

NORTHERN PUYŎ

YILOU

Songhua R.

FORMER QIN

Liao R.

Hun R.

Mt. Paektu ▲

EASTERN PUYŎ

Tumen R.

Kungnae ★

KOGURYŎ

Yalu R.

Ch'ŏngch'ŏn R.

Taedong R.

P'yŏngyang ○

EAST SEA

TONGYE

Wirye [Hansŏng] ★

Han R.

PAEKCHE

Kŭm R.

Naktong R.

SILLA

Kŭmsŏng ★

YELLOW SEA

MOKCHI

MAHAN KAYA

T'AMNA

WA

0   100 mi
0   100 km

MAP 1.2   Paekche at the end of Kŭnch'ogo's reign, 375.

And the punishment by enslavement for stealing reflects property ownership, status hierarchy, and a gap between the wealthy and the poor.

Extant sources reveal more about the economy, society, and culture of Kojosŏn's northern neighbor, Puyŏ. Known for farming and livestock husbandry, Puyŏ produced good horses, fur, and gemstones. To defend property ownership and maintain social stability, Puyŏ used legal provisions similar to those of Kojosŏn. The state executed murderers and enslaved their family members. Those who stole from others had to repay the victims twelve times the value of the stolen goods. An adulterous or overly jealous wife was executed. Complementing the law code were such customs as yŏnggo ("welcoming drums") that promoted social cohesion across status boundaries. Performed on the twelfth moon to invoke a god or spirit, yŏnggo honored an ancient hunting society's tradition. The people sang, danced, and released prisoners. In the event of a war, the people made offerings to heaven, killing an ox and heating its hooves to observe patterns for fortune-telling.

Echoing the customs of Puyŏ, those of early Koguryŏ also embody a strong warrior ethos. Originating in the mountainous region of the middle reaches of the Yalu, where food production was limited, Koguryŏ maintained a harsh law code. A treasonous conspiracy or rebellion was punishable by execution by burning and subsequent beheading; the family members were enslaved. Execution awaited anyone surrendering to the enemy or returning home after losing a battle. And as was true in Puyŏ, anyone caught stealing had to repay the victim twelve times the stolen goods' value.

Koguryŏ's martial culture had a special place for women. The people worshipped both the founder Chumong and his mother, Lady Yuhwa (d. 24 BCE, trad.), as their ancestral deities. According to legend, Yuhwa, the Yalu River god's daughter, gave birth to Chumong by heaven's son. Separated from him by her angry father, who disapproved of the union, Yuhwa and the fatherless Chumong found refugee under the Puyŏ king. As Chumong grew into an adept archer, threats from the king's jealous sons forced Chumong to flee and found his own state, Koguryŏ. Subsequently, on every tenth moon, the Koguryŏ king and his officials made sacrificial offerings to the mother deity and the son deity as the central part of the autumn harvest festival, tongmaeng (or tongmyŏng, "Eastern Light"). Valuing an individual's maternal ties, the Koguryŏ people practiced uxorilocal marriage. Once wedded, a couple resided in a small abode behind the wife's parents' living quarters. Only when the couple's children had matured would they all move into the husband's parents' household. This custom would persist well into the early modern era in Korea.

Closely related to the people of Koguryŏ, the Okchŏ people nevertheless had some unique customs. They practiced virilocal marriage, according to which a betrothed young girl first moved into her fiancé's family residence. Upon her reaching maturity, and with gifts from the groom's family to the bride's, the wedding took place. For the dead, the people performed a temporary burial until the body decomposed sufficiently for the family members to collect the bones and place them in a large, underground wooden chamber that functioned as a family grave. A jar hung by the chamber's entry contained rice as an offering to the dead's spirits. Rice was a relatively precious grain for most Koreans until the modern era, but Okchŏ was blessed with fertile soil for farming. Okchŏ also abounded in marine products such as fish and salt, both of which Koguryŏ extracted as a tribute.

Also of Koguryŏ stock, the Tongye people spoke a language and kept customs similar to those of Koguryŏ, which collected indigenous products as a tribute. Both farming and fishing thrived thanks to fertile soil and abundant marine resources. The Tongye people were also skillful weavers of silk and hemp cloth. Among various local products, especially famous were birch wood bows, miniature horses, and seal skin. On the tenth moon, Tongye celebrated *much'ŏn* ("dance to heaven"), when the people made offerings to heaven. Four times more populous than Okchŏ, Tongye practiced exogamy, and an individual married outside his or her kin group.

In the south, the Samhan people, whose language and customs were distinct from those in the north, maintained a more variegated economy centered around agriculture. Possessing more arable land suitable for rice farming, Samhan agriculture benefited from iron implements, although most farmers still used wooden tools. The relative abundance of iron even allowed Samhan to export it to the Chinese commanderies and the Wa. Iron also functioned as currency for trade with other groups. Unlike the mobile traders, ordinary people lived in towns and villages, typically in partially subterranean dugout dwellings with thatched roofs or in log cabins. Mostly farmers and artisans, the population collaborated on larger projects through mutual aid organizations, *ture*, which would remain a social institution for farming communities in Korea until recent times. Given the importance of weather for farmers, *ch'ŏn'gun* ("lord of heaven"), as religious leaders, conducted sacrificial rites for heaven. Samhan spirituality also recognized sacred groves, *sodo*; not even a tribal leader could forcibly remove a criminal taking refuge within a *sodo*. Religion also promoted social cohesion. The people offered sacrifices to heaven on the fifth moon after planting and on the tenth moon after the autumn harvest. During the ensuing festivities, all enjoyed eating, drinking, singing, and dancing for days.

Among the Samhan states, Paekche maintained a language, customs, and dress that did not differ much from Koguryŏ's. Martial and fond of horsemanship and archery, the Paekche people were also neat and tidy in accouterment. As was true in Koguryŏ and Puyŏ, Paekche laws were strict and harsh. Murder, retreating during a battle, and treason all warranted capital punishment. For stealing, the punishment entailed banishment and repaying the victim twice the value of stolen goods. An official taking a bribe or stealing a state property had to repay the government three times the amount and was permanently barred from officialdom.

As Paekche and Koguryŏ turned into more centralized aristocratic kingdoms, each district's aristocrats and officials became the king's subjects. The originally tribal nature of each district became more purely administrative. In Koguryŏ, serving the king were various *taega*, who were senior members of the royal house or consort families. A *taega* maintained household retainers known as *saja*, *choŭi*, and *sŏnin*. Until the fourth century, the Chega, an assembly of all *taega* and *soga*, who were of lower rank, functioned as an aristocratic council that deliberated on serious crimes, sentencing criminals to death and turning family members into slaves. A hierarchy of inherited social status shaped an official ranking system. Divided into more than ten ranks, Koguryŏ officials, headed by the chief minister, handled political affairs. In Paekche, officials divided into sixteen ranks and headed by the high minister dealt with state matters. Silla would institute similar institutions only in the sixth century.

The central government of each of the Three Kingdoms sought to extend its control to newly incorporated territories. The state reorganized conquered areas with fortified towns (*sŏng*) and villages, in accordance with the power or prestige of indigenous ruling groups, and built local administration around these groups. The central government tried to govern the local population and extract resources directly, by dispatching officials to various parts of the kingdom, but the control of more distant regions was weak. The relative autonomy of indigenous strongmen who controlled fortresses or villages persisted for centuries.

While Silla lagged, Koguryŏ and Paekche selectively readapted aspects of China's high culture. Confucian classics played a central role in moral education of the youth and in the training of government administrators. Appreciating the power of historiography for political legitimation, each state also commissioned its official history. Sometime early in its history, Koguryŏ compiled the *Extant Records* (*Yugi*); and in Paekche, when it was undergoing a rapid expansion under King Kŭnch'ogo, Ko Hŭng (fl. 375) authored the *Documentary Records* (*Sŏgi*). Besides historiography, rituals too were critical for political legitimation, and Chinese court music found receptive ears. A Koguryŏ minister, Wang Sanak (fl. 350?), modified a seven-stringed zither sent from Jin into a six-stringed *kŏmun'go* ("black zither"), which would become a favorite instrument in traditional Korean music (*kugak*).

Along with Chinese court culture and Confucianism, Koguryŏ and Paekche officially adopted Buddhism in 372 and 384, respectively, without replacing indigenous shamanism. Competing, if not overlapping, definitions of the term *shaman* coexist. For the purposes of this book, a shaman is anyone who communicates with a spirit world while in an altered state of consciousness. Korean shamanism shares many characteristics with the shamanism elsewhere in Afro-Eurasia, including the concept of a spirit-possessed shaman (*yungsinmu*), and also displays some differences, such as a hereditary shaman (*sesŭmmu*), who inherits the ability and hence the position from a parent. Hereditary shamans tended to be daughters of female shamans, though northern Korea also had male shamans, as was true elsewhere in Afro-Eurasia. In the religious landscape of the time, Koguryŏ and Paekche rulers sponsored Buddhism to enhance royal power and promote social harmony. Still, the new religion also shared with shamanism the role of easing human anxiety about the afterlife, an anxiety not adequately addressed by the more this-worldly Confucianism, especially from the perspective of illiterate masses.

Unsurprisingly, the Buddhist practice of cremation did not immediately replace the indigenous custom of burying the dead. In the Bronze Age, an earlier practice of burying an individual of high social status in a large jar or chamber gave way to stone mound tombs. Early tombs of Koguryŏ and Paekche, in areas surrounding Kungnae and southeastern Seoul, were Bronze Age–style stone mounds, many with visibly distinct layers if not steps. The shared style suggests that the founding elite of Paekche indeed originated in Koguryŏ. By contrast, Silla buried its elites in massive stone mounds with wooden chambers protecting the dead and burial goods. Since each chamber was also covered with pebbles and then earthen soil on the top, Silla tombs were more secure from pilfering than Paekche or Koguryŏ tombs, and a greater quantity of Silla burial goods are extant.

Excavated objects, including those from tombs, suggest that metallurgy was highly developed in ancient Korea. In Koguryŏ, iron production was an essential, state-sponsored industry, and thanks to the abundance of iron ore, iron smelting technology was highly developed. Indeed, iron weapons and tools excavated from Koguryŏ sites are of high quality. An even more impressive specimen is the Seven-Branched Sword that a Paekche king sent as a gift to a Wa ruler in late fourth-century Japan. Made of steel with gold inlaid writing, this masterpiece has been preserved to this day in Japan's oldest extant Shinto shrine.

In the fourth century, various Korean states began to exert a formative influence on early Japanese civilization. Especially active was Paekche, which introduced sundry aspects of continental culture and material objects alike. When a Paekche scholar, Ajikki (fl. 375), taught Literary Sinitic to the Wa crown prince, the impressed Wa king asked whether Paekche had even better scholars. Ajikki recommended Wang In (fl. 375), who subsequently introduced such classics as the *Thousand Character Text* (Ch. *Qiaznzi wen*; Ko. *Ch'ŏnja mun*) and the *Analects of Confucius* (Ch. *Lunyu*; Ko. *Nonŏ*) to the Wa. According to Japanese researchers, the average date when the agricultural population from Korea, which accounts for about 80 percent of the present Japanese genome, merged with the archipelago's indigenous hunter population, from which about 20 percent of the present Japanese genome derives, is around 400.

Within early Korea, the everyday culture shared among various states featured many customs that continue to the present, especially relating to diet. Ancient Koreans consumed mostly plants but supplemented them with protein from land and marine animals. Among the domesticated plants were millet, sorghum, barley, rice, beans, and various fruits and vegetables, including garlic and mugwort. Besides making a wide variety of porridges, the people steamed flour milled from rice or other types of grain to make *ttŏk*. Prepared for and consumed after all kinds of religious rituals, the use of *ttŏk* in various ceremonies continues to this day. Hunting remained essential for securing meat, but raising and consuming such domesticated animals as horses, oxen, pigs, dogs, and chickens became more widespread.

In coastal regions, the diet featured a wide variety of such fish as snapper, chub mackerel, sea bass, pufferfish, righteye flounder, yellow corvina, and shark, as well as such shelled creatures as clams, mussels, abalones, conches, and river snails. Earlier food storage and preservation techniques persisted, including roasting or drying for a carcass and a whole fish, roasting for grain, and fermentation for alcoholic drinks. Salt for food came from rock salt and the saline contents of coastal reefs and seagrass.

Compared to conditions in the earlier Bronze Age, housing became more variegated. Settlements spread from low-lying hills to river deltas, where settlers pursued farming and animal husbandry. Dugout dwellings remained common in the north, including Koguryŏ, Okchŏ, and Tongye with their harsher climate, whereas in the warmer south, the people of Pyŏnhan and Chinhan lived in log cabins. In wet terrain, dwellings with column-supported floors higher above the ground were typical. Gradually, the more sophisticated, complex wooden buildings of Han China, introduced through Lelang, inspired the use of larger structures, including palaces, among the elite.

Larger housing reflects the emergence of a central aristocracy headed by a monarch as the Three Kingdoms integrated Samhan and other early states. Initially, such units as Koguryŏ's five tribal districts constituted each kingdom's capital ruling elite. Although the position of the royal house became superior to the positions of the tribal district families, each district's aristocracy controlled the territory through its officials. Nonetheless, a body comprising aristocrats from all districts deliberated on matters of consequence to the state, especially mobilizing the population in times of war. In the ensuing centuries, warfare would increase in scale and frequency among the Three Kingdoms while other polities perished.

CHAPTER 2

The Three Kingdoms,
Puyŏ, and Kaya, 391–676

Various states contributed to Korea's classical civilization, with legacies lasting to the present. The rulers of Koguryŏ, Paekche, and Silla adopted Chinese governing institutions to enhance royal power while commanding force for wars, amidst which Puyŏ and Kaya perished. The Three Kingdoms improved economic productivity by strengthening tax collection and manpower mobilization, disseminating iron farming tools, and promoting plowing with oxen. Each also produced luxury goods that required sophisticated craftsmanship to meet the demands of royals and aristocrats. Increased manufacturing and agriculture allowed surplus production, which stimulated commerce and trade. The state and elites instituted strict laws to buttress a caste-like aristocracy system, with administrators, commoners, and slaves, while promoting Buddhism for social harmony and order. Besides technological innovations and advances in astronomy and metallurgy, extant tombs, statues, and calligraphic inscriptions reflect artistic sensibilities at the time.

SHIFTING HEGEMONY

In the late fourth century, flourishing Koguryŏ emerged as a significant power in eastern Eurasia. The conquests by King Kwanggaet'o (r. 391–412?) in Manchuria greatly expanded Koguryŏ. He also extended Koguryŏ's influence to southern Korea by intervening in the conflict among Paekche, Silla,

Kaya, and the Wa. Kwanggaet'o adopted his era name, thus elevating himself to the same status as Chinese emperors who, as self-proclaimed Sons of Heaven, had been using era names for more than 500 years (Figure 2.1). In the reign of Kwanggaet'o's son and successor, King Changsu (r. 412?–91), who also used his era name, Koguryŏ gained control of the central Manchurian plain to the east of Inner Mongolia. Maintaining relations with China's rival Northern and Southern Dynasties (420–589), Changsu held both in check. Pursuing southward expansion, Changsu moved the capital from Kungnae to P'yŏngyang (427). In defense, Paekche and Silla allied (433). It did little good: Changsu took Paekche's capital Hansŏng (475), killed its king, and conquered the entire Han River valley, thus bringing central Korea under Koguryŏ's control (Map 2.1). With the incorporation of both Okchŏ and Tongye complete by then, and upon formal submission by Northern Puyŏ (494) after Changsu's death, Koguryŏ reached its maximum territorial extent. In central Manchuria, an offshoot of Puyŏ, Tumangnu (410?–726), led a poorly documented existence as the northernmost Korean state ever, barely attracting Koguryŏ's attention.

In southern Korea, Paekche reeled from the crushing defeat, and recovery took decades. Retreating south, Paekche moved its capital to Ungjin

FIGURE 2.1   Tomb of the General, believed to be the grave of King Kwanggaet'o, early fifth century. Constructed as a pyramid with seven strata, the tomb stands 14 meters tall, with each side of the base 31.5 to 33 meters long. Ji'an, Jilin, China. Photo credit: Northeast Asian History Foundation.

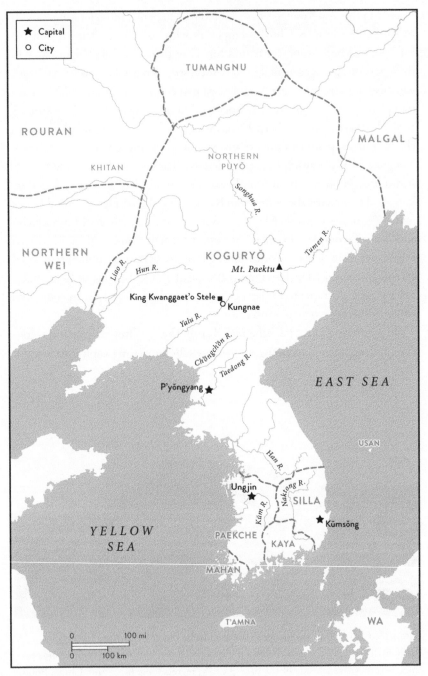

★ Capital
○ City

TUMANGNU

ROURAN

KHITAN

MALGAL

NORTHERN
PUYŎ

Songhua R.

NORTHERN
WEI

KOGURYŎ

Liao R.

Hun R.

Mt. Paektu ▲

Tumen R.

King Kwanggaet'o Stele ■
○ Kungnae

Yalu R.

Chŏngch'ŏn R.

Taedong R.

EAST SEA

P'yŏngyang ★

Han R.

USAN

Ungjin ★

Naktong R.

SILLA

Kŭm R.

YELLOW
SEA

Kŭmsŏng ★

PAEKCHE

KAYA

MAHAN

T'AMNA

WA

0   100 mi
0   100 km

MAP 2.1   Koguryŏ at the end of Changsu's reign, 491.

(present-day Kongju, South Ch'ungch'ŏng; 475). Amidst the chaos following the catastrophe, royal power remained weak as the aristocracy wielded more power until the situation stabilized in the reign of King Tongsŏng (r. 479–501), who led Paekche's recovery. His son and successor, King Muryŏng (r. 501–23), strengthened the central government's local control by posting royal kin in twenty-two administrative districts (tamno). Sometime in the late fifth or early sixth century, Paekche cornered what remained of the Mahan confederacy in the southwest (modern-day Naju).

Muryŏng's son and successor, King Sŏng (r. 523–54), pursued recovery of Paekche's homeland, an effort for which he lost his life. Moving the capital southwestward to Sabi (present-day Puyŏ, South Ch'ungch'ŏng; 538), which enjoyed better access to the Yellow Sea lanes, Sŏng pursued internal consolidation and territorial recovery. He expanded the central bureaucracy to twenty-two ministries (pu), thus completing a system of sixteen official ranks (538?). Also, the reorganization of the capital and the local administrations into five districts (pu) and five regions (pang), respectively, suggests that Paekche had completed the incorporation of Mahan (538?). Furthermore, Sŏng actively promoted royal power and social cohesion with Buddhism, which he also introduced to Japan. While cultivating close relations with the Liang dynasty (502–57) in South China, Sŏng capitalized on Koguryŏ's internal strife. In collaboration with Silla, Paekche recovered the lower Han River valley—only to be betrayed by Silla when it took Paekche's gain by surprise. Enraged, Sŏng personally led a full-frontal assault against Silla, only to be ambushed, captured, and beheaded (Figure 2.2). Silla was now Paekche's mortal enemy.

By then, ascendant Silla had been pursuing internal consolidation and territorial expansion since the late fourth century. After repelling the marauding Wa from Silla, King Kwanggaet'o had stationed his troops in Silla. While adopting Chinese institutions and ideas through Koguryŏ, Silla sought to break free from Koguryŏ interferences. In the early fifth century, Silla accepted Paekche King Tongsŏng's proposal for an alliance. As Silla's rulers continued their effort to effect a more centralized governing system, in the late fifth century the court reorganized the capital's original six villages as six districts (pu). Silla's transformation into a more centralized monarchy accelerated under King Chijŭng (r. 500–14). Making Silla the official name of the state, Chijŭng changed the royal title from maripkan to king, posted centrally appointed officials in local administrations (505), and subjugated an island state in the East Sea, Usan (modern-day Ullŭngdo; ?–1022), extracting tribute (512).

FIGURE 2.2 Guze Kannon statue, possibly a life-size depiction of King Sŏng, sixth or seventh century. Housed at a famed Japanese Buddhist monastery, Hōryū-ji, the wooden statue stands 178.8 centimeters tall. A conventional view is that it depicts Prince Shōtoku (574–622) of Japan. According to a medieval Japanese compilation of ancient records on and legends about Shōtoku, regarded by many as a reincarnation of Sŏng, the latter's son, who felt responsible for his father's death, had commissioned the statue in Sŏng's image. Source: Hōryū-ji, Nara, Japan. Photo credit: *Hōryūji ōkagami*, vol. 51 (Tokyo: Tōkyō bijutsu gakkō, 1918), via Wikimedia Commons.

Chijŭng's son and successor, King Pŏphŭng (514–40), continued both consolidation and expansion. Pŏphŭng further improved the governing organization by instituting the Ministry of War (517); promulgating a law code (520); completing a system of seventeen official ranks with standardized dress colors (520?); and fully incorporating the lower-level bureaucratic organization of each administrative district (*pu*) into the central bureaucracy (520). Pŏphŭng also accommodated new groups in the centralized political system by completing the "bone rank" (*kolp'um*) system (520?), which recognized an aristocracy of "sacred bones" (*sŏnggol*) and "true bones" (*chin'gol*) above six "head ranks" (*tup'um*), and by adopting Buddhism as the official religion (528). Externally, his armies conquered a member of the Kaya confederacy, Kŭmgwan Kaya (532). The confident king even adopted an era name, Silla's first.

The pace of Silla's military expansion accelerated under Pŏphŭng's nephew and successor, King Chinhŭng (r. 540–76), who also continued internal consolidation. Chinhŭng reorganized various Buddhist groups to facilitate the dissemination of Buddhism as a unifying ideology. In order to recruit talented young men, Chinhŭng transformed the existing *hwarang* ("flower lads"), a disciplined warrior youth corps, into a state-sponsored organization. The current and former *hwarang* assumed leadership in the military as warfare continued. Silla gained the entire Han River valley and conquered the coastal plains of the Hamgyŏng region from Koguryŏ and ended what remained of the Kaya confederacy by conquering Greater Kaya (42, trad.–562) in present-day Koryŏng, North Kyŏngsang (Map 2.2). Controlling the Han River valley was especially crucial, as it gave Silla a strategic advantage for continuing wars and direct access to China across the Yellow Sea. As the ultimate tribute to his feats, Chinhŭng too used an era name, replacing it three times, as he saw fit.

Before succumbing to Silla, the Kaya confederacy had undergone a period of reorganization, resurgence, and decline. In the late fourth and early fifth centuries, Koguryŏ's military presence weakened southeastern coastal member states based in Kimhae and Ch'angwŏn, dissolved the confederacy, and confined it to the western banks of the Naktong River. Less prominent member states farther north, however, were able to maintain their territories, and in the late fifth century, they reconstituted the confederacy with Greater Kaya as the new leader. In the early sixth century, Greater Kaya was nearly on a par with Silla, fighting it and forming a marriage alliance. Before long, however, Paekche and Silla's constant warfare weakened the confederacy, which was caught in the middle. After Silla conquered Kŭmgwan Kaya (532), Silla and Paekche divided the remaining southern part of the confederacy. The Silla conquest of Greater Kaya (562) ended a political collective that had never developed into a more centralized state similar to the Three Kingdoms.

Koguryŏ, Paekche, and Silla all modeled local administration after China's prefecture-county system but, in reality, relied on officials posted at strategic points while local autonomy continued. Centrally appointed

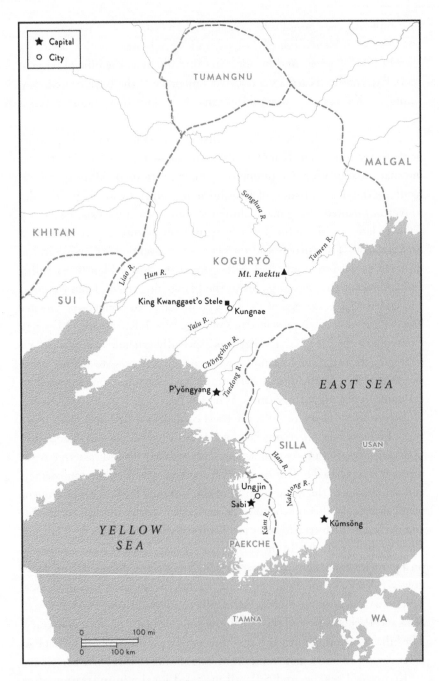

MAP 2.2   Silla at the end of Chinhŭng's reign, 590.

officials governed the highest-level local administrations, namely districts (*pu*) in the capital and provinces (*pang, chu*) elsewhere, and such intermediate-level units as fortified towns (*sŏng*) and prefectures (*kun*); local village headmen handled the lowest-level administration. Officials appointed by the center commanded their troops. In Paekche, a provincial governor (*pangnyŏng*) maintained 700 to 1,200 soldiers drafted from his province. In Silla as well, a provincial governor (*todok*) commanded his army (*chŏng*), but in 583, "oath bannermen" (*sŏdang*) began to constitute the monarch's army.

While each of the Three Kingdoms made progress with internal consolidation, a new external force posed a military threat from China. Reunifying China proper after nearly three centuries of division (589), the Sui dynasty (581–618) extended Chinese control and influence, and Koguryŏ stood its ground, allying itself with Paekche, the Wa, and the Eastern Turkic Khaganate (581–630) of Mongolia. The Koguryŏ-Sui War (598–614) commenced when Koguryŏ mobilized 10,000 Malgal (Ch. Mohe), ancestors of Jurchens and Manchus, and attacked Sui's strategic Shanhai Pass at the eastern end of the Great Wall. In retaliation, Sui struck Koguryŏ with an army of 300,000, ultimately suffering defeat at the Liao River by a Koguryŏ force of 50,000 (598). When Sui attacked Koguryŏ again, about 10,000 Koguryŏ troops led by Ŭlchi Mundŏk (fl. 612) annihilated the Sui force of over 300,000 in the decisive Battle of Salsu (612). Subsequently, Koguryŏ repelled two additional invasions (613, 614). Sui soon collapsed after its disastrous campaigns against Koguryŏ and other massive projects sparked rebellions, but the succeeding Tang dynasty (618–907) pressured Koguryŏ. To strengthen its defense, Koguryŏ constructed in its western border region a wall stretching some 370 kilometers, two to three meters high, and six meters thick (631–47). After Yŏn Kaesomun (617–66?), who was in charge of the project, gained power through a coup and enthroned a figurehead, King Pojang (r. 642–68), the Tang emperor personally led an army of 300,000, thus commencing the Koguryŏ-Tang War (645–70). After taking various Koguryŏ fortresses, Tang forces attempted in vain for two months to overcome Ansi fortress before withdrawing (645). Koguryŏ also repelled two subsequent Tang attacks (647, 648).

Repeated failures by both Tang and Sui reflect Koguryŏ's determined, well-organized resistance and the logistical challenges for a sedentary state based in China proper of conducting an extended campaign in Korea. Liaodong's climate and terrain allowed a Chinese invasion force with an extended supply line from China proper only the spring season to subdue Koguryŏ after months of long, bitterly cold winter and before the region's marshland bogged the army down in hot, humid summer weather which melted even bowstrings. Sui undertook a massive project of constructing the Grand Canal to facilitate the transport of a workforce and supplies from the Yangzi River valley (604–09), but that effort was not enough.

The tide of the Koguryŏ-Tang War turned only when Tang and Silla allied against Koguryŏ and Paekche, which by then had become Silla's scourge (648). Silla King T'aejong Muyŏl (r. 654–61), the architect of the Silla-Tang alliance before ascending the throne, fielded an army of 50,000 under the command of his brother-in-law, Kim Yusin (595–673). His army annihilated a fiercely resisting Paekche army of 5,000 and reached the capital, Sabi, joined there by a Tang force that had crossed the Yellow Sea. Weakened by internal turmoil and moral laxity among elites, Sabi fell when the Silla-Tang pincer attack overcame 10,000 Paekche defenders. A few days later, Tang troops captured the last Paekche ruler, King Ŭija (r. 641–60), in Ungjin and established the Commandery of Xiongjin (Ko. Ungjin) to control the Paekche territory (660). Surviving members of the Paekche leadership, however, elevated as king Ŭija's son, who was in Japan. Aided by Japanese troops escorting the son to Korea, Paekche loyalists recovered some 200 fortresses and attempted to retake Sabi and Ungjin. Before long, however, internal strife hurt their effort, and the victory of Silla-Tang forces over Paekche-Japanese forces at the Kŭm River effectively ended the Paekche restorationist movement (663). Tang kept all gains to itself and established the Great Commandery of Jilin (Ko. Kyerim; 663) in Silla's capital, Kŭmsŏng, and instilled conflict between Silla's King Munmu (r. 661–81), who had succeeded his father, Muyŏl, and Munmu's brother.

In the meantime, Tang and Silla successfully collaborated against Koguryŏ. Their initial pincer attack failed when Yŏn Kaesomun's army annihilated a Tang force of 100,000 (661–62). After Yŏn Kaesomun's death, however, a bitter power struggle among his three sons compromised effective resistance. P'yŏngyang fell to the Tang army, Pojang surrendered, and Tang established the Protectorate-General to Pacify the East (668). The surviving Koguryŏ leadership continued the resistance from the Hwanghae region, even retaking P'yŏngyang (669–84). When the Silla-Tang War (670–76) pitted the erstwhile allies against each other, Silla aided Koguryŏ loyalists while driving Tang troops out of the former Paekche territory. Ultimately, however, Tang and Silla crushed the remaining Koguryŏ resistance weakened by internal strife (684).

In many ways, the Silla-Tang War was a Sino-Korean war as Silla drew support from populations of both vanquished states. After initial setbacks, Silla turned the war's tide when its army of under 30,000 defeated an advancing Tang army of 40,000 at Maeso fortress (probably modern-day Yangju, Kyŏnggi; 675). In the following year, Silla won a resounding naval victory at the mouth of the Kŭm River, and Tang effectively withdrew from Korea by relocating the Protectorate-General to Pacify the East from P'yŏngyang to Liaodong. Now in control of roughly the southern two-thirds of the Korean Peninsula, Silla faced the formidable challenge of integrating its gains and governing an expanded realm.

Meanwhile, the island polity of T'amna maintained autonomy. By the sixth century, T'amna had become an organized maritime state, communicating and trading with the Three Kingdoms. Soon after the fall of Paekche, T'amna made strategic adjustments by establishing relations with both Japan and Tang China. Unlike the Three Kingdoms, T'amna remained a polity ruled jointly by three royal families claiming descent from Yang Ŭlna, Ko Ŭlna, and Pu Ŭlna, although, evidently, the Kos were first among equals in terms of representing the state in relations with others. Regardless of such protocols, T'amna seems to have maintained an economy relatively more egalitarian than that of the mainland Korean states.

STATE POWER AND ECONOMY

In the Three Kingdoms period, the state recognized private ownership to some extent while maintaining its revenue base. Dividing the population into households and assessing their assets, the government used indigenous leaders to collect "tribute": namely, grain, cloth, and unique local products. Besides tribute, military service and corvée were compulsory for males of age fifteen and above, as the government mobilized the workforce for wars and for construction and repair of royal palaces, fortifications, and reservoirs. The Three Kingdoms also required slaves skilled in crafts to supply weapons, decorative accessories, and other goods needed by the state. Government agencies responsible for producing silk and manufactured items possessed their own craftsmen slaves.

Besides the state, aristocrats also owned slaves and land as primary means of production. An aristocratic officeholder could supplement private possessions with additional slaves and a stipend village, which belonged to the state but allowed the recipient to collect much of the harvest as rent from resident cultivators and to mobilize their labor during his tenure. A royal or a meritorious official could receive additional slaves, a stipend village, and a tax village that, although state-owned in principle, entitled the recipient to rent and labor from residents and endowed the tax village as an inheritance within his family. A war too was an opportunity for aristocrats to acquire more slaves, land, and tax villages. Either as free cultivators or tenant farmers, most commoners struggled to survive, as they owed various obligations to the state and the ruling elite. Besides remitting rent and tribute in the form of grain, hemp cloth, and fruit, ordinary people performed corvée for constructing fortifications and reservoirs, cultivating ginseng fields, and raising mulberry trees—when not drafted for war.

Since free cultivators constituted the state's primary revenue base, the Three Kingdoms sought to maintain a stable agricultural economy, with various policies to increase production and offer relief in times of hardship. The government provided iron farming tools to cultivators, promoted oxen for plowing, encouraged opening up new land for cultivation, and constructed or repaired reservoirs for times of drought. Farmers themselves improved agricultural technology while clearing ravines and hillsides for cultivation. Periodic fallowing for at least a year remained the norm, as neither deep plowing technology nor effective fertilizer was available. Also, only in the fourth and fifth centuries did iron farming tools become more widely available. By the sixth century, such iron implements as plows, hoes, and picks were in broader use, while tilling with ox-pulled plows began to spread. Originally less dependent on agriculture than Paekche or Silla, Koguryŏ too became more fully agricultural in its economy within a few decades of transferring the capital from Kungnae to P'yŏngyang.

The overall productivity of the mostly agrarian economy was low, and relatively minimal commerce developed slowly. Once interstate trade began to expand in the fourth century, Koguryŏ traded with the Northern and Southern Dynasties of China and various powers of Central Asia, such as the Eastern Turkic Khaganate. Even more active, Paekche traded primarily with the Southern Dynasties and the Wa. By contrast, Silla's trade with China initially relied on Koguryŏ and Paekche as intermediaries until the conquest of the Han River valley, which allowed direct trade with China across the Yellow Sea. Much of the Three Kingdoms' interstate trade involved commodities of concern to the state and the aristocracy. Since commercial transactions were limited among the general population, markets existed only in capitals and other sizable population centers. In 490 in Kŭmsŏng, Silla opened its first market, followed by establishing the Eastern Market Regulatory Commission (509). At least in part, these developments may reflect demands of a more powerful state, the aristocracy, and the growing population of Korea and the northern vicinity as a whole.

INSTITUTIONALIZATION OF STATUS HIERARCHY

The region's population, which grew from probably several hundred thousand to 2 million, comprised caste-like status groups, among whom the aristocracy wielded political power and maintained socioeconomic privileges. Practicing levirate and uxorilocal marriage, the endogamous Koguryŏ nobility consisted of the five district leaders, including the royal house, which generally used the surname Ko. In Paekche, the royal house, surnamed either Yŏ or Puyŏ, and eight surnamed aristocratic families made up the ruling elite. And in Silla, the bone rank system recognized an aristocracy, which consisted of the Kim-surnamed sacred bones and true bones, and six head ranks—effectively determining individuals' advancement opportunities. The throne was reserved for the sacred bones until 654, when they became extinct with two female monarchs. Taking their place were the true-bone Kims, who were offshoots of sacred-bone Kims originally ineligible for the throne. By then, the true bones also included the Paks who were descendants of Silla's earlier royal house; the descendants of the last king of Kŭmgwan Kaya (who was Kim Yusin's great-grandfather); and the descendants of a Koguryŏ prince, Ansŭng (fl. 668–83). Silla also accommodated lower-level elites of Koguryŏ and Paekche with head ranks six and five, respectively, which included the descendants of former rulers of Chinhan states incorporated earlier by Silla. Men of head ranks six, five, and four were eligible for administrative positions in the central government, whereas the lowest three head ranks presumably comprised the general population.

An aristocrat participated in court politics and led troops. In Paekche, aristocrats assembled at Chŏngsaam, a rock cliff location of likely religious significance in Sabi, to discuss state matters. In Silla, the earlier tradition of tribal leaders assembling to debate political affairs continued in the form of the Hwabaek, a council of nobles headed by an aristocrat with "extraordinary rank one" (*sangdaedŭng*). The Hwabaek checked royal power, especially since the council's deliberations on all agendas, including the issue of royal succession, used the principle of unanimous consent. On at least one occasion, the Hwabaek deposed a reigning king (579). For their part, Silla monarchs sought to increase their power by expanding and strengthening the central bureaucracy with new offices and functions, including the Chancellery Office (651), which executed royal edicts.

Aristocrats of the Three Kingdoms enjoyed a luxurious life. Residing in high-walled, tile-roofed mansions with large kitchens, stables, and wells, the nobility donned silk clothing imported from China and wore accessories decorated with gemstones, gold, and silver. In Silla, sumptuary laws regulated the size and decorations of clothing, dwellings, and carriages depending on a person's hereditary rank. In Koguryŏ tomb mural paintings illustrating aristocrats' lives, even the size of a person depicted varies according to social status. The elites of Koguryŏ and Paekche alike enjoyed hunting and various games such as pitch-pot, Paduk (Ch. Weiqi; Ja. Go), and Changgi (Ch. Xiangqi; Ja. Shōgi; "Chinese chess").

The rest of the population consisted of commoners, who were mostly free cultivators, and slaves, who were owned by aristocrats or government agencies. In Koguryŏ, commoners married relatively freely. Weddings entailed no formal gift other than pork and liquor from the groom's family to the bride's; receiving anything more was regarded as selling the daughter. In the Three Kingdoms as a whole, commoners struggled to survive as they owed labor and taxes to the state. In times of war, the government drafted them to fight as infantrymen or to perform such non-combat duties as transporting supplies. Those who lost or were forced to abandon their plots due to high-interest loans and natural disasters turned into vagrants, bandits, or slaves. Since commoners performing their obligations to the state constituted the state's primary revenue base, the Three Kingdoms took such measures as King Kogukch'ŏn's Relief Loan Law to help those struggling. Smaller than commoners in population, slaves lived with their owners and worked for them or, as out-resident slaves, cultivated their owners' lands. Besides those born as slaves, conquered groups, prisoners of war, criminals, and debtors unable to repay their creditors joined the slave population. In Koguryŏ, killing someone's cow or horse was a crime punishable by enslavement.

Besides strict laws, the Three Kingdoms maintained institutions for promoting stability and social cohesion, including Silla's *hwarang*, a group that drew members from the aristocracy and commoners alike. The *hwarang*, a tight-knit group of young males, honed their skills as hunters and warriors and fortified themselves mentally through pilgrimages to sacred sites, performing sacrificial rituals to heaven, and singing, dancing, and drinking. As the *hwarang* as an institution expanded with state patronage, starting in Chinhŭng's reign, Wŏn'gwang (542–640), a key figure in the early history of Silla Buddhism, devised Five Secular Injunctions (600) for *hwarang* to heed. Reflecting Buddhist and Confucian ethics in ways appropriate for a warrior, the injunctions required serving the monarch with loyalty; honoring one's parents with filial piety; treating friends with trust; never retreating in battle; and exercising discretion when taking a life. Since an aristocratic *hwarang* eventually served in the government, the Five Secular Injunctions also functioned as a code of conduct for future leaders. Since not all *hwarang* were from elite families, the institution also helped to diffuse tension and conflict engendered by Silla's caste-like bone rank system.

Surviving descriptions of *hwarang* show that the emotional bond between two *hwarang* could be intense. When mentioning a *hwarang*, such sources rarely fail to note that he was beautiful or pretty in adornment. According to the *History of the Three Kingdoms*, Sadaham (d. 562?), a true-bone *hwarang*, and another *hwarang*, Mugwallang (d. 562?), vowed that not even death would part them as friends. When Mugwallang died not long after suffering a battle injury, Sadaham was said to have cried for seven days before his death. Their relationship seems typical of warrior cultures common throughout classical Eurasia.

EARLY CLASSICAL CULTURE

The Three Kingdoms shared many cultural similarities, despite prolonged warfare among them. Some differences marked their clothing and bowing styles, among other behaviors. Still, overall customs and languages among the inhabitants of Koguryŏ, Paekche, and Silla were much closer to one another than they were to the customs and languages of the Turks, the Chinese, the Malgal, or the Wa. Also, although the overall pace of selective adoption and modification of Chinese institutions and ideas varied among the Three Kingdoms, with Koguryŏ and Paekche far ahead of Silla, the general direction was more or less the same.

The Three Kingdoms promoted education and learning. In Koguryŏ, the State Confucian Academy in the capital offered a curriculum in Confucian classics and histories. Likely established not long after the State

Confucian Academy, youth schools (*kyŏngdang*) taught Literary Sinitic and martial skills throughout the kingdom. In Paekche, the state maintained a faculty of preceptors in the Five Classics of Confucianism (*Classic of Poetry, Book of Documents, Book of Changes, Book of Rites,* and *Spring and Autumn Annals*), history, and medicine, and aristocrats were well versed in the Chinese classics and histories. Before long, Paekche was dispatching its experts in the Five Classics, herbs, medicine, astronomy, and divination to Japan, shaping the formation of its Asuka Culture (592–710). Around the same time in Silla, the youth studied the Confucian classics. Through such texts, the Three Kingdoms promoted loyalty to the sovereign, filial piety to the parents, and trust between friends as cardinal moral virtues. Also, each state compiled histories for drawing lessons from the past and ultimately for political legitimation. In Koguryŏ, Yi Munjin (fl. 600) abridged the *Extant Records* into a five-volume *New Compilation* (*Sinjip*; 600), and in Silla, Kŏch'ilbu (d. 579) compiled the *State's History* (*Guksa*; 545) upon King Chinhŭng's command.

Promoting education and learning sparked an interest in the writing system as both an art form and a medium of communication. Engraved text on the King Kwanggaet'o Stele (erected in 414), which commemorates the warrior king's conquests, features brushstrokes of vigorous style, suggesting that calligraphy had become an essential artistic genre by then. Silla devised its writing systems, such as *idu* and *hyangch'al*, which designated certain Sinographs to represent specific Korean sounds or grammatical functions. *Idu*, in particular, would become the favored script among clerks and other low-level administrators. Simultaneously, aristocrats continued to favor Literary Sinitic in pursuing an ever-widening breadth and depth of knowledge.

In addition to classical Chinese learning, Koguryŏ and Paekche promoted Buddhism, internally and abroad. Both officially adopted the religion in the late fourth century and achieved a high-level understanding of Buddhism as a complex system of thought. Korean Buddhism as such formed the core of the two states' formative influence on Japan's Asuka Culture. A Paekche aristocrat, Norisach'igye (fl. 552), presented Buddhist sutras and statues to the Japanese king, introducing Buddhism to the archipelago (552). Although farther away from Japan, Koguryŏ's contribution was no less. Decades later, a monk from Koguryŏ, Hyeja (Ja. Eji; d. 622), taught various Buddhist sutras to Prince Shōtoku for more than twenty years, while another, Hyegwan (Ja. Ekan; fl. 625), actively disseminated Buddhism on the archipelago.

By contrast, Silla did not officially adopt Buddhism until the early sixth century, when it began to use Buddhist names and posthumous titles for monarchs who promoted the religion as a state-protecting ideology inseparable from royal power. Unsurprisingly, indigenous shamanism retained its place, as reflected in the incantatory "Song of the Comet" (Hyesŏng ka; mid-seventh century), and it was thanks to this incantation that both the comet—which the three *hwarang* who saw it took as a warning of a Japanese raid—and the raiding Japanese are said to have gone away. Nonetheless, the foundation of Silla Buddhism saw completion in the late seventh century, when Silla culture integrated the legacies of Koguryŏ and Paekche. Furthermore, continuing interactions with Tang China enhanced both the breadth and depth of Silla Buddhism. As a spiritual practice, the mature Buddhism of Silla stressed karma, a concept according to which intent and actions of a sentient being influence its future, including reincarnation, and Maitreya Buddha, a compassionate being who will appear in the future to teach the people *dharma*, the pure "cosmic law and order."

Two Silla monks, Wŏnhyo (617–86) and Ŭisang (625–702), are twin pillars of classical Korean Buddhism. A towering intellectual of the era, Wŏnhyo commanded a broad understanding of Buddhist texts. Seeking to overcome conflict among competing Buddhist schools, he argued that all emanate from the One Mind, the Buddha nature which all sentient beings embody. Unlike Wŏnhyo, who never visited Tang China, another brilliant mind and his friend, Ŭisang, did so and introduced the Hwaŏm (Ch. Huayen; Ja. Kegon; or Flower Garland) School to Silla (670). Hwaŏm taught that any phenomenon exists only as part of the entire nexus of reality. The phenomenon's existence depends on others' whole networks, all equally connected and contained in one another. Teaching Hwaŏm, Ŭisang laid the foundation for a monastic way of life by establishing religious orders, founding such famous monasteries as Pusŏk-sa in Yŏngju, North Kyŏngsang, and by training many disciples.

Both Wŏnhyo and Ŭisang also explained key Buddhist concepts in ways more readily understandable by the ordinary people. Wŏnhyo propagated Pure Land Buddhism, which emphasized a sincere faith in Amitābha Buddha, the guardian of the Pure Land—the celestial realm of a buddha or bodhisattva—who secures one's salvation by admission into the paradise. Ŭisang popularized worship of Avalokiteśvara, a bodhisattva that embodies all Buddhas' compassion, yet deliberately postpones Nirvana—permanent release from the painful, endless cycle of reincarnations—to help the suffering sentient beings. Ŭisang and many other Silla monks traveled to Tang China to enhance their understandings of Buddhism and introduced new schools to Korea. Wŏnhyo's teachings also influenced Japan's Asuka Culture.

Besides Buddhism and Confucianism, the Three Kingdoms were receptive to Daoism, which emphasizes living in harmony with the Dao ("Way"), the source, pattern, and substance of all that exists. Introduced from China, Daoism complemented indigenous shamanistic beliefs. Some bricks excavated from Paekche tombs are inscribed with mountain and river motifs that symbolize living in harmony with nature. In contrast, gilt-bronze incense burners depict an ideal world of immortal hermits. Koguryŏ tomb mural paintings show the Four Deities who, representing the Daoist gods of four directions, protect the dead in the afterlife. During Pojang's reign, the kingdom's strongman, Yŏn Kaesomun, even promoted Daoism as an official belief system of higher status than Buddhism or Confucianism. In Silla, Daoist ideals inspired the overall landscaping of Anapchi, a royal palace complex constructed in the seventh century in Kŭmsŏng. The building site, the artificial pond, and its three small islands embody the ideal of all things in harmony with nature.

Astronomy, meteorology, and mathematics attracted attention as ways of better understanding the natural world. The Three Kingdoms made astronomical and meteorological observations, and the *History of the Three Kingdoms* records instances of solar eclipses, lunar eclipses, comets, and unusual weather—all matters of concern for a good harvest and royal legitimacy. Koguryŏ produced astronomical charts showing constellations, and some extant Koguryŏ tomb mural paintings depict these heavenly bodies. Sometime between 632 and 647, Silla's interest in astronomical phenomena led to the construction of the Ch'ŏmsŏngdae ("star-gazing tower"), the oldest surviving observatory in Asia, if not the world.

Construction sites and remnants of the period reflect a high level of mathematical knowledge. Amidst frequent wars, the Three Kingdoms built countless fortresses, most of which were stone-wall mountain fortifications that took advantage of the terrain. No residential construction or Buddhist monastery is extant, but Koguryŏ tomb mural paintings and extant sites show some distinct characteristics of early Korean architecture. The largest known among the period's royal residences is Anhak Palace, which Koguryŏ constructed on a square-shaped lot, each side 620 meters long, during Changsu's reign in P'yŏngyang. Among monastery sites, Silla's Hwangnyong-sa and Paekche's Mirŭk-sa stand out for their grand scale. Some Buddhist pagodas, though, have survived. They testify to how the spread of Buddhism inspired the construction of pagodas to store *śarīra*, pearl- or crystal-like materials found among cremated remains of spiritual masters. Paekche painters and craftspeople contributed distinctly Paekche-style Buddhist pagodas to Japan's Asuka Culture, which also benefited from Silla's shipbuilders and water control technicians.

The elaborate burial culture of the Three Kingdoms reflects artistic and technological sophistication. An earlier Koguryŏ style of stone mound tombs gave way to earthen mound tombs. Found on the periphery of both P'yŏngyang and Kungnae, this new type employed one or more stone chambers connected by passageways. The earthen mound tombs also feature mural paintings, which offer vignettes of daily life, culture, and religion. Earlier paintings typically depict scenes from the life of the person buried, whereas later works are more abstract and can include cosmological themes such as the Four Deities. Koguryŏ conventions also influenced early Japanese tomb mural paintings. In early seventh-century Koguryŏ, Buddhist monk and painter Tamjing (579–631) introduced paper and ink stick manufacturing techniques and created a mural painting at a famous Japanese Buddhist monastery, Hōryū-ji. Also reflecting Koguryŏ influence is the Takamatsuzuka Tomb, a circular burial structure constructed at the turn of the eighth century in Asuka. Paekche too decorated the walls and ceilings of stone chamber and brick chamber tombs with paintings depicting such figures as the Four Deities. Influenced by China's Southern Dynasties, stone chamber and brick chamber tombs, which included the tomb of King Muryŏng, became more common when the capital was moved to Ungjin. Earthen mound tombs with stone chambers from the later Sabi period are smaller but of sophisticated design. By contrast, Silla tombs, which are more distinct in construction and style from Paekche and Koguryŏ tombs, generally lack mural paintings. Earlier Silla tombs were large tumuli, each with a stone chamber covered by a mound of rocks and earthen soil, but in the seventh century cave-style stone chamber tombs appeared.

Objects excavated from tombs and other sites show that metallurgy was highly developed in ancient Korea. A large number and variety of crowns of pure gold or gilt reflect impressive craftsmanship. Whether pure gold or gilded, the crowns excavated from Silla tombs are of distinct designs—embodying shamanistic symbolism associated with rulership (Figure 2.3). Dated to approximately the fifth to seventh centuries, the crowns were shaman-monarchs' headgear, worn on ceremonial occasions. Showing no sign of Chinese influence or similarity to known specimens of royal Paekche and Koguryŏ headgear, the stylistic details of Silla crowns suggest the influence of Scytho-Iranians and other ancient Eurasian steppe peoples. Each crown's tree motif, with limbs bent at right angles, represents trees of the human world, whereas two antler-like prongs symbolize the cosmic deer which travels between human and spiritual worlds—all important elements of Afro-Eurasian shamanism. By contrast, an extant gilt-bronze incense burner from seventh-century Paekche exemplifies the outstanding metallurgical craftsmanship inspired by Buddhism.

Likewise imbued with syncretic world views, performing arts occupied an influential position in daily life in ancient Korea. Depictions of dancers in Koguryŏ tomb mural paintings suggest that the Koguryŏ people were fond of dancing. Extant documents from Silla note that the *hwarang* enjoyed singing and dancing. And in Kaya, one of its kings commissioned Urŭk (fl. 551) to refashion a Chinese zither into a new twelve-stringed instrument, the *kayagŭm*. After Silla's conquest of Kaya, Urŭk gained the patronage of King Chinhŭng, who adopted the Kaya music introduced by Urŭk as Silla's court music. Promoting Kaya music and dance, Urŭk taught *kayagŭm* performance. Along with Koguryŏ's *kŏmun'go*, the *kayagŭm* would become an important instrument in Korea's *hyangak* ("local music"), also known as *sogak* ("popular music"), which began to thrive as a more refined form of indigenous music owing to the influence of Tang Chinese court music, *tangak* (Ch. *tangyue*, "Tang music"), which Silla adopted in the mid-seventh century. Including the "Song of the Comet," the oldest known works of *hyangga* ("native songs"), all with extant poetic lyrics written in *hyangch'al*, also date from this period. Composed by the Buddhist clergy and *hwarang*, *hyangga* as a genre embodies political ideology, Buddhist and shamanistic spirituality, and folk song. Besides vocal and instrumental music performances, masked dance drama likely was popular. Probably dating back to the prehistoric era, masked theater originated in villages as part of shamanistic rituals to cleanse houses and villages and to secure protection and good harvests.

The ancient Korean diet reflects rituals and festivities associated with food production centered around increasingly organized farming, fishing, and animal husbandry. Besides rice, which was the elite's staple, and barley

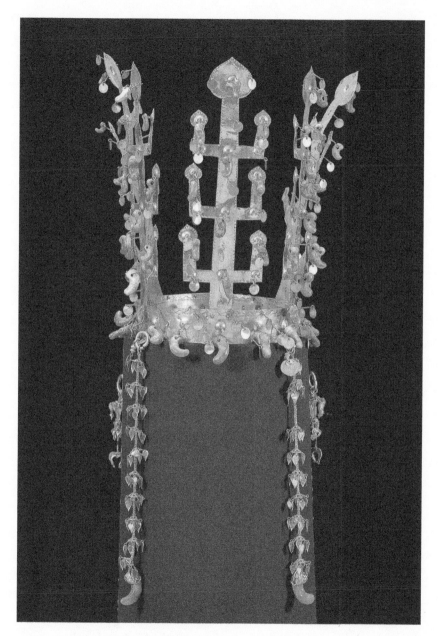

FIGURE 2.3   Silla gold crown, fifth century. Its use ceased by the seventh century, when Silla completed adopting basic Chinese-style institutions befitting a more centralized government. Source: Gyeongju National Museum. Photo credit: National Museum of Korea.

and beans, both the ordinary people's staples, the grain diet featured wheat, millet, sorghum, mung beans, and red mung beans. Rice-based *ttŏk* became a popular food, not just for rituals but also on festive occasions. Added to the plant diet already featuring acorns, chestnuts, pine nuts, and Chinese yams were lettuce, peaches, plums, Korean pears, mandarins, and ginseng, which was used as medicine. Silla elites enjoyed mandarin peel and tea, which was introduced from Tang China during Queen Sŏndŏk's reign (632–47). Improved navigational technology and aquaculture further diversified seafood sources, including sea bass, righteye flounder, yellow corvina, grenadier anchovy (*ungŏ*), flathead grey mullet, shark, dolphin, octopus, shrimp, and *tasima* (Ja. *kombu*; edible kelp). As raising chickens, pigs, oxen, sheep, and horses became more organized, the Silla government managed animal feed, the raising of sheep, pastures on islands, and meat handling. Supplementing roasting and boiling was the occasional consumption of fresh meat (beef, pork, and poultry) and seafood in such raw dishes as *yukhoe* and *hoe*. Although elites also used ice collected during the cold season to preserve food, all classes preserved food through drying meat in thin strips (*yukp'o*) and by using fermentation and salt, the production and distribution of which the Silla government oversaw through various agencies. Besides fermented pastes (*chang*) used as preservatives and condiments, honey, oil, Sichuan peppers, and ginger became popular. Among the increasing variety of preserved food, *kimchi* became an important side dish (*panch'an*)—at that time, made from salted radish (*tchanji*) prepared with fermented paste or salted seafood (*chŏtkal*).

Advances in food storage techniques were paralleled by housing design innovations. In Koguryŏ, royal palaces, ancestral shrines, Buddhist monasteries, government buildings, and elites' homes all had tile roofs, whereas the ordinary people lived in thatched-roof dwellings. All buildings used wooden columns, rafters, and cross-beams. As most people sat and slept on the floor, they warmed it with heating flues and *ondol* in the winters. *Ondol*-heated homes, however, were not standard among the elite, as they possessed chairs, tables, and beds; hung thick fabric sheets for insulation; and covered the floors with rugs and other textile materials, which were also suitable for doors, windows, and walls. A larger house had a kitchen, butchery, barn, and stable. Houses in Paekche differed little from those of Koguryŏ, and by the seventh century the *ondol* floors used in Koguryŏ had become common. What is known about houses in Silla, likewise fitted with *ondol* floors, comes from the sumptuary laws. They prohibited the true-bone aristocracy, who lived in luxurious homes, from having any feature reserved for royal palaces, including a room over 24 *ch'ŏk* (about 5.6 meters) long; eaves with decorated tiles; a gable with a fish-design decoration (*hyŏnŏ*), which symbolically warded off fire; any decoration with gold, silver, or brass; *tanch'ŏng*, a five-colored decoration on the underside of the roof extending over the main structure; steps made of polished stones or comprising more than two conjoined, parallel flights of stairs; a lot wall covered with a decorative roof (*yangdong*) or coated with limestone plaster; and a floor made of such luxury materials as hawksbill sea turtle shell or agarwood. Homes of people of head rank six or lower could not have gates in four directions or an inner gate; five or more horses; or a floor made of rosewood or littleleaf boxwood. Those of head rank four or below could not have a room over 15 *ch'ŏk* (about 3.5 meters) long or a roof over wells. Quality of life would become even more variegated in the following century of relative peace and prosperity.

CHAPTER 3

The Northern and Southern States, 676–918

Silla and Parhae (698–926) perfected classical Korean civilization. In the south, the expanded Silla enjoyed decades of stability and prosperity. Parhae arose as a multiethnic state in the north, with a distinct Buddho-Confucian culture that combined Koguryŏ legacies with China's and Central Asia's influence. Besides acquiring institutions and ideas from both China and Central Asia, Silla culture integrated the legacies of Koguryŏ and Paekche. Nevertheless, Silla rulers' pursuit of royal absolutism through more centralized, bureaucratic governance could not overcome aristocratic resistance. In its final decades, the Silla state's increased extractions from farmers sparked rebellions. Also, head rank six intellectuals and increasingly autonomous local strongmen (*hojok*) turned against the rigid Silla order based on the bone rank system—rallying around two new states, Later Paekche (900–36) and T'aebong (901–18; formerly Later Koguryŏ until 904, Majin until 911). Meanwhile, Parhae, weakened by internal strife, faced the threat of the rapidly expanding Khitan Liao dynasty (916–1125) from the west.

THE RISE AND FALL OF EARLY CENTRALIZING REGIMES

Upon winning the war against Tang China, Silla monarchs employed their expanded economic base and increased military capacity to enhance royal power with more robust bureaucratic governance. Munmu's son and successor King Sinmun (r. 681–92) mounted a massive purge of his father-in-law, Kim Hŭmdol (d. 681), and his supporters for treason, and this effectively reconstituted the political leadership, as the increased authority of the chief minister of the Chancellery Office checked the power of the Hwabaek. While the true bones continued to monopolize critical positions, the throne promoted sixth head rank men of learning and scholarship. Accordingly, Sinmun established the State Confucian College (682) as the highest educational institution, in order to inculcate Confucian values, especially among future administrators. Sinmun also reorganized the central government, the military, and local administration centered around nine provinces (*chu*) and five secondary capitals (*sogyŏng*; 685). The central government allocated official's land among incumbent officials but abolished stipend villages.

The proper functioning of Silla's central government in Kŭmsŏng relied on many key institutions. Headed by the Chancellery Office, various bureaucratic agencies assumed a more comprehensive range of administrative functions. Under the chief minister, who was now more powerful, the Department of Personnel and twelve other departments (*pu*) handled administrative work divided among them. The Department for Surveillance of Official Conduct functioned as an auditing agency, checking corruption and unlawful conduct among government personnel. And the State Confucian College supplied new administrators, who were more strongly imbued with Confucian moral values.

Outside Kŭmsŏng, Silla bolstered its more centralized governing system with a multi-tier system of provincial administration. Since Kŭmsŏng was located in the southeastern corner of a greatly expanded realm, Silla established five secondary capitals at strategic points and appointed a true bone to administer each. Silla also divided its kingdom into nine provinces, which performed administrative functions in overseeing prefectures (*kun*) and counties (*hyŏn*). The central government appointed officials to administer provinces, prefectures, and counties but entrusted low-level administrative duties to local village headmen who reported to centrally appointed officials. Other administrative districts, such as *hyang* and *pugok*, fulfilled more specialized obligations to the state. As an additional measure for maintaining control, the central government dispatched inspectors general to monitor local officials and kept local notables in Kŭmsŏng as *sangsuri*, who were not only liaisons between the center and the localities but also de facto hostages.

Complementing the civil administration was a streamlined military organization. As the core of the central army, Sinmun installed nine oath bannermen, who constituted his personal army (687). He also sought to integrate diverse groups into the military organization by recruiting from originally non-Silla populations, including those of Paekche, Koguryŏ, or Malgal background. Outside Kŭmsŏng, Sinmun stationed ten provincial armies throughout the kingdom (685?). Each province had one such army, except the northern frontier region, Hansan (or Han), which maintained two, since unrest continued for some time.

To the north of Silla, the Koguryŏ and Malgal populations remained restless before establishing a new state, Parhae. Tang China's Protectorate-General to Pacify the East forcibly relocated tens of thousands of Koguryŏ's population, if not more, to regions as far away as northwestern China. Still, the effort was in vain, as the former captive king, Pojang, whom Tang had sent back to Liaodong as a vassal ruler (676–77) with some Koguryŏ and Paekche subjects, rebelled. Even after Tang removed him (681) and subsequently reestablished his descendants as kings of Lesser Koguryŏ (685–820s) as a Tang vassal state, the remaining Koguryŏ population continued to collaborate with the Malgal, the Khitans who descended from the Xianbei, and others in resisting Tang rule. Among them, a former Koguryŏ general likely of Malgal descent, Tae Choyŏng (King Ko; r. 698–719), led Koguryŏ and Malgal populations to eastern Manchuria, an area less affected by the turmoil. After defeating pursuing Tang troops, Tae established—in Kuguk ("Old State") at Mount Dongmou (present-day Dunhua, Jilin)—his kingdom, Parhae (698).

Tae Choyŏng's son and successor, King Mu (r. 719–37), expanded Parhae and ended the military threat of Tang and Silla once and for all. Mu not only recovered much of the former Koguryŏ territory but also incorporated Tumangnu farther north (726) and various Malgal tribes in the east. In response, Silla fortified the border while Tang enlisted the Heishui tribe of Malgal to pressure Parhae from the east. Mu was enraged when the Tang court protected his brother after the two had a fallout, and the Parhae-Tang War (732–33) commenced when a Parhae fleet raided a Tang garrison in Shandong and clashed with Tang troops in Liaoxi. To check Tang and Silla, Parhae reached out to the Second Turkic Khaganate (682–744), a new nomadic confederacy in Mongolia, and to Japan, where Parhae envoys spoke of their state as the revived Koguryŏ. Collaborating with the Turks and Khitans, in 733, Parhae defeated Tang in battles. Upon Tang's request, Silla dispatched an army under Kim Yusin's grandsons' command to see if lightning strikes twice, only to be thwarted by harsh winter weather. The failures of Silla and Tang effectively ended the war and commenced an era of a balance of power in Northeast Asia that would last about 150 years. Expressing self-confidence, Mu used era names, and his successors would continue the practice. In fact, subsequently, no China proper–based state would ever attempt to invade Korea, settling instead for a symbolic acknowledgment of the Chinese emperor as the universal ruler by a Korean state as China's tributary.

In the long reign of Mu's son and successor, King Mun (r. 737–93), Parhae focused on internal consolidation. Eventually, normalizing relations with Tang, Parhae selectively adopted Tang institutions for the central government. As part of an ongoing administrative reorganization, Mun transferred the principal capital three times: from Kuguk to Chunggyŏng ("Central Capital," present-day Helong, Jilin; 742) to Sanggyŏng ("Upper Capital," modern-day Ning'an, Heilongjiang; 756) to Tonggyŏng ("Eastern Capital," present-day Hunchun, Heilongjiang; 785). To the south, relations with Silla were neither hostile nor friendly, and no exchange of envoys is known.

By contrast, around the same time, Silla began to suffer political instability. In the reign of King Kyŏngdŏk (r. 742–65), a stronger monarchy supported by an expanded central bureaucracy aroused more fierce opposition from the aristocracy. The governing system superficially resembled its Tang model. Still, since the true bones monopolized all department head positions, provincial governorships, and army command posts, monarchs' attempts to enhance royal power by strengthening bureaucratic governance had a limit. Not only did the revival of stipend villages and the increased number of monastic lands strain the government's finances but the true bones also used their expanded economic bases to fund private armies amidst the power struggle at the court. The murder of Kyŏngdŏk's son and successor King Hyegong (r. 765–80), the first regicide in Silla since 417, effectively marked the end of not only the continuous succession by Muyŏl's direct descendants but also their efforts to effect a stronger monarchy based on bureaucratic governance while checking aristocratic power. In the early ninth century in Silla, royal succession politics turned into a bloody free-for-all among the true bones, and royal power plummeted. The political leadership became a de facto coalition of rival aristocratic factions, and Kŭmsŏng gradually lost control of the provinces. Locally based individuals such as Chang Pogo (787–846), a self-made merchant prince, entered the fray, although none was strong enough to secure a lasting presence in central politics.

Meanwhile, Parhae's power reached its apogee during the reign of King Sŏn (r. 818–30), after a brief period of instability following Mun's rule. Transferred back from Tonggyŏng (793), the principal capital would remain at Sanggyŏng until the kingdom's end. For twenty-five years, though, royal succession was highly irregular, and six monarchs reigned before Sŏn, a descendant of Tae Choyŏng's brother, ascended the throne. By the end of Sŏn's reign, Parhae had gained control of much of the present-day Russian Maritime Province by subjugating the remaining Malgal tribes. Parhae also incorporated Liaodong by conquering Lesser Koguryŏ, an independent kingdom with former Koguryŏ, Paekche, and Malgal populations that had existed since Tang lost control of that region in 755. Impressed, Tang referred to Parhae as a "flourishing state in the east" (*haidong shengguo*).

By the time of Sŏn's reign, Parhae's overall administrative system was entirely in place. The central bureaucracy consisted of the Two Chancelleries and the Six Ministries, modeled after the Tang system. The Great Minister headed the Department of State Affairs, which handled all matters of state. Under him, the Chief Minister of the Left supervised three of the Six Ministries, the Ministry of Loyalty for personnel administration, the Ministry of Benevolence for finances, and the Ministry of Righteousness for rites; and the Chief Minister of the Right oversaw the Ministry of Knowledge for military affairs, the Ministry of Propriety for punishment, and the Ministry of Integrity for public works. Although the overall organization reflects the Tang system, nomenclature and various agencies' actual functions show significant modifications. Controlled by the civilian administration, a central army of ten "guards" (*wi*) protected the royal place and the principal capital, beyond which local administration featured five capitals (*kyŏng*) and fifteen provinces (*pu*; Map 3.1). Spread out across the kingdom, all five capitals were at strategically important locations. Below the fifteen provinces on the administrative hierarchy were sixty-two districts (*chu*), among which three (Yŏngju, Sokchu, and Tongju) reported directly to the central government, and, farther down the hierarchy, some one hundred counties (*hyŏn*). The central government appointed all local officials down to the county level but entrusted chiefs (*suryŏng*), most of whom were Malgal, with the lowest-level administration. Only the centrally appointed local officials exercised command of regional armies, which the central government supplemented with select units stationed at strategic points in the frontier regions.

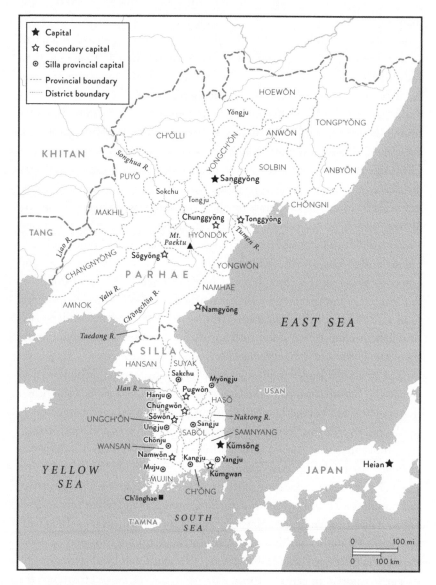

Legend:
- ★ Capital
- ☆ Secondary capital
- ⊙ Silla provincial capital
- --- Provincial boundary
- ··· District boundary

KHITAN

Songhua R.

PUYŎ

Sokchu

Tongju

MAKHIL

TANG

Liao R.

CHANGNYŎNG

Sŏgyŏng ☆

PARHAE

Mt. Paektu ▲ HYŎNDŎK

Chunggyŏng ☆

CH'ŎLLI

YŎNGCH'ŎN

HOEWŎN

Yŏngju

ANWŎN

TONGP'YŎNG

SOLBIN

ANBYŎN

★ Sanggyŏng

☆ Tonggyŏng

CHŎNGNI

Tumen R.

YONGWŎN

Yalu R.

AMNOK

Ch'ŏngch'ŏn R.

NAMHAE

☆ Namgyŏng

EAST SEA

Taedong R.

SILLA

HANSAN

SUYAK

Sakchu ●

Myŏngju ⊙

USAN

Han R.

Pugwŏn ⊙

Hanju ⊙ ☆ Chungwŏn

HASŎ

UNGCH'ŎN

Sŏwŏn ☆

Ungju ⊙

Naktong R.

⊙ Sangju

SABŎL

SAMNYANG

Chŏnju ⊙

WANSAN

Namwŏn ☆

Kangju ⊙ ⊙ Yangju

★ Kŭmsŏng

Muju ⊙

☆ Kŭmgwan

JAPAN

Heian ★

YELLOW SEA

MUJIN

CH'ŎNG

Ch'ŏnghae ■

T'AMNA

SOUTH SEA

0   100 mi
0   100 km

MAP 3.1   Major administrative centers and boundaries of Silla and Parhae, 830.

Records on Parhae's final decades of existence are sparse, but certainly, by the end of the ninth century, the kingdom had become militarily weak. To the west, the Khitans grew strong before establishing the Liao dynasty, thanks to declining Tang power and a vacuum following the Kyrgyz Khaganate's (550–1219) takeover of the Uyghur Khaganate (744–840), which had earlier supplanted the Second Turkic Khaganate. Also, Parhae may have suffered from an internal power struggle, as suggested by extant sources, but little information on the court politics is available.

In the mid-ninth century in Silla, true-bone aristocrats came to terms among themselves, and royal succession became more peaceful again. Still, decades of bloody power struggle had taken a toll. By the reign of Queen Chinsŏng (r. 887–97), refusals by the financially ruined commoners to pay their taxes were widespread. When the central government attempted to collect taxes by force, the desperate rebelled, including two farmers, Wŏnjong (fl. 889) and Aeno (fl. 889), in Sangju, North Kyŏngsang (889). Chinsŏng attempted reform by promoting a Confucian scholar of head rank six, Ch'oe Ch'iwŏn (857–908+), who had studied in China and served in the Tang government before returning home. Ch'oe proposed Ten Urgent Points of Reform (894), but deterred by the entrenched true-bone elites, he resigned soon after Chinsŏng's abdication. Among the warring rebel leaders, two established independent states in the early tenth century, commencing the era of the Later Three Kingdoms (Map 3.2).

The first rebel leader to do so was Kyŏnhwŏn (r. 900–35), who vowed to avenge the humiliation of Paekche and called the kingdom he established (Later) Paekche. Formerly a Silla military garrison officer posted in the southwest, Kyŏnhwŏn brought the region's military forces and local strongmen under his sway and established his capital in Wansan (modern-day Chŏnju, North Chŏlla). Also gaining control of much of the Ch'ungch'ŏng region, Later Paekche made use of that region's high agricultural productivity and population. Building on his earlier experience as a garrison officer dealing with maritime trade, Kyŏnhwŏn actively courted various post-Tang Chinese states. Nonetheless, his overly hostile attitude toward Silla and excessive tax levy on his population failed to win over additional local strongmen.

Farther north, in central Korea, Kungye (r. 901–18) vowed to avenge the humiliation of Koguryŏ and established his state, T'aebong. Born an illegitimate son of a Silla king, Kungye likely was a victim of power struggles in Kŭmsŏng. Before ascending the throne, he joined bandits in Pugwŏn

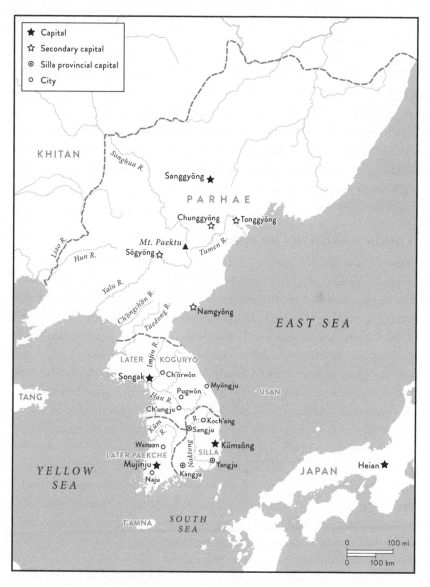

MAP 3.2   The Later Three Kingdoms and Parhae, 901.

(modern-day Wŏnju, Kangwŏn) and gained control of central Korea, including the Kangwŏn and Kyŏnggi regions. After extending his sway to the Yesŏng River valley of the Hwanghae region, Kungye declared the founding of revived Koguryŏ, with its capital in Songak (present-day Kaesŏng), and even adopted an era name (901). Continuing to expand his territory and solidify his new state's foundation, Kungye changed his kingdom's name, first to Majin (904), then T'aebong (911). Kungye moved the capital to Ch'ŏrwŏn, Kangwŏn (905), as he pursued a new social order by instituting a bureaucratic system intended to replace the Silla bone rank system. Kungye, though, not only overburdened the population with an excessive tax to fund incessant warfare but also turned despotic. Claiming to be the omniscient Maitreya Buddha, he ruthlessly sought out and killed anyone deemed disloyal, including his wife and sons. Before long, a group of leading generals and officials overthrew him (918).

ECONOMY: GROWTH AND DECLINE

Before its demise, the state of Silla pursued economic policies for stabilizing the livelihood of free commoners while checking aristocratic power. The throne abolished stipend villages for officeholders, curtailed tax villages granted to royals and meritorious officials, lowered the land tax to one-tenth of the harvest, and strengthened relief programs for the poor. When Silla's economy was healthy, its backbone was the "well-fields" (chŏngjŏn), which the state designed after an earlier Chinese land distribution method. The concept derived from a Sinograph, jing (Ko. chŏng 井, "well"), which represented the theoretical appearance of land division: a square plot divided into nine identically sized sections with the eight outer sections privately cultivated by individual households and the center section communally cultivated for a landowning aristocrat. Besides working the land for his household to pay the land tax, every male from sixteen to sixty was required to perform military service and corvée. Treating villages as basic tax assessment units, the central government also collected such indigenous products as hemp cloth, silk thread, and fruit as local tributes. To facilitate tax collection and workforce mobilization, the government maintained a triennially updated record of population, landholdings, number of cows and horses, and local specialties for each village.

The resulting increase in production and population stimulated trade. The government supplemented the existing East Market with West Market and South Market to accommodate expanded commerce in the capital. To facilitate the production of goods sought after by the aristocracy, such as gold and silver, silk products, culinary vessels, furniture, and ironware, the state organized government agencies so that their craftsmen, including slaves, manufactured and supplied the products. Besides domestic commerce, interstate trade expanded after the Silla-Tang War ended. Also, trade with Japan increased in the eighth century. Booming interstate trade in Northeast Asia even attracted Arab merchants to Silla, which imported such luxury goods as silk, rugs, glassware, and gold jewelry from China and the Middle East. In Shandong and in the lower Yangzi River valley, Silla maritime activities gave rise to pockets of Silla residential communities, administrative agencies, inns for travelers, and Buddhist monasteries. In the mid-ninth century, when the power of the Silla and Tang governments began to wane, the thriving sea trade invited piracy, of goods and people alike. Chang Pogo established the Ch'ŏnghae garrison (828–51; present-day Wando) with the Silla court's permission, wiped out piracy, and gained control of maritime trade routes through the Yellow Sea and the East China Sea, before meddling in court politics led to his downfall.

Even in the era of stability and prosperity that ended in the mid-eighth century, the Silla economy had limitations. The expanded realm increased the revenue base for the state and the overall economic base for the aristocracy. Besides land grants from the state, aristocrats possessed other types of land such as ranches, as well as slaves, typically through inheritance or purchase. And improved agricultural productivity increased commodity production and the capital's population alike. Nonetheless, fallowing for a year or more continued, due to limited fertilization technique. Landholdings of aristocrats and Buddhist monasteries were most fertile, whereas the state's primary revenue base, the tax-paying commoners, cultivated less productive plots. Even in bountiful times, a commoner household had little left after tax remittance. Many also worked the land belonging to others, only to owe half or more of the harvest to the landlord. Not only did military and corvée obligations often interfere with farming but having to repay loans at high interest rates, a significant source of income for aristocratic lenders, also harmed commoners.

In the mid-eighth century, new problems began to weaken Silla's economy. Self-cultivators suffered as aristocrats expanded their estates and as Buddhist monasteries with elite patronage or ties amassed further holdings.

Aristocratic recipients of tax villages and revived stipend villages overburdened commoner cultivators. In times of hardship, the desperate became slaves of government agencies, monasteries, or aristocrats. Slaves produced such necessities as food and clothes for their owners, managed their estates, and cultivated their land. As the population of private slaves increased, the state's tax base decreased. Also, as the central government gradually lost control of the provinces in the late ninth century, estate owners stopped paying their taxes, in the end hurting the state and the ordinary commoners alike.

In the north, the Parhae economy was similar to Silla's in terms of its productive activities and living standard. Possessing estates, Parhae aristocrats, of mostly Koguryŏ descent, enjoyed a luxurious life. Trade with Tang China imported such essential items for elites as silk and books. By contrast, the general population, of Koguryŏ or Malgal backgrounds alike, struggled to survive as the state required three obligations from them: land tax assessed on such harvests as millet, barley, and beans; tribute submitted in the form of hemp cloth, silk, and leather; and corvée for such government projects as construction or repair of royal palaces and office buildings.

The Parhae economy was based on agriculture, handicraft manufacturing, and commerce and enjoyed relative stability through the ninth century. Given Parhae's location in the colder climate region, dry-field farming was the mainstay of agriculture, but some warmer, coastal areas farther south sustained wet-paddy rice farming. Well-developed ranching raised oxen, pigs, horses, and sheep. Handicraft manufacturing produced a wide range of goods using iron, copper, gold, and silver; such textiles as hemp cloth and silk; and ceramics. Through trading these products, domestic commerce was well developed in cities such as Sanggyŏng, modeled after Tang China's capital Chang'an (present-day Xi'an), one of the world's most cosmopolitan metropolises at the time—with ethnoreligious groups from much of Eurasia present. Parhae also exported horses, fur, deer antlers, musk-scented items, ginseng, Buddha statues, and pottery. Major imports from Tang China included such goods in high aristocratic demand as silk and books. The Parhae-Tang trade followed Liaoning land routes and the Yellow Sea lanes. In Dengzhou, Tang maintained inns specifically for a large number of frequent Parhae visitors. The Parhae-Japan trade volume too was sizable, as the personnel of each trade mission numbered in the hundreds. For trade with Silla, Parhae established a permanent land route stretching from Sanggyŏng to northeastern Silla and passing through Tonggyŏng and Namgyŏng ("Southern Capital," possibly modern-day Hamhŭng, Hamgyŏng) and then following the eastern shore to reach Silla. The use of the route peaked at the turn of the ninth century. Parhae also traded with the Khitans, although little is known of that activity.

SOCIAL INTEGRATION: THE CENTER AND THE PERIPHERY

The combined population of Silla and Parhae likely did not increase much over this period. Around 700, the total was roughly 2 million, and even by the early tenth century, it may have been 2 to 4 million. Harvest irregularity, the state's harsh exactions, and epidemic disease probably prevented more rapid population growth. Among the various types of epidemic disease, smallpox likely ravaged Silla and Parhae, especially in cities and towns. In both states' final decades, widespread vagrancy among commoners and chronic warfare could have lowered the birth rate and increased the death rate.

Until the late ninth century, Silla's social hierarchy based on the bone rank system remained stable. In addition to wielding political power as aristocrats, true bones resided in Kŭmsŏng and maintained villas in the vicinity. They followed the latest fashion trends and enjoyed a comfortable living with luxury goods imported from Tang China and the Middle East. Below the true bones, men of head rank six and five found more advancement opportunities in officialdom, thanks to King Sinmun and his immediate successors. They sought to enhance royal power with more robust bureaucratic governance. By contrast, as distinctions among the three lowest head ranks faded, their respective rank holders became no different from ordinary commoners. And at the bottom of the social hierarchy, slaves probably changed little in population, since the enslavement of war prisoners had virtually ceased.

In the late eighth century, commoner cultivators' living conditions began to decline with a prolonged, violent power struggle among the ruling elite. As aristocrats expanded their estates and Buddhist monasteries amassed their own land as well, the number of free cultivators declined. The central government burdened the rest of the cultivator population with more taxes and other obligations. Residents of such special administrative districts as *hyang* and *pugok* suffered even more. The residents were legally commoners, but the government required such additional responsibilities as producing manufactured goods in high demand by the state and the aristocracy. Toward the end of the ninth century, recurring natural disasters and the government's chronic revenue shortage further increased tax burdens on commoners. Those who lost their plots became tenant farmers, if not resorting to slash-and-burn farming on hillsides, vagrancy, or even banditry.

As the power of the Silla central government grew weaker, local strong-men of diverse backgrounds became autonomous. Including Kungye and the descendants of King Muyŏl based in Myŏngju (present-day Kangnŭng, Kangwŏn), many were true-bone aristocrats or head rank six men who had lost out in the power struggle in Kŭmsŏng and had reestablished themselves in the provinces. Others, such as the founder of the Koryŏ dynasty (918–1392), Wang Kŏn (temple name T'aejo, r. 918–43), hailed from maritime merchant families who had accumulated wealth through the Yellow Sea trade. Includ-ing merchants like Wangs and Chang Pogo, those who interacted with the Chinese used Chinese-style surnames. Some, such as Kyŏnhwŏn, were garrison officers or locally prominent individuals like village headmen. Regardless of their backgrounds, autonomous local strongmen possessed revenue bases and manpower, including armies. Fortifying their home bases, many called themselves "castle lords" (sŏngju) or generals. They recruited talented advisors from those expressing discontent toward Silla, especially Confucian scholars of sixth head rank who had studied in Tang China and Sŏn Buddhist monks. Critical of the Silla bone rank system, many disaffected intellectuals, for whom the political establishment had no meaningful role, left the government, as did Ch'oe Ch'iwŏn, if not joining the rising local strongmen.

Much less is known about Parhae's multiethnic society. In a diplomatic document presented by his envoy to the Japanese court, King Mu declared that Parhae had recovered Koguryŏ's territory and inherited the customs of Puyŏ. In reality, since Tang had forcibly relocated much of the Koguryŏ population to China and since a significant population of Koguryŏ elites had fled to Japan, the majority of the Parhae population were Malgal, and those of Koguryŏ descent were numerous mostly at the elite level. Besides those with the royal surname Tae, the Parhae aristocracy included families with such Koguryŏ surnames as Ko. Holding all critical positions in the government, aristocrats generally resided in one of the five capitals or re-gional administrative centers with their slaves and the general population. Some Malgal who had assisted the founder Tae Choyŏng were able to join the ruling elite or wield local power as chiefs who managed local affairs. Regardless of ethnicity, Parhae's educated elites studied in Tang China, where many passed the "guest and tributary examination" (bingongke) for foreigners.

At times, the students from Parhae and Silla competed fiercely for the highest honor. Although Parhae adopted many Tang government institutions, the customs of Koguryŏ and Malgal shaped the people's daily life.

Extant sources on the Northern and Southern States period provide some suggestive details on gender and sexuality, and documented depictions of Queen Chinsŏng of Silla are revealing. Chinsŏng ascended the throne, likely in her early twenties, when both of her elder brothers had reigned and died without leaving a legitimate son (887). Initially, her husband, who was also her father's brother, exercised power as the regent, but upon his death, she ruled in person (888). The *History of the Three Kingdoms* and the *Memorabilia of the Three Kingdoms* portray her as tall and well-built, misbehaving and lustful, and recruiting and showering favors on a select group of beautiful young men while neglecting matters of state. Before long, Chinsŏng's lovers and their cronies took over the court, and rampant corruption incapacitated the government, which lost control of the provinces. Entrusted by the queen with reform, Ch'oe Ch'iwŏn described her as unselfish, not greedy, speaking only when appropriate, and strong-willed—unbending once she had made her decision. Suffering from various illnesses, she enjoyed pastimes before abdicating, and then dying six months later, only in her early thirties (897). The third and the last female monarch in Korean history, Chinsŏng would subsequently receive harsh treatment in orthodox Confucian historiography that idealized royal succession through a worthy legitimate male heir, even though such writers venerated Ch'oe as a founding figure in the history of Korean Confucianism.

LATE CLASSICAL CULTURE

State-sponsored Confucian education assumed greater importance in the Northern and Southern States period. As mentioned, in Silla, King Sinmun instituted the State Confucian College as the highest-level institution providing Confucian education (682). Decades later, King Kyŏngdŏk reorganized it as the State Confucian University (747), staffing it with instructors for such texts as the *Analects of Confucius* and the *Classic of Filial Piety* (Ch. *Xiaojing*; Ko. *Hyogyŏng*). The curriculum stressed loyalty to the ruler and filial piety as cardinal moral virtues. Going further, King Wonsŏng (r. 785–98), the founder of a new Kim line of monarchs, instituted the Three-Grades Reading Examination, which tested candidates for recruitment to official posts on their knowledge of the Confucian classics (788). The examination did not become the primary method for staffing an officialdom that remained bound to the bone rank system but it facilitated dissemination of Confucian learning among elites. Likewise, Parhae instituted the Directorate for Education, which oversaw all aspects of state-managed education: classics learning and more practical studies alike.

Achieving a high level of erudition, many scholars produced noteworthy achievements in various branches of knowledge. Both Parhae and Silla sent students to Tang China, where some, such as Ch'oe Ch'iwŏn, competed successfully in the guest and tributary examination for foreigners and even served in the Tang government. Including Ch'oe, such Silla students tended to be from head rank six families. Among them, Kangsu (d. 692), who came from a family of Greater Kaya descent, was exceptionally skilled in composing diplomatic documents. Another scholar of sixth head rank, Sŏl Ch'ong (b. 658), the son of Wŏnhyo, commanded an expansive knowledge of the Confucian classics and improved the existing indigenous script, hyangch'al, to aid others in the learning of Literary Sinitic. Not limited to Confucian learning, Silla elites authored works on a wide range of subjects. A true bone, Kim Taemun (fl. 704), wrote Chronicles of the Hwarang (Hwarang segi), which is a collection of biographies of hwarang; Lives of Eminent Monks (Kosŭng chŏn); and Record of Hansan (Hansan ki), which is a geographical treatise on expanded Silla's northernmost province, where he served as the governor. None of these works is extant, but these titles suggest that he sought to understand Silla culture as distinct from the culture of Tang China. Indeed, the bulk of extant Silla hyangga lyrics written in hyangch'al come from this period.

While the pursuit of knowledge in various branches appealed to secular elites, Buddhist clergy sought to achieve a deeper understanding of Buddhist teachings. Certainly, shamanism continued to complement Buddhism, as a popular religion rich with such ritual contents as "Song of Ch'ŏyong" (Ch'ŏyong ka), which served all as an incantatory hyangga, especially for warding off the Great Spirit of Fever (Yŏlbyŏng taesin) responsible for such illnesses as smallpox, measles, and malaria. Indeed accommodating shamanistic practices, many Silla Buddhist monks also traveled to China, where they participated in the latest intellectual discussions among cosmopolitan Buddhist circles. Some even visited India to study the religion in its birthplace. Among them, Hyech'o (704–87) wrote a vivid account of places he visited in South and Central Asia, Memoir of the Pilgrimage to India's Five Kingdoms (Wang o Ch'ŏnch'ukguk chŏn). In Parhae, Buddhism built on the traditions of Koguryŏ and thrived mainly among the ruling elite. King Mun styled himself a Chakravartin (Ko. Chŏllyun sŏngwang), in Buddhism, an ethical, benevolent universal ruler and, in a way, the secular counterpart to a Buddha. More than ten grand monastery sites and various Buddha statues excavated in Sanggyŏng indeed suggest Buddhism flourished in Parhae.

In Silla, a desire to disseminate Buddhist sutras fostered a flourishing print culture, which stimulated overall knowledge production and calligraphy. Considered the oldest extant printed text globally, the Great Dharani Sutra—an early eighth-century scroll discovered inside a three-story stone pagoda at Pulguk-sa—reflects Silla's highly developed paper manufacturing technology. The paper of the scroll, made from the paper mulberry tree, is of such high quality and durability that the material has survived to the present. Skillful woodblock carving allowed a faithful reproduction of the text's calligraphy, in which Kim Saeng (b. 711) pioneered a simple yet unique style. The Silla print culture also facilitated the reception and spread of new knowledge in astronomy and mathematics. Silla adopted the Xuanming calendar, which Tang China had devised in 822 and which calculated one year as 365.2446 days, impressively close to 365.2425 days—the average of Gregorian calendar years across the complete leap cycle of 400 years.

Little has survived of Silla and Parhae constructions and sites, yet that little has yielded some insights on mathematical and architectural knowledge during the Northern and Southern States period. Almost nothing of Silla royal palaces and houses remains. However, extant constructions such as the pagoda at Pulguk-sa and Sŏkkuram, a grotto serving as a hermitage for Pulguk-sa, are revealing (Figures 3.1 and 3.2). Both are representative works of late Silla Buddhist architecture. Constructed in 751, Pulguk-sa expresses the ideal of a Buddha-land through harmony, proportion, and balance, whereas Sŏkkuram, completed some twenty years later, symbolizes a spiritual journey into Nirvana. No standing structure of Parhae is extant, but the excavated sites of the royal palace and monastery still show that such constructions were integral parts of the capital, Sanggyŏng. As was true in its Tang model, Chang'an, Sanggyŏng's main road stretched southward from the palace, and an outer wall surrounded the city.

Burial cultures of Parhae and Silla likewise integrated influences of Tang China, Buddhism, and earlier indigenous practices. Following Buddhist practice, cremation became the norm among elites. In Silla, the burial construction style gradually changed from larger stone-mound wooden chamber tombs to

FIGURE 3.1   Pulguk-sa, Kyŏngju, North Kyŏngsang Province. Photo credit: Cultural Heritage Administration.

smaller, corridor-style stone chamber tombs. A new construction trend featured a burial mound at its base surrounded by a ring of rectangular decorative stones, each carved with an image of one of the twelve "branch" deities according to the East Asian zodiac. As depicted, each god combines a human body with the head of one of the twelve branch animals—rat, ox, tiger, rabbit, dragon, snake, horse, ram, monkey, cock, dog, and boar. Among the good number of Parhae burial structures excavated is the tomb of Princess Chŏnghye (738–77), the daughter of King Mun. Its artifacts reflect Parhae's sophisticated, eclectic culture. As a corridor-style stone chamber tomb, its intersecting triangular ceiling resembles a late Koguryŏ tomb. An inscribed text provides information on Chŏnghye's life, and mural paintings depict her attendants.

Craftspeople of the Northern and Southern States period produced outstanding depictions of Buddhas and bodhisattvas, some freestanding, others relief figures (Figure 3.3). A masterpiece, the Buddha statue at the center of the main chamber of Sŏkkuram is made so that a viewer entering the grotto can sense movement in the sculpture, which employs both relative symmetry and realism in balance. As the bodhisattva carvings on the walls

FIGURE 3.2   View of Sŏkkuram, showing protective deities and other guardians in the entry-way leading to the stone Buddha statue. Photo credit: Cultural Heritage Administration.

around the statue also employ realism, the designer of Sŏkkuram seems to have intended the grotto to imbue a visitor with a sense of entering an ideal Buddhist realm—gradually leading the pilgrim from the natural simplicity of the entrance on a low-lying hillside into the refined, purified inner space. Parhae too produced masterpiece Buddha statues, many of which the kingdom exported. In the monastery sites of Sanggyŏng and Tonggyŏng, archeologists have excavated sculptures that reflect the stylistic influence of Koguryŏ. Made of baked clay, each work positions two Buddhas seated next to each other, rather than the triad of Buddhas flanked by two bodhisat-tvas common in the earlier masterpieces of the Three Kingdoms. Given the cosmopolitan characteristics of Parhae's capitals, the design may reflect Zoroastrian or Manichean dualism's influence, if not intense early Christian struggles with the relative importance and relationship between the human and divine natures of Christ.

In addition to Buddhist statues and relief images, other extant works demonstrate a high level of craftsmanship. Works from Parhae's well-developed ceramic production tend to be bright and shiny, although varying greatly in type, size, shape, and color. Masonry was no less impressive, and among other features, high-quality bricks and roof tiles with bold yet straightforward inscribed patterns show Koguryŏ influence. Among the far smaller quantity of metallurgical works extant are Silla Buddhist monastery bells of quality artistry. In the late seventh century, Silla began to cast many such works, including the Sangwŏn-sa Bell and the Bell of King Sŏngdŏk (r. 702–37), the son and successor of King Sinmun. The Bell of King Sŏngdŏk, in particular, is famous for its solemn yet clear tone and delicate carvings of flying heavenly maids. Made of bronze containing zinc, the bell owes its mystical sound to Silla's outstanding metal casting technique.

In the late seventh and early eighth centuries, Silla transmitted diverse aspects of classical Korean civilization to Japan's Asuka Culture, albeit on a scale more limited than earlier transmissions from Paekche. Among other philosophical tools, Hwaŏm thought, as introduced by Simsang (d. 742), facilitated the spread of Hwaŏm Buddhism in Japan. Also, the Confucian ideas studied by Sŏl Ch'ong influenced the Japanese court, which was actively adopting continental institutions in pursuit of a more centralized bureaucratic government based on a law code. The destruction of Paekche, however, gradually alienated Japan from Korea. In the late eighth century, when the Japanese court relocated to Heian (modern-day Kyoto), a tendency to reject continental influence and look down on Silla grew stronger.

By contrast, Silla continued to embrace new institutions and ideas from cosmopolitan Tang China, including Sŏn Buddhism, which had become increasingly popular since its introduction in 784. Critiquing doctrinal schools that stressed intellectual understanding and knowledge of the teachings of sutras and other texts, Sŏn schools emphasized self-control, meditation, gaining insight into the Buddha-nature, and personal application of such wisdom in daily life, especially for the benefit of others. To this end, Sŏn sought a direct understanding of the Buddha-nature through meditation and learning from an accomplished teacher. Growing demand for reform within the late Silla Buddhist world accelerated the spread of Sŏn, which challenged not only establishment Buddhist teachings but also the existing ecclesiastical organization. Sŏn eventually became the guiding ideology among local strongmen, as many Sŏn monks hailed from such families. In collaboration with local strongmen, the Sŏn clergy established home monasteries in various regions, among which the most prominent became known as the "nine mountain schools." Spreading from such bases, Sŏn enriched regional cultures as distinct from the true-bone aristocratic culture

FIGURE 3.3   A Parhae Buddhist stele, 834. Standing 73.3 centimeters tall, the inscription records the era name of the Parhae ruler at the time. The text also records an individual as a vassal prince appointed by the Parhae monarch. Source: Ohara Museum of Art, Kurashiki, Japan. Photo credit: pressapochista via Wikimedia Commons.

of Kŭmsŏng. In particular, octagonal layered stupas containing relics of venerable monks and steles commemorating their lives became popular. Displaying the sophistication and sense of balance of late Silla artistic style, relic stupas and memorial steles symbolize the transmission of awakening experience or enlightenment from the teacher to the disciple as valued in Sŏn. Moreover, these works reflect the growth of local strongmen as political forces patronizing Sŏn. Along with Silla intellectuals of the sixth head rank who desired social reform, the Sŏn clergy laid the ideological foundation for the eventual victor among the Later Three Kingdoms, and the unifier, the Koryŏ dynasty.

Simultaneously, geomancy ("wind and water"; Ch. *feng shui*; Ko. *p'ungsu*) became popular, especially among local strongmen. Such Silla monks as Tosŏn (827–98) had introduced geomancy, popular in Tang China. Understanding topography in an organic sense, geomancy recognized auspicious and inauspicious sites, especially when proper locations for capitals, royal palaces, residences, and family graves were being selected. Fundamentally concerned with the effective use of the entire terrain, late Silla geomancy encouraged the identification of auspicious locales outside Kŭmsŏng, thus rejecting old Silla's world view, which privileged the capital and its true-bone elites. Tosŏn did much to popularize geomancy by disseminating his topographical knowledge to address the ordinary people's desire for peace and stability. His ideas especially appealed to the local strongmen who believed that their home bases were auspicious and that they destined to succeed in pursuing their political ambitions, if not the kingship itself.

Parhae's and Silla's residential structures, including royal palaces, continued to use various wooden and *ondol* floorings, depending on the household's climate and social status. In the summer in Silla, and perhaps in Parhae as well, rice was cooked over a charcoal burner, instead of a furnace connected to the household's overall *ondol* system. The floors in Silla homes were covered with rugs and other textile materials, which were also used for doors, windows, and walls. Since these features were similar to those of earlier Koguryŏ homes, Parhae most likely maintained identical customs.

Likewise, the diet in both Parhae and Silla embodied elements of change and continuity. Not only did rice remain the elite's staple, but Koreans as a whole also enjoyed a great variety of *ttŏk*. Cultivation of rice, wheat, millet, cluster mallow, and beans was widespread in Parhae, whereas in Silla, rice, barley, millet, and beans were the essential crops. Besides grain, the people in Silla grew scallions, cucumbers, eggplants, walnuts, pine nuts, and ginseng. Common fruits in Parhae included plums, Korean pears, and grapes, among which both pears and grapes were used for *ttŏk*. In addition, animal husbandry was widespread in Parhae, with people raising oxen, pigs, horses, and dogs. In Silla, livestock farming was common, centered around chickens, oxen, pigs, horses, and dogs. Hunting, with the assistance of dogs, supplemented the slaughter of domesticated animals as a source of meat. The people in Parhae hunted deer, Siberian musk deer, rabbits, bears, and tigers. Fishing was also common as Parhae's abundant lakes, rivers, and seashores offered flathead grey mullet, crucian carp, shark, octopus and Korean common octopus (*nakchi*), snow crab, hawksbill sea turtles, and *tasima*. Not only were most of these available also in Silla but clams and seaweed further enriched the diet there. In both states, sea salt was critically important as a preservative, condiment, and essential ingredient for such derived condiments as fermented pastes. In Parhae, fermented bean pastes (*toenjang*) of Tonggyŏng, sesame oil, and honey, in particular, were valued. In Silla, fermented pastes of all kinds, dried meat, dried fish, and salted seafood were favorites. The overall similarity in customs between Parhae and Silla at the classical period's end awaited only the political unity of the Koryŏ dynasty that would herald Korea's post-classical period.

The Post-Classical Period

PART II

The Post-Classical Period

CHAPTER 4

Early Koryŏ, 918–1146

K oryŏ established the first united monarchy of the land that the An-
glophone world would eventually call "Korea." The new order, based
on local strongmen and head rank six intellectuals, instituted an examination system to recruit central officials, who constituted a new aristocracy. Koryŏ also accommodated refugees from Parhae, repelled attacks by the
Khitan Liao dynasty, and then traded with Liao and also with China's Song
dynasty (960–1279), the Jurchens, and the Japanese. The state supported
its personnel with Stipend Land Law (976), expanded cultivated land, and
promoted commerce and manufacturing. The aristocrats who commanded
wealth were hereditary functionaries descended from local strongmen—
above commoners and the lowborn, mostly slaves. Many local functionaries
(*hyangni*) and soldiers entered officialdom, whereas commoners performed tax,
tribute, corvée, and military obligations. While elites pursued a deeper understanding of Confucianism, Buddhist intellectuals sought the unity of the
doctrinal and Sŏn schools. Buddhism, shamanism, geomancy, and Daoism
shaped daily life and a culture wherein architecture, sculpture, celadon ware,
and print technology reflected master craftsmanship.

THE ESTABLISHMENT OF THE FIRST UNITED MONARCHY

The Koryŏ founder, King T'aejo, was keenly aware of his place in history.
For his state, which he proclaimed to be the successor of Koguryŏ, he chose

the name Koryŏ. T'aejo also adopted an era name, Ch'ŏnsu ("Heaven be-
stowed [mandate]"), thus assuming the status of a universal ruler. He embraced continuing waves of a mass exodus from internally weakened Parhae,
which Khitan Liao ultimately conquered (926). Even bestowing his surname,
Wang, on a Parhae prince, T'aejo accommodated the refugees and settled
them between the capital, renamed Kaegyŏng (formerly Songak; present-
day Kaesŏng), and P'yŏngyang, which he designated as Sŏgyŏng ("Western
Capital"). Using the latter as a base, T'aejo pushed the border northward
up to the Ch'ŏngch'ŏn River and occupied a buffer zone between Koryŏ
and Liao. To secure a continental ally, he established relations with one of
the Five Dynasties (907–60) of northern China proper and began to use
Chinese era names (933). Simultaneously, T'aejo courted Silla, the totter-
ing yet prestigious ancient state. Earlier, when Kyŏnhwŏn of Later Paekche
sacked Kŭmsŏng and killed the king, T'aejo had aided Silla, thus winning
the trust of its people (927). Subsequently, the new Silla monarch elevated
by Kyŏnhwŏn, King Kyŏngsun (r. 927–35), surrendered his state to Koryŏ
(Figure 4.1). Earlier in the year, when Kyŏnhwŏn defected to Koryŏ after
losing his throne to the eldest son, T'aejo received him warmly and then
conquered Later Paekche (936). Farther away, he received a tributary mission
from the East Sea island state of Usan and granted the visitors Koryŏ offices
(930). From the island state to the south, T'amna, T'aejo secured ritual submission and recognized its visiting prince as the hereditary ruler of the isle
(938). Indeed, Koryŏ established Korea's first united kingdom.

T'aejo instituted a political system that retained Kungye's basic bureaucratic structure and modified both the Silla and the Tang systems. Awarding
key positions to "foundation merit subjects," who had helped him ascend
the throne, and to cooperative local strongmen, T'aejo married the women
of prominent local strongman families: six queens and twenty-three royal
concubines. At the same time, he sought to extend the central government's
power by appointing local inspectors general and maintaining *kiin* (*sangsuri* in
Silla), who resided as members of local strongman families in Kaegyŏng and
were de facto hostages. Mindful of the new political order's future, T'aejo
authored *Ten Injunctions* (*Hunyo sip cho*) that admonished his successors. His
concerns were not unwarranted: T'aejo had twenty-six sons by his queens
and concubines, and during the two subsequent reigns, a violent power
struggle ensued among his fathers-in-law advocating for their respective
royal grandsons.

FIGURE 4.1   Portrait of King Kyŏngsun by Yi Myŏnggi (b. 1756), 1794. Living forty-three years after surrendering his kingdom, Kyŏngsun lay low during the turmoil, and historically, no Kim family has made a credible claim of descent from him. His posthumous fame grew as succeeding dynasties honored him as the virtuous last monarch of Silla. Today, some 300 Kim-surnamed descent groups that have been claiming descent from him since late Chosŏn account for about ten million Koreans. Source: Gyeongju National Museum. Photo credit: Cultural Heritage Administration.

T'aejo's fourth son and the fourth Koryŏ ruler, King Kwangjong (r. 949–75), succeeded in enhancing royal power through suppressing the influence of foundation merit subjects and local strongmen, purging thousands. Kwangjong weakened their economic and military bases as well as expanding the state's revenue base, the commoner population of free cultivators, by instituting the Slave Review Law (956), which not only returned slaves to their rightful owners but, more importantly, freed those who had been wrongly enslaved in the chaotic decades of the Silla-Koryŏ transition. Kwangjong also sought to replace the political establishment with a new Confucian-educated officialdom by instituting the government service examination system (958). And by standardizing officials' dress according to nine court ranks, which effectively replaced Silla's hereditary head ranks, he created a clear hierarchy for the ruling elite. To further enhance his stature as a universal ruler, Kwangjong adopted imperial nomenclature and such era names as Kwangdŏk ("Illustrious virtue") and Chunp'ung ("Great abundance").

Building on Kwangjong's works, his nephew and the sixth monarch, King Sŏngjong (r. 981–97), pursued more centralized governance led by Confucian scholars with mostly Silla's sixth head rank backgrounds. Upon accession, Sŏngjong solicited policy recommendations from mid-level and higher officials. Among them, Ch'oe Sŭngno (927–89), who hailed from a sixth head rank Kyŏngju (formerly Kŭmsŏng) Ch'oe family, submitted "Twenty-Eight Urgent Points of Reform" (982), of which twenty-two are extant. Besides assessing the achievements and shortcomings of Sŏngjong's predecessors so that the king could draw lessons from the past, Ch'oe advocated further promoting Confucianism and curtailing excessive expenditure on Buddhist ceremonies. Taking up Ch'oe's proposal, Sŏngjong reformed the official recruitment system, giving preferential treatment to those who passed the government service examination, in order to promote more individuals with an in-depth knowledge of Confucianism.

The early Koryŏ recruitment system struck a compromise between meritocracy and aristocratic privilege with the examination and the protection appointment ("shadow privilege") systems. The examination featured three types of competition. The most prestigious composition examination required policy essays based on literary talent, whereas the classics examination tested knowledge of the Confucian classics. Regarded less highly, the "miscellaneous examination" recruited technical officials with expertise in law, accounting, or geography. Legally, all males except the lowborn could compete. In reality, the composition and classics examination candidates came mostly from the aristocracy and upper-stratum local functionary families, who were descendants of local strongmen during the Silla-Koryŏ transition. Even the miscellaneous examination was realistically accessible only to a small number of educated commoners. At the same time, the protection appointment system provided a safety net for less talented members of the ruling elite by allowing appointments without passing an examination for the descendants of monarchs and merit subjects; and for the sons, grandsons, sons-in-law, brothers, and nephews of mid-level or higher officials, that is, those of the top five court ranks on the nine-rank hierarchy, with each rank divided into senior and junior levels.

Completed by the end of Sŏngjong's reign, early Koryŏ officialdom comprised civil and military officials, together known as *yangban* ("two orders"; 995). Simultaneously holding one of the nine court ranks, an officeholder served either in or outside Kaegyŏng, depending on the post. Modeled after the Tang antecedent, the Two Chancelleries and Six Ministries formed the core of the reorganized administrative organization (995). Outside the capital, the central government had earlier established twelve provinces (*mok*) throughout the realm (983). Each provincial governor (*moksa*) regulated and incorporated local strongmen into an increasingly centralized governing system as hereditary local functionaries.

Undergoing further modification, the early Koryŏ system of local administration saw completion during King Hyŏnjong's reign (r. 1009–31). The design divided the realm into a capital district (Kyŏnggi), which surrounded Kaegyŏng, five provinces (*to*), and two border regions (*kye*); and designated major administrative centers as three secondary capitals, four protectorates (*tohobu*), and eight districts (*mok*; Map 4.1). To each province, an intermediate-level local administration without a standing bureaucracy, the court dispatched a commissioner to perform an inspection tour of the prefectures (*kun*) and counties (*hyŏn*) constituting the province. By contrast, the court appointed a military commander for the northern and eastern border regions established for the northern frontier zone and the eastern shore. Instead of prefectures or counties, each border region consisted of garrisons.

The authority of the central government extended only gradually. The court began to appoint officials for prefectures, counties, and military garrisons, but among the prefectures and counties, the appointments were only for the "control prefectures" (*chugun*) and "control counties" (*chuhyŏn*). Each

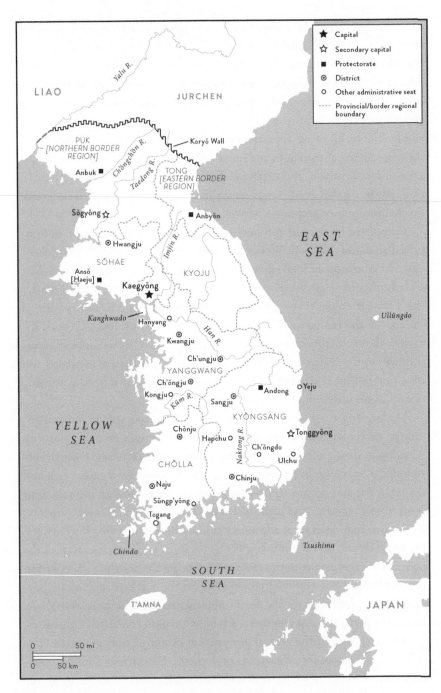

LEGEND:
★ Capital
☆ Secondary capital
■ Protectorate
⊙ District
○ Other administrative seat
- - - Provincial/border regional boundary

LIAO

JURCHEN

Yalu R.

PUK
[NORTHERN BORDER
REGION]

Koryŏ Wall

Anbuk ■

Ch'ŏngch'ŏn R.

Taedong R.

TONG
[EASTERN BORDER
REGION]

Sŏgyŏng ☆

Anbyŏn ■

Hwangju ⊙

Imjin R.

EAST
SEA

SŎHAE

KYOJU

Ansŏ
[Haeju] ■

Kaegyŏng ★

Kanghwado

Hanyang ○

Han R.

Ullŭngdo

Kwangju ⊙

Ch'ungju ⊙

YANGGWANG

Ch'ŏngju ⊙

Kongju ○

Andong ■

Yeju ⊙

Kŭm R.

Sangju ⊙

KYŎNGSANG

YELLOW
SEA

Chŏnju ⊙

Hapchu ○

Naktong R.

Tonggyŏng ☆

Ch'ŏngdo ○

Ulchu ○

CHŎLLA

Chinju ⊙

Naju ⊙

Sŭngp'yŏng ○

Togang ○

Chindo

Tsushima

SOUTH
SEA

T'AMNA

JAPAN

0   50 mi
0   50 km

MAP 4.1   Major administrative centers and boundaries of Koryŏ, 1050.

control prefecture oversaw subordinate prefectures (*sokkun*), subordinate counties (*sokhyŏn*), and unique local administrative districts, that is *hyang*, *pugok*, and *so*. A control county had subordinate counties, *hyang*, *pugok*, and *so* under its jurisdiction. Subordinate prefectures and subordinate counties outnumbered the control prefectures and control counties. In a subordinate prefecture or a subordinate county, neither of which had an official appointed by the central government, hereditary local functionaries performed such essential administrative duties as collecting taxes and local tribute and mobilizing a workforce for corvée and military service. In the case of distant T'amna, Koryŏ turned the island into a prefecture (1105) before downgrading its status to a county (1153), but kept the indigenous Ko royal house, allowing the leader to inherit princely positions.

Also completed during Hyŏnjong's reign, the early Koryŏ military organization consisted of central and local armies. The central military comprised Two Armies, which consisted of royal guards, and Six Divisions, which handled capital and frontier defense. Serving in the Two Armies and Six Divisions as low-level officers were hereditary professional soldiers, *kunban* ("soldiery order"), who were recorded on the army register (*kunjŏk*); for his services, the government provided a *kunban* with soldier's land. By contrast, garrison armies in the two border regions and county armies in the five provinces conscripted males aged sixteen to sixty from among ordinary commoners.

The military rose to the occasion for its first true test, the Koryŏ-Khitan War (993–1019). As Khitan Liao was at war with Song China, to which Koryŏ remained well disposed, Liao attacked Koryŏ with an army of about 60,000 to secure its flank and demanded that Koryŏ cede whatever former Koguryŏ territory it was holding and end relations with Song. After a negotiation, Liao withdrew when Koryŏ promised to establish relations with Liao in return for the latter's recognition of Koryŏ as Koguryŏ's successor and of Koryŏ control of six districts between the Ch'ŏngch'ŏn and Yalu Rivers—to facilitate direct communication between Liao and Koryŏ, as the latter argued (993). Subsequently, when a military strongman, Kang Cho (964–1010), deposed King Mokchong (r. 997–1009), Liao attacked Koryŏ with an army of 400,000, ostensibly to punish Kang. After routing Kang's army of 300,000 and taking some fortresses, Liao withdrew, finding its rear supply lane insecure (1010). When Liao attacked Koryŏ yet again, Kang Kamch'an (948–1031) commanded 208,000 Koryŏ troops and annihilated

100,000 Liao troops in the Battle of Kwiju (1018–19). Koryŏ then strengthened its defense by constructing a city wall around Kaegyŏng and building a long wall along the northern border. Unable to continue its war with both Koryŏ and Song, even though the latter was not performing well militarily, Liao came to terms with both. This peaceful trilateral balance of power in eastern Eurasia would last a century.

In the postwar era, early Koryŏ officialdom, centered around the Two Chancelleries and Six Ministries, saw completion during King Munjong's reign (1046–83). Headed by a chancellor, one of the Two Chancelleries, the Secretariat-Chancellery, comprised *chaesin* who, as first- and second-rank officials, deliberated on matters of state, and remonstrance officials, who not only protested what they deemed the monarch's wrongful policy decisions and improper behaviors but also ratified personnel actions and policy measures in collaboration with surveillance officials. The second of the Two Chancelleries, the Executive Department, oversaw the Six Ministries' policies. Other key organs included the Security Council, which transmitted royal commands and handled urgent military matters; the Finance Commission, which handled financial affairs and accounting; the Military Council, which assembled *chaesin* to deliberate on affairs of state; and the Directorate-General of State Affairs, wherein five lower second-rank officials, *ch'usin*, who headed the Security Council, did likewise. Concurrently holding the highest-level offices in the Six Ministries and other major organs, the *chaesin* and *ch'usin*—together known as *chaech'u*—exercised political leadership.

Early Koryŏ officialdom operated as a system of checks and balances thanks to the Censorate. Constituting the Censorate personnel were the Secretariat-Chancellery's remonstrance officials and the Office of the Inspector General, which performed policy critiques and personnel inspection. Although not of high ranks, the Censorate officials had the power to ratify personnel actions and policy measures, protest improper royal behaviors, and even send back royal commands that they deemed wrongful. As some aristocratic families, however, became overly powerful, with multiple marriage ties to the throne, the functional integrity of the Censorate and other vital organs of the central government gradually decreased. By the beginning of the twelfth century, a political storm was brewing as prominent families competed for power while a new external challenge loomed on the horizon.

In the north, the ascendant Jurchens of eastern Manchuria began to disrupt the peaceful trilateral relations among Koryŏ, Khitan Liao, and

Song China. Descended from the Malgal and divided into various tribes, the Jurchens had been enjoying considerable autonomy under Liao since the fall of Parhae. For its part, Koryŏ sought to keep the Jurchens content by offering various incentives. Nonetheless, the Jurchens occasionally raided the border and the Koryŏ tributary island state of Usan to the extent that the islanders could no longer continue farming, and Koryŏ placed Usan under the jurisdiction of a coastal militia commissioner in Yeju (modern-day Yŏnghae, North Kyŏngsang; 1022). By 1104, advancing Jurchens gained control of the Tumen (Ko. Tuman) River basin and increased their military pressure on Koryŏ. Taking up the recommendations of a high official, Yun Kwan (1040–1111), King Yejong (r. 1105–22) created the Special Military Corps, composed of a cavalry unit, an infantry unit, and a unit of Buddhist warrior monks. Yun commanded them with success in repelling the Jurchens and fortifying the newly acquired territory (1107). After pressures from Yun's political enemies and promises of annual tribute from the Jurchens, Koryŏ returned the acquired territory (1109). Before long, a new leader united the Jurchens, founded the Jin dynasty (1115–1234), conquered Khitan Liao (1125), and wrested the Yellow River valley from Song China (1126). When Jin demanded submission as a vassal, Koryŏ assented, as Yi Chagyŏm (d. 1126), who was wielding supreme power as a royal in-law, did not want to jeopardize his position.

Yi was a member of the Kyŏngwŏn (present-day Inch'ŏn) Yi family, which had been in power for some eighty years with marriage ties to the throne. The rise of Kyŏngwŏn Yi to prominence began when King Munjong married a daughter of Yi Chagyŏm's grandfather, Yi Chayŏn (1003–61). As the father of the wife of King Yejong and the wife of Yejong's son and successor, King Injong (r. 1122–46), Yi Chagyŏm even purged Yejong's confidants and played a critical role in helping Injong ascend the throne despite Yejong's doubts about his son's abilities. As Yi and his supporters abused their power, those loyal to Injong organized themselves as a political force. In response, Yi staged a coup with the support of a military man, Ch'ŏk Chun'gyŏng (d. 1144), who soon switched sides, throwing his support behind the king who then banished Yi (1126).

In the aftermath, Injong pursued reforms geared toward enhancing royal power, improving the people's livelihood, and strengthening military defense, but the ensuing policy debate produced a new conflict. Leading more reform-minded figures from the provinces were Myoch'ŏng (d. 1135), who was a Buddhist monk from Sŏgyŏng, and his supporters, who used geomancy in arguing that Kaegyŏng's energy had been depleted and that auspicious Sŏgyŏng, the final capital of Koguryŏ, was full of vigor. Constructing a new palace for the king in Sŏgyŏng, Myoch'ŏng partisans urged Injong to assume an imperial title and attack Jin. In contrast, conservatives centered around Kim Pusik (1075–1151), a Kyŏngju Kim aristocrat descended from local functionaries of the former Silla capital, defended the status quo. When Injong wavered, Myoch'ŏng staged a rebellion from Sŏgyŏng, which was ultimately suppressed by the government army under Kim's command (1135–36). This outcome marked the victory of pragmatist Silla successionism over Koguryŏ successionism and the entrenchment of the socioeconomic interests of the Kaegyŏng aristocracy.

REVITALIZED AGRARIAN ECONOMY

Early Koryŏ reformed the tax collection and workforce mobilization systems that were in disarray by the final decades of Silla. King T'aejo not only prohibited local strongmen from overtaxing the population but also fixed the land tax at one-tenth of the harvest, the same rate applied in the Silla levy system before its collapse. When the early Koryŏ administrative reorganization was complete, both the Ministry of Taxation and the Finance Commission handled revenue management. The state budgeted for general expenditures, military defense, officials' stipends, and royal house expenses. Each government agency had land allocated to cover its costs, but an agency could secure funds through other means when that allocation was insufficient. The government also granted land tenure to incumbent officials and others who served the state and their beneficiaries, and each tenure holder collected land tax from commoner cultivators. To take stock of its resources, the government conducted land and household surveys. Land registers recorded each cultivated plot's owner and size, whereas household registers (*hojŏk*) documented families centered around married couples or extended families.

Utilizing the registers, the state levied land tax, local tribute, military service, and corvée on all except the lowborn. To assess land tax, the government classified rice paddies and dry fields into three grades in terms of productivity. Each prefecture or county mobilized its commoner population to transport the collected grain to tax granaries, from which government-authorized ships transported the tax grain to Kaegyŏng. Also, determining the quantity of other products needed by various agencies, the government levied local tributes on prefectures and counties, collecting them annually or as required, depending on the product. Control prefectures and control counties levied tribute on their respective subordinate administrative units. Local functionaries were instrumental in collecting tribute from households at the village level and in conscripting males aged sixteen to sixty for corvée and military obligation. The government also levied taxes on fishers and merchants.

The state's de facto competitors in exacting funds from the free population were land tenure holders. Instituted by King Kyŏngjong (r. 975–81), who built on his father and predecessor Kwangjong's efforts to effect a stronger monarchy, the Stipend Land Law of 976 granted land tenure in eighteen grades to civil and military officials, soldiers, and *hanin* ("idlers"), who were officeless sons of officials of the sixth court rank or lower. The system entitled a tenure holder to collect land tax on the harvest of resident cultivators and firewood from woodlands. In principle, the land reverted to the government when the tenure holders died or no longer performed their duty. Still, the government also allocated land to the surviving beneficiaries of those who died after serving the state and various institutions essential for the well-being of the state or the royal house. Accordingly, an official of fifth rank or higher was eligible for "merit-protection land," which he could transfer to a descendant as an inheritance. Along with protection appointments, merit-protection land was crucial for maintaining a family's aristocratic status. The state even granted land to *hanin*, thus allowing less talented members of the ruling elite to maintain their lifestyles. Likewise, a soldier's land was transferable to a central army soldier's heir inheriting the military obligation. Furthermore, surviving relatives of lower-level officials and soldiers received pension land. And the royal house, government agencies, and Buddhist monasteries maintained royal estate land, government agency land, and monastic land, respectively, to cover their expenses.

Most of the cultivated land, however, was in privately owned "people's land" (*minjŏn*) plots, which aristocrats and commoners acquired through inheritance, transactions, and reclamation. The state guaranteed ownership of a plot of people's land as a private holding that could be bought, sold, inherited, transferred, or leased, and was thus immune to arbitrary takeover. Entitlement to all that the land could produce also bound the owner to a land tax. An aristocrat's primary income sources and assets were inherited landholdings and slaves, a rank land (*kwajŏn*), and a government stipend for holding an office. Such an aristocrat collected one-tenth of the harvest from his rank land and received grain or silk twice a year as stipends from the government. Tenant farmers and slaves typically cultivated the aristocrat's land, and the owner collected one-half of the harvest through deputies who oversaw the cultivators. Each year, a slave owner also collected hemp cloth and grain as "personal tribute" (*sin'gong*) from out-resident slaves who lived separately from the owner to take care of the latter's properties elsewhere. Aristocrats increased their landholdings through land reclamation, buying financially strapped commoners' plots at a low price, or, using political clout or high-interest rates, outright taking over such land. Certainly, most commoners struggled to make ends meet, as they generally cultivated whatever people's land they inherited, state-owned land, or someone's private plot. Day labor and weaving hemp cloth, ramie fabric, or silk were additional sources of household income. Commoner cultivators also tried to increase their harvests through land reclamation and new farming techniques.

The early Koryŏ economic policy entailed measures to aid commoner cultivators. To encourage land reclamation and to disseminate new farming techniques, the government offered rent subsidies or temporary tax exemptions to those who cultivated wasteland or weed-grown fallow land. If such a plot had an owner, then the state subsidized any rent that the cultivator owed; if it was unowned, the cultivator became the new legal owner. Other measures that the government took to aid commoner cultivators included (1) prohibition against their mobilization for corvée or "miscellaneous obligations" during busy farming seasons; (2) price equalization granaries to keep the market price stable, through either selling or buying grain as needed; (3) capping the interest rate at 100 percent of the principal; (4) emergency relief granaries for storing grain in reserve in ordinary times and distributing it among the poor during famines; and (5) reduced tax or corvée, if not an exemption, in times of natural disaster.

In contrast to commoners, slaves were not free, but they at least enjoyed minimal economic security. Among public slaves, whose owners were various state agencies, "service slaves" received remuneration for work at palaces or government offices. In contrast, out-resident slaves lived in the provinces to cultivate state-owned land and to submit a legally prescribed portion of the harvest to the agency that owned them. Similarly, a private slave, who was the property of an aristocrat or a Buddhist monastery, could be a resident slave, who lived with the owner and performed domestic work, or an out-resident slave, who lived separately from the owner, cultivated the owner's land, and submitted a required portion of the harvest as personal tribute. Since out-resident slaves could also cultivate someone else's land or pursue other economic activities, some achieved a degree of financial security comparable to that of a landed farmer.

In the mostly subsistence-level, agrarian economy of early Koryŏ, the state managed much of the handicraft manufacturing. Limited in scale and scope, handicraft manufacturing mostly entailed producing goods necessary for the government and the royal house, such as weapons and silk. Each agency maintained a roster of master artisans and other skilled laborers, from whom it procured such necessary goods as weapons, furniture, goldware, silverware, silk fabric, and horse trappings. Also, the government mobilized private artisans and commoner cultivators for additional handicraft products as needed. Furthermore, residents of *so* were required to submit such goods as thread, fabric dye, paper, ink sticks, tea, ginger, and mined gold, silver, iron, and copper as a local tribute. By contrast, individual household production formed the mainstay of private handicraft manufacturing. As the state encouraged silk production by raising mulberry trees, commoner cultivator households produced ramie fabric and silk for their own use and submission as a local tribute. Additionally, Buddhist monasteries had monks, nuns, and slaves skilled at making hemp cloth, ramie fabric, roof tiles, wine, and salt.

Despite limited production through handicraft manufacturing, commerce flourished in early Koryŏ, centered around the cities. In Kaegyŏng, the government set up the City Market with state-operated shops. Customers were mostly government officials and aristocrats, and the Bureau of Capital Market Supervision oversaw transactions. Also, Kaegyŏng and such other cities as Sŏgyŏng and the former Silla capital, Tonggyŏng ("Eastern Capital"), featured stores that sold books, medicine, wine, and tea, all government produced. Additionally, occasional markets allowed urban residents to buy and sell daily necessities. In the countryside, officials, local functionaries, commoner cultivators, and artisans gathered near government offices where they bartered hemp cloth, rice, and other essential commodities. Bringing goods to rural markets, peddlers traveled from village to village to sell such items of daily use as salt in exchange for hemp cloth or grain, and they bought grain and handicraft products from monasteries, and sold them at country markets and villages.

In early Koryŏ, hemp cloth and grain functioned as de facto currency, but the government began to issue money as commerce flourished. Minted in Sŏngjong's reign, *Kŏnwŏn chungbo* (996), an iron coin, is Korea's first known money. A century later, King Sukchong (r. 1095–1105) issued copper coins, *Samhan t'ongbo* (1101?), *Haedong t'ongbo* (1102), and *Haedong chungbo* (1103?). Supplementing these coins was silver money shaped like Korea, or a bottle, *Hwalgu* (1101), which was made of one *kŭn* (about 630 grams) of silver and worth more than 100 bolts of hemp cloth. None of this currency, however, achieved wide circulation, as commercial transactions and trade continued to favor hemp cloth and grain as means of exchange.

While a limited yet steady volume of domestic commerce flourished, Koryŏ's trade with other states and peoples grew. Near Kaegyŏng, the island of Pyŏngnando at the mouth of the Yesŏng River thrived as a port for interstate trade, mostly with Song China. Using trade routes across the Yellow Sea, Koryŏ imported from Song sundry goods used by elites and exported such handicraft items as paper and local products like ginseng. In the north, Khitan Liao and the Jurchens paid with silver for Koryŏ farming tools and food items. In the late eleventh century, the Japanese began to trade mercury and sulfur for food, ginseng, and books from Koryŏ. Central Asian merchants brought mercury, herbs, spices, and corals, and spread descriptions of Koryŏ to the Middle East and the West, distant places about which Korea's population would know little until the early modern era.

SOCIAL REORGANIZATION AND THE NEW ARISTOCRACY

Early Koryŏ's total population probably remained between 2 million and 4 million, without sustained growth. Preventing a steady population increase were low fecundity, harvest irregularity, famine, poor nutrition, and epidemic diseases. Among the diseases, smallpox repeatedly ravaged Koryŏ, although it evolved into a childhood disease of less demographic consequence by the twelfth century. Also, high vagrancy among the poor in times of hardship likely helped to hold down birth rates, which, if true, must have hurt both the state and its aristocratic proprietors.

Lording over the population, aristocrats lived and worked in Kaegyŏng. Most families producing officeholders in the tenth century were descended from local strongmen, such as Kang Cho and Kang Kamch'an, or from Confucian scholars of Silla's sixth head rank backgrounds, such as Ch'oe Sŭngno. The families that began to produce officials somewhat later came from local functionary families, as did the aristocrat Kim Pusik. Accordingly, "ancestral seat" (*pon'gwan*) indicated a family's origin as of late Silla or early Koryŏ. By the end of T'aejo's reign, every local elite family was using a surname. Comprising central officials and their immediate kin, the aristocracy virtually monopolized central offices through the examination and protection appointment systems. The ruling elite included the royal Kaesŏng Wang and the families of officials of at least the fifth court rank. They all were eligible for protection appointments and merit-protection land tenure. Although a monarch could father children by many women, only some of the direct male descendants of King Hyŏnjong enjoyed standing as bona fide members of the royal house and married royal princesses; all the other princes fathered by a king either became Buddhist monks or assumed maternal surnames. The most prominent families produced high officials, especially *chaech'u*, for generations. Besides attaining such positions, an aristocratic family sought to enhance its prestige through marriage ties to other prominent families. Becoming a royal in-law also meant political clout, and the leading families like the Kyŏngwŏn Yi married a number of their daughters to kings.

Elites enjoyed a life of luxury. Besides rank land, an aristocratic officeholder was eligible for merit-protection land. The state allowed heirs to inherit, and many used their political influence to take over private and government-owned lands illegally. While living in a primary residence in Kaegyŏng, the wealthiest also possessed countryside villas and large pavilions. For an outing, male and female aristocrats rode horses, were escorted by attendants, and visited tea houses serving the best imported Chinese tea. An aristocrat who committed a crime could suffer banishment to a provincial locale. Still, the destination was often the ancestral seat, where patrilineal kin served as local functionaries and thus as a de facto local elite who could extend courtesies.

The early Koryŏ aristocracy remained open to new members, drawn mostly from those in and outside Kaegyŏng whose social status was lower than that of aristocrats but higher than that of ordinary commoners. Among them were *kunban*; *namban* ("southern order"), who were royal palace functionaries; *chamnyu* ("miscellaneous kinds"), who were low-level clerks in central government agencies; postal station functionaries; and local functionaries. As agents of the state, they performed their duties on a hereditary basis and thus held appropriate land tenures. In the tenth century, the integration of each region's local strongmen as upper-stratum local functionaries was crucial for creating a more centralized governing system, which offered them an incentive: access to officialdom through passing the government service examination. As local elites, functionary families monopolized township headman and assistant township headman positions for generations and married among themselves.

Much of the population that such agents of the state dealt with in daily life consisted of commoners. They included free cultivators, merchants, and artisans, who generally resided in major military or political centers (*pu*), localities of some sociopolitical importance (*chu*), prefectures, or counties. The majority of the commoners were free cultivators, also known as *paekchŏng* ("white-clad males"), on whom the state imposed tax, local tribute, military, and corvée obligations. Compared to the *paekchŏng*, the residents of special administrative districts like *hyang*, *pugok*, and *so* performed physically or financially heavier duties for the state. Those living in *hyang* or *pugok* generally pursued farming, whereas most *so* residents were handicrafters or miners. Regardless, all people of *hyang*, *pugok*, and *so* had to present special handicraft products and local minerals, and thus they could not move as freely as other commoners. The central government could punish a prefecture or county for a rebellion by demoting it in status to a *hyang*, *pugok*, or *so*. Also required to perform special obligations to the state were the residents of postal station districts and military garrison districts, who generally assisted with communication and transportation.

In their lives full of hardship, commoners received modest relief through state initiatives and self-help. The government instituted the Eastern and Western Bureaus of Relief (1049) in Kaegyŏng to provide medical care for the sick and shelter for the homeless; the Endowment for Emergency Relief (1076), which used the endowment interest to offer relief to the poor; and the Government Dispensary (1112), which provided free medicine. In times of disaster, the government set up the Directorate-General of Relief and Rehabilitation or the Directorate-General of Emergency Relief as an ad hoc agency to offer help to those affected. For their part, commoner farmers maintained a sense of shared identity through daily rituals and collective labor. For example, each community's "incense association" (*hyangdo*)—which buried juniper on the seashore as a religious activity of seeking salvation through meeting the Maitreya Buddha—exercised leadership with projects requiring a considerable workforce, such as constructing Buddha statues, stone pagodas, and monasteries.

At the bottom of the society were the lowborn, the vast majority of whom were chattel slaves who could be bought, sold, inherited, and transferred between owners. In times of hardship, many financially struggling commoners turned themselves into slaves. Also, to maintain an adequate supply of unfree labor, both the state and officialdom instituted laws to the effect that an offspring of a slave and someone of higher social status was a slave—typically with the mother being a slave. The lowborn also included hereditary female entertainers, *kisaeng*, who appear in extant records as government slaves. Possibly originating as Later Paekche's itinerant basket makers, who constituted an outcast group, they became skilled also in needlework, medicine, and music, and the Koryŏ state trained the pretty ones in singing and dancing through special schools. The state kept a roster of such *kisaeng* for prompt mobilization on such occasions as the Yŏndŭng (lantern lighting) festival, which celebrates the birth of the historical Buddha, and the P'algwan (Eight Vows) festival, which had its origins in an earlier shamanistic ritual of making offerings to various native deities. The hereditary role of *kisaeng* also gradually expanded to include the entertainment of officials and visiting dignitaries.

Although Koryŏ instituted laws influenced by China's Tang Code, early Koryŏ society generally followed indigenous customary laws. A penal code maintained five forms of punishment: beating on the buttocks, flogging with a stick, imprisonment, banishment to a remote locale, and execution by either strangulation or beheading. The Confucian cardinal virtues of loyalty and filial piety meant that treason and unfilial conduct were seen as heinous crimes. Yet, the moral stance also allowed a degree of leniency. The state granted even a criminal sentenced to banishment a leave of seven days if their parent had died. And the sentence for a convict with a parent who was seventy or older and had no other family member to look after them was suspended. On legal matters other than serious offenses, local officials possessed great judicial power and thus exercised discretion.

In early Koryŏ, a married couple of a husband and a wife from families of equal social status formed the center of a family organization. Males and females married around age twenty and age eighteen, respectively. Continuing an earlier Silla custom, marriage between close relatives such as first cousins was common for the royal house. The practice continued despite occasional prohibitions by the throne. Also, marriage between a male and a female of the same surname and same ancestral seat remained prevalent for the surnamed population as a whole, including local functionaries. However, once a family joined the capital aristocracy, the practice ceased.

Among siblings or between husband and wife, one sex was not superior to another in terms of rituals, propriety, or inheritance share. Household registers recorded children by birth order, and parents divided the inheritance equally among children. Also, a married male with a daughter but without a son did not adopt a son of a brother or a patrilineal cousin, since the daughter could perform the ancestral rites for her deceased parents. Accordingly, mourning rituals for one's paternal and maternal relatives differed little. Reflecting widespread uxorilocal marriage, a married male was recorded on the household register of his wife's family and residing with those household members was common. As mentioned, the protection appointment system covered an eligible official's sons-in-law and grandsons through a daughter, aside from patrilineal descendants. Likewise, meritorious service to the state resulted in rewards for one's parents and parents-in-law. Moreover, a woman could remarry relatively freely, without any discrimination against her offspring from such a union.

In Korea's gender history, the seventh Koryŏ monarch, Mokchong, is the first ruler to have an acknowledged same-sex relationship. Ascending the throne at nineteen, Mokchong favored Yu Haenggan (d. 1009), who was beautiful in appearance, and maintained a sexual relationship with him. As Mokchong increasingly cited illness when declining to give an audience, Yu and his allies wielded power until Kang Cho staged a coup, executed Yu, deposed the king, and not long thereafter killed him. Compiled by the Chosŏn dynasty (1392–1910), the rulers of Koryŏ's successor state, Confucian official histories of Koryŏ portray not just Kang negatively for committing regicide but also Mokchong himself—not so much for the same-sex relationship per se as for neglecting the duties of an ideal Confucian ruler.

EARLY POST-CLASSICAL CULTURE

Koryŏ monarchs upheld Confucianism as the guiding ideology for governance. During the dynastic founder's reign, such sixth head rank individuals as Ch'oe Ŏnwi (868–944), Ch'oe Ch'iwŏn's cousin, recommended statecraft based on Confucianism. The government service examination system instituted by Kwangjong to recruit officials well versed in the Confucian classics was a milestone. By the end of Sŏngjong's reign, the ideology was firmly in place, with a system of government-managed Confucian schools established.

This period's representative Confucian scholar is another head rank six figure, Ch'oe Sŭngno, whose twenty-eight recommendations for reform advocated a new society based on Confucianism as the governing ideology while also recognizing that Koryŏ should not blindly follow all aspects of Chinese civilization. Taking up Ch'oe's proposal, Sŏngjong reorganized the existing higher learning institutions as the State University (992) and dispatched instructors of the classics and medicine to the provinces.

The initially reformist impulse of Confucianism gradually gave way to more purely intellectual or literary concerns with the establishment of the new, Kaegyŏng-based aristocracy. Active during Munjong's reign, Ch'oe Ch'ung (984–1068), a son of a local functionary of Haeju, raised the quality of Confucian learning from a collection of Chinese exegetical studies from Han through Tang to a more profoundly philosophical engagement. Upon retirement from officialdom, Ch'oe founded the Nine-Course Academy to promote Confucian education in the countryside (1055), and contemporaries and posterity alike praised him as the "Confucius of the East" (haedong Kongja). By the early twelfth century, in Injong's reign, Kim Pusik represented the mid-Koryŏ Confucian learning that regarded the Confucian classics as its foundation and promoted appreciation for good prose and poetry.

The Koryŏ state established schools to promote Confucianism in general and to train government officials in particular. Founded in Kaegyŏng, the State University featured a Confucian studies division, which comprised the Kukcha ("Sons of the State"), T'aehak ("Grand Learning"), and Samun ("Four Gates") colleges, and a technical studies division that taught law, calligraphy, and accounting. The Confucian studies division admitted sons of civil and military officials of the seventh court rank or higher. In contrast, the technical studies division accepted sons of lower-rank officials, functionaries, and commoners. Outside Kaegyŏng, newly established provincial schools educated the sons of local functionaries and commoners.

By the eleventh century, private education was flourishing through the Twelve Assemblies. Especially prestigious among them was the Lord of Munhŏn Assembly, which was Ch'oe Ch'ung's Nine-Course Academy renamed after his posthumous title of honor (siho). As those educated at such private academies excelled in government service examinations, the best students flocked to them, and the State University as an institution of higher learning declined. In response, Yejong reorganized the university to offer expert lectures and set up an endowment to put the overall public education system on a more secure financial footing.

Besides education and statecraft, official historiography came under Confucian influence more strongly than ever before. Compilation of reign-by-reign "veritable records" (*sillok*) began immediately after T'aejo's reign, but none survived the Koryŏ-Khitan War. Thereafter, Hyŏnjong's court re-compiled the veritable records for the reigns of all of his seven predecessors, a project completed during the reign of Hyŏnjong's son and successor, King Tŏkchong (r. 1031–34). Still, not even this compilation nor any of the subsequent veritable records of Koryŏ monarchs is extant. During Injong's reign, Kim Pusik and other officials took up a royal command and compiled the *History of the Three Kingdoms*, the oldest surviving Korean work on the region's history. Based on the *Old History of the Three Kingdoms* (*Ku Samguksa*), which was completed in early Koryŏ, the *History of the Three Kingdoms* employs an annals-treatise format from a rational Confucian perspective. By then the general standard for official dynastic histories in China, this format features the "main record" (*pon'gi*), which provides a chronological account, and also a collection of treatises on various subjects, including biographies. Despite T'aejo's proclamation of Koryŏ as the successor of Koguryŏ, Silla successionism gained strength. The *History of the Three Kingdoms* emphasizes Silla's legitimacy in the succession of dynasties before Koryŏ.

Besides Confucianism, Buddhism too enjoyed state sponsorship and appealed to all social groups. While acknowledging Confucian ideology and the indigenous customs of Korea, T'aejo also constructed many Buddhist monasteries in Kaegyŏng. In his *Ten Injunctions*, T'aejo emphasized Buddhism's importance for the state's well-being and urged his successors to conduct both the Yŏndŭng and P'algwan festivals with great fanfare. As a part of the examination system instituted by Kwangjong, the ecclesiastical examination granted each passer a court rank and certified his status as a member of the clergy. State Preceptor and Royal Preceptor positions reserved for the clergy symbolized Buddhism's authority, which ostensibly transcended secular authority. Furthermore, the court provided monasteries with land and granted the clergy exemptions from tax, local tribute, and corvée. Besides state sponsorship, Buddhism enjoyed aristocratic patronage, as the ruling elite valued Confucianism and Buddhism as complementary teachings. Accordingly, the royal house and aristocrats became the primary patrons of such large monasteries as Hŭngwang-sa in Kaegyŏng (1067). For the ordinary people, incense associations, which functioned as socio-religious collectives, embodied facets of Buddhism and geomantic and indigenous shamanistic practices.

Early Koryŏ Buddhism as a complex belief system underwent a notable transformation. While Sŏn Buddhism remained popular, the efforts of Kyunyŏ (923–73), who further explained the stages of bodhisattvahood, disseminated the Hwaŏm School of Buddhism. Along with the Pŏpsang (Ch. Faxiang; Ja. Hossō; or Consciousness-Only) School, which teaches that an understanding of reality derives from one's mind rather than empirical experience, Hwaŏm flourished, with royal and aristocratic patronage. In the eleventh century, Ŭich'ŏn (1055–1101), a monk who was born King Munjong's fourth son and was based in Hŭngwang-sa, led an effort to overcome the tensions that had arisen among various schools. While seeking to unify doctrinal Buddhism around Hwaŏm, for unifying Sŏn he established a monastery, Kukch'ŏng-sa (1095), as the base for the Ch'ŏnt'ae (Ch. Tiantai; Ja. Tendai; or Lotus) School, which he introduced from Song China (1097). Through Ch'ŏnt'ae, which stressed both scriptural study and meditative practice, Ŭich'ŏn tried to accommodate a more textual study-oriented approach among Sŏn schools. Thanks to his effort, the clergy flocked to Ch'ŏnt'ae, but neither the state nor the wealthy Buddhist establishment fully addressed various abuses producing socioeconomic problems. Upon Ŭich'ŏn's death, Koryŏ Buddhism became divided again and remained centered around elites.

Early Koryŏ efforts to move toward a more overarching understanding of Buddhist thoughts culminated with the state-commissioned carving of a set of woodblocks for the *Tripitaka Koreana*. This undertaking gathered all three types of known Buddhist scriptures written in Literary Sinitic, namely: Buddha's teachings as fundamental doctrines; ethical clauses and codes of daily life as rules to be followed; and the commentaries by clergy and lay scholars on doctrines and precepts. The massive project demanded a systematic exposition of Buddhist doctrines. Carving the *Tripitaka* woodblocks was also a devotional act, motivated by a desire to enlist the Buddha's power against the Liao invaders at the time, and the project's completion took seventy-six years (1011–87). Some surviving print copies suggest a high level of early Koryŏ print technology. After the carving of the woodblocks, Ŭich'ŏn collected commentaries on the *Tripitaka* from Koryŏ, Song, and Liao and compiled the *Comprehensive Catalog of the New Compilation of the Teachings of*

All Schools (Sinp'yŏn chejong kyojang ch'ongnok). Lasting more than a decade, the project saw the publication of more than 4,700 books, including earlier Silla works.

Alongside Buddhism and Confucianism, Daoism flourished as an influential school of thought. Concerned with the pursuit of good fortune in life and immortality thereafter, Daoism offered prayers to innumerable gods for protection from calamities, the well-being of the state, and the prosperity of the royal house. First constructed in Yejong's reign, Daoist temples conducted such rituals as worship of heaven and the stars. Koryŏ Daoism was neither a religion of systematized thoughts nor an institutionalized organization, developing instead as a folk religion that integrated Buddhist ideas and prophecy. Nonetheless, per T'aejo's instruction, the state sanctioned the P'algwan festival, as it combined Daoism and folk religion with Buddhism in performing rituals in worship of famous mountains and rivers.

Indeed, shamanism as a folk religion continued to complement Buddhist and Daoist practices. Not only did dancing to a late Silla *hyangga*, the "Song of Ch'ŏyong," remain popular as an incantatory practice at community levels, but members of the court, to varying degrees, also held shamans in high esteem. In fact, in the twelfth century, the court's interest in shamanism increased, in part thanks to Yejong, who commissioned shamans to perform rain rituals during a prolonged drought (1121). His successor, Injong, continued the practice, sometimes having more than 300 female shamans pray for rain.

Acquiring a considerable body of prophetic beliefs, geomancy too remained influential. Initially, the notion that both Kaegyŏng and Sŏgyŏng are auspicious inspired T'aejo and his immediate successors to recognize Sŏgyŏng as a secondary capital and to attempt to expand the territory northward. By Munjong's reign, when the prospect of further expansion had vanished, many believed that Hanyang (modern-day Seoul) was an auspicious site. Accordingly, the court upgraded Hanyang's status to Namgyŏng ("Southern Capital") and built a royal palace, which kings occasionally visited, whereas the relative importance of the former Silla capital, Tonggyŏng, declined. As exemplified by Myoch'ŏng's rebellion, court politics continued to heed geomancy for its concern with the state's well-being and future.

Dynamic interactions among geomancy and various other systems of thought inspired a well-developed print culture. Building on Silla's legacy, Koryŏ raised woodblock print technology to a higher level, as suggested by the *Tripitaka Koreana*. The state also sought to increase paper production by encouraging the cultivation of paper mulberry trees and maintaining an agency to oversee all aspects of production and distribution. As paper manufacturing technique improved, Koryŏ began to produce a more durable white paper with a smoother surface, more suitable for brush writing and woodblock printing, even exporting it to Song China, where it was well regarded.

Advances in print culture facilitated knowledge production and dissemination in astronomy, medicine, shipbuilding, and architecture. Building on classical legacies and innovations from China and the Islamic world, early Koryŏ astronomy continued to use and improve the Xuanming calendar with astronomical observations. Accordingly, the Institute of Astronomic Observation, later renamed the Directorate of Astronomical Observation, oversaw officials who performed their duties at various observatories. Surviving records on solar eclipses, sunspots, and comets show that early Koryŏ astronomy attained a level of development comparable to that of the Islamic world, where astronomy was most advanced. In medicine, the government played a leading role, as instructions offered by the Directorate of Medicine and administration of examinations in medicine maintained a pool of competent physicians. In shipbuilding, Koryŏ constructed vessels as large as 96 *ch'ŏk* (approximately 29.76 meters) long—whereas three centuries later, Christopher Columbus's largest ship during his 1492 voyage to the New World, the *Santa María*, would be about 19 meters long. Shipbuilding was crucial for increased maritime trade with Song and for tax grain transport using coastal sea lanes. Likewise, Koryŏ made practical use of architecture, especially for palaces and Buddhist monasteries. None is extant, but the royal palace site in Kaegyŏng, Manwŏltae, shows traces of a magnificent palace complex built on a high embankment on a slope with various buildings standing on the rising steps.

A combination of aristocratic refinement and Buddhist spirituality resulted in commissions to master artisans for a variety of artworks. Handicraft manufacturing produced sundry necessities of the aristocracy's daily life and Buddhist rituals. Among these necessities was outstanding porcelain, produced following the traditions of Silla and Parhae and also adopting Song technique. It assumed a unique style, and the craftsmanship reached its peak in the twelfth century. Appreciated in Song, the most famous porcelain was the celadon, with a unique jade green color. Subtle color, a great variety of shapes, and delicate decorative patterns reflected the naturalistic taste of Koryŏ (Figure 4.2). Metal craftsmanship too was well developed and employed especially for Buddhist ritual artifacts. A sophisticated silver inlay technique allowed inscribing a bronze surface and filling the spaces with silver strings. Representative works include bronze incense burners decorated with silver inlays and bronze ritual ewers decorated with willow and animal motifs.

Early Koryŏ aristocracy's refined taste is also evident in calligraphy and painting, much of it influenced by earlier Chinese masters. The firm, vigorous style of the early Tang Confucian scholar and calligrapher Ouyang Xun (557–641) was popular. An especially renowned early Koryŏ calligrapher was the Buddhist monk T'anyŏn (1070–1159), whose style found inspiration in Wang Xizhi (303–61), a Jin dynasty Chinese official and a master of all forms of calligraphy. Early Koryŏ paintings are of two distinct types: works of professional painters affiliated with the Bureau of Painting, and literati paintings by aristocratic scholars and Buddhist clergy. Among professional paintings, content illustrations (functioning as the table of contents) on the front covers of Buddhist sutras to aid in hand copying or printing the text formed an important genre.

Compared to the visual arts, the performing arts blended a wider array of styles and traditions, indigenous and imported. Early Koryŏ music featured two broad categories: aak (Ch. yayue, "elegant music") and hyangak. Koryŏ embraced aak when the Song emperor sent Yejong a gift of musical instruments, costumes, and ritual dance accessories (1116). After that, aak evolved into one of the three genres of Korean court music. At the same time, while hyangga, with their poetic lyrics written in hyangch'al, declined as elites composed more poems in Literary Sinitic, hyangak produced many popular songs, such as "Taedong River" and "Ode to the Seasons" (Tongdong). Koryŏ music featured about forty musical instruments, including some imported from Song. Masked plays too were popular among all groups. Not limited to villagers, masked plays formed a favorite performance genre for royal banquets, and the Directorate-General of Masked Dance Drama supervised performances.

Each year, a rich array of cultural activities brought Koryŏ together in celebration on many special days. On New Year's Day, the people performed ancestral rites, offered one another greetings of good wishes, and played various games. On the third day of the third moon, the Double Third Festival (Samjinnal) celebrated spring's arrival. On the fifth day of the fifth moon,

FIGURE 4.2   Koryŏ celadon, twelfth century. Source: National Museum of Korea.
Photo © Eugene Y. Park 2021.

the Double Fifth Festival (Tano) brought all outdoors for polo, swinging
(*kŭne*), and wrestling (*ssirŭm*). Then on the fifteenth day of the sixth moon,
the people of Tonggyŏng celebrated Yudu with an ancient Silla custom of
all the people washing their hair in a stream that flowed eastward to flush
away the bad luck. And on the fifteenth day of the eighth moon, all reveled
in the autumn harvest festival, Ch'usŏk, with a performance of ancestral
rites followed by eating, singing, dancing, and drinking.

Tempered by Buddhism, the early Koryŏ diet was more plant-based than
earlier Korean cuisine had been. Black adzuki beans and peas were some of the
new crops, but rice and barley mixed with millet remained staples. Along with
tofu processed from soybeans, soybean sprouts enriched the diet and found a
medical use when dried. Functioning as two essential components of a meal were
pap, a bowl of steamed grain, and a soup (*kuk*), for which the primary ingredient

could be clams, taro, sea mustard (*miyŏk*), *tasima*, or fermented bean paste. A common substitute for *pap* was red mung bean porridge, *k'alguksu* (handmade, knife-cut wheat flour noodles), or buckwheat noodles. Many households raised cucumbers, eggplants, radishes, scallions, and cluster mallow among various vegetables, and as the government occasionally issued a Buddhist prohibition against slaughter, meat consumption became less common. Besides vegetables, marine products were popular, including seaweed, horned turban, oysters, abalone, mudfish, crab, and shrimp, among which salted tiny shrimps (*saeujŏt*) served as an essential seasoning ingredient. Besides salt, condiments included black pepper, which was introduced from Song China, vinegar, sesame, and sesame oil. Also, from China, sugar supplemented other sweeteners such as honey and grain-based syrup (*mullyŏt*). Aside from a growing variety of *ttŏk*, other grain-based confections became popular, often accompanying tea or alcoholic drinks of all sorts. More essential than distillation, fermentation, or drying for food processing or preservation was salt, on which the government maintained a monopoly. Fish and meat were preserved with salt and cinnamon, respectively, before drying. When fresh vegetables were unavailable for consumption in winter, salted radish was eaten; the radish leaves and stems were stored with fermented paste for the summer. Making *kimchi* entailed fermenting the salted vegetable seasoned with garlic and ginger.

As was also true of the food culture, early Koryŏ housing customs reflected both continuity and change. A house was a wooden structure with a varying combination of wooden and *ondol* floorings. Homes of elites had tile roofs, whereas the ordinary people lived in thatched-roof dwellings. Regardless, even the wealthiest elites lived in single-story homes constructed at sites deemed auspicious according to geomantic principles. According to one account attributed to Tosŏn, a one-story house, as an embodiment of *yin* (Ko. *ŭm*), is desirable because the Koryŏ realm as a whole is mountainous, an embodiment of *yang* (Ko. *yang*). Even in Kaegyŏng, which was expansive but overall had an uneven surface, with gravels and hillside ridges, no more than one or two out of ten houses used tile roofs, and the rest were small, thatched-roof homes. Royals and aristocrats slept on beds and used comfortable, spacious platforms covered with silk paddings for sitting or resting, but most people, in and outside the capital alike, slept on the floor—using the *ondol* floors in winter months. The culture of daily life, including housing, would experience some change due to turmoil and warfare in late Koryŏ.

CHAPTER 5

Late Koryŏ, 1146–1392

Koryŏ underwent a prolonged decline before its collapse. Monarchs remained figureheads under a century-long military rule (1170–1270), which suppressed rebellions by poor farmers and slaves while weathering the Koryŏ-Mongol War (1231–59). After a century of Mongol domination (1259–1356), during which men from diverse backgrounds entered officialdom, Koryŏ broke free, only to suffer Wakō raids from the east and also demands from China under the Ming dynasty (1368–1644). During the decades of incessant warfare, the state relied on private armies of military men, among whom Yi Sŏnggye (1335–1408) rose to power and usurped the throne with the support of reformist scholar-officials. Despite the sociopolitical turmoil, agricultural productivity increased, thanks to technological innovations, while commerce centered around urban markets grew. Handicraft manufacturing expanded as the bulk of production shifted from state-contracted craftspeople to Buddhist monasteries and farming households. Late Koryŏ also produced the world's first moveable metal type printing, cannons mounted on warships, and paintings by master artists of secular and Buddhist themes alike.

THE DECLINE AND FALL OF KORYŎ

Conflict among competing factions of the ruling elite persisted after the court suppressed Myoch'ŏng's rebellion. Injong's son and successor, King

Ŭijong (r. 1146–70), fostered a circle of confidants, with whom he increasingly pursued a life of pleasure while neglecting duties. As the hedonistic court dominated by royal favorites and aristocratic civil officials mistreated military officials, the latter became discontent. Also, the rank and file who were no longer receiving the soldier's land were disgruntled.

With a violent coup, the military took over the court and initiated a military rule that would last a century. Leading the coup, Chŏng Chung-bu (1106–79), Yi Ŭibang (1121–74), and other military officials slaughtered en masse the civil aristocrats, eunuchs, and royal favorites against whom they held grudges, and replaced Ŭijong with his younger brother, King Myŏngjong (r. 1170–97). Retaining civil officials who were cooperative, the military wielded power through the Council of Generals, a deliberative body composed of the highest military officials. Monopolizing key positions in officialdom, military strongmen competed among themselves for supreme power, as each sought to acquire more land, slaves, and troops for a de facto private army. The bloody power struggle continued for a generation.

Among these military strongmen, Ch'oe Ch'unghŏn (1149–1219) gained supreme power and achieved political stability through four generations of Ch'oe House rule (1196–1258). At the beginning of that rule, Ch'oe Ch'unghŏn presented to Myŏngjong a set of reform measures, the Sealed Memorial of Ten Points (Pongsa sip cho; 1196). Preferring to wield power and govern through his institutions rather than the existing bureaucracy, Ch'oe created the Directorate-General for Policy Formulation as the highest deliberative organ and coordinated his private army's activities through the General Military Council. Relying on loyal troops, he vigorously suppressed uprisings by discontented commoner cultivators and slaves. The reform produced little improvement, as Ch'oe himself was bent on acquiring more land and slaves while strengthening his army.

His son and successor, Ch'oe U (1166–1249), further solidified the Ch'oe House rule's military base. He established the Three Special Patrol Troop Units to serve as the regime's crack troops. Wielding political power not only through the Directorate-General for Policy Formulation, Ch'oe U also set up the Personnel Authority at his mansion and handled all personnel matters through this new institution. He also promoted a new generation of civil officials, who displayed both scholarly talent and administrative capacity, giving them advisory roles. As Ch'oe remained focused on wielding supreme power and restructuring governing institutions to that end, his regime neglected the overall well-being of the country and the people while a catastrophic military threat loomed in the heartland of Asia.

In Mongolia, Chinggis Khan (r. 1206–27) brought all the Mongol tribes under his sway and founded an empire that would come to control East and Central Asia, Persia, and the East European steppe by the mid-thirteenth century. A nomadic people, the Mongols under his leadership conquered North China, taking it from the Jurchen Jin dynasty and hence initiating direct contact with Koryǒ. Increasingly overbearing and demanding, the Mongols used the murder of their envoy as he was returning from Koryǒ as a pretext to attack, thus setting off the Koryǒ-Mongol War lasting a generation. Ch'oe U prepared for the conflict by moving the court from Kaegyǒng to the island of Kanghwado at the mouth of the Han River (1232) and by ordering the population to seek refuge on islands or in mountain fortresses. As Ch'oe kept the Three Special Patrol Troop Units in reserve for the regime's security, Koryǒ could rely only on its regular government armies of dwindling strength, militias, and monk armies, one of which, under the command of the monk Kim Yunhu (fl. 1232–63), repelled the Mongol army at Ch'ǒin fortress (present-day Yongin, Kyǒnggi). Even the exploited residents of special administrative districts and slaves resisted the invaders, but overall the general population suffered tremendously during the war.

The throne and those who opposed the continuing military rule desired to come to terms with the Mongols, doing so after overthrowing the military with Mongol aid. After a military strongman overthrew the last Ch'oe House leader (1258), King Kojong (r. 1213–59) agreed to submit to the Mongols, who allowed Koryǒ to exist as a vassal state rather than outright destroying it, as they had done to states elsewhere (1259). After the court returned to Kaegyǒng, as a term of surrender and as the military rule finally ended (1270), the Three Special Patrol Troop Units, which had resisted peace, revolted, elevated a royal scion king, and continued their resistance. On retreat, they relocated from Kanghwado to an island in the southwest, Chindo, and then moved again to T'amna. Ultimately, joint military operations of the Koryǒ and Mongol troops crushed the revolt (1273). Meanwhile, Koryǒ paid the price for continuing its existence as a Mongol vassal state, as the Mongols not only downgraded the status of the Koryǒ monarchy and governing institutions to that befitting a vassal but also annexed Koryǒ's northeast (1258), northwest (1269), and T'amna (1273).

The Mongol Yuan dynasty (1271–1368), ruled by Chinggis Khan's heirs in eastern Eurasia, imposed itself, meddled in Koryŏ's internal affairs, and made demands. Every Koryŏ heir apparent married a Yuan princess, whose personal entourage typically promoted Yuan interests. In keeping with these interests, the Yuan dynasty established Zhengdong ("Eastern Expedition") Province (1280–1356) to facilitate military operations against Japan; controlled the Koryŏ military through the Patrolling Myriarchy; and posted special officials, *darughachi*, to be in charge of administration, especially tax collection. Yuan twice attacked Japan (1274, 1281), and on both occasions, Koryŏ had to contribute troops and supplies. Additionally, Yuan demanded young, unmarried females as "tribute women" (*kongnyŏ*), gold, silver, hemp cloth, ginseng, medicinal herbs, and falcons, the favored companions of Mongols as hunters.

Mongol Yuan pressures and the machinations of pro-Yuan elements shaped Koryŏ's internal politics. Many social newcomers joined the elite, especially Mongolian language interpreters, falconers, and others with skills valued by the Mongols; those with marriage or other forms of personal ties to Yuan; and members of the Koryŏ crown prince's entourage during his residence at the Yuan court—as a de facto hostage—before ascending the throne. Such individuals and their kin expanded their agricultural estates at the expense of financially struggling commoners, turning many into slaves and shrinking Koryŏ's revenue base. After Yuan returned the northwest (1290) and T'amna (1301), Koryŏ kings pursued a reform centered around Confucian scholar-officials. Initiated by King Ch'ungsŏn (r. 1298, 1308–13), the reform mainly targeted government personnel and their estates' abuses. The effort made little difference as heavy-handed Yuan interference and obstruction of its henchmen in Koryŏ proved too strong.

When Yuan power declined rapidly in the mid-fourteenth century, King Kongmin (r. 1351–74) took bold steps to break free from Yuan overlordship. Unlike his predecessors unhappily married to Mongol princesses, Kongmin and his Mongol queen, Princess Noguk (d. 1365), were a loving couple (Figure 5.1). She likely was the driving force behind his effort. Kongmin purged such leading pro-Yuan figures as Ki Ch'ŏl (d. 1356), whose sister was the Yuan crown prince's mother (1356). The Kis and other pro-Yuan elements had been abusing their power and amassing agricultural estates. In the same year, Kongmin also prohibited Mongol customs, restored the earlier governing institutions that Yuan had downgraded, abolished Zhengdong

FIGURE 5.1   A Chosŏn portrait of King Kongmin and Princess Noguk, no date. The painting is one of many that have survived in association with shaman rituals. This is the only known depiction of a Korean monarch and his wife together before the era of photography. Source: Kongmin Wang sindang at Chongmyo, Seoul. Photo © Eugene Y. Park 2021.

Province, and recovered the northeast from Yuan. Furthermore, his armies repeatedly invaded Liaodong to regain former Koguryŏ territory, though they could not secure the region (1357, 1370, 1371).

Interests of the throne and the aristocracy clashed. Kongmin abolished the Personnel Authority, which had been limiting royal power and obstructing the advancement of a new generation of Confucian scholar-officials. Also, while neglecting duties, Kongmin, who was overcome with grief after Princess Noguk's death (1365), put his confidante and a former monk, Sin Ton (1322–71), in charge of the Directorate-General of the Regularization of Land and Slaves, so that those that powerful families had wrongfully taken could be returned to their rightful owners and the wrongly enslaved could be manumitted (1366). Unsurprisingly, the political establishment pushed back, ultimately forcing Kongmin to break with Sin Ton partisans (1370). Nonetheless, the king and Sin Ton were able to promote some reform-minded Confucian scholar-officials, most of whom were descendants of those who had risen from local functionary status under military rule. As a relatively new generation of central officials, some sided with the old aristocracy while others supported more progressive reform. Pursuing Nature and Principle Learning, also known as Neo-Confucianism, they sought to end abuses stemming from the corrupt Buddhist establishment and rapacious aristocrats. As such reform-minded scholar-officials advocated a powerful state, they elicited resistance from conservatives who obstructed their advancement and tried to withhold rank lands and stipends.

At the same time, Koryŏ, finally liberated from Yuan domination, weathered military pressure from all directions, ultimately repelling all incursions. The Red Turbans, who were Han Chinese influenced by a millenarian religious movement, rebelled against Yuan and invaded Koryŏ twice (1360, 1361–62). For its part, Yuan attacked Koryŏ for renouncing the Yuan overlordship (1364). Wakō raids increased in frequency and scale from the sporadic appearances that had begun in the thirteenth century from the south. As pirates based primarily on the Japanese Archipelago's Tsushima and Kyushu islands, the Wakō initially pillaged Koryŏ's southeastern coastal regions, but before long, even Kaegyŏng was vulnerable. Because Yuan had virtually dismantled the Koryŏ military organization, Kongmin turned to leading political players' private armies. Two military men, Ch'oe Yŏng (1316–88) and Yi Sŏnggye, stood out, winning one battle after another and thus gaining popular support. Whereas Ch'oe Yŏng hailed from the old aristocracy, Yi

Sŏnggye, a descendant of Yi Ŭibang's younger brother, was from the family of a local strongman, Chŏnju Yi, of the Yuan-controlled northeast, which that family had helped Kongmin recover.

Upon Kongmin's assassination following a palace intrigue, Yi Inim (d. 1388) wielded actual power almost throughout the reign of Kongmin's child and successor, King U (r. 1374–88), before Yi Sŏnggye gained power. Not only reverting to a pro-Yuan policy, which eventually put Koryŏ in a difficult position as the ascendant Ming dynasty took over China proper and the periphery, Yi Inim partisans also expanded their landholdings at the expense of the state and the commoner cultivators. Moreover, U came of age as a dissolute monarch. Eventually, Ch'oe Yŏng and Yi Sŏnggye—joining together to get the upper hand against the Wakō and securing the support of reformist scholar-officials—staged a coup, killed Yi Inim partisans, and gained power (1388). Before long, however, the two clashed over the direction of reform, including foreign policy. When Ming China demanded that Koryŏ cede the northern territories that Koryŏ had recovered from Yuan, Ch'oe advocated confronting Ming while Yi urged accommodation. When Ch'oe, backed by U, fielded against Ming an invasion force of some 38,000 under the command of the reluctant Yi and another general, those two, upon reaching the island of Wihwado in the middle of the Yalu River, turned their army around and marched back to Kaegyŏng, took over the court, and replaced U with his son, King Ch'ang (r. 1388–89), still a child.

When Yi Sŏnggye gained power, the reformist Confucian scholar-officials who supported him disagreed over the direction of reform while Koryŏ took on the offensive against the Wakō. A military expedition dispatched a fleet of at least 100 warships fitted with cannons and about 10,000 troops for a successful raid on Wakō bases on Tsushima (1389) while such moderates as Yi Saek (1328–96) and Chŏng Mongju (1337–92) sought in vain to pursue reform within the general framework of Koryŏ institutions. The moderates wanted to end the more blatant abuses associated with large private estates. In contrast, more radical reformers, such as Chŏng Tojŏn (1342–98), advocated curtailing private ownership of land by the influential. Rallying around Yi Sŏnggye, the radicals gained power when they accused Ch'ang and his father U as Sin Ton's progeny, deposed the boy-king, killed both him and U, and elevated a figurehead, Kongmin's seventh cousin, King Kongyang (r. 1389–92). Subsequently, Yi Sŏnggye partisans instituted Rank Land Law, with which they expanded the state's revenue base and weakened the economic base of their adversaries (1391), and eliminated Chŏng Mongju and other moderates who stood in their way. Finally, deposing Kongyang, they elevated Yi Sŏnggye to the throne, thus ending the nearly five-century Koryŏ rule of the Wang royal house. Underlying all the rhetoric of reform were the evolving economic interests of competing political players.

ECONOMIC GROWTH WITH A WEAK STATE

In late Koryŏ, not only did royal power suffer but the state also nearly went bankrupt. The earlier stipend land system had collapsed as the aristocracy monopolized land ownership and kept land within families as an inheritance for generations. Taxable land for the central government continued to decrease, especially as armed strongmen and their agents grabbed land during the military rule. Under the subsequent Mongol Yuan suzerainty, both the throne and the state were at the mercy of Yuan exactions and the avarice of pro-Yuan elements at the court. And in the final decades of Koryŏ, continual Wakō raids took a heavy toll on Koryŏ resources. Even with the salt monopoly instituted to increase the government's revenue (1309), no new economic measure could turn the tide. When more radical reform advocates rallied around, as Yi Sŏnggye instituted the Rank Land Law to expand the state's revenue base, they were already determined to replace Koryŏ with another state, under Yi.

Although the state struggled financially, the late Koryŏ economy produced some noteworthy advances in agriculture. In the twelfth century, the amount of farmed land increased, thanks to marshland cultivation and reclamation of shore land. During the Koryŏ-Mongol War, when the court took refuge on Kanghwado, land reclamation on the island's shores and nearby coastal regions across the sea got underway. Furthermore, irrigation facilities improved. Including such facilities as Pyŏkkolje (in modern-day Kimje, North Chŏlla) and Susanje (in present-day Miryang, South Kyŏngsang), earlier reservoirs and connected waterways with embankments underwent renovation. Expansion of smaller reservoirs also became common.

Besides irrigation facilities, other innovations improved overall farming technology. Not only did cultivators use such improved tools as short half-moon hoes and plowshares, but ox-drawn deep plowing also became the standard. Also, fertilizer application methods became more advanced as burning and grinding the weeds from fallow land for use as compost gave way to using animal feces–derived manure and green manure. As fallowing began to decrease albeit gradually, the amount of land suitable for cultivation increased, even enabling dry-field farming that yielded three harvests in two years. Among rice paddy farmers in some parts of southern Korea, the direct seeding method, which used the same plot from seeding to harvest, was replaced by seedling transplantation, which entailed planting seeds in one field and transplanting seedlings to another for a better harvest. Moreover, a wider variety of crops became available, including many improved types of existing harvest grains. Other crops, however, were entirely new, including cotton, thanks to seeds introduced from Yuan China by Mun Ikchŏm (1331–1400). Late Koryŏ agriculture further benefited from the dissemination of the latest Chinese farming techniques, through such Yuan works as the *Essentials of Farming and Sericulture* (*Nongsang jiyao*), which the polymath Yi Am (1297–1364) introduced to Koryŏ.

With improving agricultural technology, a subsistence economy transitioned to one more circulation based. As handicraft manufacturing by private artisans and monasteries spread, commerce in Kaegyŏng expanded beyond the city wall. Such harbors as Pyŏngnando, at the mouth of the Yesŏng River, became transportation and commercial hubs. As peddlers became more active in rural areas, commerce in urban and rural regions expanded, markets became more extensive and more specialized. The rice, fish, salt, and porcelain trade took advantage of the tax grain shipping lanes. New land routes gave rise to inns (*wŏn*), which turned into commercial centers. By requiring government agencies, officials, and monasteries to buy from and sell to commoner cultivators and make proxy tax payments, the state integrated commoners into the more circulation-based economy. In the process, some merchants and handicraft manufacturers not only amassed wealth but also acquired government offices. None, though, achieved aristocratic status, nor altered the existing social hierarchy.

SOCIAL TURMOIL: CRISIS AND OPPORTUNITIES

In late Koryŏ, a more sustained population increase began along the major rivers and in the interior valleys. Without a doubt, the Koryŏ-Mongol War restrained growth. Even by the end of Yuan China's overlordship, the total population was no more than 3 to 4 million, reflecting no real increase since the Silla to Koryŏ transition. Some new trends, though, contributed to sustained growth. By about 1250, newly compiled tracts on medicine were devoting attention to obstetrics and pediatrics and decreasing infant mortality. At least among aristocratic households, the better medical practice began to improve life expectancies, although benefits for the rest of the population were likely more limited. Despite Wakō raids for three decades or so, Korea's population was well launched on a growth trajectory that would continue for nearly three centuries, as was also true in both China and Japan.

The elite among late Koryŏ's increasing population amassed wealth at the expense of both the state and free cultivators. Upon the military coup of 1170, the power struggle among military men and the collapse of the regular, central administrative system placed the court at the center of a free for all that involved strongmen and those individuals, mostly local functionaries from the south, entering officialdom as the first members of their families to do so. Aristocrats and their agents still sought to secure the most important positions in officialdom and acquire more land. As wealthy landlords continued to expand their holdings, the most powerful among them possessed massive agricultural estates with major mountains and rivers as boundaries. Such landlords treated the commoners cultivating their estates as personal slaves.

Unable to stand increasingly harsh exactions, some suffering commoners and slaves rebelled. When the Resident Governor of Sŏgyŏng, Cho Wich'ong (d. 1176), led an armed rebellion against the military strongmen at court, many commoner cultivators joined it (1174). Even after the central government suppressed the rebellion (1176), the general unrest did not cease for many years. It included uprisings by two brothers, Mangi (fl. 1176–77) and Mangsoi (fl. 1176–77) from the *so* of Myŏnghak in Kongju (1176–77), and by an alliance of Kim Sami (d. 1194) in Mount Unmun (in modern-day Ch'ŏngdo, South Kyŏngsang) and Hyosim (fl. 1193–94) in Ch'ojŏn in Ulchu (present-day Ulsan) (1193–94). The rebels typically expressed grievances toward avaricious local officials, but some based in the southeast used Silla restoration as their rallying cry. Upon Ch'oe Ch'unghŏn's rise to power, popular uprisings decreased in frequency and scale, thanks to his two-pronged approach of appeasement and suppression. His slave, Manjŏk (d. 1198), reignited uprisings, but the Ch'oe House suppressed all. Rather than protesting just against rapacious government agents, Manjŏk declared that he was fighting against status discrimination, rhetorically questioning whether kings, nobles, generals, and ministers are of separate breeds.

During the Koryŏ-Mongol War and the subsequent Mongol domination, the population suffered tremendous hardship while the court and the aristocracy enjoyed relative security and comfort. As the Ch'oe House insisted on resistance without using its best troops or making adequate preparation for protecting the population from the invaders, acute food shortages also afflicted sieges. And whenever a fortress fell, the Mongols slaughtered most inhabitants and took the survivors away as captives. Even in the postwar era, the ordinary people suffered from a long list of Yuan demands and rapacious aristocrats while struggling to recover from the devastations of the war.

The century-long Mongol domination produced a significant volume of human and material traffic between Koryŏ and Yuan China. Those with military merit, fluent in the Mongolian language, or married to Mongol nobility found advancement opportunities in Koryŏ society. Some among them, especially those with Yuan backing, even joined the Koryŏ aristocracy. Also, Mongol customs became popular, including hairstyle, dress, language, and given names, all of which were widespread among royals and aristocrats, including those who willingly or unwillingly moved to China. Most did so as wartime captives, political hostages, young, unmarried females, or vagrants. To meet the Yuan demand for tribute women, the Directorate-General for Marriage Recruitment (1274–1355) targeted and rounded up unattached women, wives of treasonous criminals, and daughters of Buddhist clergy who had broken their vows. Through them and other Koreans who arrived in China, Koryŏ dress, dining ware, and cuisine spread, and were known as "Koryŏ style" (Gaoli yang).

Shortly before Koryŏ broke free from Yuan domination, the Wakō became a new source of pain and suffering for the population. Unable to produce enough food for themselves, the Wakō resorted to raiding. A typical raid took both grain and inhabitants, after the initial round of slaughter, rape, and pillage. At the peak of the onslaught in the 1370s, the Wakō struck dozens of times each year, laying waste wherever they went. Many coastal regions became uninhabitable, to the extent that the government withdrew local administrative staff farther inland.

As a survival strategy, the ordinary people relied on various mutual aid organizations, especially incense associations. More purely religious collectives in the earlier period, the late Koryŏ incense associations promoted their members' sundry interests. As such, incense associations turned into farmers' organizations that managed a wide range of activities involving not just popular religious rituals, such as a village making an offering to heaven, but also communal labor, weddings, and funerals. Rather than Confucianism, a mix of Buddhist, Daoist, and more purely indigenous religious practices shaped rituals.

Known marriage customs yield insights on gender and family in late Koryŏ society, reflecting a century of Mongol domination. The Yuan demand for tribute women lowered the typical wedding age to the early teens, as parents hurriedly married off their daughters when necessary. Also, unlike the earlier Koryŏ custom of a male having one wife, in late Koryŏ he could be married to two or more wives of relatively equal, legal, and social standing—except for kings, who might marry Yuan princesses who would be superior in status to a king's Koryŏ wife. Likewise, the children of a man's multiple wives enjoyed relatively equal legal and social standings in terms of eligibility for office among his sons and property inheritance among his sons and daughters alike—with the notable exception of the children mothered by a king's Yuan-princess wife and as opposed to his Koryŏ wives. Reformist Confucian scholar-officials, who tended to advocate the ideal of one husband married to one wife, criticized polygamy, although their chosen leader Yi Sŏnggye himself had two wives for about twelve years before his first wife's death. As a young man from the northeast, Yi married his first wife from a local strongman's family from his home region, the northeast. In contrast, his second, much younger wife was someone he married after establishing himself as a political player in Kaegyŏng—and she hailed from a family of central officials. The marriage custom would change in the subsequent Chosŏn period with the increasing application of Confucian cultural norms as deemed proper by the state and the elite.

LATE POST-CLASSICAL CULTURE

Confucian scholarship's influence continued to grow among elites and those of middle social status, especially local functionaries. The military coup of 1170 was a setback for Confucian learning, as some powerful aristocratic families suffered destruction, but the impact was temporary. A *hyangak* piece from Kojong's reign, "Song of Confucian Scholars" (Hallim pyŏlgok), suggests that the erudite still commanded respect. A century later, King Kongmin restructured the State University, which had undergone many name changes, as the Confucian Academy (1362), removing technical studies and offering a more purely Confucian curriculum.

While Confucianism's influence as a moral philosophy increased, nativist reflections on Korea's history grew amidst unrest and warfare. Representative works include the *Lay of King Tongmyŏng* (*Tongmyŏng Wang p'yŏn*; 1193?) and *Lives of Eminent Eastern Monks* (*Haedong kosŭng chŏn*; 1215), aside from the *Memorabilia of the Three Kingdoms* and the *Poetic Record of Emperors and Kings*. Composed by Yi Kyubo (1168–1241), a civil official, scholar, and writer, the *Lay of King Tongmyŏng* is an epic poem eulogizing the feats of the founder of Koguryŏ. As a hymn, the verse reflects Yi's Koguryŏ successionist sentiment. Yi's contemporary and a Hwaŏm monk, Kakhun (d. c. 1230), authored the *Lives of Eminent Eastern Monks*. The extant parts feature biographies of more than thirty-five monks. Decades later, Iryŏn (1206–89), a Sŏn monk, wrote the *Memorabilia of the Three Kingdoms*, a rich repository of ancient folk tales and other transmitted accounts centered around Buddhism. Acknowledging Tan'gun as the progenitor of the Korean people, the *Memorabilia of the Three Kingdoms* includes the story of Tan'gun's founding of Kojosŏn. Likewise, the *Poetic Record of Emperors and Kings*, by Yi Sŭnghyu (1224–1300) , narrates Korean history from Tan'gun on and highlights Koryŏ's autonomy by placing Korea's history on the same footing as China's.

Meanwhile, the turmoil following the 1170 military coup produced religious organizations that advocated Buddhism's return to the fundamentals, and Chinul (1158–1210) played a leading role (Figure 5.2). A Sŏn monk, Chinul criticized the Buddhist circles for pursuing merely fame and profits. Emphasizing scripture reading and meditation as the duties of the clergy, Chinul formed a reformist religious association (*kyŏlsa*), Susŏn, based at Songgwang-sa, a Chogye School monastery in Sŭngp'yŏng (modern-day Sunch'ŏn, South Chŏlla; 1190). The Susŏn gained support from the reformist clergy and the local laity while popularizing Chogye as a leading Buddhist school. Stressing the importance of Sŏn and doctrinal approaches as inseparable in their fundamentals, he propagated the concept of "sudden enlightenment followed by gradual cultivation" (*tono chŏmsu*), according to which an effort to achieve awareness of oneself as a Buddha must be accompanied by persevering cultivation. As such, Chinul's teachings, which accommodated doctrinal schools with Sŏn at the center, effectively completed Koryŏ Buddhism's long-standing orientation toward the notion of the oneness of Sŏn and doctrinal approaches.

Other prominent monks followed Chinul's footsteps in revitalizing Buddhism. Under the leadership of Hyesim (1178–1234), the influence of

FIGURE 5.2   Portrait of Chinul, 1780. The painting is one of sixteen housed in the hall of state preceptors at Songgwang-sa, honoring its venerable monks from the Koryŏ period. The hall likely housed the original version of Chinul's portrait in the late fourteenth century. Source: Songgwang-sa, Sunch'ŏn. Photo credit: Cultural Heritage Administration.

Susŏn grew further. Arguing that Confucianism and Buddhism are the same, Hyesim stressed the cultivation of the mind and laid the foundation for late Koryŏ intellectuals' eventual embrace of Neo-Confucianism. His contemporary, Yose (1163–1245), rebuilt a monastery, Mandŏk-sa in Togang (present-day Kangjin, South Chŏlla), and organized his reformist religious association, Paengnyŏn (1211), to address the laity's spiritual needs. Promoting the Lotus Sutra, which emphasizes sincere repentance for one's harmful actions, the Paengnyŏn too elicited an enthusiastic response from the local people.

Buddhist revitalization efforts by various reformist religious organizations received a boost from the state-sponsored project of carving a new set of *Tripitaka* woodblocks. Kojong's court commissioned this undertaking not only to replace the earlier set destroyed during the Koryŏ-Mongol War but also as a devotional act of seeking the Buddha's power to repel the invaders. Managed by the Directorate-General of Tripitaka, from 1233 to 1248, the project entailed carving more than 80,000 woodblocks (Figure 5.3). The *Tripitaka Koreana* arguably stands out as the premodern world's best *Tripitaka*, a vast amount of text of impressive accuracy with almost no erroneous or missing characters, not to mention its fine calligraphy.

FIGURE 5.3   The *Tripitaka* woodblock collection. Source: Haein-sa, Hapch'ŏn, South Kyŏngsang Province. Photo credit: Cultural Heritage Administration.

During the period of Mongol Yuan overlordship, the reformist impulse of Buddhism grew weaker. Tied to the aristocracy, the Buddhist establishment again became fraught with abuse. Many leading monasteries possessed a large amount of land and actively pursued commerce; such dealings were rampant among the clergy. In response, Pou (1301–82) prioritized uniting and reorganizing various Buddhist schools. Still, such reformists could not overcome the Buddhist establishment's vested interests and the political leadership's interests also in maintaining the status quo. Before long, Chŏng Tojŏn and other members of a new generation of scholar-officials who found inspiration for reform in Neo-Confucianism began to criticize the abuses, if not Buddhism as a whole.

The introduction of Neo-Confucianism from Yuan China in the late thirteenth century made a decisive impact on late Koryŏ. In China, in contrast to the florid parallel prose popular from the Han through the mid-Tang dynasties, the Classical Prose (Guwen) of the late Tang and Song dynasties favored clarity and precision, and Neo-Confucianism was a grand synthesis by Zhu Xi (1130–1200) of Song. As reflected in its traditional name, Nature and Principle Learning, Neo-Confucianism pursued philosophical inquiry into problems of human nature and principles of the universe. Introducing Neo-Confucianism to Koryŏ (1290), an eminent scholar-official, An Hyang (1243–1306; Figure 5.4), disseminated its study from his home town, Sunhŭng (in modern-day North Kyŏngsang). One of his disciple's students, Yi Chehyŏn (1287–1367), interacted with Yuan scholars and deepened his understanding of the Nature and Principle Learning at the Hall of Ten Thousand Books (Man'gwŏndang), which King Ch'ungsŏn built in the Yuan capital (1314; in present-day Beijing), where he resided after Yuan had deposed him. Upon returning to Koryŏ, Yi taught many students, thus contributing to Neo-Confucianism's dissemination beyond its epicenter in Kyŏngsang. He also wrote a number of historical works, including the co-authored Concise History (Saryak; 1357), which emphasized notions of orthodoxy and moral obligation guided by "great principle and moral obligation" (taeŭi myŏngbun), but only his commentary is extant. One of his students, Yi Saek, further propagated Neo-Confucianism through teaching the likes of Chŏng Mongju, Chŏng Tojŏn, and Kwŏn Kŭn (1352–1409) during Kongmin's reign.

Intellectuals pursued the Nature and Principle Learning as a holistic system of thought for reforming their society. Generally coming from local functionary families that had begun to produce central officials after the military coup, Neo-Confucian scholars stressed applicable teachings relevant

FIGURE 5.4   Portrait of An Hyang, 1318? This is a copy commissioned for the provincial school in Sunhŭng by its magistrate when the court commissioned the original portrait for the Koryŏ shrine of Confucius (1318). Source: Sosu Museum, Yŏngju, North Kyŏngsang Province. Photo credit: Cultural Heritage Administration.

to daily life rather than metaphysics. Accordingly, they valued two works in particular, Zhu Xi's *Family Rituals* (*Jia li*; 1169), which is a manual for the private performance of initiation, wedding, funeral, and ancestral rituals; and *Elementary Learning* (*Xiaoxue*; 1187) by Liu Zicheng (1134–90), who compiled the work, following his teacher Zhu Xi's instructions, as a moral primer for children.

Late Koryŏ's overall intellectual fervor motivated the invention of the world's first movable metal type printing technology. A culmination of accumulated expertise in carving high-quality woodblocks, making durable paper with a smooth surface, compounding suitable ink, and casting bronze type, the invention likely occurred at the turn of the thirteenth century, considering that in 1234 on Kanghwado, the court arranged for the printing with movable metal type of a new edition of the *Prescribed Ritual Text of the Past and Present* (*Sangjŏng kogŭm yemun*), which Injong had commissioned a century earlier. Predating the first movable metal type printing in the West by more than two centuries, the edition has not survived, but the *Anthology of Great Buddhist Priests' Sŏn Teachings* (*Paegun hwasang ch'orok pulcho chikchi simch'e yojŏl*; 1377) compiled by the monastery Hŭngdŏk-sa (in modern-day Ch'ŏngju, North Ch'ungch'ŏng) is still the world's oldest extant work printed using movable metal type.

Advances in print technology facilitated knowledge production and dissemination in various fields, including astronomy and medicine. Although repeatedly reorganized and renamed, the Directorate of Astronomical Observation continued to oversee all aspects of astronomical observations and of devising the official calendar. Ch'ungsŏn's court adopted Yuan China's Shoushi calendar (1281), which used spherical trigonometry to obtain measured data for calendar calculation, and fixed the year at 365.2425 days—the same calculation as was found for the Gregorian calendar three centuries later, in 1582, in the West. Koryŏ made the Shoushi calendar its own, fully understanding the calendar's theoretical foundation and calculation methods. In medicine, Koryŏ built on earlier Tang and Song achievements by developing cures and prescriptions adapted to local needs. New medical manuals prescribed indigenous herbs. These manuals include Korea's oldest extant herbal guide, *Emergency Remedies Using Indigenous Medicine* (*Hyangyak kugŭp pang*; 1236), covering various ailments and more than 180 kinds of indigenous herbal medicine.

Late Koryŏ advances in knowledge also produced gunpowder, firearms, and modified warships. Yuan China strictly guarded the technique of making gunpowder, but Ch'oe Musŏn (1325–95), a military official and an inventor who was convinced that firearms were essential for repelling the Wakō, learned from a Chinese gunpowder craftsman the essential ingredients: sulfur, slack or fine coal, and potassium nitrate. With perseverance, Ch'oe was finally able to make gunpowder on his own. Upon his repeated recommendation, the government established the Directorate-General of Fire Bombs (1377–88), for which he supervised the production of gunpowder and cannons. Under his leadership, technology for manufacturing cannons rapidly improved, and before long, Koryŏ was producing eighteen different kinds. Deploying them, Ch'oe won a resounding victory against the Wakō at Chinp'o at the mouth of the Kŭm River (1380). Capitalizing on earlier advances in shipbuilding, Koryŏ also mounted cannons on warships, and subsequently, shipbuilders modified these vessels' design to improve their stability when cannons were being fired.

Besides technology and knowledge, late Koryŏ produced crowning achievements in fine arts. The quality of jade green celadon with an inlay declined after its golden age during the court's Kanghwado period. Still, high-quality works of calligraphy and painting continued to be produced throughout the late Koryŏ period. The flowing, elegant calligraphy of Yuan China's Zhao Mengfu (1254–1322) was popular among Koryŏ scholar-officials, including Yi Am, whose own calligraphy achieved celebrated fame. In literati painting, the so-called Four Noble Ones became the main subjects—the plum blossom, the orchid, the bamboo, and the chrysanthemum—but none of these works is extant. Royals, aristocrats, and professional painters also produced more colorful, vibrant paintings that employed greater realism. An extant work attributed to Kongmin, *A Hunt in the Mountains of Heaven*, reflects the influence of Yuan China's Northern School, which was known for proper attention to detail, the use of color, and highly refined traditional modes and methods as employed by professional painters. Buddhist paintings have survived in far greater number, as demands of the royal house and aristocratic families seeking good fortune through prayers produced many works on the theme of praying for reincarnation in the Pure Land. Embodying the spirituality of Pure Land Buddhism, such paintings commonly depict the triad of Amitābha Buddha; Mahāsthāmaprāpta, a bodhisattva representing the power of wisdom; and Avalokiteśvara.

In daily life, though, the Buddhism-inspired food culture centered around vegetables changed considerably with Mongol influence. Meat consumption increased as Koryŏ accommodated Mongol officials, visiting or resident.

Domesticated animals commonly butchered for meat were oxen, horses, pigs, chickens, geese, and ducks, but dog meat was also popular among ordinary people. Also consumed were such wild animals as boars, rabbits, deer, Siberian roe deer, pheasants, and sparrows. New foods introduced from Yuan further enriched the diet, including *sŏllŏngt'ang*, a stew made from ox bones, mostly leg bones, brisket, and other cuts; dumplings (*mandu*); wine; and *soju*, a clear, colorless distilled alcoholic beverage made from rice, wheat, or barley. Many households raised cucumbers, eggplants, radishes, scallions, cluster mallow, and calabashes for side dishes. A typical side dish, soybeans enjoyed a medical purpose when dried, while the beans were important for consumption by themselves and for making tofu. Additionally, many homes raised bracken, *songi* (Ja. *matsutake*) mushrooms, and lance asiabell (*tŏdŏk*). Some common fruits were pears, plums, peaches, apricots, Korean cherries, *yuja* (Ja. *yuzu*), mandarins, persimmons, jujubes, chestnuts, pine nuts, and Chinese quinces. Watermelon, introduced from Yuan, became popular only toward the end of the Koryŏ period, whereas grapes were abundant enough for wine making. As many people acquired a taste for milk, also introduced from Yuan China, the government maintained a standing agency to supply milk, used mainly as a primary ingredient in rice-milk porridge (*nakchuk*).

Relations with Yuan China wielded a lasting influence on housing culture as well. As was true in the earlier period, building and living only in single-story homes, as influenced by geomancy, elites split the year between an *ondol* floor in the cold season and a wood floor in the warmer months. In contrast, *ondol* floors were the norm in ordinary people's homes. In the final decades of Koryŏ, Chŏng Mongju and other Confucian scholars advocated a new addition for a home, a family shrine (*kamyo*) that housed the spirit tablets (*wip'ae*) of the male household head's immediate patrilineal ancestors. Such a shrine was constructed to be higher than the rest of the house and situated in the northeast. As the direction of *yang* where the sun rises, east symbolizes life, whereas north is the position of the superior individual who faces south, as monarchs do when giving an audience. The custom of building a family shrine for one's home began to spread among officials as more of them turned to Neo-Confucianism as a new, guiding ideology—arguably heralding the beginning of Korea's early modern era.

PART III

The Early Modern Era

CHAPTER 6

Early Chosŏn, 1392–1567

E arly Chosŏn built on the achievements of Koryŏ. The monarch consulted with high officials, and the Censorate checked their power. The state promoted farming while regulating commerce, but as agricultural productivity increased, the surplus stimulated private manufacturing and trade, giving rise to rural markets. The *yangban*, the aristocracy, no longer defined by officeholding but rather by descent, increasingly evaded tax, tribute, corvée, and military obligations, thus overburdening the ordinary commoners who relied on mutual aid organizations for survival. Emerging *yangban* lineages used community compacts (*hyangyak*) to reshape local society according to Confucian moral norms while denigrating remarried women and illegitimate children. While Buddhism and shamanism remained important, especially among women and nonelites, Neo-Confucianism triumphed as the official ideology. For wider dissemination of moral primers, farming manuals, and medical treatises, the state devised a phonetic alphabet, *han'gŭl*. Still favoring Literary Sinitic, intellectuals pursued encyclopedic learning. In contrast to Koryŏ, the ideal simplicity of a scholar's life found expressions through paintings, calligraphy, and white porcelain wares.

A REORGANIZED MONARCHY AND CONFUCIAN STATECRAFT

The Chosŏn founder, Yi Sŏnggye, also known by his posthumous temple name as King T'aejo (r. 1392–98), reigned in consultation with the high officials who had elevated him to the throne (Figure 6.1). Giving in to their unbending pressures, in May 1394, T'aejo ordered a massacre of the male members of the Koryŏ royal house. For two decades, the authorities killed any additional royal Wang they apprehended. In November 1394, T'aejo moved the capital from Kaegyŏng to Hansŏng (present-day Seoul), and fitted the kingdom's new political, economic, and cultural center with a city wall, Kyŏngbok Palace and other royal residences, a royal ancestral shrine, altars where the monarch performed rites of sacrificial offering to the spirits of soil and grain, government schools, city markets, and roads. Among the state counselors and ministers who wielded actual power and advised T'aejo was the new dynasty's architect, Chŏng Tojŏn. While refuting Buddhism for what he deemed its destructive influence on morality, Chŏng advocated Confucian statecraft, with the people as the foundation.

T'aejo's ambitious fifth son and the third Chosŏn ruler, King T'aejong (r. 1400–18), reigned as a strong monarch after eliminating Chŏng and others who supported rival candidates for royal succession. To bolster royal power, T'aejong abolished all private armies (1400), placing their troops under royal command both in name and actuality; increased the number of royal guard troops; instituted the military examination to recruit military officials (1402); and made the Six Ministries present matters of state directly to him rather than to the State Council for deliberation and approval (1414). T'aejong also expanded the state's revenue base by conducting a cadastral survey (1405–13), confiscating most of the Buddhist monastic lands (1406), instituting the Identification Tag Law to prevent vagrancy among males aged sixteen to sixty and then abolishing it due to widespread complaints (1413–16), and manumitting those wrongly enslaved (1417). Self-assured, T'aejong issued an edict of toleration ending the persecution of royal Wangs (1413).

With royal power secure and a healthy economy, T'aejong's son and successor, King Sejong (r. 1418–50), completed all Confucian statecraft's primary institutions. He established the Hall of Worthies (1420–56) inside the palace as a policy research organ where scholarly junior officials advised the throne by conducting research and participating in royal lectures. Unlike T'aejong, Sejong made the State Council first deliberate on matters forwarded by the Six Ministries before presenting a consensus for royal approval (1436), although he attended to personnel and military matters. Mindful of the propriety required for Confucian governance, Sejong adopted the Five Rites, which judiciously combined existing court rituals with indigenous precedents and Tang, Song, and Ming practices. In pursuit of the Kingly

FIGURE 6.1 Portrait of King T'aejo Yi Sŏnggye, 1872. A copy by Cho Chungmuk
(fl. 1846–72) and seven others for T'aejo's shrine in Chŏnju. He wears a dragon robe,
the everyday dress of the monarchs of China (from Sui to Qing), Korea (Koryŏ and
Chosŏn), Ryukyu, and Vietnam (Nguyen). Since yellow, the color of the center,
was reserved for emperors, T'aejo as a Ming vassal could have donned a red robe, as
would King Sejong (r. 1418–50) from 1443 and his successors until 1897, but instead
chose blue, the color of the direction east. Source: Royal Portrait Museum, Chŏnju,
North Chŏlla Province. Photo credit: Cultural Heritage Administration.

Way, which idealized governance based on the monarch's benevolence and virtue, Sejong was committed to the Confucian concept of the people as the state's foundation. Accordingly, he sought to propagate Confucian morality as the social norm, beginning with the scholar-official elite, by admonishing them to follow Zhu Xi's *Family Rituals*.

After Sejong's reign, royal power declined sharply. His well-groomed, diligent eldest son and successor, King Munjong (r. 1450–52), died prematurely, and Munjong's only son and successor, King Tanjong (r. 1452–55), ascended the throne as a child. Such high officials as Kim Chongsŏ (1383–1453) and Hwangbo In (1387–1453) wielded political power until the boy king's ambitious uncle staged a bloody coup (1453). Subsequently usurping the throne, King Sejo (r. 1455–68) took many measures to enhance royal power. Besides reverting to T'aejong's system of the Six Ministries presenting all matters directly to the throne (1455), Sejo abolished the Hall of Worthies, which had produced many officials who challenged his legitimacy (1456); discontinued royal lectures, which had been providing a forum for policy debate (1456); and filled key positions with trusted royal kin, whose political participation his grandfather, T'aejong, had restricted.

The early Chosŏn governing institutions saw completion in the reign of Sejo's grandson and the ninth monarch, King Sŏngjong (r. 1469–94; Gregorian 1495). Promulgation of the Great Code of Administration (Kyŏngguk taejŏn) formalized the governing ideology for Chosŏn society (1485). Also, entrusting a royal archive, Office of the Special Counselors, and the counselors themselves with remonstrance functions revived in a modified fashion the Hall of Worthies, as the special counselors held concurrent positions for the restored royal lectures (1478). Because high officials and other significant political figures participated, a royal lecture was not so much an occasion for the king to pursue scholarship as an institution for the monarch and his officials to debate and deliberate on policies in the context of whatever classic that they were reading.

As institutionalized by the Great Code of Administration, the Chosŏn central government replicated the Koryŏ system in many ways. As was true in Koryŏ, officialdom comprised civil and military officials. Each official held one of nine court ranks, each divided into senior and junior levels. As the highest organ of the government, the State Council oversaw all state matters, including policy execution by the Six Ministries. Accordingly, various government agencies subordinated to the Six Ministries performed a wide range of specialized functions. At the same time, high officials of the State Council and Six Ministries coordinated the overall execution of policies by participating in significant deliberations and royal lectures.

A system of checks and balances vis-à-vis the throne and high officials was more robust than its Koryŏ precedent. Together known as the Three Offices, the Office of the Inspector General, the Office of the Censor General, and the Office of the Special Counselors monitored the conduct of government personnel, critiqued policies, and prepared a wide range of official documents. Not even the king could arbitrarily stifle the remonstrance of the Three Offices. Although not among the highest ranks, the Three Offices appointments generally went to men of moral probity and scholarship. And barring any unusual circumstance, such officials eventually attained minister or top state counselor positions.

The central bureaucracy featured other vital organs. The Office of the Royal Secretariat transmitted documents of royal command and selectively presented memorials and other documents addressed to the king. The Bureau of State Records compiled and preserved historical works. The Confucian Academy functioned as the institution of higher learning. The State Tribunal handled criminal cases involving aristocrats or matters of consequence to the state. And the Hansŏng Magistracy oversaw the administration and security of the capital.

For jurisdictions outside Hansŏng, the court appointed officials at provincial and county levels. The Chosŏn state, which was more powerful than its predecessors, divided the realm into eight provinces and appointed a governor for each to supervise magistrates (Map 6.1). A provincial governor wielded the power to administer, adjudicate, and audit and also to exercise military command. Also, adjusting the court rank of a magistrate according to the size of the population under his jurisdiction, Chosŏn merged smaller prefectures and counties with larger counties, altogether numbering some 330 counties, and appointed a magistrate for every county, which was classified as a regional center (*mok*), major defense command (*taedohobu*), defense command (*pu*), major county (*kun*), or minor county (*hyŏn*). Such special administrative districts of Koryŏ as *hyang*, *pugok*, and *so* either became regular counties or merged with larger counties. As for Chejudo (formerly T'amna), Chosŏn abolished the hereditary princely position held by the Ko royal house (1402). Representing the king, magistrates throughout the kingdom performed duties as administrators, judges, and military commanders. Assisting each magistrate was a local *yangban* bureau, which also supervised local functionaries, who were no longer the local elite, and promoted Confucian social mores. In Hansŏng, each county maintained a capital liaison office headed by incumbent officials who were native sons. Capital liaison offices ensured that local *yangban* bureaus served the central government's interests, which was an issue of concern.

This concern arose out of the reality that the central government appointed officials for neither of the two subcounty local administration levels, district (*myŏn*) and subdistrict (*ri*). Each district comprised a number of subdistricts, each a natural village or, in counties of higher population density, several neighborhoods (*tong*). The central government sought to facilitate control of villagers with the Five-Family Unit System, which aggregated five neighboring households into one neighborhood under a leader who oversaw all five homes. To monitor local conditions, from time to time the court dispatched to each province a secret inspector (*amhaeng ŏsa*), who traveled incognito and reported directly to the king on his findings.

The more centralized state of Chosŏn reorganized military institutions that were in disarray in late Koryŏ. Mirroring the Koryŏ precedent, the military organization comprised both central and local armies. Constituting the capital army by 1457, the Five Guards protected royal palaces and the city wall, and a high civil official held the commanding position concurrently with his civil post. With infantry at its core, the Five Guards also included "armored soldiers" (*kapsa*), who were salaried professional soldiers recruited through tests and eligible for court ranks, and other select units. Local armies consisted of land troops and marines, and in early Chosŏn, they served in regiments (*yŏng*) or at garrisons at strategic points. Sejo adopted a regional command garrison system, according to which a province maintained one or two army commands. Headed by a provincial army commander, each command oversaw several regional garrisons, each commanded by a magistrate. Similarly, provincial naval commanders led marines, but people were reluctant to serve since marines' duties were more arduous and dangerous than those of land troops. Backing up the regular forces were reserves drawn from clerks, technical learning students, commoners who performed socially denigrated duties, and slaves. Active-duty soldiers served either in Hansŏng or at strategic locations in border regions on a rotation basis, and upon fulfilling the commitment, a conscript became eligible for court rank. Incumbent officials, government school students, and

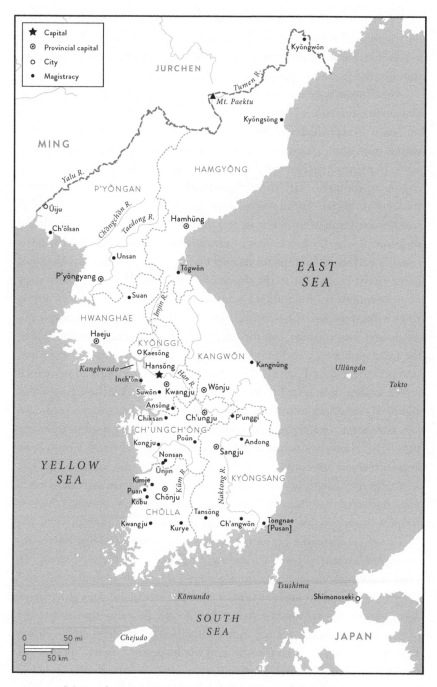

MAP 6.1   Major administrative centers and boundaries of Chosŏn, 1454.

local functionaries were exempt from military duties. Handled by active-duty personnel were the newly constructed city and town walls, chains of beacon fires for military emergency communication, and a network of post stations that facilitated general government communication and transport.

The Chosŏn state recruited officials through the government service examination, protection appointment, and recommendation systems in order to staff such an expanded administrative system, the most centralized yet. The examination system featured civil, military, licentiate, and technical examinations. In principle, all except the lowborn, most of whom were slaves, were eligible to compete. Still, the civil and military examinations also barred the sons of officials found guilty of corruption; the sons and grandsons of remarried women, whom the state and the aristocracy deemed immoral; and illegitimate sons. Both examinations featured regular competitions held triennially and special competitions held on felicitous occasions for the royal house or the king's visit to the shrine of Confucius. The preliminary stage of the triennial civil and military examinations selected candidates according to provincial quotas, the second stage chose thirty-three and twenty-eight candidates, respectively, and the final stage, a palace examination held in the royal audience, merely ranked all finalists. Taking the civil examination initially required passing the classics or licentiate examinations, which served as admission tests for the Confucian Academy. Also held triennially, technical examinations recruited specialists in foreign languages, medicine, law, astronomy, and accounting, with a fixed quota for each subject. Besides passing an examination, one could become an official through a protection appointment or one could receive a high official's recommendation and pass a simpler test. Eligibility criteria for protection appointments were much more restricted than those of Koryŏ, and attaining a high office was difficult for protection appointees who had never passed the civil examination.

Chosŏn instituted a personnel management system suitable for the reorganized bureaucracy and its leading candidate pool, the aristocracy. To prevent corruption, nepotism, or oligarchy, a system of "mutual avoidance" (sangp'i) prohibited the appointment of close relatives to the same government agency or posting a magistrate in his home locale. To assure the impartiality of personnel decisions, the selection of an official of the fifth rank or lower required approval by both the Office of the Inspector General and the Office of the Censor General. Furthermore, a superior periodically evaluated a subordinate's performance in consideration of promotion or demotion.

These institutional mechanisms, which were supposed to enhance central-ized governance through more rational personnel management, worked perhaps too well—eventually dividing officialdom into more conservative senior officials and more reform-minded junior officials.

In the mid-fifteenth century, a new generation of aristocrats that was more committed to Neo-Confucian moral norms began to form a political force, Sarim ("Rusticated Literati"). At the time, the leading political players were Hun'gu ("Meritorious Old Elite"), who had become powerful as merit subjects for helping Sejo ascend the throne, had amassed land and slaves, and continued to reorganize the government according to Official State Learning, which was the study of a government-sanctioned curriculum. By contrast, the Sarim emphasized local autonomy and statecraft of the Kingly Way, which they saw as based on morality and "righteous principle" (ŭiri). Hail-ing primarily from yangban families of the capital region or Kyŏngsang, the Sarim challenged the Hun'gu's central political position. Especially promi-nent among the Sarim were Kim Chongjik (1431–92) and his disciples, who entered the political arena during Sŏngjong's reign. As civil examination graduates, the Sarim mainly filled the bureau section chief positions of the Six Ministries and the Three Offices' remonstrance positions. In such capacities, they scrutinized the conduct of the Hun'gu and the king alike. Since Sŏngjong promoted the Sarim as a counterweight against the Hun'gu, a balance of power continued throughout the reign.

By contrast, Sŏngjong's son and successor, King Yŏnsan'gun (r. 1494–1506), pursued absolute monarchy by pushing back both the Hun'gu and Sarim. Yŏnsan'gun was keen on suppressing the Sarim's remonstrance, and two rounds of bloody purges cast most Kyŏngsang-based Sarim out of power (1498, 1504). The increasingly despotic Yŏnsan'gun pursued hedo-nism, wasting government revenue and even confiscating Hun'gu officials' assets. Unable to tolerate the tyranny any longer, the Hun'gu staged a coup, dethroned Yŏnsan'gun, and elevated his younger half-brother, King Chung-jong (r. 1506–44).

The Sarim gradually expanded their presence in officialdom in the reigns of Chungjong and his successors. Since royal power had reached a new low, Chungjong sought to improve his position vis-à-vis his Hun'gu minders by promoting the Sarim. Accordingly, in 1515, he advanced Cho Kwangjo (1482–1519), a well-reputed Sarim from the capital aristocracy, and Cho's supporters through a recommendation system, the Examination for the Learned and

Virtuous (Hyŏllyangkwa). Securing remonstrance positions in the Three Offices, Cho led mostly Kyŏnggi-based Sarim to promote their views as "public opinion" (kongnon): that is, as a general consensus representing the common good. They pushed ahead with such agendas as strengthening the institution of the royal lecture; increasing remonstrance activities; revoking the recognitions and privileges of unworthy merit subjects; abolishing the Office of Astrological Rituals, for promoting what they deemed superstitious practices; disseminating the *Elementary Learning*; and ending abuses of tribute contracting that had appeared during Sŏngjong's reign and had spawned corruption as government agencies secured goods through contracted merchants. The Hun'gu fought back, successfully pressuring Chungjong, who had grown tired of the Sarim's endless moralizing, to purge Cho and other Sarim officials (1519). Nonetheless, the Sarim remained a significant force, as Chungjong subsequently promoted them again to check Hun'gu power. Upon the accession of Chungjong's son and successor, King Injong (r. 1544–45), the Sarim regained power with the support of Injong's maternal kin—only to be cast out again when the maternal kin of Injong's half-brother and successor, King Myŏngjong (r. 1545–67), purged them (1545). Meanwhile, in local society, the Sarim solidified their prominent positions through such new institutions as private academies and community compacts.

In a world that the elite increasingly understood in terms of Confucian moral hierarchy, Chosŏn interacted with Ming China within the framework of "serving the great" (sadae). The early Chosŏn foreign policy toward Ming acknowledged a China-centered world order, according to which the Ming emperor was the universal ruler. For the most part, Ming China confined the various obligations of its tributaries to ritual protocols, rarely meddling in internal affairs, and Chosŏn was no exception. Initially, the Ming demand for the extradition of Chŏng Tojŏn, for a document that the emperor found offensive, prompted Chŏng to launch preparations to invade Liaodong, but then T'aejong, on his way to power, killed Chŏng (1398). Once relations normalized in T'aejong's reign, Ming was content to allow autonomy, while Chosŏn derived such benefits as high international standing, enhanced royal power, continuing inspirations from the Chinese civilization, and access to the Chinese market.

To the north, Chosŏn exercised a more comprehensive range of policy options vis-à-vis the Jurchens. From the outset, T'aejo, who himself was from the northeast, had personal ties to many Jurchens and took an interest in incorporating the entire region south of the Tumen River into Chosŏn. In Sejong's reign, Chosŏn established a more robust military presence in Hamgyŏng and secured the Tumen and Yalu Rivers as its northern border (the same as the modern-day Sino–North Korean boundary). Nonetheless, as Hamgyŏng remained vulnerable to Jurchen raids, Chosŏn maintained a carrot-and-stick policy. To encourage the Jurchens to submit, Chosŏn offered such incentives as official posts, court ranks, land grants, dwellings, and access to regulated trading outposts in such border region locales as Kyŏngsŏng and Kyŏngwŏn in Hamgyŏng. Jurchen raids, nonetheless, did not cease, and each time Chosŏn responded with a punitive expedition. At the same time, Chosŏn sought to solidify its control of the frontier regions by settling agricultural colonists from its three southernmost provinces in the north and allocating offices to influential northern residents.

For dealing with various island states to the east and south, Chosŏn followed the principle of "neighborly relations" (*kyorin*). Toward Japan, Chosŏn undertook two military campaigns against Tsushima as Wakō raids recurred. The first expedition mobilized a fleet of at least 100 warships and about 10,000 troops (1396–97), but details of the outcome are unknown. The more extensive second operation, commanded by Yi Chongmu (1360–1425), dispatched a fleet of 227 warships and 17,000 troops and succeeded in obtaining the domain lord's promise to stop Wakō raids (1419). Thereafter, as the Japanese pleaded for permission to trade, Chosŏn allowed regulated trade at the locations of present-day Pusan, Chinhae, and Ulsan. Chosŏn also maintained contact with various Southeast Asian states, including the Ryukyus, Siam, and Java, and envoys from these states presented indigenous products as gifts. Chosŏn reciprocated with clothing, dyeing material, and stationery supplies. Relations with the Ryukyus, in particular, were friendly. Chosŏn made meaningful contributions to Ryukyu culture with such gifts as the Confucian classics, Buddhist scriptures, Buddhist monastery bells, and fans. Also, whenever Chosŏn fishers were shipwrecked in the area, the Ryukyu government rendered assistance with repatriation.

In the sixteenth century, relations with Japan deteriorated. When Chosŏn imposed more restrictions on trade, the Japanese often breached agreements and even turned violent. In 1510, Japanese riots at the three ports prompted Chosŏn to establish the Border Defense Command (1510). Initially set up as an ad hoc body, the Border Defense Command soon turned into a permanent deliberative council for dealing with all security matters. In 1555, more than seventy Japanese ships pillaged the Chŏlla shore, and Chosŏn temporarily discontinued official relations with Japan, which increasingly resented the continuing Chosŏn and Ming restrictions on East Asia's expanding international trade.

AGRARIAN ECONOMIC GROWTH

Ideologically critical of commerce, the early Chosŏn state continued the Koryŏ economic policy that prioritized agriculture to secure the people's livelihoods and thus the state's primary revenue base. Besides repeated attempts to enforce the Identification Tag Law (1413–16, 1459–69), the government instituted the Five-Family Mutual Surveillance Law (1485) to prevent vagrancy effectively and sought to expand cultivated land, increase agricultural productivity, and lighten the commoner cultivators' tax burden. For tax assessment, Chosŏn retained the traditional concept of *kyŏl* ("stack"): an officially assessed amount of harvest produced by a measure of land. Sejong's court redefined a *kyŏl* so that one *kyŏl* of the highest-grade land increased from the measure set in Koryŏ during Munjong's reign of 6,573.1 square meters to roughly to 9,859.7 square meters (1444)—thus decreasing the taxable amount of harvest per area unit.

Chosŏn maintained a land tenure system geared toward securing its revenue base, which primarily comprised commoner taxpayers, and toward financially supporting government officials. Rank land tenure granted to each official entitled him to one-tenth of the harvest from resident cultivators. The assignment was limited to Kyŏnggi, and in principle, the land reverted to the state upon the tenure holder's death or treason. The government, though, allowed a deceased official's widow who did not remarry to keep a portion as "fidelity land" (*susinjŏn*), or if she were dead, the children could keep a portion as "fostering land" (*hyuryangjŏn*). Since rank lands in some circumstances and merit-subject lands were inheritable, the state land available for tenure began to dwindle before long. The government replaced the Rank Land Law with the Office Land Law (1466–1556), limiting land tenure to incumbent officials. Then in Sŏngjong's reign, local government offices began to collect tax based on a given year's assessed harvest and redistributed that tax grain to office land tenure holders, instead of allowing them to collect more than one-tenth of resident cultivators' harvest, as had been the practice for some time. Even the new system became untenable before the government stopped granting any more land tenure (1556). However, state-owned forests, fisheries, and salt ponds continued to provide additional revenue for the government.

The Chosŏn state's primary revenue base was a land tax, supplemented by some special taxes. In principle, all landowners had to submit one-tenth of the harvest as land tax, but in reality, landlords, most of whom were aristocrats, often passed on their obligations to resident tenant farmers. The government annually assessed each locale's harvest and adjusted the levy accordingly. To rationalize the system, Sejong stipulated that taxable land be classified into six grades of productivity and that a given year's harvest be assessed according to a nine-fold classification. The readjusted levy amount was payable in kind with such crops as rice and beans, and in times of natural disaster, cultivators received a temporary tax reduction or exemption. Besides the tax levied on any cultivated land owned, handicrafters and merchants also had to pay special taxes. Government personnel transported the collected tax grain from various counties to shoreline or riverside tax granaries. The tax grain then reached capital granaries via the Yellow Sea lanes from the granaries in Chŏlla, Ch'ungch'ŏng, and Hwanghae; via the North Han River from Kangwŏn; and via the Naktong River and the South Han River from Kyŏngsang. While keeping some in reserve as rice, the state used the rest of the tax grain to pay for the Chŏnju Yi royal house's expenses, government events, officials' stipends, military provisions, public medical services, and relief for the poor.

Chosŏn also continued the Koryŏ practice of collecting local tribute by assigning product quotas for all counties and levying them on individual households. These products included handicraft goods, minerals, marine products, fur, fruits, and medicinal ingredients. Since keeping an accurate record of local products for every county and revising the quotas accordingly was difficult, a county often had to procure goods elsewhere to meet the government quota. Thus, compared to the land tax, remitting the local tribute was more onerous for taxpayers and the local authorities.

Additionally, males from age sixteen to sixty performed military and corvée obligations. The military service entailed either active duty on a rotational basis or, as a support taxpayer, covering an active-duty soldier's expenses. In early Chosŏn, aristocrats and commoners alike performed their duties, whereas incumbent officials, administrative clerks, local functionaries, government school students, and slaves were exempt. Besides contributing as support taxpayers, aristocrats typically served in elite or ceremonial guard units. In the late fifteenth century, however, they began to shun active duties, as well as the corvée through which the state mobilized eligible males for such projects as constructing or repairing royal tombs, fortification walls, and reservoirs. The government generally refrained from mobilizing commoner cultivators during the busy farming season. A new regulation devised in Sŏngjong's reign mobilized one male for every eight *kyŏl* of cultivated land and limited his corvée to no more than six days per year, although arbitrary mobilization remained frequent.

As proprietors of the state, the *yangban* aristocracy maintained an economic foundation that consisted of stipend, rank land, privately owned land, and slaves. An officeholder received an annual stipend that comprised grain, bolts of hemp cloth, and paper money, with the quantity of each determined by his rank. Most *yangban* were landlords whose holdings tended to be in Kyŏngsang, Chŏlla, and Ch'ungch'ŏng, all of which had more fertile soil than did the rest of Korea, and each holding tended to be an agricultural estate. Slaves cultivated an aristocrat's land, but if slave labor was not sufficient, then a landlord turned to local tenant farmers, collecting half the harvest from each. Some *yangban* managed their land personally by maintaining residences and storage near their holdings. Still, for the most part, they relied on local relatives and, from time to time, dispatched their personal slaves to provide supervision. As aristocratic landholdings began to increase in the late fifteenth century, more commoner cultivators became vagrants, and landlords took them in, treating them as agricultural slaves.

In early Chosŏn, an aristocratic landlord typically owned anywhere between 10 and 300 or more slaves. Some purchased slaves, but more commonly, the owners inherited them or acquired them as their existing slaves produced offspring. Relevant laws were such that the offspring of a slave inherited slave status regardless of the other parent's status, even if that parent were an aristocratic father. Slaves performed such duties as taking care of the household, cultivating the land, and weaving for their owners. The majority of slaves lived apart from their owners, as out-resident slaves who cultivated or managed their owners' land. From each out-resident slave, the owner annually collected a personal tribute of a bolt of cotton cloth and paper money. During much of the fifteenth century, the state was mostly successful in prohibiting *yangban* landlords from taking over free cultivators' plots.

As the state, landlords, and cultivators alike built on late Koryŏ advances and innovations, agricultural production continued to increase. Besides promoting land reclamation and irrigation facility improvement among landlords and cultivators, the government developed new farming techniques, including the use of manure, improved fertilizer application, and tools, and disseminated them through such farming manuals as *Straight Talk on Farming* (*Nongsa chiksŏl*; 1429), which was based on the experience of Korean farmers with regard to storage of seeds, improving soil quality, and seedling transfer, and the *Comprehensive Compilation for Agricultural Practices* (*Kŭmyang chamnok*; 1492). As landowners, *yangban* scholar-officials themselves were eager to build or repair irrigation facilities and import the latest agricultural technology from Ming China. Even in the south, where the climate and the terrain were more suitable for rice paddies, spring drought limited seedling transfer to some locales. The rice transplanting technique, though, soon spread to the rest of the region and enabled double-cropping, with rice as the fall harvest and barley as the summer harvest. Double-cropping probably began in the late sixteenth century in the southwestern coastal plains, but until the seventeenth century, royal edicts generally prohibited it for fear of a barley crop failure in the winter and resulting famine. For such dry-field crops as barley, millet, and beans, three harvests in two years became widespread. Also, the cultivation of such cash crops as medicinal herbs, fruit, and cotton increased. Throughout much of the fifteenth century, commoner cultivators enjoyed improved living conditions compared to late Koryŏ. Cultivated land registered with the government tripled from some 500,000 *kyŏl* at the end of Koryŏ to more than 1.6 million *kyŏl* by the mid-fifteenth century.

Expansion of the agrarian economy sustained flourishing handicraft production. Early Chosŏn maintained a government-run handicraft industry, which was more effectively managed than Koryŏ's. To secure necessary goods, each government agency kept a record of registered crafters. Some 2,800 in Hansŏng and more than 3,500 in the eight provinces produced such goods as clothing, stationery, movable type, gun powder, weapons, and eating ware. Government artisans received just enough remuneration to cover their meal costs while performing their obligations. Such artisans supported their households by selling whatever goods remained after meeting their quota and paying the tax; when not on duty, they produced goods for their profit. In the sixteenth century, as the early Chosŏn systems of tax collection and workforce mobilization broke down while commerce continued to grow, the number of independent artisans increased. They produced mainly farming tools and other goods for use by the ordinary people and luxury items for aristocratic households. Self-sufficient cultivator households produced such daily necessities as silk, ramie fabric, and hemp cloth and also cotton cloth as cotton cultivation became more widespread.

Compared to Koryŏ, early Chosŏn regulated commercial activities more strictly. Among the four occupational categories that the aristocracy recognized, scholars ranked at the top, followed by farmers, artisans, and merchants. Both the throne and the ruling elite generally believed that un-regulated commerce would produce extravagance and waste, hurt agriculture, and widen the gap between the rich and the poor. Given this perspective, the early Chosŏn state maintained a minimal network of roads and transportation modes for commerce. In Hansŏng, only government-licensed merchants could set up shops along the main avenue, Chongno. The government allowed the merchants of Kaesŏng, formerly the Koryŏ capital, to move to Hansŏng and levied shop tax and merchant tax on them. In return for supplying the royal household and government offices with various goods, capital merchants received monopoly rights for specific merchandise, and the Bureau of Capital Market Supervision prohibited illegal commercial activities. Known as the Six Licensed Shops, those who sold silk, ramie fabric, hemp cloth, cotton cloth, paper, or marine products especially prospered. In the provinces, rural markets spread with increased agricultural productivity. Worried that cultivators might neglect farming, the government restricted such markets, but many opened periodically, typically every five days. Traveling throughout the kingdom, peddlers, who carried goods on their backs, sold produce, handicraft items, marine products, and medicinal materials at rural markets. The government tried to promote paper money and copper coins, *Chosŏn t'ongbo* (issued in 1427), but the ordinary people generally conducted market transactions using rice and cotton cloth as de facto currency.

Besides controlling domestic commerce, early Chosŏn also restricted international trade. Officially authorized merchants accompanied Chosŏn envoy visits to China and conducted trade both for the government and for their own profit. Regulated by the government, Chosŏn merchants also traded with the Jurchens and the Japanese, through northeastern border outposts and the Japan House in Tongnae (in modern-day Pusan). The commodity trade involved mainly cotton cloth and food items. The government prohibited purely private international trade, but by the sixteenth century, many merchants conducted such trade illegally—often with the support of influential political figures, who then pocketed a share of the profits.

By the early sixteenth century, several developments had transformed the early Chosŏn economy in ways that increased hardship for commoner cultivators. Tenancy increased, owing to natural disasters, usury, and tax burdens, while such powerful aristocrats as merit subjects continued to expand their holdings. Tenant farmers owed half their harvest to their landlord. Also, the increasingly common evasion of active-duty military service by *yangban* overburdened ordinary commoners with such obligations. In the late fifteenth century, Chosŏn entered a long period of relative security from external threats, and the government began to allow conscription-age males to hire substitutes, but the cost was too burdensome for an ordinary commoner. Furthermore, as tribute contracting increased in volume, with intermediaries pocketing profits, farmers' obligations became more onerous. Moreover, corrupt magistrates and local functionaries abused the Grain Loan System, which maintained emergency relief granaries and price equalization granaries to aid those in need and to release grain to stabilize market prices. And government agents filled their pockets by using various extortion strategies to charge borrowers more interest than the stipulated amount. In the end, a growing number of free cultivators who could no longer meet their obligations to the state or their landlords abandoned their plots, thus increasing the tax burden on other taxpayers.

The state responded with various measures, but, on the whole, such efforts could not stem the tide. To provide additional food sources, the government disseminated new methods for processing mixed grain, acorns, and even tree bark. Also, landed local aristocrats sought to stabilize agrarian society by establishing privately run granaries and instituting community compacts that outlined residents' duties and obligations, determined primarily by social status. Such reform-minded scholar-officials as Yi I (pen name Yulgok; 1536–84) and Yu Sŏngnyong (1542–1607) advocated a new tax system replacing the onerous local tribute with rice, which functioned as de facto currency, and the more public-minded magistrates began to implement the new system. Such aristocrats, who were proprietors of the state, were rare.

ARISTOCRACY, *CHUNGIN*, COMMONERS, AND THE LOWBORN

While many free cultivators suffered in the sixteenth century, the overall expansion in agricultural output sustained population growth throughout the early Chosŏn period. As of 1392, the remarkable long-term phase of growth during which the total population of 3 to 4 million as of 1350 would triple by 1700 was likely well underway. The gain suggests that it was proceeding in a sustained fashion despite periodic setbacks due to famine, disease, and war. Improved efficiencies in primary production drove commercialization, urbanization, and diversification in material goods. In the fifteenth century, a large-scale, state-sponsored migration of agrarian Koreans from the south to the north began, as discussed earlier.

The government conducted a household survey triennially. For each administrative jurisdiction, the state assigned local tribute and military service quotas based on the population recorded on household registers. Since those responsible for local tribute and military service were males aged sixteen to sixty, available official statistics understate the actual population. When Chosŏn was first established, the total population probably was between 5.5 million and 7.5 million. As of Sejong's reign, Hansŏng's population was about 100,000. About half of the kingdom's population lived in the three southernmost provinces, Kyŏngsang, Chŏlla, and Ch'ungch'ŏng, and this pattern would persist throughout the Chosŏn period. Among the rest of the provinces, Kyŏnggi and Kangwŏn accounted for about 20 percent and Hwanghae, P'yŏngan, and Hamgyŏng about 30 percent of the total population.

Chosŏn institutionalized a hierarchy that divided the population into four status groups. The highest, the *yangban*, had become a hereditary aristocracy by the beginning of Chosŏn, and by law, an increasing number of members of the Chŏnju Yi royal house more than four generations removed from a Chosŏn monarch through direct male descent became *yangban*. The status group just below the *yangban* comprised *chungin* ("middle people"): government-employed technical specialists, capital government office and local functionaries, noncommissioned military officers (*kun'gyo*), and illegitimate children of aristocratic men by commoner concubines. The rest of the free population formed the third status group, commoners, most of whom were farmers. Below the commoners were the lowborn who were unfree. Most were chattel slaves, but some were *kisaeng*. Since an offspring of parents who were not of the same social status generally inherited the lower status, over a few generations, a descent line could easily fall in status from aristocrat to slave.

A distinction between the *yangban* (or simply *pan*) and the "ordinary" (*sang*) set the aristocracy apart from the rest of the population. A closed status group of aristocrats, *yangban*, comprised not just civil and military officials of aristocratic descent, which traced at least as far back as late Koryŏ, but also their kin. Possessing land and slaves, *yangban* sought official careers through the government service examination, protection appointment, or recommendation systems. As potential government officials with economic means, aristocratic males from childhood could devote themselves to studies focused on Confucian texts and received training in prose, poetry, and calligraphy. Supporting an aristocratic lifestyle were various institutionalized privileges sanctioned by the state, which the aristocracy managed through officialdom. *Yangban* enjoyed exemption from tax and corvée obligations on the grounds that they were serving the state as scholars and officials. And in the late fifteenth century, exemption from active-duty military service also became increasingly common. At the same time, the aristocracy did what it could to prevent others from joining its ranks. In the fifteenth century, some nonaristocrats of talent passed the prestigious civil examination and attained civil offices, but *yangban* officials scrutinized such appointees until that attention effectively ended the hapless victims' careers.

Below the aristocracy but above the commoners were *chungin*. As state-employed technical specialists, capital government office and local functionaries, or noncommissioned military officers, *chungin* generally remained in their respective occupational groups for generations, married within such a group, and resided near the government agencies where they worked. Likewise, being neither aristocrat nor commoner, illegitimate children of aristocratic men and commoner concubines also married among themselves and passed down their status to the next generation. Barred from the civil and military examinations, some obtained lower-level military offices or technical positions. Although denigrated by the aristocracy, specialist *chungin* in particular held their ground as their services were essential to the state. Among them, interpreters who accompanied envoys to China or Japan even made profits from officially approved trade. Hereditary local functionaries still wielded significant influence, as centrally appointed magistrates were neither familiar with local conditions nor served for a long term. Nonetheless, the *yangban* who relocated from the capital and established themselves as landed local elites increasingly subordinated the functionaries.

Below the *chungin* were the commoners, who constituted the majority of the population. Most were free cultivators, but the commoner population working as handicrafters and merchants continued to grow. Commoners were legally eligible to take the government service examinations, but in reality, devoting themselves to years of intensive study in preparation for the examination was not feasible for most; responsible for land tax, local tribute, corvée, and military service, all of which as a whole was burdensome, they struggled to survive. Handicrafters worked either for the government or private customers, whereas market merchants and peddlers performed commercial transactions under government regulation. As the early Chosŏn economic policy prioritized agriculture while restricting commerce, merchants were inferior to farmers in social status. Early Chosŏn also treated some commoners who performed certain socially denigrated duties as de facto lowborn. These individuals included marines, government office runners, State Tribunal guards, beacon fire station soldiers, post station staff, and tax transport workers. Before the late fifteenth century, occasional military campaigns against the Wakō or domestic rebellions offered rare opportunities for acts of military merit that could result in an office or a court rank for a commoner. Still, even such attainment did not enable that commoner to become a *yangban*.

At the bottom of Chosŏn's society were the lowborn. Most were chattel slaves, who were transferable, as commodities, through a financial transaction, inheritance, or gift exchange. In general, an offspring of a slave was a slave regardless of the other parent's status. As was true in Koryŏ, a resident slave lived and worked in a private household or at a government office, whereas an out-resident slave who managed the owner's property elsewhere, typically a landholding, resided onsite and periodically remitted personal tribute. The lowborn also included *kisaeng*, including female government slaves who had become such entertainers. The most highly regarded were those well versed in prose, poetry, or painting. In principle, the government allowed only aristocrats to hire *kisaeng* for special occasions, rather than going to *kisaeng* houses, but in reality many royals and ordinary *yangban* patronized such venues.

Most commoners struggled with hardship, and government aids were insufficient. In addition to the Grain Loan System for free cultivators, various state-managed facilities offered relief and medical care to the population, including the Government Dispensary, which sold medicinal ingredients; the Eastern and Western Bureaus of Relief, which assisted the capital residents in need; the Bureau of Public Aid which did likewise in the provinces; and the Eastern and Western Bureaus of Vagrant Relief which provided shelter and food to the homeless. Nonetheless, many vagrants resorted to banditry in times of hardship, robbing goods being transported to the central government or to *yangban*. Among them, Im Kkŏkchŏng (1504–62), who was active in Hwanghae and Kyŏnggi during Myŏngjong's reign, reportedly took from the rich and gave to the poor before being captured and executed.

Chosŏn did not have judiciary organs separate from executive entities. In Hansŏng, the Office of the Inspector General, the State Tribunal, the Ministry of Punishments, the Hansŏng Magistracy, and the Bureau of Slave Administration all handled legal cases. Elsewhere, governors and magistrates did likewise in their respective jurisdictions. Depending on the nature of a case, a litigant unsatisfied with a ruling might be able to appeal to another agency. A complainant might even appeal to the king by beating the Sinmun'go, a special drum that the government maintained outside the palace, or by beating a gong during his majesty's outings. To minimize frivolous cases, the government maintained strict criteria for the types of issues that could be so appealed, and a violator suffered punishment. At first mostly concerning slave ownership or status, legal cases increasingly involved disputes over ancestral gravesites, as the elite funerary culture transitioned from Buddhist cremation to Confucian burial and as organized lineages associated with particular locales arose.

Early Chosŏn generally relied on the Great Code of Administration and the Great Ming Code, rather than on customary laws as Koryŏ had done. While retaining Koryŏ's five forms of criminal punishment, for most crimes, Chosŏn otherwise applied the Great Ming Code, one of the most important law codes in Chinese history. Punishments were particularly severe for treason and violation of a cardinal Confucian virtue, and such crimes resulted in punishment of not just the culprit but also that person's parents, siblings, spouse, and children. For a crime of such a kind deemed especially heinous, the government even punished the entire community from which the criminal hailed by penalizing the magistrate with a low performance score, if not outright dismissing him, and by downgrading the administrative status of the county.

While the rule of codified law gained ground, in early Chosŏn customary laws did continue to govern such fundamentally important human bonds as kinship. In continuation of the ancient custom of uxorilocal marriage, a newlywed couple resided at the wife's natal home. Also, while a new law gave the eldest legitimate son an additional fifth of the inheritance from the parents, each of the sons and daughters received an equal share of the remainder of the estate, as was customary. Furthermore, siblings could take a turn in performing or sharing responsibilities for ancestral rites, rather the eldest legitimate son having to assume all the duty. Reflecting such a standing among women, some extant early Chosŏn portraits of officials show both the husband and wife (Figure 6.2).

This convention ceased in the sixteenth century, however, as Chosŏn officialdom pursued ideal patriarchy by devising new laws that emphasized filial piety and chaste widowhood. Marriage was a matter of decision for the parents, and the minimum legal ages for weddings were fifteen for males and fourteen for females. Although by law a husband could be married to only one wife, he could maintain concubines. After decades of debate, the Great Code of Administration prohibited a widow's remarriage and barred illegitimate sons, as well as the sons and grandsons of remarried women, from the civil or military examinations. In the same spirit, the state made provisions for recognizing and honoring filial sons and chaste wives.

In many ways, Lady P'yŏngsan Sin (studio name Saimdang; 1504–51) epitomizes the kind of womanhood increasingly idealized by the Chosŏn elite, both in her lifetime and in the centuries thereafter. Born into a family of *yangban* officials, she was not only the wife of a minor official and the mother of talented children, including the celebrated Yi I, but also a scholar, writer, poet, and painter. Reflecting the ancient marriage custom, Saimdang was born at her mother's home village in Kangnŭng and later gave birth to and raised Yi I there before moving in with her parents-in-law in Hansŏng. Both her husband and her mother-in-law were supportive of Saimdang's pursuit of learning and arts. Her posthumous fame as a virtuous woman would also grow thanks to Yi I's stature as a Confucian luminary, especially since his intellectual heirs became dominant in post-1623 politics and shaped the cultural landscape.

THE BEGINNINGS OF EARLY MODERN KOREAN CULTURE

The early Chosŏn state's efforts to control knowledge production and shape moral norms motivated Sejong and his scholar-officials to invent a Korean phonetic alphabet, *han'gŭl*. Although used since early times, none among the then existing writing systems—Sinographic, *idu*, and *hyangch'al*—was capable of transliterating the Korean language as used in daily life or was easy enough for the ordinary people to learn. Such limitations hindered the state and the aristocracy's effort to promote a stable, *yangban*-centered society by propagating Confucian morality. Also, as full-fledged participants in Sinitic civilization, the elite desired to standardize Korean pronunciation of Sinographs.

FIGURE 6.2   Portrait of Chief State Councilor Ha Yŏn (1376–1453) and his wife, Lady Sŏngju Yi (1390–1465), nineteenth century. Source: Paeksan Academy Shrine, Muju, South Chŏlla Province. Photo credit: Cultural Heritage Administration.

As proudly noted in *Correct Sounds for the Instruction of the People* (*Hunmin chŏngŭm*; 1446), *han'gŭl* is far easier to learn than Sinographs and allows a more direct expression of one's thoughts as orally articulated. Using *han'gŭl*, the government subsequently compiled *Songs of Flying Dragons* (*Yongbi ŏch'ŏn ka*; 1447), which praises virtues of the Chŏnju Yi royal house, and *Songs of the Moon's Reflection on a Thousand Rivers* (*Worin ch'ŏn'gang chi kok*; 1449), which extolls the Buddha's virtues. During the succeeding reigns, the court produced *han'gŭl* editions of various Buddhist scriptures, farming manuals, moral primers, and military strategy texts. Although unable to replace Literary Sinitic as the elite's preferred written language, *han'gŭl* became a commonly used script among government functionaries, as their recruitment test required proficiency. *Han'gŭl* literacy likely began to increase among the ordinary people as well.

Expanding on Koryŏ educational institutions, Chosŏn maintained a system of government-run schools at three levels. Rather than an interconnected component of a comprehensive education system, each was an independent institution. Replicating its late Koryŏ namesake in Kaegyŏng, the new Confucian Academy in Hansŏng housed the state shrine of Confucius and served as the kingdom's sole institution of higher learning, admitting those who passed the classics or literary licentiate examination. Satisfactory academic performance and fulfillment of all curricular requirements made students eligible to take the civil examination. Besides the Confucian Academy, Hansŏng featured government institutions of secondary education, the Four Schools (*sahak*), located in the capital's eastern, southern, western, and central sections. Outside Hansŏng, each county maintained a public school where students performed rites in honor of select Confucian worthies, especially native sons, and received secondary-level education. For each county school (*hyanggyo*) as such, the central government appointed a preceptor or an instructor, depending on the school's size and location.

Supplementing the state education system were a far greater number of private schools throughout the kingdom. Initially, all were village schools that provided primary education to commoners and those of higher social status who could not enter one of the Four Schools or a county school. Students generally ranged in age from eight to sixteen. While serving as the magistrate of P'unggi in Kyŏngsang, Chu Sebung (1495–1554) founded Chosŏn's first private school for more advanced study, the Paegundong Academy (1543; later renamed Sosu Academy) where he befittingly honored the famous native son and Confucian worthy An Hyang. The Paegundong Academy and others that followed brought together students from leading local *yangban* families to perform rites in honor of renowned scholars or merit subjects and pursue learning and scholarship. The government encouraged the establishment of private academies, and by the end of Myŏngjong's reign, a total of twenty-six were flourishing, among which fifteen were in Kyŏngsang. Each province had at least one.

Besides honoring past worthies, the compilation and study of history were essential for affirming Chosŏn's legitimacy in the succession of dynasties from a Confucian perspective. Continuing the Koryŏ tradition, each new Chosŏn reign compiled the veritable records for the preceding reign, in effect producing an abridged, heavily edited version of draft daily records. Also, many new works narrating the history of pre-Chosŏn eras appeared. Chŏng Tojŏn compiled the no longer extant *History of the Koryŏ State* (*Koryŏ-guk sa*; 1395), which justified the Koryŏ-Chosŏn dynastic change. Such self-legitimizing historiographical projects of Chosŏn continued, culminating in Munjong's reign with the *History of Koryŏ* (*Koryŏ sa*; 1451), which employs an annals, treatises, and biographies structure, and the *Essentials of Koryŏ History* (*Koryŏ sa chŏryo*; 1452), which uses only the annals format. Not limiting the scope to Koryŏ, Chosŏn also compiled the entire history of Korea. Commissioned by Sŏngjong, the eminent civil official and a scholar Sŏ Kŏjŏng (1420–88) compiled the *Comprehensive Mirror of Korea* (*Tongguk t'onggam*; 1485), which presents history from Kojosŏn through Koryŏ in an annals format. New works followed in the next century, including the *Concise History of Korea* (*Tongguk saryak*; early sixteenth century) by Pak Sang (1474–1530), also a prominent civil official and a scholar.

Drawing lessons from history, early Chosŏn sought to strengthen centralized governance and military defense, as reflected in many new geographical treatises and maps. A group of erudite officials prepared and presented to T'aejong the *Integrated Map of Borders Regulating States and Capitals throughout History* (*Honil kangni yŏktae kukto chi to*; 1402), which is East Asia's oldest extant map of the world (Figure 6.3). The map shows Korea disproportionately large compared to China, whereas disproportionately small Japan comprises merely a few islands. Knowledge of the world farther west, including Europe and Africa, was limited. Early Chosŏn subsequently produced increasingly accurate maps, including the *Map of the Realm of Korea* (*Chosŏn pangyŏk chido*; 1557 or 1558), which is also extant. At the same time, more detailed maps of Korea appeared, including the *Map of Eight Provinces* (*P'alto to*; 1402), which T'aejong commissioned, and the *Map of Korea* (*Tongguk chido*; 1463), the production of which was overseen by the renowned civil official and scholar Yang Sŏngji (1415–82), during Sejo's reign, but neither of these maps has survived. The court also commissioned such works as the *Newly Compiled Geographical Treatise on the Eight Provinces* (*Sinch'an p'alto chiriji*; 1432), Korea's first government project of this kind, and the *Survey of Korea's Geography* (*Tongguk yŏji sŭngnam*; 1481). Again, neither has survived, but both reportedly provided detailed information on each county's topography, local products, transportation, customs, history, and notable personalities. Later, Chungjong commissioned an updated version of the *Survey of Korea's Geography*, the *Augmented Survey of Korea's Geography* (*Sinjŭng Tongguk yŏji sŭngnam*; 1530), which is extant.

While mapping its domain in the physical world, early Chosŏn also pursued projects in ethics and rituals, befitting its place in the Confucian moral universe. Sejong commissioned the *Illustrated Guide to the Virtues of the*

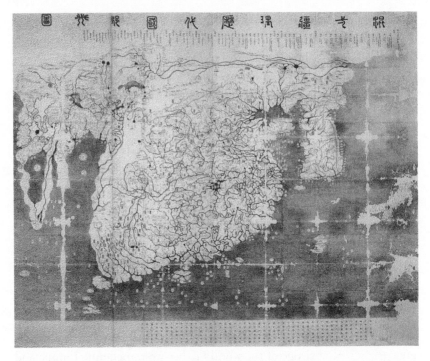

FIGURE 6.3   A pre-1459 hand-copied edition of the *Integrated Map of Borders Regulating States and Capitals* throughout History. Source: Tokiwa Museum of Historical Materials. Photo credit: Kyujanggak Institute for Korean Studies, Seoul National University.

Three Bonds (*Samgang haengsil to*; 1432), which featured vignettes of exemplary loyal subjects, filial sons, and virtuous women. Decades later, Sŏngjong's officials compiled the *Manual for the Five Categories of State Rites* (*Kukcho orye ŭi*; 1474), which reviewed auspicious (ancestral) rites, family (capping and wedding) rites, guest rites (concerning diplomatic embassies), military rites, and mourning rites. In the sixteenth century, the Sarim, who were promoting the twelfth-century Song Chinese works *Elementary Learning* and *Family Rituals*, prepared moral primers, such as the *Illustrated Guide to the Virtues of the Two Human Relationships* (*Iryun haengsil to*; 1518), which emphasized moral imperatives for elder and younger brother relationships and friendships. To disseminate Zhu Xi's *Essential Knowledge for Children* (*Tongmeng xuzhi*; c. 1163), a treatise on education for the young, the Sarim published a new, woodblock edition of that work (1517).

At the same time, the Chosŏn state moved swiftly to codify governing standards to reflect Confucian tenets. The architect of the new dynasty, Chŏng Tojŏn, compiled the Administrative Code of Chosŏn (Chosŏn Kyŏngguk chŏn; 1394) and the Mirror for Governance (Kyŏngje mun'gam; 1395). Another leading figure in the politics of dynastic change, Cho Chun (1346–1405), followed up with the Six Codes of Governance (Kyŏngje yuk chŏn; 1397). A legal compilation of more lasting impact went into effect decades later with the Great Code of Administration, a project that began in Sejo's reign and saw completion during Sŏngjong's reign. Comprising codes on personnel, taxation, rites, war, punishments, and public works, this code would remain the foundation of the overall Chosŏn legal system for two centuries.

In interpreting and applying Confucianism for the new governing order, differing views arose among the scholar-officials. Not limiting themselves to Nature and Principle Learning, such advocates of Official State Learning as Chŏng Tojŏn and Kwŏn Kŭn addressed various issues also by selectively drawing from Han-Tang Chinese Confucianism, Buddhism, Daoism, geomancy, and even folk religion. They held in high regard the *Rites of Zhou* (*Zhou li*) as a treatise on institutions of early China's Zhou dynasty and hence a guiding text. Thus, the Official State Learning scholars pursued an overall objective of "wealthy state, powerful army" (*puguk kangbyŏng*) through institutional reform and reorganization. By contrast, the Sarim, who began to form a political force during Sŏngjong's reign, built on the moral teachings of more moderate reformers of late Koryŏ, such as Kil Chae (1353–1419), who refused to serve Chosŏn, instead retiring from officialdom. The Sarim stressed governance based on a moral transformation of the people rather than on law codes. Criticizing merit subjects and royal in-laws for arrogance and corruption, the Sarim sought to apply Nature and Principle Learning to governing institutions.

Stressing morality and self-cultivation, the Sarim showed a keen interest in human nature. Among them, Sŏ Kyŏngdŏk (pen name Hwadam; 1489–1546) and Yi Ŏnjŏk (1491–1553) were pioneering figures in the development of two key concepts in Neo-Confucian metaphysics: *i* (Ch. *li*), the underlying pattern and order of nature as reflected in its organic forms; and *ki* (Ch. *qi*), the vital force or psychosomatic energy that forms part of all things and materializes all things as defined by *i*. Sŏ not only understood the cosmos more in terms of *ki* than *i* but was also open to Buddhist and Daoist thoughts.

Likewise interested in both Buddhism and Daoism, Cho Sik (pen name Nammyŏng; 1501–72) advocated putting learning into action. Such ideas, as articulated by Sŏ and Cho, formed a distinct intellectual trend in the mid-sixteenth century. By contrast, Yi Ŏnjŏk advanced ideas overall more centered around *i*—a position more influential among later intellectuals. Among them, Yi Hwang (pen name T'oegye; 1501–70), in particular, made decisive contributions. Authoring such works as *Essentials of Master Zhu's Writings* (*Chuja sŏ chŏryo*; 1561), Yi Hwang constructed his system of thoughts reflecting Zhu Xi's teachings while considering the realities of Chosŏn. Emphasizing the mind and heart together as the basis for moral action, his thoughts are rich in fundamentalism and idealism.

During Chungjong's reign, Chosŏn intellectuals expressed varied reactions to Ming Chinese Yangmingism, which criticized Neo-Confucianism for absolutizing and formalizing tendencies and, instead, stressed actual practice. The ideas of a multitalented Ming scholar-official and general, Wang Yangming (1472–1528), constituted the main intellectual opposition to Neo-Confucianism based on Zhu Xi's teachings. Belonging to the School of Mind, Yangmingism emphasized that one can obtain *i* from the heart without seeking it externally. Although this was appealing to many Chosŏn intellectuals, Yi Hwang criticized Yangmingism for challenging the orthodoxy of Zhu's thoughts. Especially as Yi's teachings gained a large following, mainstream Chosŏn scholarship condemned Yangmingism as heterodoxy.

Whereas Neo-Confucianism triumphed as the dominant system of thought, the position of Buddhism and shamanism as officially sanctioned religions deteriorated. Certainly, the royal court, the aristocracy, and the ordinary people alike continued to seek out Buddhist clergy and shamans. For example, *yangban* families sponsored the printing of Buddhist sutras to gain merit and hired shamans to ward off evil spirits in times of pestilence. Nonetheless, soon after the dynastic change, the government took drastic measures against Buddhism, even though T'aejo himself was a devout Buddhist. The state confiscated land and slaves from Buddhist monasteries. Also requiring all monks to register, the government set a strict limit on the number of registered clergy and collected registration fees. Moreover, the state merged the Buddhist schools into just two, the Sŏn and doctrinal schools. Sejong, also a devout Buddhist, recognized only thirty-six monasteries for the entire kingdom, shutting down the rest. Nonetheless, as the government could not weaken Buddhism's appeal across status boundaries overnight, the religion retained such official roles as conducting prayer rituals for the Chŏnju Yi royal house's well-being and for the repose of deceased royals. Buddhism even enjoyed a revival under Sejo, who was increasingly guilt-ridden while also resenting Confucian moralizing on his usurpation. He established the Directorate-General for Sutra Publication, which oversaw the translation of Buddhist texts into *han'gŭl* and their dissemination. During Sŏngjong's reign, persistent anti-Buddhist criticism by the Sarim, whom the king promoted politically, began to distance at least the male elite from Buddhism, gradually confining its rituals to monasteries in the mountains. In Myŏngjong's reign, Buddhism enjoyed another revival, thanks to the vigorous patronage of the king's mother, the dowager Queen Munjŏng (1501–65), who entrusted Pou (1515–65; not to be confused with the Pou of late Koryŏ mentioned previously) with a mission of revitalizing Buddhism and even restored ecclesiastical examinations. Upon her death, however, the downfall of her natal kin and Pou effectively ended the resurgence.

Likewise, both Daoism and shamanism lost ground, with their number of temples and ceremonies reduced, although their influence remained pervasive in Chosŏn culture. Recognizing that heaven-worship rituals enhanced the power of the state, the government maintained the Office of Daoist Rituals and implemented *ch'oje*, a ritual for worshipping the sun, the moon, and the stars. Also, geomantic ideas and prophetic beliefs remained influential, as reflected in transferring the capital from Kaegyŏng to Hansŏng and in the aristocracy's general concern for selecting auspicious sites for ancestral graves. Moreover, such practices as shaman rituals, worship of local mountain gods and the Three Gods, who have power over conception, childbirth, and the health of the newborn, and village offering rituals had deep roots in popular culture. In particular, seasonal customs melded with Confucian thoughts, gradually turning into new rituals for ancestral worship and seeking village well-being. As Buddhist-style cremation gave way to grave burial, a desire to secure auspicious sites for the living and the dead alike became even more pronounced.

Accompanying new trends in belief systems, the utilitarian tendencies of the early Chosŏn state and its intellectuals built on late Koryŏ achievements and produced technological innovations. The government and the ruling elite alike valued technology to enrich the state, strengthen the army, and secure the people's livelihood. Combining the indigenous body of knowledge with knowledge introduced from China and beyond, early Chosŏn technology produced some noteworthy advances in architecture, astronomy, meteorology, medicine, military technology, and print culture.

In architecture, Koryŏ's primary concern with Buddhist monasteries gave way to prioritizing such secular structures as royal palaces, government offices, and schools. Sumptuary laws regulated the size and decoration of buildings according to the owner's social status, and the overarching concern was to enhance royal authority while maintaining the existing social order. Chosŏn constructed a city wall for Hansŏng and built the Kyŏngbok Palace as the king's residence, soon followed by the Ch'angdŏk and Ch'anggyŏng Palaces. Once the Sarim made inroads into court politics, construction of private academies increased, and these schools began to spread throughout the country in the sixteenth century. Typically located in a quiet, secluded village area conducive to reflecting on nature, a private academy had a lecture hall as its central structure, flanked by a Confucian shrine and a dormitory as eastern and western chambers. The architecture of these private academies possesses a unique beauty that combines the layouts of aristocratic homes and Buddhist monasteries in a more practical manner.

As was true of architecture, concerns of practicality motivated studies in astronomy and meteorology. From the outset, Chosŏn devised astronomical charts. T'aejo's court had the *Chart of the Constellations and the Regions They Govern*, based on astronomical charts drawn up in Koguryŏ, carved in stone. Sejong's court devised a new chart, *Calculation of the Motions of the Seven Celestial Determinants* (*Chilchŏng san*; 1444), which calculated locations of the sun, the moon, and the five inner planets, based on the Chinese Season-Granting Astronomical System (Shuoshi lifa) and the Islamic Astronomical System (Huihui lifa). Thanks to this new chart, Koreans accurately calculated the paths of major heavenly bodies for the first time, with Hansŏng as the reference point. Appointed by Sejong, Chang Yŏngsil (1390?–1450?), a technician and former government slave, who had been born the son of a *kisaeng* and a Chinese émigré, oversaw the invention or assembly of many observational instruments, including armillary spheres, an equatorial triquetrum, clepsydras (striking water clocks), scaphe sundials, and rain gauges. Especially noteworthy was a clepsydra with a precise mechanical device that automatically produced time signals (1434). The government set up standardized rain gauges throughout the kingdom and employed surveyors' rods and triangulation devices for land surveys and cartography.

The field of medicine saw advances and innovations based on indigenous adaptations of a body of knowledge introduced from China. Continuing scholarly investigation into medicinal ingredients and cures better suited to Korea produced such works as *Compilation of Native Prescriptions* (*Hyangyak chipsŏng pang*; 1433), commissioned by Sejong, and *Classified Collection of Medical Prescriptions* (*Ŭibang yuch'wi*; 1477), an encyclopedia also commissioned by Sejong but completed only during Sŏngjong's reign. These studies systematized the era's pharmacological knowledge.

At the same time, military matters attracted much attention and produced innovations. Sejong commissioned *Records on Gunpowder Weaponry* (*Ch'ongt'ong tŭngnok*; 1448), which, though no longer extant, reviewed the manufacture and deployment of various firearms. Munjong commissioned *Mirror of Korea's Military Matters* (*Tongguk pyŏnggam*; early 1450s), which discussed military history from Kojosŏn through Koryŏ. And Sŏngjong ordered the compilation of *Battle Formations* (*Chinpŏp*; 1492), to serve as a guidebook for military training. As the state maintained an active interest in systematic explications of military matters, overall weaponry underwent further improvements. A leading figure of the overall effort was Ch'oe Musŏn's son, Ch'oe Haesan (1380–1443), whom T'aejong entrusted with overseeing firearms production. Among such weapons, cannons achieved a range up to 1.25 kilometers, and *hwach'a* ("fire carts") with a range of up to two kilometers were capable of launching up to 100 arrows, each 1.1 meters long with a gunpowder-filled paper tube attached to the shaft just below the head. In military shipbuilding, T'aejong commissioned "turtle ships," which were armored attack vessels, and *pigŏdosŏn*, which were smaller but faster battle craft, but none is extant.

Advances in various branches of knowledge benefited from improvements in movable type printing and paper-making techniques. T'aejong's court set up a type foundry, which cast a new set of about 100,000 copper types (1403). A generation later, Sejong's court cast its own set of more than 200,000 copper types (1434). Not limited to movable type, overall printing technology developed further during Sejong's reign. The earlier method of using beeswax to affix movable types in their proper positions for a text gave way to assembling type in galleys, a new technique that doubled the printing productivity. At the same time, the court established the Paper Manufactory to oversee the production of a wide variety of papers.

Besides advances in technology with practical applications, early Chosŏn culture featured such unique artistic masterpieces as *punch'ŏng* and white porcelain. Replacing the gold and silverware that the Koryŏ aristocracy had favored, *punch'ŏng* is stoneware with a bluish-green tone. Coated with a white slip, the surface features painted decorative designs using iron pigment. In the fifteenth century, workshops throughout Korea produced *punch'ŏng* along with *onggi*, a form of earthenware made more purely for the storage of food for government offices and private clients. In the sixteenth century, *punch'ŏng* production declined and gradually gave way to more sophisticated white porcelain. As the ascendant Confucian literati culture valued frugality and pragmatism, white porcelain became popular for its aesthetic simplicity and purity compared to earlier styles of pottery.

The early Chosŏn culture produced a wide range of illustrative art. Along with professional court painters, aristocratic literati selectively adopted China's painting styles to develop new modes, which also subsequently influenced Japanese paintings under the Ashikaga shogunate (1336–1573). Building on earlier traditions, Chosŏn styles of landscape painting that arose in the sixteenth century employed powerful brush strokes in expressing literati sensibilities through depictions of the Four Noble Ones. Simultaneously, many outstanding calligraphers appeared, as calligraphy, painting, prose, and poetry remained core genres of *yangban* literati culture. For educating the general population, the government printed and disseminated illustrated moral primers.

Besides the visual arts, the state employed the performing arts to transform the people morally, and music played a key role. Sejong commissioned Pak Yŏn (1378–1458), a civil official and a musician, to improve existing musical instruments and invent new ones. The king himself composed such works as *Enjoyment with the People* (*Yŏminnak*; 1447) and devised *Mensural Notation* (*Chŏngganbo*; 1447 or earlier), East Asia's oldest music scoring system that indicates a note's length and pitch. Additionally, Sejong facilitated the development of *aak* as court music by standardizing various pieces and scores. Decades later, Sŏngjong commissioned a scholar-official, Sŏng Hyŏn (1439–1504), to compile the *Canon of Music* (*Akhak kwebŏm*; 1493), an illustrated treatise on musical notation, instruments, accessories, and staging for performance in all three styles of music prevalent at the time: *aak*, *tangak*, and *hyangak*. This treatise contributed significantly to the preservation and further development of traditional Korean music. Among the ordinary people, *tangak* and *hyangak* had merged into *sogak* by the mid-sixteenth century. *Sogak* featured various types of song with lyrics in Korean, including *kasa*, a form of sung poetry; *sijo*, which were vernacular musical verses composed by aristocrats before they evolved into written verses; *kagok*, vocal music for mixed female and male singers; and folk music.

The early Chosŏn food culture featured both earlier customs and the new, increasingly influenced by the Confucian ideology of the state and elites as it affected daily life. Beginning with the *yangban*, the performance of ancestral rites (*chesa*) and the emergence of organized lineages as social collectives further enhanced the richness of food preparation and serving. Offering the best sacrificial food to an ancestral spirit being honored and serving the best dishes to guests occupied a central position in *yangban* culture. Underpinning the generosity was a diet centered around nine edible seeds: rice, barley, wheat, millet, sorghum, corn, Korean sorghum (*tangsŏ*), beans, and red mung beans. Dishes and soups made use of vegetable ingredients that were more or less the same as those used in late Koryŏ; though besides matsutake (Ko. *songi*) mushrooms, the diet also featured shiitake (Ko. *p'yogo*) mushrooms and *sŏgi* mushrooms (*Umbilicaria esculenta*). Complementing the plant diet were more than fifty marine products, mostly the same as those featured in Korean cuisine today. Besides salted tiny shrimps, salted Korean anchovy (*myŏlch'ijŏt*) became a favorite seasoning ingredient for *kimchi*. In comparison, meat consumption remained more or less limited to elites and special occasions, when it featured beef, pork, poultry, and pheasant. During the peak summer heat, dog meat was popular as a more affordable yet rich protein source to nourish the body. Also, horses past their usefulness as modes of transportation were slaughtered for processing as dried meat.

As with the diet, the early Chosŏn housing culture embodied all the essential elements that would continue to be used for centuries. A household's socioeconomic status along with geomantic principles and local climate determined the residential structure's location and layout. The initial architectural planning considered the wife's "inner room" (*anpang*), the kitchen, the main gate (*taemun*), and an outhouse the "four pillars" (*saju*). Climate was a critical factor for the location and layout, especially among the ordinary people, thus producing regional variations. Among *yangban* and *chungin*, climate considerations focused on the wife's inner room, as they were more concerned with geomancy. The average size of such a house increased to accommodate an extended family. An accompanying development influenced by Confucian social norms was a stricter spatial partitioning into male living quarters (*sarangch'ae*), where the household head received guests, and female inner quarters (*anch'ae*). Considerations of each resident's age and social status might also factor into the planning. In addition, a family shrine had become a standard feature of a larger house. For a smaller, modest dwelling, for which such an arrangement was not feasible, spirit tablets enclosed in a small wall closet (*pyŏkkam*) or a hanging scroll painting of a family shrine (*kammo yŏjae to*) with the spirit tablets affixed performed the same function. The variations in housing culture according to the residents' social status reflected socioeconomic realities and sumptuary laws. In 1395, T'aejo allocated the land in Hansŏng according to social status. In 1431, Sejong issued a set of laws that set the maximum allowed size of a house, ranging from 10 *k'an* (the distance between two columns) for an ordinary commoner to 60 *k'an* for a *taegun* ("grand prince"), a royal prince mothered by a queen. Violations persisted, as suggested by the court's continuing issuance of regulations from time to time, including restrictions against painted columns and polished stones for homes. The early Chosŏn housing culture reflects a degree of lingering tension between the stable, status-based social hierarchy that the state idealized and the social reality. The gap would only widen in the next era of turmoil and transition.

CHAPTER 7

The Mid-Chosŏn Crisis and Recovery, 1567–1724

M idway through Chosŏn dynastic rule, Korea coped with formidable challenges. The ruling elite formed political parties
(*pungdang*), each with an intellectual lineage representing regional interests. Partisan politics entailed policy debates, personal ani-
mosities, and purges. Gradually excluded from court politics, rural *yangban*
utilized community compacts to strengthen their positions as local elites.
Some nonelites who grew rich from expanding commerce and manufacturing became more influential in local society, but most struggled to survive.
Sympathetic to their plights, some *yangban* intellectuals pursued Practical
Learning (Sirhak), which sought to stabilize the agricultural economy
based on free cultivators. Others turned to Yangmingism and studied subjects such as astronomy and medicine. Introduced from China, Western
Learning (Sŏhak), which encompassed Catholicism and other branches of
European knowledge, also broadened Korea's cultural horizons. Besides
vernacular narrative fiction and other forms of literary work, mid-Chosŏn
landscape paintings, genre paintings, and white porcelain reflect facets of
daily life.

PARTISAN POLITICS AND WARS

The Sarim triumphed when King Sŏnjo (r. 1567–1608) ascended the throne,
but the political establishment soon became divided. The Sarim who had

been leading political players during Myŏngjong's reign were more conservative, whereas the Sarim who became more prominent upon Sŏnjo's
accession advocated reform. As the conflict between the two intensified, the
initial division produced the Westerners (1575–1680), who tended to be the
conservative Sarim, and the Easterners (1575–89), generally the reformist
Sarim. Drawing from its intellectual tradition, each party pursued particular agendas. Leading the Easterners were those who had inherited the more
i-centered thoughts of Sŏ Kyŏngdŏk from Kaesŏng, Cho Sik from South
Kyŏngsang, or Yi Hwang from North Kyŏngsang, and some political newcomers also joined the party. By contrast, the Westerners typically gathered
around the disciples of a capital aristocrat, Yi I, whose thoughts stressed
i and *ki* equally, and around the more eclectic Sŏng Hon (1535–98), also
from Hansŏng. More powerful, the Easterners eventually divided over the
handling of alleged treason by Chŏng Yŏrip (1546–89), who had criticized
his teacher, Yi I, and then switched parties, moving from the Westerners
to the Easterners. In fighting against the Westerners, who wanted Chŏng
executed, moderate Easterners became the Southerners (1589–1910), who
were mostly of the Yi Hwang School, and the hawks became the Northerners (1589–1910), generally of the Cho Sik School. Initially, the Southerners dominated. During the mid-Chosŏn period, the Three Offices' role
changed from remonstrance to a ruling party's instrument of attack against
the opposition. Also, bureau section chiefs in the Ministry of Personnel
and the Ministry of War pursued power by purging their adversaries, abusing their right to recommend their successors and to control mid- and
lower-level appointments.

Embroiled in such strife, the political leadership was little prepared for
the devastating East Asian War (Imjin War; 1592–98). Reunified by Toyo-
tomi Hideyoshi (1537–98) after more than a century of incessant internal
warfare, in 1592, Japan landed an invasion force of roughly 200,000 on Korea.
In the initial engagements, the overall Chosŏn army of some 8,000 troops
performed poorly. Abandoning Hansŏng before it fell to the enemy, Sŏnjo's
court fled north and requested military aid from Ming China. The Japanese
navy also sought to secure sea lanes, in order to supply and collaborate with
the land army, but the Chosŏn navy under Yi Sunsin (1545–98) thwarted
these efforts. Based in Chŏlla, Yi's fleet won a series of victories against
the enemy. By securing the southern shore, the navy successfully defended
Chŏlla, a grain-rich region, and prevented the Japanese from sustaining their

military operation farther north. Also, former officials and local *yangban* organized "righteous armies" (*ŭibyŏng*), with ordinary commoners as the rank and file. The Buddhist clergy did likewise with their armies, under the royally sanctioned command of a venerable monk, Hyujŏng (1520–1604). Although inferior in number and armament to the Japanese, the righteous armies effectively deployed their superior knowledge of the terrain and guerilla tactics in delivering significant damage to the enemy. Furthermore, in the course of the war, the government army's combat capacity improved through collaboration with the righteous armies.

The tide of war turned in the following year, although its conclusion took six years. The arrival of 50,000 Ming troops was critical, and a joint Chosŏn-Ming counteroffensive recovered P'yŏngyang (1593). In a decisive conflict at Haengju fortress to the northwest of Hansŏng, a combined effort of some 3,000 Chosŏn government troops, more than 6,000 righteous army fighters, and local residents fought off a siege by some 30,000 Japanese. Driven back to the coastal regions of Kyŏngsang, the Japanese began to negotiate a truce with Ming, while Chosŏn used the opportunity to regroup. When more than three years of negotiation failed, the Japanese renewed an all-out offensive with about 141,000 troops (1597). Later in that year, a collaboration of 175,000 Chosŏn and 100,000 Ming troops stopped the enemy's further northward advancement with a crucial victory in Chiksan, Ch'ungch'ŏng. Meanwhile, Yi Sunsin's fleet routed the Japanese in the Battle of Myŏngnyang, and the invaders retreated to the south coast. Sensing futility, the dying Hideyoshi ordered his troops to withdraw from Korea (1598).

The East Asian War changed the power dynamics within the Chosŏn political leadership. During the conflict, the Border Defense Command at the core of the power structure began to expand, and its membership eventually came to include such significant officials as the three highest state counselors, both incumbent and former; all ministers and second ministers except those of public works; military division commanders; the directors of the Office of Royal Decrees and the Office of Special Counselors; and the magistrate of Kanghwa. In addition to military affairs, almost all important issues came under its purview, including foreign policy, finances, social policy, and personnel. The deliberative mechanism centered around the State Council and the Six Ministries became defunct. By the end of the war, the Northerners, who were especially active as righteous army leaders in southern Kyŏngsang, had replaced the Southerners as the ruling party.

A string of initial battlefield defeats also forced Chosŏn to reorganize its military. The newly created Directorate-General for Military Training (1593) commanded a division of three corps, namely musketeers, archers, and "killers" (*salsu*), who were close-combat swordsmen, pikemen, and spearmen. Replacing commoner conscripts, the Directorate-General troops were salaried professional soldiers. Provincial armies too underwent reorganization, with a regional command garrison system centered around newly created *sogo* armies intended to recruit from the entire population (1594). As the *yangban* continued to shun serving, however, *sogo* troops quickly became all commoners and slaves. In contrast to the full-time Directorate-General for Military Training soldiers, the *sogo* troops were intended to be mobilized only in the event of an enemy attack; otherwise, they went on with their livelihoods and received part-time military training.

None of these efforts by the state prevented tremendous destruction and suffering during the East Asian War. The population drastically decreased due to slaughter by the Japanese, famine, and epidemics, and the amount of land under cultivation dwindled. Pillaging and arson by the enemy destroyed royal tombs; various cultural edifices, such as Pulguk-sa; artworks; and countless books. The more discriminating Japanese rounded up sets of movable type, books, and paintings, as well as taking tens of thousands of Koreans as captives, holding *yangban* women for ransom, and retaining individuals with valuable skills. Among the latter were Neo-Confucian scholars, print technicians, and potters. Neo-Confucian scholars and potters in particular made decisive contributions to Japan's own Neo-Confucian learning and ceramic craftsmanship.

A decade after the war, the two countries normalized their relations. Emerging victorious upon Hideyoshi's death, the Tokugawa shogunate (1600–1868) sought stability. When the new regime relayed through the lord of Tsushima a desire to restore formal relations, the Chosŏn court dispatched an eminent monk and a former righteous army commander, Yujŏng (1544–1610), who was one of Hyujŏng's main disciples, to assess the situation in Japan and to repatriate captives. Yujŏng brought some 3,500 compatriots back, and at the request of the shogunate, Chosŏn dispatched official envoys (1607). Subsequently, Chosŏn and the shogunate agreed on reestablishing formal relations and regulated trade at the Japan House in Tongnae (1609).

Meanwhile, to the north of Korea, the Jurchens grew rapidly in power. Nurhaci (r. 1616–26) brought all tribes under his sway and founded the Later

Jin dynasty (1616–1912; renamed Qing in 1636). Later Jin expanded southwestward against Ming China, which responded with an offensive and requested military aid from Chosŏn. King Kwanghaegun (r. 1608–23), who had ascended the throne with Northerner support upon the sudden death of his father, Sŏnjo, sought to keep war-devastated Chosŏn out but ultimately succumbed to the Ming demand and the pressures of his officials. Kwanghaegun dispatched to Liaodong a force of about 10,000 musketeers and 3,000 archers under Kang Hongnip (1560–1627), instructing him to do his best not to engage the Later Jin forces but also to respond according to the tide of the conflict. In a series of clashes, the combined Ming-Chosŏn army of between 103,000 and 133,000 suffered a crushing defeat by about 60,000 Later Jin troops, and Kang surrendered with 7,000 survivors (1619). Subsequently, Ming continued to request more troops, but Kwanghaegun declined. In the interim, the powerful Northerners dominated officialdom until the Westerners staged a coup, deposed the king, and purged the Northerners (1623).

Elevating Kwanghaegun's nephew, King Injo (r. 1623–49), the Westerners, who advocated an openly pro-Ming policy, wielded power with the Southerners as a junior partner. Unlike the earlier Northerners, who had divided into factions with conflicting interests, the Westerners and the Southerners were more cohesive political parties, each with a distinct intellectual orientation and regional base. Each party also included largely capital-based *yangban* families producing mostly, if not only, military officials who provided the muscle in tumultuous, sometimes violent, politics dominated by prominent civil officials. Mutually recognizing their respective positions, the Westerners and the Southerners maintained a de facto coalition. Chastened by the East Asian War and wary of Later Jin, Injo's court sought to improve military defense by supplementing the Directorate-General for Military Training troops with three new professional armies, the Royal Division (1623), the Anti-Manchu Division (1624), and the Namhan Defense Division (1626).

The new regime's pro-Ming policy soon invited disasters. Citing avenging Kwanghaegun as a pretext, Later Jin invaded Chosŏn with about 30,000 troops. In the ensuing Chŏngmyo War (1627), the Chosŏn government troops and righteous armies collaborated. Among the militia leaders, Chŏng Pongsu (1572–1645) in particular stood out—defeating an enemy force in Ch'ŏlsan, P'yŏngan, and rescuing thousands of Chosŏn captives. With its supply line in danger, the Later Jin army withdrew, after stipulating an elder brother–younger brother relationship, with Chosŏn as the inferior. Continuing to grow in power, Later Jin subsequently changed its ethnonym and the dynastic name, to Manchu and Qing, respectively, and demanded that Chosŏn transfer its allegiance as a tributary from Ming to Qing. When rebuffed, Qing invaded with an army of 140,000, setting off the Pyŏngja War (1636–37; Gregorian 1637). Injo and his court fled to Namhan fort, where they held out for three weeks before capitulating.

Postwar Chosŏn maintained formal relations with Qing in the context of tributary obligations to the new suzerain, but anti-Manchu sentiment persisted. Subjugation under a people whom Chosŏn had long regarded as barbarians was traumatic to Koreans regardless of status, and anti-Manchu sentiment was widespread. In the reign of Injo's son and successor, King Hyojong (r. 1649–59), a desire to avenge the humiliation and to repay the grace of Ming for aid during the East Asian War fueled the Northern Expedition Policy. Promoting such anti-Qing figures as the revered Neo-Confucian luminary Song Siyŏl (1607–89), the renowned scholar-official Song Chun'gil (1606–72), and the prominent military official Yi Wan (1602–74), Hyojong repaired fortifications and pursued a military buildup in preparation for invading Qing, but he died before realizing his ambition. In the reign of his son and successor, King Hyŏnjong (r. 1659–74), the Westerner-Southerner coalition collapsed as two rounds of Rites Controversy (1659, 1674) over proper mourning rituals, with implications for the royal legitimacy of Hyojong, turned the two parties into implacable enemies. Amidst the turmoil, Chosŏn abandoned the Northern Expedition Policy.

Hyŏnjong's son and successor, King Sukchong (r. 1674–1720), continually shifted his endorsement from one party to another. Upon purging the Southerners after accusing them of treason (1680), the Westerners split into Patriarchs (1680–1910) and Disciples (1680–1910). Led by Song Siyŏl, the Patriarchs valued "great principle and moral obligation" (taeŭi myŏngbun) while seeking to secure the people's livelihood. The Disciples centered around Yun Chŭng (1629–1714), who had earlier studied Zhu Xi's works under Song Siyŏl, and they tended to be more pragmatic and also advocated active development of northern frontier regions. As Sukchong played one party off against the other, his confidantes, such as royal kin and personal favorites, became more influential. The increasing concentration of power in the upper echelons of officialdom incapacitated the remaining organs of remonstrance, effectively barred local yangban from political participation, and eroded a multiparty political system's foundations. These developments destroyed the balance of power among competing political parties and ultimately threatened royal power. Upon realizing the danger, Sukchong initiated the Policy of Impartiality, which put the monarch at the center of politics and made personnel decisions ostensibly based on individual merits regardless of party affiliation.

During Sukchong's reign, Chosŏn also came to terms with Qing, which continued to expand beyond China proper after conquering Ming. Such leading scholar-officials as Yun Hyu (1617–80) sought to revive the Northern Expedition Policy in response to the Revolt of the Three Feudatories (1673–81) in China, and the implementation of the Palace Guard Division (1682) that completed a new capital army, called the Five Military Divisions. Ultimately, though, Chosŏn had to abandon the policy, as Qing decisively suppressed the revolt and continued to expand as a well-governed, militarily powerful, and culturally sophisticated empire. As such, Qing promoted China's traditional culture and selectively adopted aspects of Western "barbarian" culture. Learning about new institutions and ideas, Chosŏn envoys who visited the Qing court related their observations through official reports and travelogues.

Despite the disparity in power, the normalized Chosŏn-Qing relations were such that the two agreed in Chosŏn's favor when a border dispute arose. Qing sought to keep its ancestral homeland of Manchuria off-limits to others, but many Koreans crossed the Tumen River into the region to gather ginseng or for hunting. Representatives from both Chosŏn and Qing surveyed Mount Paektu (Ch. Changbai) and its vicinity, agreed on the boundary, and erected a marker stele (1712). Its inscription stated that the border corresponded to the Yalu River and the "T'omun," but the latter's identity would later generate another dispute between the two countries in the late nineteenth century.

Chosŏn maintained peaceful relations with Tokugawa Japan as well. Whenever a new shogun assumed office, he requested an envoy from Chosŏn, which acquiesced, and from 1607 to 1811, Chosŏn dispatched an envoy twelve times. On each occasion, the shogunate received with utmost propriety and hospitality a Chosŏn delegation of some 300 to 500 members. Besides performing diplomatic functions, each visit was a rare opportunity for cultural exchange for both countries' elites and intellectuals. Valuing peaceful, stable relations with Chosŏn, the shogunate was also pragmatic in handling any outstanding territorial issue. During Sukchong's reign, a fisherman, An Yongbok (fl. 1693–97), not only confronted Japanese fishermen who frequently appeared on the shores of Ullŭngdo and Tokto (Ja. Takeshima) but obtained from the shogunal authorities an acknowledgment that the islands belonged to Chosŏn (1693). Subsequently, the shogunate reaffirmed that position, through the lord of Tsushima (1697).

ECONOMIC RECOVERY AND TRANSFORMATION

Before the East Asian War, neither the Chosŏn state nor the aristocracy, which was embroiled in expanding partisan strife, solved various problems afflicting the economy, and the ordinary commoners suffered. Ever onerous local tribute became even more burdensome with tribute contracting, which enabled such intermediaries as tribute merchants and government personnel to pocket profits. Spreading corruption and the deteriorating finances of farming households also reduced the state's revenue base and workforce for the army. The financially strapped government increased the military cloth tax, the remittance of which exempted a male of conscription age from military service, and the commoners who could no longer bear the burden abandoned their land. The accompanying collapse of the corvée system made the government mobilize wage laborers to construct or repair fortification walls and roads. Still, paid wages were not enough to restore the financial security of commoner taxpayers.

The East Asian War effectively ruined the largely agrarian Chosŏn economy. The population was decimated, especially in the southeast, which bore the brunt of the initial Japanese onslaught; a preponderance of those who survived the slaughter died from starvation or epidemic. Abandoned cultivated land was ruined, although eventually, the invaders sought to promote cultivation in the southern coastal regions under their occupation and collect a portion of the harvest. During the war, the financially strapped Chosŏn government granted offices, court ranks, or manumission to grain donors, depending on the contributor's status and the contribution amount. Such donors won an exemption from military service. Such rewards were well beyond the means of most commoners, for whom the general obligations to the state did not decrease. At the end of the war, the total area of registered land was some 300,000 kyŏl, a drastic decrease from the antebellum level of 1,500,000 kyŏl. The postwar government attempted to expand its revenue base by enforcing the Identification Tag Law (1610–12, 1626–27, 1675–1894?), undertaking a cadastral survey, and promoting land reclamation.

Simultaneously, the postwar political leadership attempted to reform the overall land tax, but the initial effort was an outright failure. In 1635, the government abandoned the earlier nine-fold classification system for the harvest and instead fixed the land tax at a particular volume measure of rice per *kyŏl* of land. While somewhat lowering the rent rate per se, the reform burdened most commoners even more. Besides the rent, the reform also required a farming household to cover such additional costs as wear and tear of tools, material transport, and processing fees. Thus the levy on such a household could be several times greater than the rent itself.

Instituted as a more overarching reform, the Uniform Land Tax Law, which gradually replaced local tribute produced mixed results. First implemented as a pilot program in Kyŏnggi (1608), the government gradually put the law into effect elsewhere in the following century, except in P'yŏngan, where a different yet comparable law went into effect in 1647. According to government quotas, the uniform land tax replaced local tribute—which used to hold every taxable household responsible for local products—with remittance in rice, hemp cloth, cotton cloth, coins, or any combination thereof, depending on a plot's assessed *kyŏl*. The new system increased three-fold the amount of rice remittance required per *kyŏl* of land. The government used the revenue to pay tribute merchants on advance contracts to procure necessary goods for various agencies. The tax burden somewhat decreased for tenant farmers and minimal plot owners, but the law also forced many farmers to sell local products on the market to acquire rice, hemp fabric, cotton fabric, or cash to pay the land tax. The new system also gradually produced abuses similar to those of the earlier tribute contracting, as tribute merchants and government agents pocketing profits overburdened the ordinary commoners.

Likewise, a parallel military reform produced mixed results. Implementation of the Five Military Divisions, which institutionalized a de facto professional army, gradually increased the number of conscript-age males paying their way out of active duties with military cloth tax payments, which the government used to cover the expenses of the new units. Besides the Five Military Divisions, though, provincial governors and provincial army commanders levied their military cloth tax on the population to the effect that commoner households were overburdened with military cloth tax imposed by two or three different government agencies. The levy varied from two to three bolts of cloth, depending on the taxpayer's assigned military unit.

While the state grappled with tax reforms, the relationship between land-lords and tenant farmers evolved from one based on status hierarchy to one that was more economic. After the wars, *yangban* aristocrats invested much effort into land reclamation. They expanded their holdings by buying up land from financially struggling cultivators, and tenancy became the norm for commoners by the end of the eighteenth century. Nonetheless, landlords also began to recognize a tenant farmer's right to continue cultivating the same land and lowered the rent or kept it the same. In general, *yangban* lived off the rent collected from tenant farmers, and at harvest time, the wealthiest landlords collected from 1,000 *sŏk* (135,000–180,000 liters) to 10,000 *sŏk* (1.35 million–1.8 million liters) of rice each year, either selling it on the market or using it to acquire more land. Some amassed wealth as financiers by fund-ing merchants or lending money for high interest. *Yangban* who were unable to adjust to such economic changes became impoverished, even tilling the soil themselves.

Some farmers improved their economic positions. They enhanced produc-tivity through reclaiming land; repairing irrigation facilities; and improving farming tools, fertilization techniques, and management methods. Such cul-tivators also increased productivity per unit of land by maximizing seedling transfer techniques and cultivating both rice and barley each year, harvested in the fall and summer, respectively. In the seventeenth century, the govern-ment ended its prohibition against double-cropping as the fear of barley crop failure in the winter cold ceased. Barley cultivation became especially popular as landlords excluded from rent assessment any barley cultivated from rice paddies. A tenant farmer could remit either a fixed portion or a fixed amount of harvest as rent, and regardless, payment with cash became increasingly common. As improved seedling transfer technique decreased the workforce required for weeding, the average size of a plot per cultivator increased. Most landlords, many self-cultivators, and some tenant farmers increased their assets through cultivating more land. The income of households that pursued larger-scale farming increased, and many even became wealthy. Such cash crops as cotton, vegetables, tobacco, and medicinal herbs generated additional income for farming households. Simultaneously, as both the number of markets and the number of days each market stayed open increased, so did the volume of commodities in circulation and the number of transactions. As demand for rice as not just a staple but also a transaction commodity increased, more cultivators converted dry fields to rice paddies.

To an extent, commercialization of agriculture gave some leverage to tenant farmers, as they secured some advantageous terms and conditions through tenancy disputes with landlords. The tenancy right secured during the period was such that a landlord could not arbitrarily evict a tenant. The rent, which used to be half of the harvest, changed to a fixed amount in either cash or kind per year. Thanks to a fixed rent, secure tenancy, and cash crop cultivation, the incomes of diligent tenant farmers who negotiated the market economy well increased; some farmers even became landlords through land reclamation or purchase.

Far more cultivators, however, lost their plots. As the variety of taxes, the high-interest loans, and the cost of various rites of passage overburdened many farmers, those who were desperate or impoverished sold their holdings at giveaway prices, and *yangban* and merchants of means acquired such land. As large-scale cultivation became more common, the landlords who used to have tenant farmers cultivate most of their holdings while personally cultivating some plots themselves revoked tenancy; instead, such landlords directly managed the land with slaves and hired farmhands. For tenant farmers, securing tenancy became harder than losing it. Uprooted cultivators moved to cities, towns, mines, and river ports, where they sold goods or worked for wages. The outflow of such farmers from rural villages produced new towns near mines and ports, including Suan in Hwanghae; Kanggyŏng in Ŭnjin, Ch'ungch'ŏng; and Wŏnsan in Tŏgwŏn, Hamgyŏng.

The growth of the urban population and the expanding coverage area of the Uniform Land Tax Law increased demand for manufactured goods, in private transactions and delivery to government agencies alike. Since tribute merchants made bulk purchases from the market, demand for such goods increased. Private handicrafters were able to conduct business relatively freely as long as they paid the crafter tax. Their products were more competitive than government artisans' in terms of quality and price. Private handicrafters produced and sold their goods at their worksites, including iron smithies and porcelain stores, and increasingly joined the tribute merchants who had been the leading actors in commerce. Besides taking orders from tribute merchants and private merchants, manufacturers secured funds and raw materials on their own for their production. As commerce and manufacturing expanded, coins became a common means of making transactions. Seeking to facilitate the circulation of money, Injo's court minted coins for use in Kaesŏng, in a pilot program. Its successor, Hyojong's court, began to circulate coins more widely.

With expanding commerce, ports became new hubs for transactions more extensive than those at inland markets. In early Chosŏn, ports had been important mainly for the transport of tax grain and rent collected from tenant farmers, but by the eighteenth century, such ports as Kanggyŏng and Wŏnsan had become commercial centers. Making use of such ports, coastal shipping merchants, inland market brokers, and coastal trade brokers actively pursued commerce. Among coastal shipping merchants who secured goods from various locales and sold them at ports, the Han River merchants became big traders. Based along the banks of the Han River, their ships also traveled along the western and southern shores of Korea, trading rice and salt and other marine products. When such a loaded coastal merchant ship entered a port, inland market brokers and coastal trade brokers played their respective roles, conducting business in commodity transport and storage, lodging, and financing. Such brokers were also active at large rural markets.

Meanwhile, international trade increased as well. In the north, expanding trade with Qing China, starting in the mid-seventeenth century, featured officially sanctioned open markets near the Sino-Korean border. Chosŏn exported silver, paper, cotton cloth, and ginseng while importing silk, medicinal herbs, and stationery from Qing. In the south, a booming trade with Tokugawa Japan went through the Japan House in Tongnae. Chosŏn merchants sold ginseng, rice, and cotton cloth, as well as bringing Qing imports into the transaction venue. From the Japanese, Chosŏn merchants bought silver, copper, sulfur, and black pepper. Private merchants were active in trade with both countries, including the merchants of Tongnae, Kaesŏng, and Ŭiju, P'yŏngan. Among them, Kaesŏng merchants profited as the middlemen between Ŭiju and Tongnae merchants, whereas Ŭiju merchants amassed wealth as leading actors in Chosŏn-Qing trade. In the mid-seventeenth century, when the Chosŏn government began to allow private mining (while taxing it), the increased demand for silver due to expanding trade with Qing stimulated silver mining development. By the end of the century, almost seventy silver mines were in operation, attracting an increasingly socially mobile population to hillside locales.

THE CENTER AND STABILIZATION OF LOCAL SOCIETY

Mid-Chosŏn Korea's overall population achieved remarkable growth, fueled by an expansion in agricultural output. Sometime in the sixteenth century before the East Asian War, the population total surpassed 10 million, of which a growing number resided in Hansŏng. Reflecting a significant dip due to the East Asian, Chŏngmyo, and Pyŏngja Wars, the total population roughly a century later, as of 1678, was about 10 to 12 million. But by then the remarkable long-term growth that had begun in the fourteenth century had resumed. Sustaining that growth were improved efficiencies in predominantly agricultural production that drove commercialization, urbanization, and diversification in material goods. More Koreans moved to towns and cities, even while the majority still lived in villages in the larger river basins: some close by major rivers, others deep in interior valleys. In the eighteenth century, the population of Hansŏng surpassed 200,000. All the same, the overall population growth was slowing as Chosŏn encountered constraints in terms of population size, urban settlement, and elite lifestyles, and also due to the hardship among the ordinary people not being adequately addressed by the political leadership.

At the top of the social hierarchy, the *yangban*, the aristocracy, bifurcated into those in the capital region, who remained active in the central political arena, and the rest, who became more purely local elites. Constituting no more than about 2 percent of the population, as was true in other early modern, sedentary, literate Afro-Eurasian societies, the mid-Chosŏn *yangban* as a status group began to subdivide as political partisan identities crystallized in the seventeenth century. In local society, landed aristocrats continued to wield power, as in each county, its local *yangban* advised the magistrate through a local council (*hyanghoe*) and lorded over the population. At the end of the sixteenth century, virtually every rural county had a number of leading patrilineal kin groups: each a lineage claiming descent from a renowned scholar or official who had first settled in the county. And by the early eighteenth century, most such local *yangban* families were no longer producing examination passers or officeholders. Thus shut out of court politics, by then dominated by the Patriarchs based in Hansŏng and its vicinity, for generations local elite lineages provided members of the local council. They diligently recorded the members in a local council roster (*hyangan*). Local elite families also maintained exclusive marriage ties among themselves, although occasional adoptions involving a descent group's capital and local branches continued into the eighteenth century. Since the typical natural village had decreased in size by the mid-seventeenth century, the villages controlled by *yangban*, especially, enjoyed considerable autonomy.

Effecting the local social order were the Sarim-inspired *yangban* who upheld Neo-Confucianism as the guiding ideology for social control. The Sarim actively promoted *Elementary Learning*, which the aristocracy regarded as the introductory text on morality and rituals. In one county after another, the local elite devised a community compact, introduced by Cho Kwangjo during Chungjong's reign. Highlighting mutual aid organizations and activities, the Sarim imbued community compacts with Confucian ethics centered around the Three Bonds (the relationships of subject to ruler, child to parents, and husband and wife) and the Five Moral Imperatives (the morality informing the relationships of subject to ruler, child to parents, husband and wife, younger brother to elder brother, and friend to friend). In doing so, the Sarim sought moral transformation of the entire community through education and rituals. Simultaneously, community compacts performed such functions of local autonomy as maintaining public safety and social order, especially after the East Asian War, when local *yangban* lineages exercised leadership in rebuilding their communities. Local elites acquired a wide range of cultural trappings that set them apart from the rest, including an increasingly voluminous family genealogy (*chokpo*), which recorded the relationships among the members of each lineage, ancestral gravesites, and family shrines. They studied at private academies that honored Confucian worthies from prominent local lineages (Figure 7.1) and brought the local political leadership to weigh in on court politics through debates and memorials to the throne.

Hardly immune from moral failings, local *yangban* could engage in extortion vis-à-vis the population, and nonelites used various means to hold their ground. Especially important to the ordinary farmers' survival strategy were *ture*, which were collaborative community labor groups, and incense associations, which remained, as before, village collectives with shared Buddhist and popular religious customs. Often overburdened by the state and bullied by local *yangban*, ordinary farmers relied on *ture* and incense associations for such occasions as a community member's death in particular and in times of hardship in general. Pallbearer associations arose among incense associations.

A small yet growing number of affluent nonelites improved their positions in local society. When Jurchen raids became more frequent and intense in the late sixteenth century, military examinations became more frequent and more extensive in scale but also recruited candidates from more diverse social backgrounds. The mid-Chosŏn wars accelerated this trend and offered opportunities for performing acts of military merit. The commoners who did so mainly received honorary offices and court ranks, whereas meritorious slaves won manumission. In the postwar era, once the financially strapped government instituted a system of granting

FIGURE 7.1   Tosan Academy. Established by local literati in 1574 in Andong, North Kyŏngsang Province, to honor Yi Hwang, in the following year the academy received its name and charter from King Sŏnjo. Tosan not only became the epicenter of learning in the southeast but eventually also played a role in disseminating Neo-Confucianism in Tokugawa Japan. Photo credit: Cultural Heritage Administration.

offices and court ranks and issued blank appointment certificates to grain donors, state-sanctioned status trappings became more widely available to illegitimate sons of *yangban*, commoners, and even former slaves. Furthermore, as economic factors began to define social relations more than status did, male slave–female commoner marriages increased in number. Earlier, the application of the Great Code of Administration was such that an offspring of a mixed commoner-lowborn union generally inherited the lowborn status. In the seventeenth century, that offspring's status began to change back and forth between commoner and lowborn, depending on the views of the political party in power.

The most successful among those who achieved upward social mobility in the mid-Chosŏn era were *chungin* who lived and worked in Hansŏng, although a glass ceiling kept them below the aristocracy. Unlike their provincial analogs—local functionaries who were caught in the middle as agents of state power and were often despised by the local *yangban* above and the general population below—the capital *chungin* in the seventeenth century formed a closed status group of state-employed experts who married spouses, adopted heirs, and kept genealogical records all among themselves. Including interpreters, physicians, jurists, astronomers, accountants, calligraphers, musicians, administrative functionaries, and noncommissioned military officers, the capital *chungin* hailed from families descended from commoners who had made their way up by 1600 or so, although some were descendants of illegitimate sons of aristocrats. Nevertheless, no examination degree, court rank, or office could turn a *chungin*, no matter how wealthy or well educated, into a bona fide aristocrat, and society-wide knowledge of who the real *yangban* were would persist well into the twentieth century. Nonetheless, as many nonelites found ways for advancement in life, local aristocrats increasingly locked out of central officialdom turned to cultural means to distinguish themselves from the rest.

NEO-CONFUCIAN HEGEMONY AND CULTURAL PLURALISM

Among the Chosŏn elite, the teachings of Yi Hwang and Yi I crystalized as the twin pillars of intellectual orthodoxy in early modern Korea. In *Ten Diagrams on Sage Learning* (*Sŏnghak sip to*; 1568), a memorial submitted to Sŏnjo, Yi Hwang argued that a sovereign follows sages' learning. Introduced to Japan after the East Asian War, his thoughts also influenced Neo-Confucianism's subsequent development in Tokugawa Japan. In comparison to Yi Hwang, whose idealism emphasized the primacy of *i*, Yi I's thoughts embodied more pragmatic, reformist tendencies. Through such writings as a memorial, *Questions and Answers at the Eastern Lake* (*Tongho mundap*; 1569), and a book presented to Sŏnjo, *Essentials of the Learning of the Sage* (*Sŏnghak chibyo*; 1575), he put forth a full range of ideas for addressing various problems of Chosŏn society through reorganizing the governing system and reforming the tax system. The *Essentials of the Learning of the Sage* particularly urges wise officials to teach the sages' wisdom to their sovereign to transform his disposition.

A deeper understanding of Neo-Confucianism fostered distinct schools of thought that centered around private academies and defined emerging political parties. During Sŏnjo's reign, disciples of Yi Hwang, Cho Sik, and Sŏ Kyŏngdŏk generally constituted the Easterner party, while students of Yi I and Sŏng Hon tended to be Westerners. When the Easterners divided into Southerners and Northerners, the latter, many of whom were Cho Sik's disciples, became dominant during Kwanghaegun's reign. Not bound by a notion of moral obligation based on righteous principles, the Northerners advocated neutrality vis-à-vis the expanding conflict between Chosŏn's suzerain, Ming, and ascendant Later Jin. Critical of this stance were the Southerners, who were generally students of Yi Hwang, and the Westerners. When the Westerners dominated officialdom for decades after staging a coup that enthroned Injo, the Yi I School and the Yi Hwang School—as represented by the Southerners who were the Westerners' de facto coalition partners—eclipsed the Cho Sik School, the Sŏ Kyŏngdŏk School, Yangmingism, and Daoism, all of which lost ground in the intellectual mainstream.

The Westerners and the Southerners alike upheld Zhu Xi's interpretations of Neo-Confucianism as the orthodoxy. Their insistence on aiding Ming as the civilization under attack by barbarism invited the Chŏngmyo War and the Pyŏngja War, only to capitulate to Qing. After an intense debate among the Westerners on how to come to terms with the humiliation and the subsequent Qing conquest of Ming, those such as Song Siyŏl, who maintained an anti-Qing stance and emphasized abiding by righteous principles, became a dominant force, the Sallim ("scholars of the mountains and forests"). In addressing various problems of postwar society, Song treated Neo-Confucianism as a moral absolute. An ensuing heated debate over such complex socioeconomic issues as the Uniform Land Tax Law soon turned various schools of thought into mutually antagonistic ideological camps.

Besides policies, more purely philosophical issues such as rituals and human nature generated intense debates. In the seventeenth century, scholars bent on rebuilding postwar society along Confucian ideals developed a keen interest in studying rituals. Believing that proper rituals morally guide individuals, society, and the state, they regarded teaching and learning about rituals as requisite methods for moral governance. Increasingly in-depth scholarship on rituals inevitably produced conflicting views among various Neo-Confucian schools, culminating with two rounds of Rites Controversy. Then in the early eighteenth century, a continuing intense study among the Patriarchs, on the nature of humanity and non-human matters, generated the Horak Debate. The Patriarchs who argued that humanity and non-human matters are fundamentally distinct tended to be from Ch'ungch'ŏng, whereas those who insisted on oneness generally were from Hansŏng.

By contrast, in the late seventeenth century, some Disciples and Southern-ers began to put Neo-Confucianism in critical perspective. In their search for solutions to social problems, they turned to the Six Classics (the Five Classics and the lost *Classic of Music*) and various non-Confucian schools of early China. Among them, Yun Hyu, a Southerner, and Pak Sedang (1629–1703), a Disciple, articulated positions that did not conform with Zhu Xi's teachings. Both Yun and Pak invited harsh criticism, first from the Westerners, and then, after the Westerners divided, the Patriarchs, who branded the two as "despoilers of the true Way," distorting orthodoxy and promoting heterodoxy. More flexible in understanding Neo-Confucianism were the Disciples. They built on the Sŏng Hon School's teachings, which were more eclectic, and even accommodated both Yangmingism and Dao-ism. In the early eighteenth century, one of a small number of Disciple intellectuals interested in Yangmingism was Chŏng Chedu (1649–1736), who systematically studied and established Yangmingism as a distinct school of thought in Chosŏn. Recognizing the ordinary people's agency, he advocated putting moral teachings in action through such reforms as the abolition of the hereditary status system.

For a more comprehensive approach to addressing a wide range of so-cioeconomic issues, a growing number of intellectuals turned to Practical Learning. Criticizing Neo-Confucian debates on metaphysics as "empty learning," these individuals, mostly Southerners from Hansŏng and vicinity, pursued Practical Learning by searching for solutions to various problems arising from postwar socioeconomic changes. Influenced by Qing China's Evidential Learning, which emphasized empiricism and textual criticism, Practical Learning's scope expanded to include agriculture-centered reform, commerce- and industry-centered reform, and studies about Korea through all branches of knowledge. A founding figure in Practical Learning was Yi Sugwang (pen name Chibong; 1563–1628), who, in his exhaustive *Topical Essays of Chibong* (*Chibong yusŏl*; 1614), pushed the limits of cultural knowledge and understanding of his time by commenting on an impressive range of issues. Another pioneering scholar, Han Paekkyŏm (1552–1615), presented a carefully researched study of historical geography in his *Treatise on Korean Geography* (*Tongguk chiriji*; 1615).

Among Practical Learning scholars, Yu Hyŏngwŏn (pen name Pan'gye; 1622–73) advocated a comprehensive, agriculture-centered reform. In his magnus opus, modestly titled *Pan'gye's Occasional Notes* (*Pan'gye surok*; written

1659?–64?), which would be published a century after his death, Yu proposed a land reform geared toward supporting self-cultivators, and his inspiration was the equal-field system of land ownership and distribution in China from the Six Dynasties (222–589) to the mid-Tang period. In this system, the state owns all land and distributes plots according to each recipient's ability to work. After a recipient's death, the land reverts to the state for reassignment, although provisions allow inheritance of land that requires long-term development. Modifying the model to suit the Chosŏn hereditary status system's reality, Yu advocated redistributing land according to status, that is, officials, scholars, and farmers, and rationalizing tax and military service systems to improve the living conditions for self-cultivators. In doing so, Yu criticized abuses associated with *yangban* privileges, government service examinations, and slavery.

Many of Yu's contemporaries privileged agriculture. Sin Sok (1600–61) wrote *Compilation for Farmers* (*Nongga chipsŏng*; 1655), which contributed to disseminating new techniques centered around rice farming, including seedling transfer. As commercial agriculture spread and cultivators turned to a broader range of crops, a demand for manuals on horticulture, sericulture, and livestock husbandry increased. Reflecting this trend are such works as Pak Sedang's *Manual on Farming* (*Saekkyŏng*; 1676) and an unpublished text by Hong Mansŏn (1643–1715) titled *Farm Management* (*Sallim kyŏngje*), both of which discuss further advances in agricultural technology at the time.

Besides food production, medical care remained a lingering concern in the postwar era, and many new writings reflect advances and innovations. Hŏ Chun (1539–1615), a court physician born an illegitimate son of a military official, authored *Exemplar of Korean Medicine* (*Tongŭi pogam*; 1610), a significant contribution to traditional East Asian medicine. In particular, its categorization of symptoms and remedies under the various organs affected—rather than by ailment—was innovative at the time. Widely recognized as an outstanding medical treatise, the *Exemplar of Korean Medicine* was also published in China and Japan. A generation later, another court physician, Hŏ Im (c. 1570–c. 1650), who was born a son of a court musician-turned-slave father and a slave mother, authored *Clinical Acupuncture and Moxibustion* (*Ch'imgu kyŏnghŏm pang*; 1644), which offers a comprehensive survey of two of the most important treatment therapies in East Asian medicine.

Beyond eastern Eurasia, Practical Learning drew from Western Learning, which subsumed Western Europe's technology, philosophy, and Roman

Catholicism. In the seventeenth century, Chosŏn envoys who visited Beijing, the capital of Ming-Qing China, gained an introduction to Western institutions and ideas as presented by Jesuit missionaries and their writings. While Catholicism remained no more than a curiosity for Chosŏn intellectuals, some of whom even thought of it as a strange variant of Buddhism, many aspects of Western technology attracted more interest. Reflecting the influence of Western Learning are Yi Kwangjŏng's (1552–1629) world maps and Chŏng Tuwŏn's (b. 1581) cannons, telescopes, and self-sounding clocks. Led by efforts of the polymath Kim Yuk (1580–1658) and others, Chosŏn adopted the calendar of Qing China, after six decades of debate. Developed by the Jesuit scholar-missionaries Johann Schreck (1576–1630) and Johann Adam Schall von Bell (1591–1666) with Xu Guangqi (1562–1633), a Ming scholar-official, this was China's final lunisolar calendar, indicating both the lunar phase and the time of the solar year. The calendar calculates twenty-four solar terms and the days of each year more precisely and provides more accurate solar and lunar eclipse predictions than previously. Building on such advances, others in Korea directly engaged with Western Learning, including Kim Sŏngmun (1658–1735), the first Korean known to have argued for heliocentrism.

During the seventeenth century, Chosŏn also came into contact with the West through two groups of Dutch sailors shipwrecked near Chejudo while on their way to Nagasaki, Japan (1627, 1653). The government assigned three survivors of the first group, including Jan Janse de Weltevree (1595–1653+), to the Directorate-General for Military Training. They taught Koreans how to manufacture and use Dutch cannons. Weltevree, who adopted a Korean name, Pak Yŏn, and his two countrymen fought alongside Chosŏn troops during the Pyŏngja War, which only Pak survived. He lived the rest of his life in Chosŏn, marrying a Korean woman and leaving behind artisan descendants. By contrast, all survivors of the second group, except at least one who left descendants in Chosŏn, eventually escaped to Japan and returned to the Netherlands. Among them, Hendrik Hamel (1630–92) subsequently wrote a book about his time in Chosŏn, the earliest known first-hand European account of Korea.

Besides Hamel's account, new popular genres of Chosŏn painting vividly depict the land and its people that the Western visitors must have seen. In part a reaction against the "barbarian" Manchu conquest of China, a growing pride in native culture was beginning to manifest itself through new styles that sought to express sensibilities and scenery unique to Chosŏn. Traditional landscape paintings underwent indigenization as artists employed realism for the natural scenery of their country, rather than the idealized natural world as expressed in earlier literati paintings. At the same time, professional artists produced genre paintings, capturing an increasingly wide variety of daily life scenes. Such works and realistic landscape paintings alike accommodated a balanced combination of contrasting Chinese styles of painting, the more colorful, refined Northern School and the Southern School, which is characterized by somewhat more impressionist ink wash paintings with expressive brushstrokes.

Nestled in the picturesque mountains and never far from creeks, Buddhist monasteries continued to attract nonelites in general and women across status boundaries. Among them were benefactors who funded the construction or renovation of monasteries, including some *yangban* and a growing number of such social newcomers as wealthy farmers, artisans, and merchants. Rebuilt in the seventeenth century, the P'alsang Hall ("Hall of Eight Pictures") at Pŏpchu-sa in Poŭn, Ch'ungch'ŏng (1626), the Maitreya Hall at Kŭmsan-sa in Kimje, Chŏlla (1635), and the Kakhwang Hall at Hwaŏm-sa in Kurye, Chŏlla (1702), are all large-scale, multistoried constructions with internally interconnected structures. At such venues, the ancient faith offered solace, especially to the ordinary people struggling with the devastation of war.

Buddhism's popular appeal drew its strength from solid intellectual foundations. During the East Asian War, the valor of Hyujŏng and his disciples, who served as his lieutenants, and many other monk warriors dispelled any lingering notion of Buddhism as escapist or anti-social. Inspired by Wŏnhyo of Silla and Chinul of Koryŏ, Hyujŏng sought to unify Buddhist doctrinal study and practice. Since his time, he has been the central figure in Korean Buddhism, and most schools of modern Korean Sŏn trace their lineages back to Hyujŏng through Yujŏng and three other main disciples. Typical of the lifestyles of late Koryŏ and earlier Chosŏn Sŏn monks, Hyujŏng and his disciples all began their training with Confucian and Daoist studies before turning to Sŏn, which they pursued as itinerant monks wandering through the mountains from one monastery to another. They engaged in the central component of Sŏn practice, *kongan* (Ch. *gong'an*; Ja. *kōan*) meditation, wherein a *kongan* is a story, dialogue, question, or statement used to provoke fundamental doubt and to test a student's progress as a Sŏn monk. Many subsequent eminent monks offered new interpretations of methodology in

Sŏn study, but Hwaŏm studies also underwent a revival. Although Hwaŏm no longer existed as an organized doctrinal school, Hyujŏng, his disciples, and most later Sŏn monks like them were all well versed in Buddhist scriptures and Hwaŏm teachings.

In lighter moments, Koreans turned to various creative genres for entertainment. In the seventeenth century, an increasing segment of the population across social boundaries participated in the production or consumption of *sijo* and narrative fiction, both written in *han'gŭl*. Elites continued to express their feelings and emotions through poems in Literary Sinitic, as did Hŏ Ch'ohŭi (pen name Nansŏrhŏn; 1563–89), who lived a short life filled with grief, and more than half of her 213 known poems express a desire to enter the world of Daoist immortals. Increasingly using *han'gŭl*, though, aristocrats, *kisaeng*, and others expressed such concerns of everyday life as poverty and love through *sijo*. In comparison, works of vernacular narrative fiction even offer a sharp social criticism. For example, *Tale of Hong Kiltong* (*Hong Kiltong chŏn*), attributed to Hŏ Kyun (1569–1618), who was Nansŏrhŏn's brother and an aristocratic official personally close to illegitimate sons of aristocrats, attacks discrimination against such offspring and rampant corruption among government officials. In stark contrast, masked plays form a more purely folk cultural genre. When Injo's court abolished the Directorate-General of Masked Dance Drama (1634), the ancient genre finally lost state patronage, and performers had to rely on private patrons. Seventeenth-century masked plays featured performers who wore masks, mimed, spoke, and sometimes sang. Each performance included significant dramatic content with masked characters who portrayed humans, beasts, birds, and supernatural beings.

In the culture of daily life, fruits and vegetables introduced in the mid-Chosŏn era further enriched the diet. Whether brought over from a neighboring country as seeds by an individual or by migrating cultivators, new crops included chili peppers (sixteenth century; China and Japan), corn (sixteenth century; China), tomatoes (seventeenth century; China), pumpkins (early seventeenth century; China), and apples (1658; China). The speed at which the cultivation and consumption spread varied widely. Apples would not be more widely grown until the late nineteenth century, when Western Protestant missionaries introduced new varieties, whereas chili peppers made an immediate impact. Especially in their powdered form, chili peppers enabled Korean cuisine to feature a far broader range in flavor, seasoning, and spiciness. Thanks to chili peppers, *kimchi*, the primary side dish for a

Korean meal, assumed its present form. Among elites and others who could afford fancier meals, the types of side dishes served in addition to *kimchi* and condiments, and their layout, became standardized according to the number of items (*ch'ŏp*): three, five, seven, nine, or twelve.

In mid-Chosŏn, the housing culture had acquired most of its lasting characteristics, especially as reflected in regional variations. In the north, the floor plan tended to be square, with a courtyard in the middle to minimize surface area exposed to the elements. All rooms were connected, and the roofed, wood-floored living room (*taech'ŏng*) with one side open to the courtyard was small, if not absent. Houses in Hamgyŏng, in particular, had a *chŏngjuk'an*—a transitional, yet distinct, *ondol* floor space between the inner room (*anpang*) and the wood-burning stove—for kitchen work, eating, and breaks. In parts of P'yŏngan and central Korea with a milder winter, many houses used a floor-plan comprising two lines of rooms joined at a 90-degree angle. Homes in the Kaesŏng area had the inner chamber and the kitchen facing south for maximum sunlight, whereas in Hansŏng, the kitchen was situated close and diagonally to the inner room. In the warmer, more humid south, mainly in Chŏlla and Kyŏngsang, rooms with many windows and doors, a spacious living room, and the kitchen were all connected and formed a single line to maximize ventilation. Out in the East Sea, on Ullŭngdo where snowfall is heavy in the winter, the islanders lived in log cabins with an outer barrier of thin wood panels or dried reeds touching the eaves for added protection against snow and wind. And to the south of Chŏlla, in likewise windy Chejudo, the islanders covered the exterior of the house with piles of rocks and secured the roof with ropes. Befitting Korea's southernmost region, the furnace was used not so much to heat an *ondol* floor as for cooking, which also made use of charcoal. Regardless of the region, the mid-Chosŏn housing culture as a whole would thrive well into the twentieth century.

CHAPTER 8

Late Chosŏn Renovation and Decline, 1724–1864

ate Chosŏn enjoyed prosperity during Yŏngjo's and Chŏngjo's reigns (1724–1800), before the decades of breakdown that followed. These rulers' Policy of Impartiality promoted royal prerogatives and good governance but failed when succeeding kings ascended the throne unprepared or as minors and were all dominated by royal in-laws. In most counties, local *yangban* hegemony collapsed as wealthy nonelites secured a presence in local administration in collaboration with magistrates. As some commoners became great merchants, private handicraft manufacturing eclipsed government-licensed production and new towns appeared. The commercial boom increased demand for wage labor, hence reducing the slave population. For most commoners, living conditions declined in the decades of consort family oligarchy, when corruption rampant among magistrates and their agents overburdened the population. Spreading discontent drove some to Catholicism, others to such uprisings as the Hong Kyŏngnae Rebellion (1811–12; Gregorian 1812). Most vented their frustrations through various popular cultural genres, including *chapka* ("miscellaneous songs"), vernacular narrative fiction, masked plays, and *p'ansori* musical storytelling.

FROM ENLIGHTENED MONARCHY TO ARISTOCRATIC OLIGARCHY

Sukchong's second surviving son, King Yŏngjo (r. 1724–76), succeeded his sickly, heirless elder brother, King Kyŏngjong (r. 1720–24), and more fully implemented the Policy of Impartiality (Figure 8.1). After suppressing a rebellion by Yi Injwa (1694–1728) and some extremist Disciples (1728) who accused him of killing Kyŏngjong, Yŏngjo promoted political moderates that supported the Policy and its rationale of putting the public good over partisan interests. Accordingly, Yŏngjo not only rejected the lofty Sallim claim that they represented public opinion but even shut down a large number of private academies that functioned as Sallim operation bases. Also, to curb abuse of power by bureau section chiefs of the Ministry of Personnel, Yŏngjo sought to end the practice that allowed them to recommend their successors and fill the Three Offices' positions. Still, the section chiefs would not entirely lose their power to recommend successors until the next reign. As Yŏngjo implemented the Policy of Impartiality more fully, royal power increased as the deciding voice on the overall governing ideology. Achieving greater political stability, Yŏngjo took steps to improve the people's livelihoods through such measures as the Equal Service Law, intended to reduce the burden of military service on taxpayers (1750); abolition of cruel punishments; and enforcement of a system of three reviews for all death sentences. His court also undertook a long overdue update of the Great Code of Administration by compiling the Amended Great Code (Sok taejŏn; 1746). The Policy of Impartiality, though, did not entirely end partisan politics. Instead, increased royal power merely kept the intensity of strife at a lower level. Putting his only surviving son, Prince Sado (1735–62), to death was a tragic consequence of both factional intrigue and the mental breakdown of a son who could not live up to the demanding father's expectations.

Succeeding Yŏngjo, Sado's son, King Chŏngjo (r. 1776–1800), judiciously yet decisively weighed in on partisan issues and sought to curb the influence that the royal in-laws and eunuchs had gained during Yŏngjo's reign as the monarch's confidants. Accordingly, Chŏngjo promoted the Disciples and the Southerners, both parties marginalized from the political establishment since the early part of Yŏngjo's reign, and also rural scholars. To check the power of political parties that pursued their own interests and garner support for his policies, Chŏngjo instituted a system of recommended civil officials (ch'ogye munsin), which selected the most outstanding among new appointees and mid- to low-level officials for group study and training sponsored by the throne. Likewise, he fostered Kyujanggak, a royal library, as a de facto political organ. Establishing it as an archive to collect and preserve the writings of past monarchs and other books, Chŏngjo vested it with the combined functions of acting as the royal secretariat, administering civil examinations, and educating civil officials (1776). Also, he bolstered his position with a

FIGURE 8.1   Portrait of King Yŏngjo, 1900. Painted by Ch'ae Yongsin (1848–1941) and Cho Sŏkchin (1853–1920), this is a copy of the original work of 1744, no longer extant. Source: National Palace Museum of Korea.

new royal guard, the Robust Brave Division (1785). Subsequently, Chŏngjo relocated his father's tomb to Suwŏn, in Kyŏnggi, where he began to construct a walled city, Hwasŏng (1789). Envisioning a new city, if not a new capital, he stationed the Robust Brave Division there and invited merchants and artisans to set up their shops. Furthermore, the king increased county magistrates' power by entrusting them with direct management of the community compacts, thus curbing local *yangban* power. Projecting the throne's enhanced power with the state, Chŏngjo commissioned an updated law code, the Comprehensive Great Code (Taejŏn t'ongp'yŏn; 1785).

The concentration of power around the throne that Chŏngjo effected ultimately paved the way for an oligarchy of consort families upon his death (1800). In the succeeding three reigns, together spanning over sixty years, when two monarchs ascended the throne as minors and the third as distant kin unprepared for the role, the Andong Kim and P'ungyang Cho in-laws wielded paramount power. The partisan debate over issues ceased, and the supply pool for officialdom became effectively confined to a dozen or so capital-based *yangban* lineages, including those of the royal in-laws themselves. The Border Defense Command continued to function as the core political organ, while officeholders below them performed more purely administrative duties without the power of remonstrance.

The oligarchy, as such, failed to govern the country effectively. The consort families and their allies excluded from the deliberative process various politically marginalized groups that Chŏngjo had promoted. Also, on tax matters, the county magistrates, whose authority had increased during Chŏngjo's reign, collaborated not so much with local *yangban* as with local functionaries and wealthy social newcomers. As the appointment and promotion of those paying bribes became rampant, rapacious officials filled their pockets by imposing unjust taxes and surcharges on the population. Furthermore, as the population began to decrease, after frequent natural disasters led to widespread famine and epidemics, the tax burden on struggling ordinary farmers only increased. With spreading discontent, outright resistance became more frequent as Korea underwent significant socioeconomic changes.

ECONOMIC LIBERALIZATION AND STAGNATION

Yŏngjo's Equal Service Law had somewhat shifted the tax burden from ordinary farmers to wealthy commoners, but the positive effect did not last long. The law fixed a conscript-age farmer's military cloth tax at one bolt per year. Still unable to tax the aristocracy, the government levied a fixed amount of rice per *kyŏl* of land on commoner landlords; one bolt of military cloth tax on some commoners of higher social status in exchange for the post of "select military officer" (*sŏnmu kun'gwan*); and fishing and boat taxes. Ultimately, however, such levies calculated to make up for the shortfall from exempting *yangban* fell on tenant farmers, as commoners of means colluded with local functionaries in falsifying household and military registers. Those who were unable to maintain even tenancy and were uprooted from the land became wage laborers who worked for government offices, which mobilized them for public construction and repair projects, and for wealthy cultivators.

While most farmers struggled to survive, private merchants became more active in the eighteenth century. This was true especially among the private merchants conducting transactions just outside the capital city wall, but those at such provincial cities as Ŭiju, P'yŏngyang, Kaesŏng, and Tongnae became increasingly active as well. Private merchants expanded their business spheres by trading commodities and maintaining branch operations, thus connecting local markets. Among them, Kaesŏng merchants, who set up branch operations throughout Korea, amassed wealth mainly through ginseng cultivation and sale as well as foreign trade. In contrast, Han River merchants expanded their business by taking up shipbuilding and other types of manufacturing. Connecting village markets to one another, peddlers maintained a guild to protect their interests and promote solidarity. As traveling merchants who played a significant role in connecting producers and consumers, peddlers took advantage of the varying dates when local market were held.

By the mid-eighteenth century, the growth of private merchants had led to an integrated, countrywide network of more than 1,000 local markets. Each attracted farmers, handicrafters, and merchants from the locale and its vicinity on a fixed date. Typically, such markets were open every fifth day, but many in booming commerce areas were open daily. In the late eighteenth century, mutually dependent markets formed regional networks. A number of them became commercial hubs, including Songp'a in Kwangju, Chŏlla; Kanggyŏng in Ŭnjin, Ch'ungch'ŏng; Wŏnsan in Tŏgwŏn, Hamgyŏng; and Masan in Ch'angwŏn, Kyŏngsang. These hubs, in turn, constituted a countrywide network of commercial transactions.

Thus, in the late eighteenth century, many commoners began to make profits through handicrafts or mining. In rural areas, village handicraft manufacturing evolved from a self-supplying activity to for-profit production. As producing goods as commodities became more widespread, some farming households pursued more professional production, mainly of clothing fabric and tableware. Simultaneously, alluvial gold mining began to flourish and to attract commercial capital, as both mining itself and smelting became easier. Since developing new mines was highly profitable, many pursued illegal mining, which generally relied on group collaboration and partnerships. Typically, mining operation experts who had contracts with mine owners secured capital from merchants and used the funds to hire mining business experts, miners, and smelting workers.

Responding to economic liberalization in the late eighteenth century, the government began to permit people to remit taxes and pay rent with coins. Buying goods became possible as long as one possessed *Sangp'yŏng t'ongbo*, the only officially minted coin for the whole kingdom (issued 1678–1894). Coins were not only a means of exchange but also an investment. Even though the quantity of minted coins increased considerably, inadequate circulation led to a shortage of coins at markets, as landlords and merchants hoarded or used them for usury. With the monetization of the economy, money orders and promissory notes too became more widespread. The spreading phenomenon was symptomatic of a society wherein money increasingly affected an individual's social standing, even though inherited status continued to matter.

ACCELERATING STATUS MOBILITY

After centuries of growth, Korea's population fluctuated erratically in the 10 to 14 million range during the period from about 1700 to 1864. The stabilization of the Hansŏng population around the 200,000 level reflects the overall demographic stability before the late nineteenth century. Elsewhere, smaller towns likely stopped growing or even declined. Not only did the state's revenue base cease to expand, increasing artisanal output, such as cloth manufacturing, migrated into the hinterland, closer to raw materials and lower-cost land and labor. Overall geographical mobility probably intensified. Changes in agricultural practice and rural social organization created new needs and possibilities that spurred a movement to pursue work. Generally, nonelites who ended up in urban areas also faced greater exposure to disease and other harms.

By contrast, the de facto one-party rule at the court offered little incentive for local aristocrats to move to Hansŏng. No longer holding an examination degree, a court rank, or an office, most *yangban* had to be content with their status as local aristocrats. Those worse off cultivated their land, if not struggling to survive as tenant farmers. Even the aristocratic lineages that had maintained standing as local elites found their positions being challenged by such social newcomers as wealthy commoners, who, backed by magistrates, secured local council seats. No longer controlling an entire county's general population with a community compact, local *yangban* lineages settled for a neighborhood compact (*tongyak*) or kin group solidarity among themselves. By the eighteenth century, single-surname or lineage villages had sprung up throughout the country, each with its private academy and shrine honoring prominent ancestors.

Initially, a phenomenon limited to the aristocracy, patrilineal lineage as a form of social organization spread across status boundaries. In principle, a woman could not own property, and daughters lost the right of inheritance. Upon wedding, a couple no longer took up residence at the wife's natal home but instead at the husband's. Along with loyal subjects and filial sons, the state honored chaste widows, regardless of status (Figure 8.2). Performance of ancestral rites by the eldest legitimate son became the norm, and accordingly, such a son received the lion's share of inheritance as the lineage heir. Since an illegitimate son was ineligible for heirship, a father without a legitimate son adopted a brother's or a patrilineal cousin's legitimate son, even if only distantly related. And posthumous adoptions became common—even for those long deceased without heirs. Accordingly, compiling one's genealogy as a record of membership in a patrilineal descent group; believing that all those with the same surname and ancestral seat are of common ancestral descent; and tracing one family's ancestry back to the classical period or to China all became widespread. To a considerable extent, membership in a particular lineage associated with a locale defined an individual's social identity.

FIGURE 8.2 (OPPOSITE)   An idealized depiction of Ch'oe Yŏnhong (1785–1846), 1914. During the rebellion by Hong Kyŏngnae (1780–1812), not only did Ch'oe—a government *kisaeng* and a concubine of her local magistrate—perform a proper funeral for him and his son after the rebels had killed them, she sheltered and looked after the magistrate's injured brother at her house. The court honored her for righteousness and chastity by relieving her of *kisaeng* duties and granting her a farmland plot. More than a century later, Ch'ae Yongsin painted an imagined portrait of Ch'oe holding a baby, possibly her son by the magistrate. Source: National Museum of Korea.

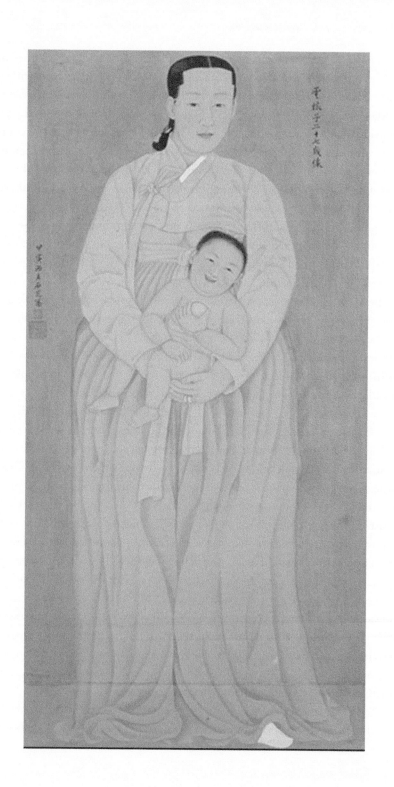

The spread of this focus on lineage as a social phenomenon that crossed status boundaries reflected some nonelites' growing influence, and among these nonelites, aristocratic men's illegitimate sons and specialist *chungin* made gains. As both Yŏngjo and Chŏngjo appointed and promoted such individuals, illegitimate sons of *yangban* fathers began to petition the court to remove the remaining restrictions on their access to certain prestigious offices reserved for bona fide aristocrats, and their effort encouraged specialist *chungin* to do likewise. Among the latter, many of whom accumulated wealth through their expertise in various areas, interpreters were exceptionally knowledgeable about the world beyond East Asia and aware of the rise of the West. Since their duties were vitally important in foreign relations, interpreters assumed an expanding role in introducing new knowledge, especially Western Learning.

Besides such *chungin*, many commoners were well-to-do. In Hansŏng, skilled laborers were in high demand due to overall booming commerce and larger-scale construction projects. They enjoyed a living standard comparable to that of their counterparts in China and Western Europe, the most affluent parts of the world at the time. Outside the capital, some commoners accumulated wealth through acquiring cultivated plots and improving farm management. Possessing rice paddies, dry fields, or both, wealthy farmers wielded a degree of influence in local society. Working with the state power centered around the magistrate and local functionaries, in many counties, wealthy commoners secured a presence in local councils, if not even taking them over. No longer primarily representing local *yangban* interests, the council turned into the magistrate's advisory group on tax-related matters, as social newcomers actively assisted with tax collection. For its part, the central government not only continued to grant court ranks, offices, and blank appointment certificates to grain donors but even sold local council memberships. These status trappings gained new local elites exemption from military service and other obligations to the state. Along with *chungin*, many wealthy commoners attained a level of education and cultural sophistication comparable to what *yangban* possessed. In particular, an increasing number of specialist *chungin*, capital functionaries, merchants, crafters, and wealthy farmers pursued literary activities formerly monopolized by the aristocracy. In their lighter moments, the social newcomers patronized *kisaeng* houses, previously off-limits to them.

At the same time, the position of slaves improved, and in the late eighteenth century, the unfree population began to decrease rapidly, for various reasons. Grain donation and military merit allowed some slaves to win manumission and even acquire court ranks and offices. More importantly, the ruling Patriarchs sought to increase the tax-paying commoner population. In 1731, the government began to treat an offspring of a slave father and a commoner mother as a commoner, as had been the case for some time for offspring of a commoner father and a slave mother. Also, a growing number of slaves ran away from their owners and became farmhands, slash-and-burn farmers, wage laborers, or peddlers. This phenomenon overburdened the remaining government slaves with personal tribute obligations, and this, in turn, pressured them to run away as well. The government responded by reducing the amount of tribute and attempting to round up the runaways, albeit in vain. Furthermore, as maintaining public slaves became financially less viable, the government converted them from paid service slaves to tribute-paying out-resident slaves. By the late eighteenth century, however, collecting personal tribute from government slaves had become unfeasible. In the reign of Chŏngjo's son and successor, King Sunjo (r. 1800–34), the state manumitted all of some 66,000 slaves attached to government offices in Hansŏng (1801). Compared to public slaves and ordinary farmers, private slaves were more vulnerable to cruel treatment, and the number of those running away continued to increase. Rather than spending money searching for or catching runaway slaves, private owners found it financially more sensible to hire wage laborers.

The increasing population of wage laborers was symptomatic of a more liberalized economy. While court politics were dominated by consort families, spreading corruption exacerbated the exploitation of ordinary farmers by magistrates and local functionaries. The Three Administrative Abuses, which involved land tax, military cloth tax, and grain loans, rampant corruption, and exploitation stemmed from the oligarchy at the court. Thus the throne was powerless to address them even after receiving reports from secret inspectors. Moreover, nationwide flooding in 1820 and the spread of cholera in the following year decimated populations. As the repercussions lingered for years, countless farmers' living conditions deteriorated further, and hungry vagrants filled the roads.

Spreading social problems and sightings of Western ships enhanced the appeal of alternative beliefs among the populace. Predictions of a future based on some prophetic texts became popular, and widespread rumors about the end of the world, dynastic change, disturbances, rebellions, or wars fueled unrest. Among such texts, *Record of Chŏng Kam* (*Chŏng Kam rok*), which probably dated back to the early seventeenth century following the wars, was an especially popular "secret writing" (*pigi*) at the time. Also of growing appeal was Maitreya worship, which promoted happiness otherwise unattainable in this life. Several self-proclaimed Maitreya Buddhas gained followings.

Likewise featuring messianic belief and offering a promise of salvation, Catholicism began to spread rapidly in the late eighteenth century. Some Practical Learning scholars among the Kyŏnggi-region Southerners, who agonized over the socioeconomic problems of the time, turned Catholic, especially after a Southerner scholar, Yi Sŭnghun (1756–1801), received baptism while visiting Beijing and thus became the first Korean to be baptized (1784). Initially, the government saw Catholicism as a passing phenomenon. As the faith continued to gain a following and as Catholics refused to perform Confucian ancestral rites, the court branded it a "false teaching" that was challenging royal power and *yangban*-centered status order. Nonetheless, Chŏngjo was relatively tolerant toward Catholicism, since many Southerners who supported him espoused the religion, but soon after Sunjo's accession, great persecution commenced (1801). Subsequently, the Practical Learning figures who had led the way in propagating Catholicism and many aristocrats left the church. When the Andong Kim, some of whom were Catholics, gained power, as one of the members was Sunjo's father-in-law and kin (1805), the persecution became laxer, and the faith spread more rapidly among the people. With the establishment of a Chosŏn diocese and the arrival of European priests, who secretly entered Korea and proselytized, the number of Catholics continued to grow. Widespread discontent enhanced the popular appeal of Catholicism, which taught that all humans are equal before God.

While Catholicism won converts, an indigenous religion, Tonghak, arose as the East's response to the Western Learning (1860). Born a son of a local *yangban* and a remarried mother, the founder, Ch'oe Cheu (1824–64), was syncretic in combining Confucianism, Buddhism (wherein Pure Land Buddhism had been undergoing a revival), worship of immortals, and folk religion. The core tenet of Ch'oe's teaching emphasized worshipping God by serving humanity and preached that the people are heaven. Stressing the equality of all humans, Ch'oe advocated ending aristocratic-commoner status distinctions, abolishing slavery, and respecting women and children. Before long, the government came to see Tonghak as a threat to the existing social order and executed Ch'oe Cheu for "deluding the world and deceiving the people" (*hokse mumin*). Subsequently, his successor, Ch'oe Sihyŏng (1827–98), continued to propagate the religion and win more converts.

While new forms of spirituality gained strength, expressions of discontent became more blatant. Initially, anonymous inflammatory streamers and wall placards criticized the government. Before long, banditry was rampant in many regions, including "fire brigands" (*hwajŏk*), who were musketeers on horseback, and "water brigands" (*sujŏk*), who traveled by ships and pillaged the population on riverbanks and seashores. In 1811 (Gregorian 1812) in P'yŏngan, Hong Kyŏngnae, an educated commoner, staged an open rebellion, leading poor farmers, small to middle-size merchants, and mine laborers. Initially encountering little resistance, the rebels gained control of almost the entire region to the north of the Ch'ŏngch'ŏn River. It took the government five months to suppress the rebellion. As corruption among officials remained widespread, social unrest did not subside. Decades later, impoverished farmers upset with corrupt officials and their agents rioted in Tansŏng, Kyŏngsang (1862). In the following months, others followed across scores of counties from Hamhŭng in the north to Chejudo in the south, continuing until the early part of the next year. Unlike the Hong Kyŏngnae Rebellion, after which all apprehended participants had been executed, in this case the government punished only the ringleaders and the targets of their complaint. Such measures left untouched the fundamental cause of popular discontent, the Three Administrative Abuses.

Amidst spreading social turmoil, a drastic change affected women, as their freedom became more restricted than ever before, especially among elites. Documents of a public nature, such as genealogies and household registers of this period, generally do not even record the given names of women except those who are slaves. Among aristocrats who lived in larger dwellings, in principle, the sexes were separated from age seven, as males used the outer part of the house as their living quarters, which also functioned as a space for receiving guests, and females stayed in the inner part; and a *yangban* woman covered her head when venturing outside the house. Adhering to a rigid social hierarchy based on age, sex, and status, the society encouraged women to follow Confucian virtues as filial daughters and chaste wives. A woman had no voice in marriage, which was for her parents to arrange. Upon wedding, she became a member of her husband's family and an outsider to her own. Any of the "seven culpae" justified expelling a wife: disobeying the parents-in-law; bearing no son; adultery; jealousy; incurable illness; garrulousness; and stealing. It was expected that widows would not remarry.

Nonetheless, Confucian moral norms centered around a married patriarch did not stifle other gendered relations. Such disparaging expressions of the time as *ch'ukch'ŏp* ("keeping concubines") show that official discourse did not view concubinage favorably, but as was also true in earlier times, a male was not bound by any meaningful social or legal restriction on the number of relationships he had outside marriage, including same-sex relations. Also, palace women continued to maintain sexual relations with females outside the palace by hosting girls from ordinary families as relatives or by *taesik* ("meeting up for meals") with Buddhist nuns or widows in or outside the palace. Documents use the expression *taesik* to refer to a palace woman entering into a committed, same-sex relationship.

Active as members of close-knit male communities beyond the confines of state power or elite culture were *namsadang*, who were itinerant troupes of male performers. Headed by a chief leader, *kkoktusoe*, a *namsadang* group gave performances that integrated music, dancing with or without masks, theatrical plays, acrobatics, and stunts. Recruits to these troupes were generally boys sold by poor farming households and runaways, although reportedly some were kidnapped. Upon entering a village, the *namsadang* toured the entire community, doing several rounds of street performances, before settling at the village's open space or market square for a performance continuing into the night. Performing for food and lodgings, the members also secured extra income by rendering sexual services. Accordingly, a troupe could enter a village only with the village leader's or representative's permission. The division of labor in the troupe was strict. Reporting to the *kkoktusoe* were one or two *kombaengisoe*, whose job was to secure such permission from the village. A *ttŭnsoe* was in charge of each performance genre, assisted by several, more experienced performers, *kayŏl*; below them were novices, *ppiri*. It was up to the *kkoktusoe* to assign a particular performance genre to a *ppiri*. Until becoming good enough to become a *kayŏl*, a *ppiri* typically dressed as a female, initially running minor errands. The functional hierarchy among *namsadang* performers featured two tiers, *suttongmo*, who were male *kayŏl*, and *amdongmo* who were the cross-dressing *ppiri*. As such, the *namsadang* typified professional performers in various genres of Korea's early modern popular culture.

THE GOLDEN AGE OF EARLY MODERN CULTURE

In the eighteenth century, Practical Learning and Yangmingism influenced each other in synergy. Chŏng Chedu's scholarship on Yangmingism thrived as the Kanghwa School, so named after the island to which he retired. Since Chŏng's followers were Disciples excluded from the political arena, the Kanghwa School continued mainly through his descendants and kin. The school pushed the limits of knowledge and understanding in such areas as history, language, literature, and calligraphy, in all of which Practical Learning scholars articulated new ideas. Among them, such intellectuals of the Applied Statecraft School as Yi Ik (pen name Sŏngho; 1681–1763) advocated land reform geared toward stabilizing the farming village society. Building on the Practical Learning ideas of Yu Hyŏngwŏn, Yi proposed land reform to foster independent farmers. Advocating a system that would guarantee each household an amount of land minimally necessary for supporting its livelihood, Yi opposed buying and selling such land. He pointed out six problems as especially damaging for an ideal agrarian society: slavery, government service examinations, aristocratic status privileges, extravagance, superstitions, the Buddhist clergy, and laziness. He also engaged with Western Learning.

Yi Ik had many disciples, some of whom began to pursue the Practical Learning of the Economic Enrichment School, also known as Northern Learning, which drew inspiration from Qing China. Rather than denigrating the Qing as barbarians who had destroyed the civilized Ming, such scholar-officials who visited Beijing relayed what they observed and heard through their reports and travelogues. Some of Yi's disciples even accepted Catholicism as a part of Western Learning, though Yi himself rejected it and was receptive only to Western technology. Advocating the adoption of various Qing institutions for "wealthy state, powerful army" and for "profitable usage, popular benefit" (iyong husaeng), Northern Learning argued for promoting commerce, industry, and technological innovation. Such an inclination signified a reorientation in terms of world view, at least among some Chosŏn intellectuals: moving away from a moral argument, based on the binary of civilization versus barbarism that had been popular since the Pyŏngja War, toward pragmatism geared to betterment of their country and people. A pioneering figure in Northern Learning was Yu Suwŏn (1694–55), who, in his Idle Jottings (Usŏ; early or mid-eighteenth century), emphasized promoting commerce, industry, and technological innovation. Yu also advocated occupational equality and professionalization of scholars, farmers, crafters, and merchants. He urged improving productivity not so much through land reform as commercialized management and technological innovations for agriculture.

Northern Learning continued to flourish in the late eighteenth century and into the nineteenth century, thanks to such scholars as Hong Taeyong (1731–83), Pak Chiwŏn (1737–1805), and Pak Chega (1750–1815). Based on his experience while visiting Qing China, Hong Taeyong advocated technological innovation, abolishing *yangban* privileges, and overcoming Neo-Confucianism: all as the fundamental requisites for a wealthy state and a powerful army. In making his case, Hong criticized the notion that China was the center of the world. His contemporary, Pak Chiwŏn visited China too and made similar recommendations in his travelogue *Jehol Diary* (*Yŏrha ilgi*; 1793). Criticizing the hereditary status system as unproductive, Pak argued for promoting commerce and industry, carts and ships, and wider circulation of money. Also, he advocated increasing agricultural productivity through new farming methods, commercial farming, and improved irrigation facilities. Building on Pak Chiwŏn's ideas, his disciple Pak Chega wrote *On Northern Learning* (*Pukhak ŭi*; unpublished) after visiting China (1778). Urging his country to adopt various Qing institutions and practices, Pak Chega emphasized the importance of developing commerce and industry, expanding trade with Qing, and using carts and ships. Also, he argued that rather than encouraging frugality, the government should encourage consumption to stimulate production.

Nearly two centuries of Practical Learning scholarship culminated with some 500 works authored by a polymath, Chŏng Yagyong (pen name Tasan; 1762–1836), whose works explored a wide range of subjects. In *Design for Good Government* (*Kyŏngse yup'yo*; 1817) and *On Administering to the People's Hearts* (*Mok minsim sŏ*; 1818), Chŏng presented his thoughts on reforming central and local administration. On land tenure, he initially advocated a community land system before settling on a well-field system. Also knowledgeable about commerce, industry, and technology, Chŏng was steadfast in his conviction that technology enriches human life and thus differentiates humans from other animals. Chŏng himself designed and constructed many machines. Studying *Illustrated Explanations of Marvelous Machines* (*Qiqi tushuo*; 1627), which the German Jesuit missionary Johann Schreck had published in late Ming

China, Chŏng built a tackle and pulley system. During the Hwasŏng city wall construction, his system considerably sped up the project and reduced the cost. And Chŏng was among many Practical Learning scholars who advanced knowledge in vaccination. Researching smallpox, he critically reviewed relevant medical treatises and collaborated with Pak Chega on vaccination research, which entailed experiments before writing his *Comprehensive Treatise on Small Pox* (*Magwa hoet'ong*; 1798).

Chŏng Yagyong's breadth of knowledge reflects the trend in vibrant encyclopedic learning at that time. Representative works among those privately authored include Yi Ik's *Miscellany of Sŏngho* (*Sŏngho sasŏl*; 1760), *Complete Works of Ch'ŏngjanggwan* (*Ch'ŏngjanggwan chŏnsŏ*; posthumous) by Yi Tŏngmu (pen name Ch'ŏngjanggwan; 1741–93), and *Random Expatiations of Oju* (*Oju yŏnmun changjŏn san'go*; mid-nineteenth century) by Yi Kyugyŏng (pen name Oju; 1788–1856). In the reigns of Yŏngjo and Chŏngjo, the government also compiled an encyclopedia, *Reference Compilation of Documents on Korea* (*Tongguk munhŏn pigo*; 1797), which categorized and reviewed Korea's institutions and ideas from the past until then.

As Practical Learning examined all aspects of Korean civilization, historical scholarship flourished. Employing empirical research and critical narratives, Yi Ik rejected Sinocentric historiography to systematize Korea's history—thus contributing to a heightened awareness of Korea's historical agency. Building on this view, a disciple, An Chŏngbok (pen name Sunam; 1712–91), wrote the *Annotated Account of Korean History* (*Tongsa kangmok*; 1778), which narrated Korean history from Kojosŏn to the end of Koryŏ. An's narrative presented a unique understanding of dynastic legitimacy in Korean history. Around the same time, Yi Kŭngik (pen name Yŏllyŏsil; 1736–1806) completed *Narratives of Yŏllyŏsil* (*Yŏllyŏsil kisul*; 1776 or earlier), which presented a history of Chosŏn politics and culture through vignette-like accounts, primarily from non-official sources. By contrast, Han Ch'iyun (1765–1814) consulted some 500 Chinese and Japanese works in writing his *History of Korea* (*Haedong yŏksa*; unfinished), which contributed to a broader understanding of Korean history at the time. Other intellectuals focused on specific parts of history. For example, in his *Korean History* (*Tongsa*; published in 1803), Yi Chonghwi (1731–97) deepened readers' understanding of Koguryŏ history, and *Study of Parhae* (*Parhae ko*; 1784) by Yu Tŭkkong (1748–1807) did likewise for Parhae as Koguryŏ's successor state. Both works challenged the more conventional, Korean Peninsula–centered historiography of their time.

A desire to better understand Korea as a physical space inspired more ac-
curate scientific maps, as influenced by Western maps introduced from China.
Especially influential was *A Map of the Myriad Countries of the World* (*Kunyu wan-
guo quantu*; 1602), produced by an Italian Jesuit missionary in China, Matteo
Ricci (1552–1610), and his Chinese collaborators. Reflecting that influence, *A
Comprehensive Map of the World* (*Ch'ŏnha tojido*; late eighteenth century) shows that
Korea's geographical knowledge had progressed by leaps and bounds since early
Chosŏn—it displays all the continents where they are, although it understands
the southern hemisphere, including Antarctica, as composed of hot regions. *Map
of Korea* (*Tongguk chido*) by Chŏng Sanggi (1678–1752) was his era's most detailed
map of the realm, with a scale of one *ch'ŏk* (about 30 centimeters) representing one
ri (about 400 meters). Even more impressive is the *Detailed Map of Korea* (*Taedong
yŏjido*; 1861) by Kim Chŏngho (1804–66?), which shows mountain ranges, rivers,
ports, and the network of roads in detail. For ease of determining distance,
the map features gradation marks indicating ten *ri*.

Besides cartography, Practical Learning scholars advanced other branches
of knowledge essential for improving people's livelihoods. Mindful of the
critical importance of seasons and weather for agriculture, Yi Ik studied
Western astronomy with keen interest, whereas Hong Taeyong conducted scientific research. Subscribing to heliocentrism, Hong understood the universe
to be infinite in extent, wherein the earth is not the center—a bold claim at
the time. From this position, he also criticized the prevailing Neo-Confucian
view of China as the center of the moral universe. Hong's contemporary,
Lady Chŏnju Yi (studio name Sajudang; 1739–1821) authored *New Records for
Prenatal Care* (*T'aegyo sin'gi*; 1801), which emphasizes that both parents' health
is the foundation of the unborn child's health and gives illustrative examples
while offering a broad spectrum of advice on medical care and the living
environment. Focusing on agriculture, Sŏ Hosu (1736–99) wrote *Farming in
Korea* (*Haedong nongsŏ*; c. 1799), which contributed significantly to the farming
technology at the time. His son Sŏ Yugu (1764–1845) produced a sixteen-part
encyclopedia, *A Treatise on Managing Rural Life* (*Imwŏn kyŏngje chi*; c. 1842), which
dealt primarily with agriculture, including illustrations of various farming
tools and a list of dates of markets throughout Korea. Sŏ Yugu's brother's
wife, Lady Chŏnju Yi (studio name Pinghŏhak; 1759–1824), who was also
the niece of Sajudang's husband, managed the household herself, including
tea plant cultivation, from her forties, after the government career of her
husband ended. Drawing on the knowledge gained from her experience and

from her study of Practical Learning texts, she wrote *Encyclopedia of Women's Daily Life* (*Kyuhap ch'ongsŏ*; 1809). This work covers food recipes, wine making, weaving clothes, dyeing fabric, embroidery, sericulture, making fire, tilling soil, animal husbandry, obstetrics, first aid care, household cleaning, and warding off evil spirits, among other domestic topics.

Many other works understood Korea as a distinct cultural space. Yi Chunghwan (1690–1756) authored a human geography text, *Ecological Guide to Korea* (*T'aengni chi*; 1751), which considered each region's natural environment, products, and customs, and the dispositions of the people, and recommended desirable places for residence. By contrast, Chŏng Yagyong wrote a historical geography, *A Study of Korean Territory* (*Abang kangyŏk ko*; 1811). Simultaneously, the desire to better understand the Korean language as an integral part of the culture motivated such works as the *Glossary of Words Past and Present* (*Kogŭm sŏngnim*; 1789) by Yi Ŭibong (1733–1801), which distinguishes Korean dialects from foreign languages. Although the position of Literary Sinitic as the written language of the elite remained unchallenged, ongoing research on vernacular Korean in conjunction with *han'gŭl* produced such works as *Explication of Correct Sounds for the Instruction of the People* (*Hunmin chŏngŭm unhae*; 1750) by Sin Kyŏngjun (1712–81) and *A Treatise on Han'gŭl* (*Ŏnmun chi*; 1824) by Yu Hŭi (1773–1837).

More than ever before, many in late Chosŏn employed Literary Sinitic and *han'gŭl* alike for satires, even expressing outrage toward social injustice. For example, Chŏng Yagyong wrote in Literary Sinitic a poem wherein he exposed the Three Administrative Abuses. Even more prolific a social critic through writing in Literary Sinitic was Pak Chiwŏn. Through such works of narrative fiction as *Tale of a Yangban* (*Yangban chŏn*; late eighteenth century), *Tale of Master Hŏ* (*Hŏ saeng chŏn*; late eighteenth century), *A Tiger's Rebuke* (*Ho chil*; late eighteenth century), and *Tale of Elder Min* (*Min ong chŏn*; 1757), he poked fun at follies of aristocratic society. Stressing practicality, Pak advocated a literary style reform that would allow more accurate depictions of social reality. Accessible to a much larger readership, works of vernacular narrative fiction from the period are even more direct in attacking *yangban* hypocrisy and satirizing injustice and corruption. In *Tale of Ch'unhyang* (*Ch'unhyang chŏn*), love between a young *yangban* man and a daughter of a *kisaeng* is so pure and passionate that it overcomes the status boundary separating them. In *Tale of Sim Ch'ŏng* (*Sim Ch'ŏng chŏn*), a filial daughter who is willing to sacrifice her life for her blind father ultimately becomes the king's wife and restores her father's vision. And in *Tale of Changhwa and Hongnyŏn* (*Changhwa Hongnyŏn chŏn*), two sisters who fall victim to intra-family strife and turmoil ask the ordinary people to reflect on all the madness rampant in society.

Likewise, the era's *sijo* are revealing. Eighteenth- and nineteenth-century works tend to be more honest expressions of emotions of the ordinary people. Not bound to formalities, longer narrative *sijo* began to allow both a more comprehensive range of feelings and more subtle expression, including articulating love between a man and a woman. Also, critical attitudes toward social reality found a voice in *sijo*. As creative literary activities of educated nonelites of means such as *chungin* and wealthy commoners increased, these individuals organized fellowships of poets who gathered at scenic locations in and around Hansŏng and published anthologies of poems. Many won acceptance by the *yangban* as peers. Satirical poets like Chŏng Sudong (1808–58), who hailed from a family of interpreters, and Kim Pyŏngyŏn (also known as Kim Satkat; 1807–63), who came from a *yangban* family disgraced for his grandfather's crimes as a magistrate during the Hong Kyŏngnae Rebellion, freely crossed status boundaries and mingled with the masses.

Rather than adopting only literary forms of expression, many *chungin* became accomplished painters. Typically employed by the state as court painters, they also produced works that showed various aspects of their society and culture. Among them, Chŏng Sŏn (1676–1759) broke new ground in landscape painting. Touring scenic spots around Hansŏng and in Kangwŏn, he depicted them with realism. In his celebrated works *Mount Kŭmgang* (*Kŭmgang chŏndo*; 1734) and *Storm Lifting over Mount Inwang* (*Inwang chesaek to*; 1751), Chŏng's technique employs ink tones for mountain surfaces composed mostly of soil and distinct lines for rocky mountain surfaces. In comparison, Kim Hongdo (1745–1806) was a more versatile artist. Although he excelled in documentary paintings, landscapes, and depictions of immortals, Kim was especially famous for genre paintings imbued with a bantering spirit. His illustrations of farmers tilling the fields, autumn harvest, wrestlers, and a village school all capture in a relaxed, witty manner the essence of each individual focused on a particular activity (Figure 8.3). Kim's younger contemporary, Sin Yunbok (1758–1814?), depicted mainly the lives and pastimes of well-to-do males and also included others of lower social status, aside from moments of gendered interactions, in a manner that combined humor and sensuality.

In the early nineteenth century, the revival of more traditional literati paintings eclipsed *chungin* professional paintings, but some new trends

FIGURE 8.3   Kim Hongdo, *Washing Place*, c. 1780. Source: National Museum of Korea.

emerged. In portraiture, such artists as Kang Sehwang (1713–91) employed Western painting techniques in depicting their subjects with realism, as reflected in his self-portrait. By contrast, increasingly popular folk paintings used a seemingly rather innocent, at times even childish, manner that vividly captured ordinary people's aesthetic sensibilities. Using the sun, the moon, trees, flowers, fish, and land animals as motifs to express wishes for good fortunes and longevity, folk paintings also decorated living spaces of homes across status boundaries.

Among elites, new calligraphy styles embodied sensibilities unique to Korea, some more traditional and others innovative. Yi Kwangsa (1705–77) put forth a graceful, "true Korean landscape" (*chin'gyŏng sansu*), which is self-consciously distinct from older, more Chinese-influenced styles. Decades later, in the nineteenth century, Kim Chŏnghŭi (pen name Ch'usa; 1786–1856), who extensively studied the brush technique of Chinese and Korean traditions alike, created his own "Ch'usa style." Characterized by uniquely shaped ideographs exuding energy, the Ch'usa style broke new ground in calligraphy.

Works of larger-scale visual art such as architecture show some new trends as well. Among them, Buddhist monasteries reflect the increased influence of wealthy farmers and merchants. In the eighteenth century, such social newcomers funded the construction or reconstruction of monasteries in their home locales. More richly decorated than older structures, representative works include Sŏngnam-sa in Ansŏng, Kyŏnggi (the main hall was rebuilt in 1725), Kaeam-sa in Puan, Chŏlla (with additions in 1728 and 1733), and Ssanggye-sa in Nonsan, Ch'ungch'ŏng (rebuilt in 1739). Decades later, in Suwŏn, Chŏngjo's Hwasŏng project sought to construct a new city in harmony with the surrounding area's scenery. Also, comprehensive urban planning now took into consideration military matters and the daily life and economic activities of ordinary people, including merchants and artisans.

In the late eighteenth century, improved living standards for nonelites of means increased demand for products of master craftsmanship. More widespread use of white porcelain, found even in private households, culminated with blue-and-white pottery, which artisans produced in an ever-widening variety of shapes and decorative motifs. The media for painting on the pottery surface became more varied, and included cobalt blue iron and copper red underglaze oxides. Potters supplied products to be used for everyday consumption and also ancestral ritual wares and stationery accessories. Nonetheless, blue-and-white porcelain ware was still expensive, even though it were in high demand among well-to-do households for its unique shapes and sophisticated decorative motifs. The ordinary people more commonly used earthenware. Also, such woodcraft products as wardrobes, desks, puppetries, small portable dining tables, chairs, and ink bush cases attracted customers. Adding a more delicate touch was Hwagak craft, which makes use of thin pieces of ox horn as decoration.

In the performing arts, music allowed increasingly bold expressions of emotions and catered to an expanding audience who wanted to be entertained rather than performing rituals. The elite continued to enjoy *sijo* and *kagok*, which featured singing accompanied by instruments. The lyrics of each sung *sijo* or *kagok* were short poems, whereas ordinary people enjoyed folk songs and *chapka* ("miscellaneous songs"). In contrast, *p'ansori* was performed by professional singers and drummers who offered musical storytelling based on various works of vernacular narrative fiction and attracted an audience of all backgrounds. Its expression of emotions was direct, but the singer could also improvise in response to the audience's mood, allowing the versatility that was an integral component of the production. First mentioned in the mid-eighteenth century, the earliest *p'ansori* singers and drummers were most likely shamans and street performers catering to the ordinary people. While incorporating folk songs, *p'ansori* singers also adopted vocal techniques and melodies that catered to *yangban* and by the early nineteenth century had secured aristocratic patronage. Reflecting this trend, more purely humorous *p'ansori* lost ground to those that judiciously combined elements of comedy and tragedy. The *p'ansori* repertoire eventually comprised twelve works, among which five are extant: *Song of Ch'unhyang (Ch'unhyang ka)*, *Song of Sim Ch'ŏng (Sim Ch'ŏng ka)*, *Song of Hŭngbo (Hŭngbo ka)*, *Song of the Red Cliffs (Chŏkpyŏk ka)*, and *Song of the Water Palace (Sugung ka)*.

Combining music and dance, masked plays continued to entertain a wide audience, especially ordinary people. The more free-style masked plays became popular in local society, performed as a part of a shaman ritual devoted to the village patron deity. In contrast, staged masked plays thrived as a popular entertainment genre sponsored by urban merchants and other non-elites of means. Regardless, masked play performances engaged with social issues and satirized vices of the aristocracy and Buddhist clergy, especially their hypocrisy and corruption. Such performances even staged particular characters of lower social status, such as Malttugi and Ch'wibari, to expose follies of *yangban* characters and humiliate them.

In daily life, the emergence of *chungin* and some commoners as well-to-do consumers and the introduction of many new crops made the late Chosŏn food culture more variegated than before. A preference for beef over all other types of meat became pronounced, and beef consumption increased, albeit still confined to those of means. By the early nineteenth century, common vegetables included spinach, lettuce, ginger, cluster mallow, Korean chives, Korean mustard, chrysanthemum greens, water celery, watershield plant, water pepper, Korean angelica-tree, and such newly introduced vegetables as sweet potatoes (1764; Japan), potatoes (1824–25; China), and peanuts (1778; China). Cooking featured all food preparation methods still used in contemporary Korean cuisine. The widespread use of chili pepper powder enabled the present method of preparing enough *kimchi* for a household to last through winter months, an activity known as *kimjang*. As the most important annual event in Korean food culture, *kimjang* was typically undertaken by households on the tenth moon. For protection from cold, jars of varying sizes stuffed with a wide variety of *kimchi* were either wrapped with a layer of straw for burial in the ground with only the covers exposed or stored inside a straw shed, depending on the region.

As is true of the culinary culture, housing too assumed more features that today seem quintessential characteristics of a traditional *hanok* ("Korean house"). As socioeconomic mobility increased, a household's social status did not necessarily determine the characteristics of a residence as a physical structure. Typical *yangban* houses, however, continued to adhere to shared features rather than reflecting any regional variations, as was common in ordinary people's homes. The two types of housing nonetheless continued to influence each other. The male living quarters assumed an importance greater than ever before and became more distinct as a space for receiving guests and performing various rituals. Becoming more common in the mid-eighteenth century, another lasting late Chosŏn innovation in housing culture was the *t'oekkan*, an expanded open space under the eaves. Supported by columns below the eaves' edges and located just outside a room's doors, a *t'oekkan*, as a transitional space between the house's interior and exterior, had a wood floor. More than a walkway or sitting area outside various rooms, a *t'oekkan* also provided temporary storage space for goods being moved or delivered. *T'oekkan* increasingly became a standard feature, even among the more modest commoner houses with thatched roofs, and continued to dominate Korea's rural landscape well into the latter half of the twentieth century.

PART IV

The Late Modern Era

CHAPTER 9

Reform, Imperialism, and Nationalism, 1864–1910

K orea struggled to reinvent itself as a modern nation-state in the age of imperialism. Hŭngsŏn Taewŏn'gun (1821–98) pursued dynastic renovation while rejecting imperialist demands for trade and relations. Then the Eastern Ways–Western Implements (Tongdo sŏgi) Reform (1873–94) of King Kojong (r. 1864–1907; emperor from 1897) selectively adopted Western technology and engaged Japan with Western powers while Sino-Japanese rivalry in Korea intensified. Spreading government corruption, foreign economic infiltration, and popular discontent fueled the Tonghak Uprising (1894), which gave a pretext for China and Japan to intervene, setting off the First Sino-Japanese War (1894–95), and launched the Kabo Reform (1894–96). When Russia replaced China as victorious Japan's rival in Korea, Kojong launched a more comprehensive modernization program, the Kwangmu Reform (1897–1904), which before long was derailed by the Russo-Japanese War (1904–05) and occupation by victorious Japan. Amidst the political turmoil, the hereditary status system broke down in daily life as that life was slowly transformed by such products of Western science and technology as railroads, electricity, and medicine.

BIRTH OF A MODERN NATION-STATE

As Chosŏn's first living *taewŏn'gun* (king's father not in the line of succession) and as the de facto regent, Hŭngsŏn Taewŏn'gun, who had secured the throne for his child Kojong after a back-door negotiation with the queen dowager, sought to address Korea's problems through a conservative reform (Figure 9.1). The Taewŏn'gun enhanced royal power, which had plummeted during the previous decades of ineffectual monarchs and consort family oligarchy, through such measures as promoting political moderates loyal to him, rebuilding the Kyŏngbok Palace, abolishing the Border Defense Command, restoring the original functions of the State Council and the Three Armies Command, and compiling the Great Code Reconciliation (Taejŏn hoet'ong; 1865). He also shut down most of the private academies that local elites had been using to weigh in on court politics and exploit local populations. Likewise, the Taewŏn'gun ended the Three Administrative Abuses, which he deemed the root cause of widespread discontent. His fiscal reform was successful, even producing a revenue surplus.

At the time, some Western powers and Japan, which was pursuing its modernization and expansionism under the government of the Meiji emperor (r. 1867–1912), began to pressure Korea for relations and trade, and the Taewŏn'gun resisted. Neither the French incursion of 1866 nor the American incursion of 1871 intimidated the court into signing the kind of unequal treaties that had been imposed earlier by Britain on Qing China (1842) and by the United States on Tokugawa Japan (1854). To demonstrate his resolve to fight off all such attempts, he ordered steles erected throughout the country, each with this inscription: "Western barbarians invade our land. If we do not fight, then we must appease them. To urge appeasement is to betray the nation." The Taewŏn'gun's foreign policy as such was successful in repelling foreign incursions for the time being, but ultimately only delayed Chosŏn Korea's arguably inevitable engagement with imperialism and its need to make adjustments.

In the course of his rule, the Taewŏn'gun made two distinct groups of political enemies. His high-handed, iconoclastic leadership aroused resentment among more conservative Confucian literati, among whom the closure of most private academies and a wide range of exactions for the costly Kyŏngbok Palace construction were widely unpopular. At the same time, King Kojong, his wife Queen Myŏngsŏng, and their political supporters increasingly believed that the country must engage with the Western powers and Meiji Japan. In the end, pressures from both groups forced the Taewŏn'gun to relinquish power and retire from politics, paving the way for Kojong, now a young man of twenty-two, to begin ruling in person (1873).

FIGURE 9.1   Hŭngsŏn Taewŏn'gun, c. 1895. Source: Homer B. Hulbert, *The Passing of Korea* (New York: Doubleday, Page & Company, 1906), plate facing p. 116.

With the support of Myŏngsŏng and her natal family, the Yŏhŭng Min, Kojong pursued a new foreign policy of securing treaty relations with Western countries and Japan. After ignoring Kojong's gestures, Japan dispatched a fleet that provoked Korea's coastal artillery into firing, used the incident as a pretext to stage a more threatening display of force, a tactic it had learned earlier from the United States, and pressured Korea into signing the Treaty of Kanghwado, which allowed Japan to export goods without paying tariff and to buy Korea's grain without limit (1876). Opening Pusan and two other ports for trade with Japan, it was an unequal treaty that gave Japan extra-territoriality and the right to survey Korea's coastal waters. Subsequently, Korea also entered into treaty relations with Western powers, including the United States (1882), Britain (1883), Germany (1883), Italy (1884), Russia (1884), France (1886), and Austria-Hungary (1892). Although their terms were more favorable to Korea than those of the Treaty of Kanghwado, all were still unequal treaties in that for each signatory, Korea had to grant most favored nation status, according to which a signatory was entitled to whatever extra advantage that the next, new signatory gains from Korea.

Reactions varied among Koreans. Kojong pursued Eastern Ways–Western Implements Reform to enrich the state and strengthen the army while maintaining traditional culture. He established the Office for Extraordinary State Affairs as the organ to oversee the reform (1881); created the Special Skills Force, which was a new style regiment trained in modern military tactics and arms (1881); and dispatched official learning missions to Japan (1881), China (1881), and the United States (1883) to survey modern institutions and ideas. At the same time, the Eastern Ways–Western Implements Reform aroused resistance from the more conservative Confucian literati, who launched the Defend Orthodoxy–Reject Heterodoxy (Wijŏng ch'ŏksa) movement, which upheld their traditional world view. They protested Kojong's foreign policy by submitting memorials that opposed opening the ports and adopting Western institutions. Eventually, old-style regiment troops and the urban poor of Hansŏng, all of whom suffered from the increasing economic infiltration by China and Japan, staged a riot that became known as the Imo Mutiny and brought the Taewŏn'gun back to power (1882). Determined not to allow instability in Korea, China promptly intervened. Quashing the mutiny, the Qing army abducted the Taewŏn'gun to China, viewing him as a troublemaker.

Now more heavy-handed, Qing China exercised tight control of Korea as a tributary by meddling in its internal affairs and expanding China's economic presence. Resenting this, Kim Okkyun (1851–94) and Pak Yŏnghyo (1861–1939), who were leaders of the reformist Enlightenment Party (c. 1874–96) and inspired by the progress Meiji Japan was making with moderniza-tion, enlisted the aid of Japanese legation troops and staged the Kapsin Coup (1884). They advocated ending Korea's tributary-suzerain relationship with China, obtaining the immediate release of the Taewŏn'gun, establishing a political system with some characteristics of a constitutional monarchy, and appointing officials based on their abilities rather than hereditary status. The coup leadership announced the establishment of a land tax system based on the land value rather than the quantity of harvest; assignment of all revenue-related responsibilities to the Ministry of Taxation; and to foster free commerce, the abolition of the Office to Aid Merchants, which the government had created in 1883 to protect the interests of peddlers hurt by the opening of the ports. The ambitious enlightenment regime, however, collapsed in just three days upon Qing military intervention.

Kojong did what he could to preserve Korea's autonomy despite the expanding Chinese and Japanese presence. In seeking territorial integrity, Korea became more active in administering Ullŭngdo, as Kojong appointed an official to administer the island (1882) and encouraged settlement (1883). After the Kapsin Coup failed, Kojong sought to check Chinese interference by strengthening ties to Russia. Alarmed by this development, Britain, which had long been Russia's rival at both ends of Eurasia, temporarily occupied Kŏmundo, Chŏlla (1885–87). As significant powers jockeyed for influence in the Korean Peninsula, some individuals, such as Yu Kilchun (1856–1914), a leading progressive intellectual of the Enlightenment Party, argued for turning Korea into a neutral state.

Korea also faced a mounting internal crisis, especially as the Tonghak, who advocated equality and social reform, gained a large following. Although Kojong continued to pursue the Eastern Ways–Western Implements Reform, the Three Administrative Abuses, the payment of indemnities to major powers for various reasons, and China's and Japan's economic infiltration fanned discontent among ordinary farmers. Increasingly aware of the rapidly changing world, the Tonghak also demanded a more sweeping social reform. Led by Ch'oe Sihyŏng, the Tonghak continued to attract new members and further explicated their doctrines through publishing the founder's teach-ings under the titles *Great Collection of Eastern Doctrine* (*Tonggyŏng taejŏn*; 1880) and *Hymns from Dragon Pool* (*Yongdam yusa*; 1881). As the Tonghak improved their organization with new institutions and rituals, their presence spread beyond the three southern provinces, even making inroads into Kyŏnggi and Kangwŏn.

A corrupt magistrate was the initial spark for the Tonghak Uprising in Kobu, Chŏlla. Under the command of Chŏn Pongjun (1854–95), local farmers armed themselves and rose up against their rapacious magistrate in February 1894. Shouting, "Protect the country, preserve the people" (*poguk anmin*) and "Eliminate tyranny, save the people" (*chep'ok kumin*), the rebels quickly gained control of the entire province. Before long, however, the Tonghak leadership and the government army's field commander came an agreement that a continuing disturbance would give China and Japan a new pretext for military intervention, and in June, in Chŏnju, the two sides reached a truce, which granted the rebels a degree of autonomy. Accordingly, the Tonghak established local directorates as civilian institutions in fifty-three counties in Chŏlla to implement a sociopolitical reform on their terms. Each directorate's staff included a director, a secretary, an inspector, a steward, and a youth education officer. The truce was a little too late, as Chinese and Japanese troops were already on their way. In July, the Japanese stormed the Kyŏngbok Palace and installed a pro-Japanese government, which, as mentioned, set off the First Sino-Japanese War. The Tonghak armed themselves again and began marching toward Hansŏng. In December, in the Battle of Ugŭmch'i in Kongju, a combined Japanese-Korean government force of 5,200 annihilated the Tonghak, numbering over 20,000. The subsequent arrest of Chŏn Pongjun and other leaders ended the rebellion.

Meanwhile, the Kabo Reform government put forth a wide array of new policies concerning politics, society, and the economy. Earlier in July, the pro-Japanese cabinet of Prime Minister Kim Hongjip (1842–96) had established a supra-governmental body, the Deliberative Council, in response to popular demand for reform. Discussing all matters of consequence before seeking Kojong's approval, the council launched the Kabo Reform, which limited royal power, abolished the hereditary status system, banned a wide range of customs and practices associated with the status system, entrusted the Finance Office with revenue management, instituted a monetary system based on the silver standard, and improved the system of tax assessment. The reform entered a new phase in January 1895, when Kojong promulgated Korea's first constitution, the Great Plan (Hongbŏm). Through its fourteen articles, the king articulated his commitment to the modernization program for the country. At the same time, Kojong sought to enlist Russia as an ally. In April, the Treaty of Shimonoseki concluded the First Sino-Japanese War with Japan's victory, but later in the month, the Triple Intervention by France, Germany, and Russia forced Japan to give up one of its gains from China, the Liaodong Peninsula. As Kojong sought to strengthen ties to Russia, in October, the Japanese raided the Kyŏngbok Palace and murdered Myŏngsŏng, whom they regarded as the mastermind behind Kojong's pro-Russia policy.

Afterward, a pro-Japanese cabinet commenced the third phase of the Kabo Reform, which featured more radical measures. On the seventeenth day of the eleventh moon of 1895, the government adopted the Gregorian calendar, thus marking New Year's Day of 1896, and Kojong adopted an independent era name, Kŏnyang ("lustrous inauguration"), thus becoming the first Korean monarch since early Koryŏ to do so. Some reform measures were highly unpopular—including an edict, issued two days earlier, that every adult male cut off his topknot, a hairstyle traditionally dictated by filial piety, which prohibited tampering with one's body as inherited from one's parents. The reform also fell well short of strengthening national defense or rationalizing the land tenure system to provide minimally necessary support for the livelihood of the people, the majority of whom were tenant farmers. After all, Kojong and his cabinet were not so much reform leaders with decision-making power as de facto Japanese hostages.

Outraged by the queen's death and the haircut edict, many rural Confucian scholars and farmers formed "righteous armies" (ŭibyŏng) to fight the Japanese. With Defend Orthodoxy–Reject Heterodoxy as their cause, such Confucian literati as Yu Insŏk (1842–1915), Yi Soŭng (1852–1930), and Hŏ Wi (1854–1908) led righteous armies that quickly swelled as farmers voluntarily joined them. Kojong himself objected to the pro-Japanese Enlightenment Party's effort to limit royal power and feared for his safety after the murder of his wife. In February 1896, Kojong and his entourage fled to the Russian legation, and the Kabo Reform ended when he ordered the arrest of his pro-Japanese officials. The king's sojourn at the legation lasted a year, during which Korean government officials made a growing number of economic concessions to the great powers, including mining and logging rights.

In the meantime, emerging civic movements sought to promote the ideal of a modern nation-state through an active engagement with the masses. In April 1896, Philip Jaisohn (Ko. Sŏ Chaep'il; 1864–1951), who was a Korean-born naturalized U.S. citizen and a former member of the Enlightenment Party, and other reformists began to publish a bilingual Korean-English newspaper, *The Independent* (*Tongnip sinmun*), with the government's support, to educate the public about the Western concept of civil liberties and to publicize Korea's modernization effort among Western nations. In July, they launched the Independence Club, which organized public lectures and debates to heighten the sense of national sovereignty and popular rights among the ordinary people. In early 1897, the Independence Club's leadership began hosting the Assembly of the People (initially the Assembly of Officials and the People) as a broader, organized political base for the club.

While Russia held Japan back, Kojong capitalized on a spreading demand for him to assert national sovereignty, and he launched the Kwangmu Reform. Ending his stay at the Russian legation in February 1897, Kojong took up residence at the nearby Kyŏngun Palace (renamed Tŏksu Palace in 1907). Then in October, in response to a series of memorials urging him to upgrade the nation's status, Kojong inaugurated the Empire of Korea and ascended the throne as its first emperor, adopting Kwangmu ("martial brilliance") as the era name (Figure 9.2). Within months, various nations that had treaty relations with Korea acknowledged the new status. The ensuing Kwangmu Reform established the Land Survey Office (1898), which conducted a cadastral survey to increase the tax revenue and establish modern land ownership by issuing property deeds. Simultaneously, the reform sought to expand the industrial base for a military buildup by promoting commerce and industry. Before long, though, the emperor and his conservative officials clashed with the Independence Club. Earlier, in November 1897, the government had allocated twenty-five seats of the fifty-member Privy Council, which Kojong had established in June 1894 as an advisory group, to individuals elected by the club. As that organization became more vocal in advocating a true parliament and constitutional monarchy, it alarmed the emperor and the conservatives. Finally, in December 1898, Kojong outlawed the Independence Club. Pursuing a different vision, in August 1899, Kojong promulgated a new constitution, the National Constitution of Korea (Taehan'guk kukche), which featured a powerful emperor unrestrained by any branch of the government.

While political turmoil continued inside the country, developments abroad were increasingly unfavorable to Korea. Japan significantly strengthened its geopolitical standing by securing the First Anglo-Japanese Alliance (1902–05), and ongoing Russo-Japanese negotiations on their respective

FIGURE 9.2   Emperor Kojong, 1907. Photograph by Iwata Kanae (1870–1922+).
Source: National Palace Museum of Korea.

spheres of influence in Korea failed. Anticipating the Russo-Japanese War, Korea declared neutrality in January 1904, but in the following month, the war commenced when the Japanese attacked Russian forces and imposed the Japan-Korea Treaty of 1904 on Korea, which gave Japanese troops a free pass throughout the country. Months later, with the Japan-Korea Agreement of August 1904, again forced upon Korea, Japan began interfering in internal affairs through a Japanese-recommended foreign advisor on the Korean government's revenue matters. Besides winning a string of battles in and around Korea and Manchuria, Japan made further gains toward securing international recognition of its central position in Korea. In July 1905, Japan's Taft-Katsura Agreement with the United States recognized Japanese control of Korea and American control of the Philippines, and the Second Anglo-Japanese Alliance (1905–11) reaffirmed British support for Japan. In September, the Treaty of Portsmouth, brokered by the United States, formally concluded the war with a Japanese victory.

Japan moved swiftly to solidify its position in Korea. In November, Japan coerced Korean officials into the Japan-Korea Protectorate Treaty of 1905, which, although Kojong refused to approve it, nonetheless stripped Korea of diplomatic representation and turned it into a Japanese protectorate administered through the newly established Residency-General of Korea (1905–10). Insisting that the treaty was null and void, in June 1907, Kojong dispatched confidential emissaries to the Second Hague Peace Conference to publicize the outrage. Subsequently, in July, the Japanese replaced Kojong with his eldest son and heir, Emperor Sunjong (era name Yunghǔi; r. 1907–10), a figurehead. The subsequent Japan-Korea Treaty of 1907 stipulated a Japanese vice minister for every Korean government ministry and abolition of the Imperial Korean Army, thus giving Japan virtually full control of Korea. Brutally suppressing righteous army resistance and taking over all judiciary and police powers, the Japan-Korea Annexation Treaty of August 29, 1910, made Korea a Japanese colony.

Not focused only on taking over Korea's national government, Japan also took measures concerning Korea's territorial rights. During the Russo-Japanese War, Japan had unilaterally incorporated the island of Tokto, which had been under Korea's Ullǔngdo-based county administration since 1900, into Japan's Shimane Prefecture. Also, in exchange for the exclusive right to construct the Shenyang-Dandong railway in Manchuria, Japan recognized a Sino-Korean border region, Jiandao (Ko. Kando; 1909), as Chinese territory. Before the agreement, Korea had administered its population in Jiandao, as China and Korea had left the question of ownership open, given that the two could not agree on the "T'omun" (Ch. Tumen) River's identity in defining the Sino-Korean border in earlier relevant documents. A more recent discovery of many documents shows that the T'omun River was not the Tuman (Ch. Douman) River, although it was the latter which, per the Japanese manipulation, thus became the official Sino-Korean border.

During this time, many Koreans, including those in Jiandao, joined the righteous armies. Among them, former officials Min Chongsik (1861–1917) and Ch'oe Ikhyŏn (1833–1907) and the commoner Sin Tolsŏk (1878–1908) led the righteous armies. Japan's dethronement of Kojong and disbanding of the Imperial Korean Army intensified the resistance, which was then joined by former Imperial Korean Army officers and soldiers. Their sphere of operation expanded to include Jiandao and the Russian Maritime Province. Nonetheless, not only did Japanese troops enjoy overwhelming superiority in armament, occasionally a conflict arose between the righteous army leadership, dominated by *yangban* literati, and the mostly commoner rank and file. At one point, the righteous armies of all provinces united and marched toward Hansŏng, only to suffer crushing defeats in the vicinity (1908).

Afterward, the surviving fighters fell back on smaller scale hit-and-run operations, including some who relocated to Manchuria or the Russian Maritime Province. Among them, An Chunggŭn (1879–1910), a lieutenant general of the righteous army based in the Russian Maritime Province, leading a special operations unit, shot and killed Japan's elder statesman and former resident general of Korea, Itō Hirobumi (1841–1909), in Harbin, Manchuria. Likewise, Chang Inhwan (1876–1930) and Chŏn Myŏngun (1884–1947), both independence activists living in the United States, shot and killed a Japanese-employed American advisor to the Korean Foreign Office, Durham Stevens (1858–1908), in San Francisco. Such actions were unable to turn the tide, but they nonetheless would inspire anti-Japanese resistance for decades.

Inside Korea, as openly anti-Japanese activity became unfeasible, various patriotic organizations arose, proposing ideologies and strategies for a better-organized resistance. Initially, both the Korea Preservation Society, which thwarted Japan's demand for wasteland reclamation rights, and the Society for the Study of Constitutional Government, which pursued the establishment of a constitutional political system, were especially active.

After Japan imposed the Protectorate Treaty, such groups as the Korea Self-Strengthening Society, the Korean Association, and the New People's Association led an effort to educate the public about recovering national sovereignty. Among them, the New People's Association secretly pursued an effort to establish the Korean nation-state as a republic by establishing operation bases outside Korea for anti-Japanese fighters while improving their compatriots' socioeconomic positions.

THE INTEGRATION INTO THE WORLD ECONOMY

After the opening of the ports under the Treaty of Kanghwado, foreign trade governed by unequal treaties generally hurt Korean merchants. The treaty had no stipulation for the Chosŏn government to charge tariffs on Japanese imports. Even after a series of follow-up agreements, Korea could levy only a nominal surcharge. In the 1880s, foreign merchants began to travel and conduct business freely inside Korea, and the government had little power to prosecute any illegal activity on their part. The unequal treaties also allowed the use of foreign currencies in Korea. Such provisions resulted in an influx of mass-produced foreign goods and a massive outflow of Korean grain. Japanese merchants initially dominated Korea's foreign trade, but in the 1880s, Chinese merchants entered the scene. Before long, Korean merchants who were based at treaty ports began to participate in the new foreign trade, although they still lacked a full knowledge of developments abroad or adequate means of modern transportation. At first, Japanese and Chinese merchants mainly brought in cotton products for sale and bought Korean ox hides, rice, beans, and gold for export. Then in the late 1890s, the Japanese introduced manufactured cotton products and other factory-produced goods.

Expanding foreign trade introduced significant changes to Korea's economy. The general pattern of cotton product import and grain export hurt the economy. Domestic cotton manufacturing based on cottage industry could not compete with cheap, imported cotton products from Japanese factories, and Korean farming household income decreased. Also, as Japan's purchase of Korean rice rapidly increased, the resulting rice shortage raised the price, thus producing hardship, especially for the poor. Furthermore, even a massive outflow of precious metal was not enough to offset exotic imported goods that fueled extravagance among the affluent and increased the overall trade deficit. Nonetheless, many landlords and merchants profited from exporting rice. Using the profit to acquire more land, some became great landlords, while others bought thread from abroad to manufacture textile products.

Qing China and Meiji Japan used political and military pressures to advance their economic interests in Korea. Following the Imo Mutiny, the China-Korea Treaty of 1882, which Qing forced upon Chosŏn, paved the way for Chinese merchants, who went on to open shops in Hansŏng and conduct business in all parts of Korea. Upon setting off the First Sino-Japanese War, Japan led the way in securing from Korea such economic concessions as the right to construct railways. During Kojong's year-long sojourn at the Russian legation, meddling in Korea's internal affairs by the great powers increased, as they were intent on gaining rights for mining, logging, and building transportation and communication networks. As the guarantor of Kojong's safety, Russia, in particular, was able to expand its presence rapidly. Upon Kojong's request, Russia dispatched financial and military advisors while securing mining and logging rights. Other great powers scrambled. The United States won rights to mine gold in Unsan, P'yŏngan and to construct railway and electric power lines, while Britain, France, and Germany also gained a wide variety of concessions. Japan concentrated its effort on constructing railways across Korea to extend Japanese influence into mainland Northeast Asia. Ultimately, Japan won rights to build the Hansŏng-Pusan, Hansŏng-Ŭiju, and Hansŏng-Inch'ŏn Railways.

During the Kwangmu Reform, many government officials and well-to-do private individuals tried to resist foreign economic infiltration and build a modern national economy. Influenced by Western capitalism, bureaucrats who handled government finances led an effort to increase production and promote the industry. Instituting the Mint Bureau, the government pursued currency reform, established a central bank, and gathered Korean investors to establish business corporations. Also, the government and private individuals alike founded schools to build a workforce educated for industrial technology. When and where possible, Korea attempted to develop land and mines on its own without involving foreigners. And during rice shortages due to a bad harvest in a particular region, responsible officials temporarily banned local rice export.

Manufacturers and merchants actively invested their efforts in economic development. In such sectors as iron and brass manufacturing, which produced farming equipment and other daily necessities, rice milling, and textile weaving, they built factories, imported new machines, and raised capital to launch joint ventures, including the nation's first joint-stock company, Korean Ramie Spinning, Ltd. (1897). Merchants and officials collaborated in setting up trading companies, financial institutions, and factories. Such non-governmental organizations as the Independence Club and the Imperial Central Commerce Association presented proposals for promoting the industry, protecting Korean merchants, and resisting concession grabbing by the great powers. When necessary, merchants protested foreign economic presence by going on strikes and closing down their shops.

Ultimately, Japanese aggression stymied all such efforts. During the Russo-Japanese War, Japan forced Korea to accept a Japanese financial advisor, and subsequently, Japan gained control of the government's finances vis-à-vis revenue collection and expenditure; nationalized the royal household income, thus financially strapping Kojong and his family; and took over state land and royal estates for building railways and military bases. After the war, Japan carried out a currency reform (1905–09), which replaced the old currency with a new one and effectively reduced the Korean government, financial institutions, and businesses to bankruptcy. As Japanese migration to Korea accelerated, Japan acquired much Korean land at a giveaway price for its own settlement and other purposes. By contrast, ordinary Korean farmers could obtain only very high-interest loans from the now Japanese-controlled government, and those who defaulted on their loans lost their lands. To facilitate land acquisition in Korea, Japan set up the Oriental Development Company (1908), which brought Japanese farmers to Korea and sold them the newly acquired land for cultivation.

Various patriotic movements sought to save the nation from the Japanese economic takeover. During the Russo-Japanese War, when Japan attempted to grab a vast amount of state land with the pretext of wasteland reclamation, a vigorous resistance led by the Korea Preservation Society thwarted the attempt. As the Japanese economic infiltration accelerated in 1905, many Koreans founded business corporations. Seeking to strengthen national sovereignty through overcoming economic dependency, patriotic businesspeople and intellectuals launched the National Debt Repayment Movement (1907–08), which sought to raise funds to pay off the debt that Japan had artfully imposed on the government. Koreans from all walks of life contributed money saved through self-sacrifice, including quitting smoking or selling ornamental hairpins and rings. Still, the movement ultimately failed to achieve its goal due to Japanese obstruction. The effort, though, made a lasting social impact, as it sharpened a collective, national consciousness across status boundaries.

THE DEMISE OF THE HEREDITARY STATUS SYSTEM

Throughout Korea, social reform movements challenging the hereditary status system were gaining strength. Around 1874, the Enlightenment Party emerged as some aristocrats and *chungin* from Hansŏng and vicinity who had inherited Practical Learning ideas pursued various Western ideas and institutions for creating a modern society with equality for all. It was the more radical members of this group, such as Kim Okkyun, Pak Yŏnghyo, and Sŏ Kwangbŏm (1859–97), who had engineered the failed 1884 Kapsin Coup. They upheld equality through such manifest goals as abolishing *yangban* privileges and appointing officials from diverse backgrounds instead, based on merit. In rural areas of the south, the Tonghak too advocated the equality of all humans through such dictates as "the people are heaven," which preached worshipping heaven by serving fellow human beings. The Tonghak religion spread rapidly, especially among ordinary farmers and poor rural *yangban*, culminating in the 1894 Tonghak Uprising.

Although initiated by a pro-Japanese government and thus widely unpopular, the Kabo Reform nonetheless addressed aspirations of the Tonghak and the Enlightenment Party. The reform banned the institutionalized *yangban*-commoner distinction, slavery, child marriage, the prohibition against a widow's remarriage, human trafficking, torture during interrogations, and the assumption of guilt by association. Replacing the traditional government service examination system, the Kabo Reform instituted a new personnel system that sought to appoint officials regardless of social status, and set up a framework for a modern legal system through separating judiciary and executive powers.

Subsequent patriotic movements too endeavored to transcend status distinctions. In general, enlightenment movements, educational associations, newspapers, and magazines sought to heighten the public's awareness of such concepts as nationhood, civil rights, and equality. In particular, the Independence Club was active, as its leaders sought to educate the public about civil rights and equality. A small yet growing segment of the population read the club mouthpiece and first non-governmental newspaper, *The Independent*; attended various public lectures and debates; and despite diverse backgrounds, even joined the club. Years later, the National Debt Repayment

Movement also drew widespread support—almost regardless of sex, age, locality, and social status—thus fostering a shared national identity. Not only did a preponderance of commoners join the righteous armies that arose in the waning years of the Empire of Korea, in many cases, the command and leadership exercised by commoners significantly contributed to breaking down traditional status barriers.

Traditional status distinctions, however, also persisted and remained widespread. Certainly, marriages between the local *yangban* families who used to dominate local councils and the nouveau riche who had begun to secure memberships in such bodies in the eighteenth century became more common. By the mid-nineteenth century, the latter had more or less fully assumed the various cultural trappings that the old aristocracy had used to monopolize power, including Confucian education, proper rituals, ancestral shrines, lineage graves, and genealogies. All the same, and even though more purely professional interactions increasingly transcended old status distinctions, marriage remained a conservative social institution. Thus an illegitimate daughter of a *yangban* father either married an illegitimate son of a *yangban* male or became the concubine of a *yangban* man, and specialist *chungin* too maintained the same custom. Many non-*yangban* parents still preferred to make their daughters become concubines of males of higher social status rather than marry them to men of their own status.

Besides equality in terms of hereditary social standing, the long, still continuing improvement in women's status also began during this era. Coupled with Western influence through Christianity, both Enlightenment Thought and the Tonghak stressed all humans' equality, regardless of gender. They advocated education for women by establishing schools specifically for females. Protestant missionaries were especially active, founding Ewha School in 1886 in Hansŏng (Figure 9.3). Including Ewha and others like it, such new schools sought to educate girls and young women in literature, the arts, and the Christian mission. Before long, male reformers who had received a Western education, such as Philip Jaisohn and Yun Ch'iho (1865–1945), began advocating women's liberation through the Independence Club activities. Encouraged by these reform movements, the first Korean women's rights organization, the Ch'anyang Association (1898), issued Korea's first declaration of women's rights. Led by elite women, the group promoted women's education. Among other groups, the Association of Women Friends (1899) staged a sit-in demonstration to protest such customs as concubinage. Albeit

FIGURE 9.3   Students of Ewha School, 1900s. Everyone is shown with his or her Western nickname and Korean family name handwritten in the Latin alphabet. Source: Ewha Womans University Museum.

slowly, the government responded by establishing the first public school for females, Hansŏng Girls High School (1908). Thanks in part to such educational opportunities, more women joined political movements.

Yet the workdays of women of lower status and men of traditionally denigrated occupations changed little. Even though legally manumitted, many former slaves stayed with their former owners. Also, *kisaeng* continued to make a living as professional entertainers on demand. Those best off were former government-registered *kisaeng*, who were elegant, sophisticated preservers of traditional styles of singing and dancing. As they generally attended special *kisaeng* training schools, joined *kisaeng* unions, and eventually married, they had more stable lives than other *kisaeng* who also offered sex for money.

Unlike *kisaeng* and other professionals, many Koreans who lacked means of livelihood fled hardship by migrating to Manchuria. Just across the Yalu and Tumen Rivers, Manchuria was relatively accessible, abounded with land that could be reclaimed for cultivation, and offered resources that could support people who took up hunting or logging. A trickle that began in the 1860s turned into a wave of migrants, and by 1910, over 200,000 Koreans were living in the region, especially in Jiandao. As righteous army fighters and Patriotic Enlightenment Movement activists fleeing from Japanese suppression in Korea joined the initial wave, this Korean diaspora became a foreign base for nationalist activities. Local Korean schools heightened patriotic sentiment, supported anti-Japanese independence armies, and collaborated with nationalist groups still inside Korea.

Another major destination for Korean migrants was the Russian Maritime Province. In 1860, Russia had acquired the province from Qing China, and it was accepting Korean migrants to develop the region. Consequently, an increasing number of Koreans crossed the Tumen River into the province and cultivated land granted by the Russian government or reclaimed wasteland. By the early twentieth century, over 80,000 were living in more than 100 ethnic Korean villages, especially in Vladivostok and Khabarovsk. As they were self-governed and maintained Korean schools, the migrants effectively turned the province also into an operations base for continuing pro-independence activities.

In comparison, Korean migration to the United States was more closely regulated by both the host nation and Korea. As Hawaiian plantation owners were having difficulty finding enough laborers either locally or elsewhere, the United States requested migrant workers from Korea. Accordingly, the Korean government recruited farmers willing to work in Hawaii, and the first group arrived in 1903. Within three years, over 7,000 Koreans were living on the island. Besides working on sugar cane plantations, the migrants also worked in railroad construction and land reclamation projects, all arduous. And compared to Koreans in Russia or Manchuria, they experienced more blatant racial discrimination. As a way to overcome such hardship, these Koreans formed close-knit communities, primarily through their schools and churches. Eventually, some moved to the continental United States, Mexico, Cuba, and elsewhere in the Americas.

At nearly the same time, ethnic Chinese began to arrive and settle in Korea. Chinese migrants to other parts of Asia usually came from the South China coasts; however, 90 percent of the Chinese migrants to Korea came from East China's Shandong, just across the Yellow Sea from Korea, and most spoke Mandarin or Shanghainese rather than Cantonese. At the turn of the twentieth century, Shandong was hard hit by famine, drought, and banditry. Also, Qing China's meddling in Korea's internal affairs from 1882 to 1894 and vigorous promotion of Chinese commercial interests in Korea encouraged many Chinese to move. Thanks to their superior access to loans, Chinese merchants competed well against their Japanese counterparts. Compared to Japanese traders who tended to be more interested in quick profits, the Chinese cultivated relationships with Korean customers. Not confined to treaty ports, many also conducted business in inland regions. After starting in Inch'ŏn, they also settled at other ports and cities, especially Hansŏng, Pusan, and P'yŏngyang, as well as Sinŭiju, P'yŏngan, and Ch'ŏngjin, Hamgyŏng. The first Chinese school in Korea opened in 1902 in Inch'ŏn, and by 1910, the Chinese population in Korea was about 12,000, and it included the ancestors of contemporary Korea's largest ethnic minority. Their lives marked the beginning of the slow, ongoing transformation of Korean identity to its modern, more multicultural form.

OLD AND NEW CULTURES

In the late nineteenth century, Northern Learning evolved into Enlightenment Thought. While resisting demands for relations and trade by Western powers and Meiji Japan, the Taewŏn'gun showed keen interest in Western military technology in particular. In contrast, the Enlightenment Party advocated more broadscale adoption of Western technology to enrich the state and strengthen the military. Subsequently, during Kojong's personal rule, his Eastern Ways–Western Implements Reform sought to adopt Western technology while keeping Korean civilization intact in terms of moral values and customs. To import Western institutions and technology, Kojong invited foreign technicians and dispatched a "courtiers' observation mission" to Japan and an envoy delegation that included students to Qing China (1881). As the government implemented the Eastern Ways–Western Implements Reform, the Office of Culture and Information published a newspaper, the Machine Factory manufactured Western-style weapons, and the Mint Bureau produced new money.

Treaty ports accelerated the introduction of modern facilities for communication, transportation, electricity, medicine, and architecture. Beginning in Hansŏng, the spread of modern technology began to change daily life in many ways. The commencement of telegraph service integrated Korea into a more modern international communication network; telephone service became available in the Kyŏngbok Palace and for the elite of Hansŏng;

electric light illuminated the palace in the evenings; trolleys transported goods and people across the capital; and electricity became available for private homes in some parts of Hansŏng. After the opening of the Hansŏng-Inch'ŏn Railway, Japan constructed both the Hansŏng-Pusan and Hansŏng-Ŭiju Railways to support its military operations during the Russo-Japanese War. Such new buildings as the Myŏngdong Cathedral; the Tŏksu Palace compound's Sŏkchojŏn, where the emperor received foreign dignitaries; and Kwanghyewŏn, a modern medical facility, all employed Western architecture. The new technology benefited the people's lives in many ways, but having to rely on foreigners for its implementation and management was a heavy financial burden on the government.

For most Koreans, much more accessible and appealing were forms of technology and knowledge that built on tradition, especially in medicine. The theory of "constitution medicine" (ch'ejil ŭihak) advanced by Yi Chema (1837–1900) became particularly influential. In his Longevity and Life Preservation in Korean Medicine (Tongŭi suse powŏn; 1894), Yi classifies human physical constitutions into four broad categories: greater yang, greater yin, lesser yang, and lesser yin. The treatise recognizes that treatment of an ailment can vary depending on the patient's constitution. The work remains well regarded even today in traditional East Asian medicine.

Especially in urban areas, however, various Western ideas began to eclipse those traditional thoughts, and the concept of social Darwinism, in particular, won over the educated, starting with the Enlightenment Party. Earlier in the nineteenth century, Britain's Herbert Spencer (1820–1903) and others had applied the biological theory of evolution as laid out by Charles Darwin (1809–82) to human society. Understanding international relations in terms of the weak falling prey to the strong and the survival of the fittest, social Darwinism provided a justifying logic for the control of weaker nations by imperialist powers. Thus, not only accepted by the Enlightenment Party bent on "nurturing actual strength" (sillyŏk yangsŏng) with a prosperous state and a strong military, social Darwinism potentially also rationalized Japan's aggression against Korea.

Upon the opening of Korea's ports, both the Enlightenment Party and the government endeavored to disseminate modern education by establishing new schools. A private school, the Wŏnsan Academy, was the first to provide a modern education (1883). The government opened the Foreign Language School to train interpreters in various Western languages (1883) and the

English Academy to educate elite parents' sons in Western-style learning (1886). Following Kojong's Edict on Nation Building through Education, issued during the Kabo Reform, the government established primary schools; normal schools, including Hansŏng Teachers College (1895; present-day College of Education, Seoul National University); and foreign language schools (1895). The Hansŏng Middle School, Medical School, Commerce and Industry School, and Kwangmu School soon followed (1899). The emerging modern education system adopted such new textbooks as *Elementary School Reader for Citizens* (*Kungmin sohak tokpon*) and *Elementary Korean History* (*Ch'odŭng pon'guk yŏksa*). Simultaneously, Protestant missionaries from the United States and other countries founded private schools geared toward spreading the Christian faith, while a growing number of Korean private schools and reformed village schools sought to educate the people as members of a modern nation-state. Among these Korean efforts were schools founded in the early twentieth century by Patriotic Enlightenment Movement activists as a part of their efforts to save the nation through a curriculum designed to heighten national consciousness.

In such a milieu, the study of the nation's culture, as initiated earlier by the Practical Learning, became popular, and the Korean language attracted attention. The Kabo Reform adopted a Sino-Korean mixed script, using *han'gŭl* and Sinographs together for government documents and textbooks; thus enabling closer correspondence between the written and spoken languages. Yu Kilchun employed mixed script in writing his widely read work *Observations from Travels in the West* (*Sŏyu kyŏnmun*; 1895), which presents his understandings and thoughts about the history, geography, industry, politics, and customs of the various Western nations he visited, and which contributed significantly to disseminating the script. Subsequently, the Korean Language Institute, founded and led by Chi Sŏgyŏng (1855–1935) and Chu Sigyŏng (1876–1914), began to take stock of Korean literature and to pursue a more systematic understanding of the Korean language (1907).

The effort to heighten national consciousness through modern education also inspired new books in Korean history. Such nationalist intellectuals as Pak Ŭnsik (1859–1925) and Sin Ch'aeho (1880–1936) actively pursued historical research, on which they based their works emphasizing Korea's agency and thus inspiring patriotism. They sought to heighten people's resolve for national independence by writing biographies of individuals who saved their nations and by translating foreign works on various countries' rise and fall.

Sin Ch'aeho laid the foundation for Korean nationalist historiography, in opposition to Japanese colonial historiography, with his column, *A New Way of Reading History* (*Toksa sillon*), for the English-Korean bilingual *Korea Daily News* (*Taehan maeil sinbo*). Around the same time, Pak Ŭnsik, Ch'oe Namsŏn (1890–1957), and others organized the Society for Refurbishing Korea's Literary Legacy, which began to republish and disseminate the classics, including the works of Practical Learning scholars.

The production of works reflecting on the nation's past was accompanied by the publication of periodicals, utilizing modern printing technology, that disseminated Enlightenment Thought and promoted patriotism. Published in 1883 by the Office of Culture and Information, the first modern official gazette, *Thrice-Monthly Hansŏng Gazette* (*Hansŏng sunbo*), featured domestic news and introduced Western cultures, albeit written in Literary Sinitic and with a pro-Japanese slant, before the failure of the Japanese-supported Kapsin Coup brought an end to that effort. More than a decade later, the publishers of the Korean-language edition of *The Independent,* who were overall favorably disposed toward Britain, Japan, and the United States, employed *han'gŭl*, thus reaching for a much broader readership, while also using an English edition to publicize Korea's modernization effort among foreigners. By contrast, the *Capital Gazette* (*Hwangsŏng sinmun*) used a mixed Sino-Korean script, albeit still seeking to heighten national consciousness. When criticizing the Protectorate Treaty, the *Capital Gazette* printed a fiery editorial, "Today We Cry Out in Lamentation" (Siil ya pangsŏng taegok) by Chang Chiyŏn (1864–1921). Thereafter, the *Korea Daily News,* which greatly facilitated the dissemination of *han'gŭl*, led such patriotic efforts as the National Debt Repayment Movement and a public campaign to oppose Japan's wasteland reclamation effort. Likewise, the *Imperial Post* (*Cheguk sinmun*), also a *han'gŭl* newspaper, and *Long Live Korea News* (*Mansebo*), which was a mixed script daily, published by the followers of Chondoism (Ch'ŏndogyo; "Religion of the Heavenly Way"), the reorganized Tonghak, spearheaded a movement to recover national sovereignty and to instill patriotic fervor among their countrymen. Before long, Japan imposed pre-publication censorship, and the Newspaper Law (1907) cracked down on nationalistic journalism.

Although of more limited circulation among the general public, literary works began to introduce their readership to modern thought and to urge social awakening at the turn of the twentieth century. Around 1908, a new-style *han'gŭl* poem by Ch'oe Namsŏn, "From the Sea to Youth" (Hae egesŏ sonyŏn ege), and the so-called New Novel appeared, articulating new moral values and thus reflecting spreading social change at the time. Also, a wide variety of translated Western works, such as the Bible, *The Pilgrim's Progress* by John Bunyan (1628–88), *Robinson Crusoe* by Daniel Defoe (1660–1731), and *Gulliver's Travels* by Jonathan Swift (1667–1745), gained a readership. They not only fostered the development of modern Korean literature but also fanned a blind admiration for all things Western.

Like literature, religion increasingly engaged with the changing dynamics of ideas and forces, old and new, East and West. Treaty relations between Korea and France (1886) allowed missionaries to propagate Catholicism. Likewise, upon the arrival of Protestant missionaries from the United States and other mostly Protestant countries in the 1880s, Protestantism gradually gained a following. While Christianity won converts, the Tonghak tried to regroup after the suppression of their rebellion and eventually reorganized themselves as Chondoists (1905), under Ch'oe Sihyŏng's successor, Son Pyŏnghŭi (1861–1922), who purged the organization of pro-Japanese elements. Even more nationalistic was a new indigenous religion, Daejongism (Taejonggyo; "Great Ancestral Religion"; 1909), which worshiped Tan'gun as the progenitor of the Korean people and the national founder. As such, Daejongism actively participated in anti-Japanese movements. In part addressing the new religions in a changing world, Pak Ŭnsik's article "Search for a New Confucianism" (Yugyo ku sillon; 1909), and similar writings by a new generation of Confucian scholars, advocated a modernized Confucianism more in touch with the ordinary people—in tandem with modern education and the Patriotic Enlightenment Movement. Among Buddhists, Han Yongun (1849–1944) urged the recovery of Buddhism's distinct identity and roles in ways relevant to modern Korea.

Mirroring these trends in religion and other cultural spheres, artists dissociated from the government in increasing numbers and became professionals working for private clients. Some learned and produced Western-style artworks, such as oil paintings, but more traditional works employing realism remained the mainstream, especially in portraiture. Realistic landscape paintings and genre paintings also enjoyed a revival. Chang Sŭngŏp (1843–97) demonstrated his talent through powerful brush strokes and unique coloring techniques. Unlike his peers, most of whom came from specialist *chungin* families of court painters, Chang was a self-made man, orphaned as a child, and a creative genius who thrived as an independent painter throughout much of his career, despite a stint at the court. While his works fetched high prices among patrons across social boundaries, the ordinary people remained fond of folk paintings.

Likewise, the era's performing arts show elements of both continuity and change. A celebrated *p'ansori* singer, Sin Chaehyo (1812–84), reinterpreted and compiled songs to cater to the aristocracy while training the first group of notable female singers. Influenced by both *p'ansori* and *sinawi*, which is improvisational ensemble music accompanying shaman rituals, a new genre, *sanjo* ("scattered melodies"), emerged as instrumental solo folk music performed with an initial slow rhythm that becomes fast. In the 1890s, *ch'angga* ("sung lyric") began to grow in popularity, initially sung to *sijo* or traditional song lyrics. Adjusting to and influencing emerging new forms of poetry, freer from older rhyming conventions, vocalists began to sing *ch'angga* with more Western-style melodies. Western influence also gave rise to the New Drama movement, which received a boost when the government built Korea's first Western-style theater, Won'gaksa (1909). The venue featured productions not only of the New Drama but also a wide variety of performing arts, old and new. For the most part, *p'ansori* and masked plays remained the most popular performing arts among ordinary people. A new trend in *p'ansori* performances in Korea was the popularity of productions featuring many vocalists.

Like the entertainers, most Koreans continued to don traditional dress, but some new fashion trends emerged. The Tonghak Uprising and the Kabo Reform raised awareness of equality as reflected in accouterments. In the spirit of progress, the Enlightenment Party members and followers and many other male elites abandoned their topknots in favor of short, Western hairstyles; donned suits instead of *hanbok*; and wore socks and hard-soled shoes. A more typical fashion, though, was *hanbok* comprising pants and a basic upper garment, *chŏgori*, as before, but additionally with a vest on top of the *chŏgori* and an outer jacket, *magoja*, worn with or without an overcoat, *turumagi*. In comparison, women's fashion was more conservative, as most continued to wear the traditional skirt and *chŏgori*. Before long, a modified *hanbok* modeled after Western missionary women's dresses appeared, gradually becoming both the de facto school uniform and the everyday attire for young women of Western education. As the frequency of women venturing outside the house increased, even among elites, and as they became more socially active, many donned a *turumagi*. Outer jacket-shaped veils and skirt-shaped veils which women had been using to cover their faces while out began to give way to parasols.

Increased contact with foreign countries also introduced new culinary cultures, although these did not fundamentally change most people's diets. Besides Western varieties of apples, which spread quickly, Protestant missionaries introduced new nutritional concepts and a custom of eating a meal together with a group seated around a table. More traditionally, not only was eating alone from a personal table the norm, but a man and a woman, or a *yangban* and a commoner, sharing a table was unthinkable in a proper public setting. Also, beginning with palace personnel and capital elites, some began to use a fork along with the spoon for a meal; to consume coffee, black tea, bread, cookies, and pastries; and to experience Western cuisine and dining etiquette. Simultaneously, some Qing merchants who had entered Korea after the Imo Mutiny opened Chinese eateries, serving a variety of Chinese dishes and simpler fare such as dumplings and steamed buns with fillings. The Japanese, who began arriving in a larger number during the First Sino-Japanese War, introduced sushi, udon, fishcakes, sweet red mung bean porridge, *takuan* (pickled daikon radish), and sake.

Besides the diet and clothing alternatives now available, Korea's housing culture began to undergo a transformation. With sumptuary laws effectively abolished, *chungin* who had been frustrated by a glass ceiling for centuries were now free to build and live in houses no different from those of *yangban*. Especially in Hansŏng, well-to-do *chungin* homes began to feature a large living quarter for males and a tile-roofed main entry gate flanked by two small rooms, features previously restricted to aristocratic homes, and many *yangban* responded by replacing such a gate with a simpler one. Once the Westerners and the Japanese began to reside in Korea, with foreign government legations and consulates built in Hansŏng and the treaty ports, their architectural styles inspired the styling of some new Korean constructions, including government offices, schools, commercial buildings, and places for religious gatherings. More commonly, though, many new houses and buildings were syncretic, featuring a few of the new features such as glass windows, a brick wall, an exterior wall coated with limestone plaster, a red tile roof, a roof-top water tank, or steam-air interior heating. Although the use of glass, bricks, cement, and concrete became more common, most Koreans continued to live in typical late Chosŏn-style dwellings, with either tile or thatched roofs.

CHAPTER 10

Japanese Occupation,
1910–1945

M ost Koreans went on with their lives under Japanese occupation. Japan's overall policy underwent three phases: a military rule of coercive measures (1910–19), an "enlightened administration" that made some concessions to Koreans while cultivating collaborators (1919–31), and the wartime mobilization of Korea for Japan's expanding war effort (1931–45). The Korean nationalist response ranged from armed resistance to organized lobbying among foreign powers to self-strengthening movements to active, pro-Japanese collaboration. Until Japan's defeat by the Allies, its economic policy controlled and dedicated colonial Korea's production for Imperial Japan's glory while fostering as a junior partner a new generation of Koreans who prospered as landlords, business leaders, and industrialists. Continuing urbanization and industrialization, an expanding education system, and a colorful spectrum of Korean nationalist movements set off a social revolution. As Japan also intensified its cultural assimilation policy, patriotic Koreans promoted Korean culture, history, and language, but those of education and influence generally worked with the colonial authorities.

THE POLITICS OF COLONIAL RULE

During the first nine years of the colonial administration, Imperial Japan maintained a heavy-handed military rule. Pensioning off the former Korean government leadership, Japan replaced its Residency-General of Korea with a

Government-General of Korea (1910–45). A retired Japanese military general, the governor-general reported directly to the Japanese emperor and exercised not only legislative and judicial power but also a military command. To the extent feasible, Japan utilized willing Koreans. Although, for the most part replacing Korean provincial governors and county magistrates within two years or so after the annexation, the government-general left indigenous district heads (*myŏnjang*) in their positions as they tended to be men of influence, if not local *yangban*. Certainly not relying on them, Japan stationed more than 20,000 Japanese gendarmeries throughout Korea. Assisted by locally hired Koreans, gendarmeries had the power to conduct summary trials for minor criminal acts, subjecting only Koreans to such punishments as whipping: banned during the Kabo Reform but revived in the name of cultural sensitivity.

Unlike the ethnic Japanese who enjoyed the rights guaranteed by Japan's Meiji Constitution (1890–1947), ethnic Koreans were without freedom of speech, assembly, the press, or association. The government-general disbanded virtually all formal Korean organizations. To suppress the continuing anti-Japanese activism of Christian groups based in P'yŏngan and of the New People's Association, the authorities fabricated a conspiracy to assassinate the first governor-general, Terauchi Masatake (1852–1919). In 1911, the government-general arrested over 600 nationalist leaders, imprisoning 105 (105-Man Incident). As Japan's brutal suppression campaign continued, Korean armed resistance armies and patriotic enlightenment groups quickly lost ground. Those who survived went underground or relocated to Manchuria or the Russian Maritime Province, where they reestablished their operation bases. As the resistance groups in and outside Korea maintained covert communication, the former emperor, Kojong, played his part: secretly exhorting resistance, funding some groups, and belatedly seeking an opportunity to join one in North Hamgyŏng to head a government in exile. Kojong had waited too long, in part through being mindful of his third son, Imperial Prince Yŏng (1897–1970), who had been studying in Japan since 1907 as Japan's de facto hostage.

Colonial Korea's growing resentment toward the occupier exploded with the March First Movement. Encouraged by the principle of national self-determination that U.S. president Woodrow Wilson (1856–1924) articulated upon the ending of World War I, on February 8, 1919, Korean students in Tokyo publicly proclaimed Korea's independence. The symbolic gesture inspired Korea's nationalist leaders to do likewise on March first, the day of the funeral for Kojong, who had died suddenly in January—likely poisoned on the governor-general's secret order. The word spread fast, and the news of the declaration of Korean independence by thirty-three nationalist leaders turned the mournful crowd into protesters. Beginning in Kyŏngsŏng (Ja. Keijō; present-day Seoul), renamed from Hansŏng, demonstrations by students, members of religious groups, merchants, and wage laborers spread to other cities, towns, and villages. At first, protests were peaceful as participants cheerfully shouted, "Long live independent Korea!" Gradually, many began to attack gendarmerie stations, subcounty offices, the Oriental Development Company offices, and landlords perceived as pro-Japanese collaborators. The government-general responded decisively, mobilizing military force, and suppressing the uprising by the beginning of May. According to the government-general's record, at least one million Koreans participated in the protests, more than 7,500 were killed, and some 47,000 were arrested.

The March First Movement prompted immediate reactions from Japanese and Koreans alike. The demonstrations led to a more organized, longterm nationalist struggle, and various groups pursuing the cause joined the Provisional Government of the Republic of Korea. Established in Shanghai on April 11, 1919, the Provisional Government elected as its president Syngman Rhee (Yi Sŭngman; 1875–1965), a prominent, American-educated independence activist and the future first president of South Korea. However, the group suffered an initial setback when a covert operation to escort Imperial Prince Ŭi (1877–1955)—Kojong's second son, who was American educated as well and sympathetic to the cause—from Kyŏngsŏng to Shanghai failed, with the prince placed under de facto house arrest by the colonial authorities in November 1919. Meanwhile, in Manchuria, nationalists organized independence armies to continue guerrilla warfare against the Japanese. Within Korea, various underground patriotic organizations arose, including the Korean Patriotic Women's Society (1919–20), which collected funds for resistance activities inside and outside Korea. The March First Movement also prompted Japan to replace its military rule with what it described as "cultural rule" (or "enlightened administration"). Underneath the veneer of these more accommodating gestures of the occupier, its massive, omnipresent instruments of coercion still lurked. The governmentgeneral replaced the gendarme with regular police—half of whom were Koreans—but both the force's size and the quantity of equipment increased.

While cracking down on any expression of resistance, Japan capitalized on the expanding debate among Korean activists and intellectuals on the future course of resistance.

The debate centered around the right strategies for achieving independence and the form of government for an independent Korea. By 1919, nationalism, socialism, and anarchism, in particular, appealed to many activists and intellectuals. While nationalists pursued the ideal of an independent, capitalist nation-state, leftists advocated a socialist nation-state centered around wage laborers and tenant farmers. In stark contrast, anarchists rejected all forms of governing organization, political power, and class interests.

In the 1920s, an increasing number of the more moderate if not compromising cultural nationalists became willing to work with the colonial state. As educated, influential Koreans who saw the futility of outright resistance, cultural nationalists prioritized local autonomy rather than national independence. Also, they focused on empowering the people through economic development and education. Accordingly, cultural nationalists pushed to establish a "people's university" (*millip taehak*) and to produce goods indigenously. As their efforts gained traction, the government-general accommodated cultural nationalists, dividing and weakening overall Korean nationalist activism within the colony. The issue of whether Koreans should pursue local autonomy while accepting colonial rule was especially divisive, and Japan took advantage.

During this decade, some students were less compromising as they pursued a range of activities geared toward educating the masses and protesting Japan's discriminatory education policy. To avoid the government-general's monitoring and oppression, student activists formed secret organizations. When the death and funeral of the former emperor Sunjong sparked the June 10 Movement in 1926, such student groups collaborated with various nationalist groups on organizing demonstrations. The overall scale, however, was far smaller than the March First Movement demonstrations and was quickly suppressed by the police. Not relenting, three years later, students in Kwangju organized the Kwangju Student Independence Movement when some male Japanese students' harassment of female Korean students sparked a clash between Korean and Japanese students. The resulting anti-Japanese protests throughout the colony continued for months, again ultimately suppressed by the police (November 1929–May 1930).

At the same time in the 1920s, socialists pursued independence movements centered around class activism. Emerging in the aftermath of the March First Movement among young adults and intellectuals studying socialist thought introduced from Japan, China, and Russia, the new ideology inspired young adult associations, labor movements, and peasant movements, which not only fought persecution by the government-general but also clashed with nationalists over the general direction of the independence movement. Socialists considerably energized various socioeconomic movements that advocated the rights of wage laborers, tenant farmers, women, and youth. Before long, the nationalists who rejected prioritizing local autonomy reached out to the socialists, who in turn responded positively with the Declaration of the Society of True Friends (1926).

Agreeing to transcend their ideological differences, the two groups formed a new organization, Sin'ganhoe (New Trunk Association, February 1927). Touring the colony, the Sin'ganhoe held lectures and advocated abolition of various colonial organs that exploited Korea, rejection of opportunism, implementation of a Korean-centered education system, and improvement in the standard of living. Putting words into action, the Sin'ganhoe supported strikes by wage laborers, tenant farmers, and students. In 1929, they aided a general strike by the workers in Wŏnsan, and launched a movement to investigate the Japanese massacre of slash-and-burn farmers in Kapsan, South Hamgyŏng. Later in that year, the Sin'ganhoe also dispatched an investigation team during the Kwangju Student Independence Movement, but the colonial police thwarted Sin'ganhoe's attempt to organize a mass rally on the day of announcing the team's findings. Subsequently, the Sin'ganhoe's executive branch split over strategies for continuing the struggle, as socialists and nationalists disagreed, and the organization disbanded (1931).

Also in the 1920s, Korean nationalists outside the colony expanded their operation bases in ethnic Korean settlements in Jiandao and the Russian Maritime Province. They first sought to secure economic security, followed by offering young adults a nationalistic education and military training. At times, the independence armies crossed the Yalu and Tumen Rivers into Korea, raiding colonial government facilities and attacking the military and the police. In 1920, in Jiandao, the Korean Independence Army led by Hong Pŏmdo (1868–1943) defeated a Japanese battalion in the Battle of Fengwudong (Ko. Bongo-dong) and also collaborated with the Northern Military Administration Office Army, under the command of Kim Chwajin

(1889–1930), in routing a Japanese army in the Battle of Qingshanli (Ko. Ch'ŏngsan-ri). The Japanese troops retaliated by massacring more than 10,000 Koreans and burning down some 2,500 homes and at least thirty schools in Jiandao.

Subsequently, the independence armies reorganized themselves. In 1921, when the Japanese launched a massive counteroffensive, the independence armies retreated to Svobodny, Amur Oblast, in the Soviet Union—only to be surrounded by Bolshevik troops, suffering casualties and being forcibly disarmed. Afterward, the surviving independence armies returned to Manchuria, where they sought unity and reorganized into self-governing bodies: the General Staff Headquarters (1924), which reported to the Provisional Government of the Republic of Korea headquartered in Shanghai; the Righteous Government (1924); and the New People's Government (1925). Each maintained its army that occasionally attacked colonial installations and personnel in Korea.

In addition to the independence armies, the anarchist Heroic Corps, founded in 1919 by Kim Wŏnbong (1898–1958), and other groups targeted the organs of colonial rule, high-ranking Japanese personnel, and pro-Japanese Korean collaborators. Their major activities, given these targets, included an assassination attempt with a bomb (1919) by Kang Ugyu (1855–1920) against the newly appointed Governor-General of Korea Saitō Makoto (1858–1936); an attack against the staff office of the government-general with a bomb (1921) and an assassination attempt on a Japanese army general visiting Shanghai (1922), both by Kim Iksang (1895–1943); an attack on Chongno police station in Kyŏngsŏng with a bomb (1923) by Kim Sangok (1890–1923); and bomb attacks on the Oriental Development Company and the Industrial Bank of Korea buildings (1926) by Na Sŏkchu (1892–1926). Of course, Japan, other colonial powers, and the rest who sympathized with them as leaders of human progress saw these incidents as nothing more than terrorist attacks—all nonetheless reminders that not all Koreans accepted the Japanese rule.

Upon the triumph of militarism at home, in the 1930s, Japan intensified its exploitation of Korea to support an expanding war effort. Following its occupation of Manchuria (1931) and invasion of China proper (1937), which commenced the Second Sino-Japanese War, Japan attacked Pearl Harbor, thus initiating the Pacific War (December 1941). Japan's National Mobilization Law (1938) subjected Koreans to work in factories, mines, and labor camps in all parts of the empire. The law implemented "student volunteer corps" and conscription systems to mobilize Korean males as military support personnel. Not trusting them with arms, only the desperation toward the end of the war compelled Japan to assign combat duties to a small number of Korean draftees. Also, the Japanese government, the military, and private contractors used varying degrees of deception that effectively sent young Korean women to military camps as sex slaves, euphemistically dubbed "comfort women," for the Imperial Japanese Army. The effort became systematic in 1937 after a Japanese court ruling prohibited the government from recruiting Japanese women. The majority of up to 200,000 women who suffered that fate were Koreans (Figure 10.1).

Meanwhile, outside Korea, nationalists continued their anti-Japanese struggle in one form or another. In China proper, Kim Ku (1876–1949) founded the Korean Patriotic Organization (1931), which targeted Japanese facilities, high-profile Japanese individuals, and pro-Japanese Korean collaborators. Among its operatives, Yi Pongch'ang (1900–32) attempted to assassinate Emperor Hirohito (r. 1926–89) in Tokyo by throwing a grenade (1932), and Yun Ponggil (1908–32) used a grenade to kill several Japanese dignitaries during a celebration of Japan's occupation of Shanghai (1932). In Manchuria, most independence fighters reorganized themselves around the Korean Independence Army and the Korean Revolutionary Army. Upon Japan's occupation of Manchuria, such resistance groups collaborated with the Chinese Nationalist Party army and scored some victories against the Japanese. Likewise, communist Koreans such as Kim Il-sung and the region's Communist Party of China (CPC) army operated jointly as the Northeast Anti-Japanese United Army. Centered around the Heroic Corps, they even secured the Chinese Nationalist Party government's cooperation in organizing the Korean Volunteer Corps. In such leftist guerrilla units, women fought alongside men.

Armed Korean resistance outside Korea continued during the Second Sino-Japanese War. In Manchukuo (1932–45), the Japanese puppet state established in Manchuria, Kim Il-sung and other resistance fighters who had not suffered extermination by or surrendered to the Japanese retreated to the Soviet Union. Others in North China formed the socialist Korean Independence League (1942), which organized its own troops, the Korean Volunteer Army (1942), separate from the Korean Volunteer Corps. Collaborating with the CPC, the Korean Volunteer Army battled against Japanese troops. When the Japanese advance through China proper forced the Chinese Nationalist Party to relocate

FIGURE 10.1   Former Korean sex slaves being questioned by the U.S. Army personnel in Myitkyina, August 14, 1944. Source: National Archives and Records Administration.

to Chongqing, the Provisional Government of the Republic of Korea followed. That organization united various Korean resistance groups from its new head-quarters and established the Korean Restoration Army (1940). Declaring war on Japan, the Provisional Government contributed a small military unit to the Allied forces at the battlefront in British India and Burma, aiding them with reconnaissance (1941).

As the Pacific War's tide shifted in their favor, the Allied leaders began to formulate plans for Asia's future upon Japan's defeat, and Korea was on the agenda. In November 1943, at the Cairo Conference, U.S. president Franklin D. Roosevelt (1882–1945), British prime minister Winston Churchill (1874–1965), and the leader of the Republic of China, Chiang Kai-shek (1887–1975), agreed that Japan should relinquish all the territories it had conquered by force and that in due course Korea should become independent. Roosevelt also proposed a trusteeship for Korea; neither Churchill nor Chiang agreed.

Later in November and December of 1943 at the Teheran Conference and in February 1945 at the Yalta Conference, Roosevelt again raised the idea. Soviet leader Joseph Stalin (1878–1953), who had replaced Chiang as an Allied leader invited to the conference, agreed but also proposed a short period of trustee-ship. He promised to join the Allies in the Pacific War two or three months after defeating Nazi Germany. On August 8, three months after Germany's surrender and two days after the United States detonated an atomic bomb over Hiroshima, the Soviet Union declared war on Japan. As Soviet troops advanced across Manchukuo, U.S. president Harry S. Truman (1884–1972), who had succeeded Roosevelt and was alarmed over the establishment of communist governments by the Soviet Red Army in Eastern Europe, feared the same outcome in Korea and elsewhere in Northeast Asia. On August 10, two American officers assigned the task of defining an American occupation zone in Korea chose the thirty-eighth parallel to divide the region into pro-posed American and Soviet occupation zones. Although the Soviets could have quickly occupied the entirety of Korea, Stalin accepted the American proposal. Soviet forces began amphibious landings in Korea on August 14 and occupied northeastern Korea. On the following day, Japan offered its unconditional surrender to the Allies.

By then, Korean nationalist groups had been preparing for Korea's lib-eration. In 1941, the Provisional Government's Korean Independence Party, which Kim Ku had formed in 1930, announced the Program for the Founding of the Republic of Korea. Based on the Principle of Three Equalities of Cho Soang (1887–1958), which advocated individual-to-individual, nation-to-nation, and state-to-state equality, the program stipulated establishing a democratic republic through a general election. In the following year, in North China, various resistance groups in Manchukuo formed the Korean Independence League. In Korea, Lyuh Woon-hyung (Yŏ Unhyŏng; 1886–1947) organized the Korean National Foundation League (August 1944–August 1945). Both groups articulated principles for establishing a democratic republic. The Ko-rean Restoration Army was preparing to collaborate with the United States on invading Korea when Japan surrendered. What awaited the leadership was an economy ruined by Imperial Japan's wars of aggression.

ECONOMIC DEVELOPMENT AND EXPLOITATION

Upon annexing Korea, Japan had initiated a cadastral survey as the first step toward strengthening its control of the colonial economy (1910). Accelerated by the new Land Survey Ordinance (1912), the project sought to assess and

record land ownership, value, and use. Since the survey recognized ownership rights only when substantiated by documents, the Government-General
of Korea took over all land that was unregistered or of uncertain ownership
and also the holdings of the former Korean government and the imperial
household. For registered land, the colonial state recognized only the rights
of landlords while denying tenant farmers' customary cultivation rights,
which they had been enjoying for generations, and limited the lease term to
one year. The government-general also levied more land tax by assessing the
land value at high rates and reclassifying more land as taxable.

The colonial economic policy increased hardship among farmers, who
accounted for more than 80 percent of working Koreans. Not only did the
number of tenant farmers on fixed-term leases increase, but they also had
to pay a rent of more than half their harvest and the land tax levied by the
government-general on the landlord. Furthermore, tenant farmers suffered
from high-handed supervisors hired by landlords. Some landowners acquired
more profits from exporting rice to Japan, while more free cultivators lost
their holdings and became tenant farmers. Those who could no longer support themselves migrated to cities and became wage laborers, many joining
the urban poor. Others struggled to survive as miners or slash-and-burn
farmers. Some migrated to Manchuria, the Russian Maritime Province,
Japan, or the Americas.

Besides regulating agriculture, Japan also sought to regulate the corporate sector. The Company Ordinance (1910) required Koreans to get the
government-general's approval to start a company and even to close one. The
ordinance made it difficult for Koreans to found or maintain companies.
Conversely, the economic downturn at the end of World War I spurred Japan
to take a series of measures to aid Japanese corporations doing business in
the colony. Japan also expanded its effort to secure food supplies, including
rice, and industrial raw materials from Korea, and at a low cost.

In the 1920s, the government-general sought to increase rice production to
promote Japanese business interests and meet the increased demand for rice
in the industrialized metropole, but results were mixed. The effort entailed
expanding irrigation facilities, introducing improved rice varieties, and increasing the use of chemical fertilizers. While most landlords saw a modest
increase in their profits, tenant farmers suffered from the increase in various
fees, including those for irrigation cooperative dues and payment for fertilizers. Tenancy disputes became more common as tenant farmers protested
what they deemed unjust terms and conditions of tenancy. During a dispute

in 1923 on the island of Amt'aedo in Muan, South Chŏlla, tenant farmers confronted their landlords and the police. After a standoff lasting nearly a year, the landlords lowered the rent. As in the Amt'aedo case, early tenancy disputes tended to be about farmers' struggle for survival and were aimed at reducing rents. As was true in the previous decade, many independent cultivators fell to tenancy, and many tenant farmers became slash-and-burn farmers, whereas landlords increased their holdings. And Japan took from Korea more rice than the amount of increase in rice produced.

Simultaneously during the decade, more Japanese capital entered the colonial economy as Japan changed the corporate law so that a new Japanese company merely had to register rather than seek a permit. Japanese investment became especially heavy in such sectors as cotton textiles, food processing, and mining, and the continuing industrialization policy drove up the number of Korean industrial laborers. Suffering from long work hours, low wages, and ethnic discrimination, many joined labor movements. The 1929 general strike by workers in Wŏnsan not only received support and encouragement from sympathizers throughout Korea but even workers in other countries sent telegram messages of support. For the most part, the government-general suppressed labor movements to ensure high profitability for Japanese capital investment.

Around 1920, some Korean landlords and merchants of means began to found their own companies. Korean corporate activities increased, centered around the likes of the Kyŏngsŏng Spinning and Weaving Company, undershirt factories in P'yŏngyang, and rubber factories throughout Korea. Advocating an economic nationalism that was both self-serving and appealing to their compatriots, in the early 1920s, many Korean business leaders, journalists, and intellectuals joined hands in a movement to promote indigenous production of goods as a way of achieving economic independence. Beginning in P'yŏngyang, the movement spread to the rest of the colony and continued to the end of the 1930s. For the most part, Korean businesses could not compete with Japanese capital investment, which was fully supported by the government-general. Accordingly, most Korean business leaders managed corporations in the less competitive sectors or ran small- to middle-size factories associated with more traditional household handicraft manufacturing.

In the 1930s, the influx of Japanese capital increased more rapidly as Japan pursued Korea's industrialization. While maintaining the already industrialized part of its empire as the metropole, Japan sought to commit Manchuria to agricultural and raw material production. Korea was to be a transition zone, with mostly light industry. To support Japan's expanding war effort in China, the policy focused on northern Korea by prioritizing increasing the production of electrical power and the procurement of mining resources through cheap land and a cheap workforce. As Japanese investment increased, industries centered around metal and chemical production grew fast, especially in northern Korea. New, large factories increased the number of factory workers, who numbered one million in 1943. Not only did the Japanese possess most of the capital, the majority of the management staff and skilled workers were Japanese. Most Korean employees were unskilled laborers, suffering from all kinds of discrimination that affected their wages and promotion.

With Japan's expanding war effort and economic mobilization of the colony, hardship for factory workers and tenant farmers alike increased further. Factory workers who suffered from low wages and a lack of job security sometimes went on strikes in collaboration with tenant farmers, who suffered from high rent and insecure tenancy terms. In the 1930s, peasant movements mobilized such farmers, as socialists changed their overall strategy. Instead of working with existing, legal agricultural cooperatives, socialists tried to organize revolutionary peasant cooperatives that were illegal, but the colonial authorities' suppression thwarted the effort. The government-general sided with corporate management to maximize profit for Japanese capital and with landlords to facilitate rice export from Korea to Japan.

During the Pacific War, Japan exploited Korea to the fullest extent. The government-general tightened regulation of all economic activities to focus on military supply production and maximize mobilization of all resources. Additional revenue from increased tax levy and savings programs forced upon ordinary households subsidized military supply companies. Also, the colonial state mobilized Koreans to work at munitions factories, mines, and labor camps. As the supply shortage became acute toward the end of the war, the government-general not only intensified its effort to procure as many mineral resources as possible but even confiscated the iron gates of schools and household spoons, thus leaving no part of the society unaffected by the war.

SOCIAL REVOLUTION

Colonial Korea's population grew rapidly to unprecedented levels, and urbanization proceeded apace. As of 1910, the colony's total population was over 13 million, of which Kyŏngsŏng accounted for up to 240,000. By 1940, the capital's population had nearly quadrupled to 930,000, and Korea's total population had nearly doubled to over 25 million as of 1945. In Kyŏngsŏng, the government-general tore down such traditional structures as royal palaces and city gates, partly demolishing some and entirely eradicating others. Japan also constructed the Government-General of Korea headquarters, the city hall, the central train station, parks, and schools. Although more limited in scope, similar changes took place in provincial cities, including a growing number of new urban centers such as Taejŏn, South Ch'ungch'ŏng, a central transportation hub.

In the 1910s, the proportion of the Korean population receiving at least six years of modern education began to increase rapidly, mostly among boys. Although the government-general oversaw the public education system through Japanese officials and principals, Korea already had a sizable group of indigenous educators trained in such institutions as the Hansŏng Teachers College, and the government-general posted them at six-year "ordinary schools" (pot'ong hakkyo). Parents generally enrolled their boys if an ordinary school was reasonably nearby. In contrast, the number of girls enrolled varied widely from none in most rural areas to accounting for nearly half the student body in the cities. Girls in central and northwestern Korea were likely to receive at least six years of public schooling; those in the culturally most conservative inland regions of North Kyŏngsang were the least likely to do so.

Although the government-general ostensibly offered equal educational opportunities to Japanese and Korean children, pervasive discrimination and the self-serving colonial curriculum spurred Korean educators and students to seek alternatives. The number of private schools and reformed village schools that had appeared in the Empire of Korea decreased in the 1920s due to Japanese suppression, but night schools offered more Korean-centered educational content, including the Korean language and history. The newly founded Society for Korean Women's Education actively promoted females' schooling (1920). Furthermore, some of the leading cultural nationalists sought to raise funds to establish a university catering to Koreans. Still, they failed due to suppression by the colonial state, which continued to emphasize lower-level vocational training for Koreans. As the study of advanced modern science and technology remained out of reach for most, some concerned Korean educators founded the Invention Society (1924), which published *Scientific Korea* (*Kwahak Chosŏn*) and organized special events on its specially designated Science Day.

Led and organized by those with formal modern education, many youth groups that emerged played important roles in the post–March First Movement era. Established amidst broader public recognition of adolescents' and young adults' role in pro-independence movements, youth groups organized lectures and debates to promote nationalistic causes. They also opened night schools for those who could not attend regular schools. At the same time, youth organizations actively supported various movements, such as those promoting indigenous production of goods and establishing a people's college. Increasingly influenced by socialism, in 1923, many youth groups began to put more effort into supporting student, peasant, and labor movements.

Along with factory workers and tenant farmers, such traditionally denigrated occupation groups continued to fight against lingering discrimination rooted in the old but still widespread status consciousness. It was true that social interactions among urbanites with modern education transcended traditional status distinctions; specialist *chungin* and educated northerners tended to stop bothering with genealogy compilations; and rural elites from old *yangban* families and the nouveau riche intermarried if both families were of local counselor descent. All the same, even in the 1930s, late Chosŏn political party affiliations still mattered among the capital-region *yangban* families; the most common genre of publications approved by the government-general was genealogy; and local *yangban*-functionary distinctions persisted in more culturally conservative areas. In such a milieu, the government-general's new household registration system marked a butcher's household with the notation "butcher," or simply a red dot. Enrolling a student required a copy of the household register, and many schools refused to admit butchers' children. In 1923, in Chinju, South Kyŏngsang, butchers formed the Equity Society, which demanded equal treatment. Still, most Koreans continued to discriminate against them and their family members, if not actually joining anti-equality movements. Likewise, the *kisaeng* remained a highly visible occupational group. Integrating former *kisaeng* training schools, *kisaeng* unions flourished in such large cities as Kyŏngsŏng, P'yŏngyang, Taegu, and Pusan. Unions offered instructions in proper etiquette, musical performance, and the Japanese language—sending newly trained entertainers to upscale restaurants or arranging performance opportunities for them. From time to time, *kisaeng* acted collectively to go on a strike when their union took an unreasonable portion of their earnings. Those *kisaeng* whose service was more limited to sex work had new competition, as the authorities maintained public prostitution.

Women's overall social consciousness increased as more females received modern education, but the position of most women hardly improved. Nationalism did give many women awareness of their roles in the society and their potential to fight for the betterment of their future. Although women's movements were more concerned with Korean independence than feminism, some religious and civic organizations sought to improve women's socioeconomic position. In the 1920s, more than 200 women's movement groups arose. While most pursued gender equality, promoted literacy among females, and fought against such older customs as concubinage, some went farther. The Women's Youth Alliance (1925–26) advocated a revolutionary class struggle to achieve women's liberation by organizing the female proletariat, and the founders included wives of the Korean communist movement leaders. Another prominent group, Kŭnuhoe (Rose-of-Sharon Friendship Association; 1927–31), was active as a sister organization of the Sin'ganhoe. The Kŭnuhoe promoted women's education and female workers' rights through lectures, debates, and night schools. Upon dissolution of the Sin'ganhoe, though, the Kŭnuhoe too ceased to exist. Subsequently, Japan's wartime mobilization of young women for military camps exposed women's vulnerable position. Upon returning home to Korea, the former sex slaves further suffered from their country's gender hierarchy and patriarchy that ostracized them.

Well before the Japanese state-sponsored recruitment of sex slaves, an increasing number of Koreans, mostly the poor in search of a new life, had begun moving to other parts of the empire. In the 1920s, the demand for labor was high in Japan while Koreans could not find jobs readily in the colony, and the majority of the Korean migrants to Japan were farmers from southern Korea. The number of Koreans in Japan increased tenfold in a decade, reaching 419,000 in 1930. Due to their limited education and discriminatory treatment by the Japanese, most could only get jobs requiring physical labor. Subsequently, the National Mobilization Law (1938) conscripted 5.4 million Koreans, in order to deal with labor shortages exacerbated by the Second Sino-Japanese War. About 670,000 of them worked in Japan's factories and mines under horrid conditions, and about 60,000 died between 1939 and 1945. After the war, some would remain in Japan, and their descendants, known as Zainichi ("Japan-resident") Koreans, numbered about 474,460 as of 2019. In southern Sakhalin, under Japanese control since 1905, 43,000 Koreans would be stranded after World War II when the Soviets took over the region and did not allow them to leave.

Another major destination for Korean migrants was Manchukuo. Japan promoted Manchukuo as a pan-Asian state of "five races": Chinese, Japanese, Koreans, Manchus, and Mongols. Out of the total population of about 30,880,000 as of 1934, 29,510,000 were Chinese (including Manchus; 95.6 percent), 680,000 Koreans (2.2 percent), 590,760 Japanese (1.9 percent), and 98,431 other nationalities (.3 percent); the composition was more or less the same when the Soviets dissolved Manchukuo in August 1945. As was also true within Korea, ethnic Koreans were among Japanese militarism's agents as well as its victims. The Japanese formed a special Korean military unit (1937), which performed well against communist guerrillas and earned its Japanese commanders' respect. Also, among roughly 300 members of the Imperial Japanese Army's Unit 731, which conducted bacteriological weapons experiments on humans, some were Korean and Chinese. Based in Harbin, Unit 731 even subjected victims to vivisection, sometimes without anesthesia, and ultimately killed between 3,000 and 12,000, most Chinese, the rest Soviets, Mongolians, and Koreans.

Throughout the Japanese occupation of Korea, even larger numbers of Japanese migrated to Korea, numbering over 850,000 by 1945. Compared to those who moved to the Americas, Japanese colonists in Korea and other Japanese colonies occupied higher social niches. Predominantly government employees, merchants, and their families, most lived and worked in Kyŏngsŏng or port cities. Around 1930, some 100,000 Japanese were residing in Kyŏngsŏng where they formed the Japanese quarter. With a stream, Ch'ŏnggyech'ŏn, which flows west to east separating them, the Japanese section to the south and the Korean section to the north became known as the "South Village" and the "North Village" respectively. At the time, the South Village, as Kyŏngsŏng's political and commercial center, was the city's more modern section, fitted with government offices, banks, department stores, shops, paved roads, electric traffic signals, street lighting, and neon signs; the North Village retained a more traditional appearance. Not unique to Kyŏngsŏng, such contrast within an urban center also characterized other cities with sizable Japanese populations, including Inch'ŏn, Pusan, Masan, Kunsan (North Chŏlla), and Mokp'o (South Chŏlla).

The Chinese constituted the second largest ethnic minority group in colonial Korea, and most would remain in Korea after the end of the Japanese occupation, unlike the Japanese themselves. From 1910 to 1942, the Chinese population increased from about 12,000 to 82,661, and then by 1945 sharply decreased to 12,648, due to wartime hardship. The first wave of Chinese migrants established Chinese schools in Kyŏngsŏng (1910), Pusan (1912), Sinŭiju (1915), Namp'o, South P'yŏngan, at the mouth of the Taedong river (1919), and Wŏnsan (1923). Largely thanks to such schools, an increasing number of those born in Korea were fluent in both Korean and either Mandarin or Shanghainese. Among the early Chinese settlers, many were barbers, chefs, and tailors. Later, an increasing number worked as traders, general merchandise shop owners, food merchants, traditional East Asian medicine sellers, and travel guides.

Besides ethnic minorities, what is now referred to as the LGBT community experienced new trends. Newspaper coverage of same-sex love tended to be negative, reporting cases in association with or in the context of rape, assault, or murder, but many magazines with a readership among intellectual and literary circles sometimes depicted same-sex relationships as ideal love. The November 1923 issue of *Modern Woman* (*Sin yŏsŏng*), which catered to female high school students and young women, observed that lesbian love has more benefits than harm compared to heterosexual love, as long as it does not become a means for satisfying "dirty" lust. Lesbian love, in particular, fosters mature feelings of affection between young females while avoiding the pitfalls of male-female "puppy love"; love must be pure and noble, regardless of whether it is between a male and a female or individuals of the same sex; and any admixture of meanness and insults ultimately poisons a woman and destroys her, the *Modern Woman* declared. Women from intellectual, literary, and social circles chimed in, sharing their experiences, as did such popular New Novel authors as Yi Kwangsu (1892–1950), a male, who wrote works with gay and lesbian themes. Same-sex love especially appealed to some young women with Western-style education, most of whom had experienced a more traditional childhood when the separation of sexes before marriage was the norm in polite quarters. During the transition in ways of living, such women, some of whom were vocal in criticizing the patriarchy, appreciated or even idealized strong emotional bonds and mutual support among females. Also, even those with Western education tended to articulate a sense of weariness toward the notion of a woman exercising agency and taking the initiative in a sexual relationship with a male. Warnings against failed male-female relationships abounded in newspapers and magazines. Idealized lesbian love, then, was a practical arrangement for a young woman before attaining the status of "wise mother, good wife" (*hyŏnmo yangch'ŏ*), an expression coined earlier in Meiji Japan to label an ideal woman.

CULTURAL NATIONALISM, ASSIMILATION, AND DIVERSITY

Upon annexing Korea, Japan exercised tight control of the press and the education system to facilitate colonial rule. The government-general shut down all except a few newspapers, such as its mouthpiece, the *Korea Daily News*. The Educational Ordinance for Korea (1911), which emphasized loyal colonial subjects' duties, sought to secure the necessary workforce to industrialize the colony by promoting lower-level vocational training. An overarching goal of the colonial education system was to phase out Korean cultural identity and to assimilate Koreans into the Japanese mainstream while withholding equal rights until the colonials become worthy—whenever that might be. Despite that goal and all the associated rhetoric, discrimination against Koreans remained pervasive. Some Korean activists tried to promote a Korean-centered education, but the number of private schools and reformed village schools gradually declined due to Japanese suppression.

As a way of shaping the minds of a new generation of Koreans, the government-general invested much effort into distorting Korean history and justifying Japan's takeover. Overall, Japan's colonial historiography denied the record of Korean agency and contributions. Trained in modern methodologies in historical research, as acquired from the West, Japanese academic historians published seemingly well-researched, empirical studies that ostensibly demonstrated how Koreans had failed to keep up with the West's and Japan's regular progress. The colonial historiography also asserted that Korea's history had been a part of continental Asian history rather than its own history. After all, Koreans and Japanese were of common origins, said to the effect that Japan's brotherly protection of Korea was only natural.

In response, Koreans in intellectual, literary, and artistic circles critically reflected on their nation's past and expressed aspirations for modern nationhood. Such nationalist historians as Pak Ŭnsik, who served in the Provisional Government of the Republic of Korea, emphasized Korea's historical agency. In *An Agonizing History of Korea* (*Han'guk t'ongsa*; 1915) and *A Bloody History of the Korean Independence Movement* (*Han'guk tongnip undong chi hyŏlsa*; 1920), Pak not only condemned Japan's takeover of Korea but also offered a historical narrative that emphasized the national spirit and articulated his aspirations for national independence. While Pak resided abroad and thus could communicate such views, inside Korea, leading writers such as Yi Kwangsu stressed overcoming what they saw as Korea's backwardness, which many of them labeled as feudalism. Rejecting more traditional, Confucian moral norms, Yi's New Novels and other works laid the foundation for modern Korean literature. In the fine arts, new masters built on traditional paintings in producing new styles, including Western-style oil painting. Some works satirized Japan's colonial exploitation of Korea.

Besides keeping an eye on artistic and literary circles, the government-general closely monitored religious groups, as many pro-independence activists who stressed national spirit were members of organized religions. The Monastery Ordinance (1911) replaced the traditional Korean Buddhist system, in which the Buddhist clergy ran monasteries as a collective enterprise, with Japanese-style management practices wherein monastery abbots appointed by the government-general exercised private ownership of monastic property and rights of inheritance. Influenced by missionaries from Japanese Buddhist schools, pro-Japanese Korean Buddhist groups began to adopt such Japanese practices as a married priesthood. Simultaneously, a new indigenous religion, Won Buddhism (1916), presented a reinvented Buddhism that integrated the faith into the laity's everyday life. Compared to Won Buddhism, which enjoyed a degree of freedom, the government-general persecuted another new Korean religion, Daejongism, for its ultranationalist teachings, and its leadership fled to Manchuria. Incorporating surviving righteous army fighters, the Daejongist leaders in Manchuria formed the Chunggwang Corps, which promoted nationalist education (1911).

Reacting to the March First Movement, Japan's "cultural rule" made some concessions and began to tolerate more tempered expressions of Korean nationalism. The government-general issued publication permits to some Korean-language periodicals, including magazines and such daily newspapers as *Chosŏn ilbo* (1920) and *Tonga ilbo* (1920), followed by the colony's first radio broadcast (1927). Censorship continued, and as harsher surveillance and censorship tended to target male writers, women gained greater visibility in publishing. Besides limited freedom of the press, the government-general accorded official status to the Korean language, making it a part of the school curriculum. The establishment of Keijō Imperial University (1924) completed Japan's expanding public education system for the colony.

Such concessions by the colonial state boosted indigenous research on the Korean language and history. Led by Im Kyŏngjae (1876–1955) and Chang Chiyŏng (1889–1976), the newly founded Society for Korean Language Research (1921) not only pursued scholarship on the language but also published a magazine, *Han'gŭl*; designated a day for an annual celebration of *han'gŭl*; and provided public instruction on using the script. Historians too were active, especially as the colonial historiography gained ground with the government-general's establishment of the Korean History Compilation Committee, which began to prepare Japan's official account of Korean history (1925). Among various works of nationalist historians, Sin Ch'aeho's *Research Notes on Korean History* (*Chosŏn sa yŏn'gu ch'o*; 1925) and *Early History of Korea* (*Chosŏn sanggo sa*; 1931) delineated a unique history of Korean thoughts by highlighting various pre-Confucian religious customs and argued for recovering the national energy, which he believed that Korea lost in the mid-Koryŏ period. In contrast, An Hwak (1886–1946) presented a narrative of progress in *A History of Korean Civilization* (*Chosŏn munmyŏng sa*; 1923), which highlights the widening social base of political participation in Korean history as various institutions of local autonomy developed further, especially in the Chosŏn period.

During the decade, various religious groups that had participated in the March First Movement continued to pursue cultural nationalist activities. Chondoists were especially active, trying to educate the public through publishing their magazines. In Manchuria, the Chunggwang Corps, guided by Daejongism, reorganized itself as the Northern Route Military Command, which promoted nationalistic education and organized armed resistance. Besides cracking down on Daejongists and other groups deemed anti-Japanese, in 1920, the government-general revised the Monastery Ordinance in order to reorganize Buddhist monastery administration and oversee the thirty-one main monasteries directly, from new headquarters at Kakhwang-sa in Kyŏngsŏng. Countering such measures, the Association for Revitalization of Korean Buddhism, led by Han Yongun (1879–1944), sought to reform Buddhism to better serve society's needs while maintaining a nationalist stance. By comparison, Catholic leaders focused more on educating and enlightening the public, as did the Protestants. Some in Manchuria, however, formed an armed, Catholic, anti-Japanese resistance group, the Righteous People's

Corps, that kindled the patriotic spirit of the Catholic An Chunggŭn, who as mentioned earlier, served as a righteous army lieutenant general and fatally shot a leading Japanese statesman.

At this time, new periodicals in arts and literature engaged with the reality of colonial Korea. Influenced by socialism and emerging in the mid-1920s, the New Trend Literature movement sought to heighten class consciousness. Embodying that movement's spirit, the Class Literature movement gained a following, thanks to its dissemination by a new, internationalist literary group with an Esperanto name, Korea Artista Proleta Federacio, organized by Im Hwa (1908–53) and several others. In more subtle ways, Han Yongun articulated nationalistic sentiment in his poems. Simultaneously, such celebrated literary figures as Kim Sowŏl (1902–34) creatively expressed their feelings in tune with what they felt was their countrymen's sentiment. Other writers advocated "pure literature" more focused on literary merits and artistry. Meanwhile, the introduction of modern theater centered around the Society for Research in Dramatic Art after the March First Movement inspired stage art for the nation stripped of sovereignty. In cinema, Na Un'gyu (1902–37) produced such films as *Arirang* (1926), which reflected an intense national consciousness through cinematic visualization of Koreans' sufferings under foreign occupation.

In the 1930s, as artists and intellectuals continued to kindle the flame of resistance, three distinct approaches to Korean history emerged. Such nationalist historians as Namgung Ŏk (1863–1939), Mun Ilp'yŏng (1888–1939), and An Chaehong (1891–1965) highlighted Korea's independence and uniqueness as they combatted Japanese distortions of Korean history. Building on the work of Sin Ch'aeho and others who treated history as a means for pro-independence struggle, Chŏng Inbo (1893–1950) presented a new nationalist historiography that featured a more solidly empirical scholarship in explaining the significance of historical particularities. Simultaneously, such socioeconomic historians as Paek Namun (1894–1979) refuted the colonial historiography's stagnation theory by arguing that historical Korea had undergone development in conformity with the stages of development in the West, especially as recognized by Marxist scholars. A third group, the positivist historians, pursued a more purely empirical study of history based on evidence. They founded a Korean studies research group, the Chindan Academic Society.

In addition to rescuing and furthering the study of Korea's history, in the 1930s, a wide range of scholarly works contributed to a better understanding of Korean culture and language. Folklore studies as promoted by such scholars as Son Chint'ae (1900–c. 1965) enjoyed a boom, while Chŏn Hyŏngp'il (1906–62) devoted himself to preserving Korean cultural artifacts and preventing them from being taken to other countries. In linguistics, the expansion and reorganization of the Society for Korean Language Research into the Society for the Study of Korean generated a more active effort to disseminate han'gŭl (1931). The society's most significant achievements were the standardization of han'gŭl orthography and the designation of a standard Korean language, which the organization defined as the Korean generally spoken by Kyŏngsŏng's middle class (1933).

In part responding to a growing audience in Kyŏngsŏng and other cities, the genre of Western music imbued with Korean sensibilities and motifs came of age during this decade. Expressing a full range of the Korean people's emotions, the songs of Hong Nanp'a (1898–1941) and Hyŏn Chemyŏng (1902–60), in particular, enjoyed popularity and since then have become classics. Pursuing more advanced study of Western music theory, Ahn Eak-tai (An Ikt'ae; 1906–65) studied classical music composition in Japan, the United States, and Europe before having a successful career as a conductor in Europe and Asia. Among his works, a choral rendition of a part of the *Symphonic Fantasy Korea* would subsequently become the South Korean national anthem, "Aegukka" (Patriotic Song).

Upon Japan's occupation of Manchuria in 1931, the government-general enacted policies to mold Koreans culturally into supporters of Japan's war effort. Emphasizing that "Japan and Korea are one entity" (*Naisen ittai*) and that Japanese and Koreans shared a common ancestry, Japan sought to transform Koreans more fully into subjects of the Japanese empire—through such requirements as the recitation of many patriotic lines pledging loyalty to Emperor Hirohito—and to destroy Korean identity. The effort also entailed phasing Korean language instruction out at primary and secondary schools (1938–43). Not only did such Korean-centered educational institutions as night schools and reformed village schools lose ground, the authorities exercised strict, pre-publication censorship of two major dailies, the *Chosŏn ilbo* and the *Tonga ilbo*, and finally shut them down (1940). The government-general also suppressed the Society for the Study of Korean's ambitious project of compiling the first Korean language dictionary. Regarding the organization as a pro-independence activist group, the authorities arrested its personnel and disbanded it (1942). Besides marginalizing the Korean language, the government-general gratuitously accorded Koreans the privilege of petitioning for Japanese-style surnames and given names during a prescribed period (1939). In reality, the name change entailed not so much a privilege nor a petition as de facto coercion, since the authorities withheld such essential public services as food rationing to those who held out after the window period, and 79.3 percent of Korean householders had complied by 1940. Typically, the head of a household chose a Japanese surname that reflected the meaning, history, or pronunciation of their Korean surname, ancestral seat, or both.

Not content to make Koreans more superficially Japanese, the colonial state mobilized religious and cultural circles to support the war effort. Not only tightening control of the largest organized Korean religion, Buddhism, the government-general also required all Koreans to participate in Shinto rituals, the central part of which was to venerate Hirohito as a living god. Some Protestants resisted, suffering imprisonment or seeing their schools shut down. Japan also prodded prominent figures from religious and cultural circles to urge all Koreans—through media and in person—to sacrifice themselves for the emperor. Ultimately, most high-profile Koreans complied, offering their talents in one way or another to wartime propaganda. Such poets as Yi Yuksa (1904–44) and Yun Tongju (1917–45) who resisted died while imprisoned.

Compared to prominent figures' words and deeds, the fashion of the clothes they wore was even more powerful in setting the trend in colonial Korea. Western suits became common among men, beginning mainly with office workers, even though most combined styles old and new by donning *hanbok* with a Western-style hat and a pair of *komusin*, rubber shoes shaped like traditional Korean shoes (Figure 10.2). By the 1910s, males other than the middle-aged or older in rural areas, many of whom tended to insist on traditional style, were keeping their hair short, if not shaving, in part for easier care and hygiene. Women were more conservative, as long hair rolled into a back bun remained common. Then in the 1920s in Kyŏngsŏng, a stylist, O Yŏpchu (b. 1905), who had returned from Japan after a stint as a movie actress, opened a hair salon in the Hwasin Department Store and introduced bobbed hair, which quickly became popular among girls and women alike, especially those in urban areas where permed hair, a blouse, a skirt, stockings, and high heels began to increase in popularity. The new feminine fashion was controversial enough to fuel a social debate. Outside of those with a modern education, the opinions were mostly negative, as they

FIGURE 10.2   A Korean businessman with his wife and children, 1922. The juxtaposition of males in Western dress and females in traditional dress, even within a family, was a common sight in Korea and other colonies at the time. The practice remains widespread in contemporary postcolonial societies, including South Korea, where during a wedding, the couple's fathers don suits, whereas the mothers wear *hanbok*. Possession of the author. Photo © Eugene Y. Park 2021.

associated the latest trend with materialistic consumerism incompatible with the ideal of "wise mother, good wife." The next more dramatic change came in the 1940s when the government-general's austerity campaign imposed new dress styles. Instead of *hanbok* or Western suits, men donned khaki *kokumin-fuku* (Ko. *kungminbok*, "national dress"), European-style men's civil attire that wartime Japan promoted throughout the empire as the standard for men, with a fatigue cap and gaiters. Women wore *monpe*, Japanese farming village women's work pants, instead of skirts.

Besides clothing, the culture of everyday life saw many changes in the diet. In urban areas, not only did consumption of processed food increase, but dumplings and steamed buns with fillings served at Chinese eateries and Japanese sushi, udon, fishcakes, sweet red mung bean porridge, *takuan*, and sake all became popular. Occasionally, some Koreans ate beef steak, Western-style soup, bread, cake, sponge cake, confections, and ice cream—foods for the most part reserved for the urban upper class. The ordinary people's diet remained mostly plant-based, low in protein, and less nutritious. Although colonial Korea's overall rice production increased, rice consumption per capita among Koreans continued to decrease. As the food shortage grew acute during the Pacific War, the government-general imposed delivery quotas on rice producers with a fixed sale price. Most households had to mix rice with other grain types for meals if not serving millet or sorghum entirely. Those struggling to survive even resorted to consuming wheat bran, pine tree bark cake, bean oil dregs (more suited for feeding livestock or fertilizing plants), or dregs from distilling grain liquor.

At the same time, new types of housing appeared in the cities and their outskirts. As of 1924, only about 23 percent of houses in Kyŏngsŏng were of Korean style, and the rest were Japanese-style brick, stone, or concrete houses. Housing shortages persisted as the colonial construction code, which required the use of nonflammable material, prohibited building the thatched-roof homes still prevalent in rural areas, where running water and electricity also remained minimal. In urban areas, construction of upper-class *munhwa chut'aek* ("cultured houses"), middle-class *kaeryang hanok* ("improved Korean houses"), and middle-to-lower-class public housing, *yŏngdan chut'aek*, increased. Appearing in the 1920s, *kaeryang hanok* left out the traditional guest reception quarters while featuring framed glass doors for the entrance to the main hall from the exterior; a second gate between the house's main entry gate and the house itself; a room next to the second gate; and new decorative elements.

First constructed in the 1930s, *munhwa chut'aek* originally were homes that Japan had begun building with eclectic designs, often mixing Western and Japanese architectural elements, and had promoted as modern and cultured. A *munhwa chut'aek* was usually a two-story structure featuring new spaces such as hallways, reception rooms, bedrooms, and children's rooms. In *munhwa chut'aek* and *kaeryang hanok* alike, males and females spent more time in shared spaces than they would in traditional Korean homes. Unlike either *kaeryang hanok* or *munhwa chut'aek*, the *yŏngdan chut'aek* constructed in the 1940s consisted of attached homes, intended to address the housing shortage among urban residents, and they were concentrated in working-class neighborhoods of Kyŏngsŏng, Inch'ŏn, and new factory towns in North and South Hamgyŏng. In the outskirts of Kyŏngsŏng, the poor built and lived in hut-like dwellings with straw or straw mats used as material for the roof and coverings for the main entrance. In 1937, more than 15,000 out of some 700,000 capital residents were living in such abodes. The government-general's lofty rhetoric of progress evidently could not do away with abject poverty, which would persist for decades beyond the end of Japanese occupation.

CHAPTER 11

Establishment of Two Korean States, 1945–1960

The joint U.S.-Soviet occupation (1945–48) and Korea's division sowed the seeds for the inter-Korean conflict. The Cold War (1947–91) polarized Korean politics and established the pro-American Syngman Rhee regime in the south and the Soviet-supported Kim Il-sung regime in the north. The resulting internal turmoil, the border clashes, and the Korean War pitted South Korea, the United States, and fifteen pro-American United Nations member countries against North Korea, China, and the Soviet Union for three years (1950–53). That devastating war and the postwar politics deepened the ideological chasm between the two Koreas. Rhee's authoritarian rule collapsed with the April 19 Revolution (1960), whereas Kim began to purge rival communist factions. America aided the capitalist southern economy with recovery, and education accelerated the formation of a new middle class. In contrast, the Sino-Soviet fallout spurred North Korea to pursue a self-sufficient, nationalized economy guided by the concept of Juche (Chuch'e; "self-reliance") that upheld Kim as the subject of a leadership cult.

DIVISION, THE KOREAN WAR, AND POSTWAR POLITICS
The joy of liberation from the Japanese occupation was momentary. Dividing Korea at the thirty-eighth parallel, American and Soviet armies occupied the southern and northern parts. Korean political leaders at all levels

scrambled to organize themselves in preparation for national independence. People's committees sprang up as local deliberative bodies throughout Korea, and Lyuh Woon-hyung converted the Korean National Foundation League into the National Foundation Preparation Committee (August 15, 1945; Figure 11.1). As the committee worked with the government-general on maintaining law and order, Korean reprisals against the Japanese were minimal. Nonetheless, to leverage itself vis-à-vis the new occupiers, the committee declared the establishment of the People's Republic of Korea (September 7). Neither the Soviets nor the Americans recognized it or any other organization claiming to represent the Korean people. Instead, the Soviets administered the north through Kim Il-sung and his former anti-Japanese guerrilla comrades, the Partisans (Ko. Ppalch'isan), who quickly took over the people's committees with Soviet support. In contrast, the Americans implemented direct control through the U.S. Army Military Government in Korea (USAMGIK). In December, in Moscow, the foreign ministers of Britain, the Soviet Union, and the United States agreed to establish an interim government for Korea—with the stipulation that a U.S.–Soviet Joint Commission would devise an agreement on a four-power trusteeship for Korea, lasting up to five years. When the joint commission met, however, the two sides could not agree on which Korean political parties and social organizations to consult (March 1946).

Meanwhile, as U.S.–Soviet relations deteriorated, Korean opinions over the future of their nation became polarized. The escalating left-right ideological conflict reached its peak as the right opposed trusteeship while the left supported it. Such right-wing leaders as the pro-American Syngman Rhee pushed for a Korean government representing their positions in the south. In February 1946, in the north, the Partisans spearheaded the establishment of the Provisional People's Committee for North Korea, with Kim Il-sung as the chair. In August, the Partisans led the formation of the Workers' Party of North Korea (1946–49), which accommodated other communist factions. Devising a strategic plan for unifying Korea through communizing the south, the northern leadership began to dispatch trained guerillas to the south, where leftist uprisings against the USAMGIK continued in the Mount Chiri area and elsewhere. Nonetheless, in the south, the communists who had remained in Korea throughout the Japanese occupation as underground activists suffered persecution by the right. In October, their leader, Pak Hŏnyŏng (1900–56), fled to P'yŏngyang, where in November, he formed

FIGURE II.I   Lyuh Woon-hyung speaking during the launch ceremony for the National Foundation Preparation Committee, August 16, 1945. Source: Mongyang Memorial Foundation.

the Workers' Party of South Korea (1946–49). Although losing ground, some political moderates supported by the USAMGIK continued to advocate left-right cooperation, but the assassination of Lyuh Woon-hyung was a critical blow to the centrist cause (July 19, 1947). To this day, the group ultimately behind the killing remains unknown, though possible culprits cited are the ultra-right, Pak's domestic communists, or supporters of Kim Il-sung.

The U.S.–Soviet Joint Commission could not agree on Korea's future, and the newly established United Nations (UN), which the United States and its allies dominated, took up the question. In November 1947, the UN General Assembly passed a resolution mandating a UN-supervised general election for all of Korea, proportionate to population. Since northern Korea's population was half of southern Korea's, the Soviet Union and the northern Korean leadership opposed this plan. As Kim Il-sung and other communist leaders hurried forward with establishing their government in the north, the UN Little Assembly decided that the general election be held where feasible, as supervised by the UN Temporary Commission on Korea. Even in the south, however, opposition to the election was widespread. On Chejudo, the southern authorities brutally suppressed an anti-election protest, only to spark the Chejudo Uprising (April 3, 1948–May 1949), producing tens of thousands of casualties. While anti-election protests raged on, such nationalist leaders as Kim Ku and Kim Kyusik (1881–1950), who feared that the UN-sanctioned election would make Korea's division permanent accepted Kim Il-sung's and Kim Tubong's (1889–1961?) invitation to the North-South Joint Conference in P'yŏngyang (April 19–26, 1948). Boycotted by the right, the conference failed to produce a solution acceptable to all.

In the following months, efforts toward separate governments accelerated. In the south, the general election by secret ballot chose members of the legislature, the national assembly (May 10, 1948). These members adopted "Republic of Korea" as the nation's official name and devised a democratic republican constitution, which based its legitimacy on the Provisional Government of the Republic of Korea's spirit of independence and designated Seoul (formerly Kyŏngsŏng) as the national capital. Elected president by the national assembly (July 20), Syngman Rhee formally declared the establishment of the Republic of Korea (August 15). Subsequently, in the north, an election in which voters cast their ballot into either a black or a white box in order to vote for a particular candidate formed the Supreme People's Assembly (SPA; September 2). Six days later the People's Constitution, which designated Seoul as the nation's official capital and P'yŏngyang as the temporary capital was ratified. The next day the SPA declared the establishment of the Democratic People's Republic of Korea (DPRK), with Kim Il-sung as the premier and Pak Hŏnyŏng as the vice premier and foreign minister (September 9). With rival Korean regimes in place, the Soviet Union and the United States withdrew their armies from Korea in December 1948 and June 1949, respectively. From the establishment of the two Korean governments, each denying the other's legitimacy, until the all-out North Korean invasion in June 1950, the northern and southern forces clashed continually along the thirty-eighth parallel.

Upon its establishment, the North Korean government achieved stability quickly. The regime was relatively well grounded, with the general population as its political base, as Kim Il-sung and his Partisans, backed by the Soviet occupation force, had consolidated control through local people's committees. In June 1949, Kim and Pak's respective parties merged, forming the present-day Workers' Party of Korea (WPK). Furthermore, a sweeping land reform turned cultivators as a whole, the majority of whom used to be tenant farmers, into landed, loyal supporters of the regime. Hundreds of thousands joined the WPK. Meanwhile, by the summer of 1953, anywhere from some 600,000 up to 1.39 million landlords, those who had worked with the Japanese, and others that feared the regime's persecution had fled en masse southward. North Korea, then, had virtually disposed of its malcontents.

By contrast, internal turmoil continued in South Korea. Responding to a popular demand for punishing pro-Japanese collaborators, the national assembly passed the Law for the Punishment of Persons Who Engaged in Anti-National Activities (September 1948). Still, the reluctance of Rhee's government, which needed the political support of landlords and business leaders, blocked the legislation's full implementation. Instead, the regime prioritized dealing with widespread unemployment, high inflation, and leftist guerrillas. The continuing left-right conflict divided even the South Korean army. Refusing to suppress the Chejudo Uprising, some troops mutinied in Yŏsu and Sunch'ŏn, South Chŏlla (October 19–27, 1948). Not backing down, Rhee sought to establish order through the National Security Act (December 1948), which effectively made communism illegal, and through implementing agricultural land reforms.

Developments abroad also put South Korea in a difficult position while strengthening North Korea's stance. In China, the communists led by Mao Zedong (1893–1976) established the People's Republic of China (September 1949), forcing Chiang Kai-shek and the Nationalists to retreat to Taiwan (December) as the end of the Chinese Civil War (1927–36, 1946–50) drew near. China released 50,000 Korean Volunteer Army troops, who had fought as members of China's People's Liberation Army, and North Korea immediately incorporated them into its Korean People's Army (KPA). And thanks to heavy weaponry supplied by the Soviet Union, by June 1950, North Korea had 242 tanks and more than 200 bomber and fighter planes, whereas South Korea had just ten training aircraft and no tanks.

The continual skirmishes along the thirty-eighth parallel became the Korean War on June 25, 1950, when North Korea launched an all-out invasion on a Sunday morning (Map 11.1). On the following day, the United States convened the UN Security Council, and with the Soviet representative not present to exercise a veto, the council condemned North Korea as the aggressor. To aid South Korea, the United States and fifteen other UN member nations contributed troops to the UN Command force: Australia, Belgium, Britain, Canada, Colombia, Ethiopia, France, Greece, Luxembourg, the Netherlands, New Zealand, the Philippines, South Africa, Thailand, and Turkey. The Americans constituted the bulk of the force, with General Douglas MacArthur (1880–1964) as its commander. Aiding North Korea, about 26,000 Soviets fought unofficially during the war, mostly as air force pilots. While the UN troop strength gradually increased with waves of American units arriving, the KPA overran much of South Korea. Rhee's officials told Seoul residents not to worry, but the KPA occupied the capital within three days. Including many pro-communists, most citizens either chose to stay put or were unable to flee after a South Korean commander, in panic, blew up the only bridge across the Han River. In the ensuing weeks, the KPA pushed the battlefront to the Naktong River in the southeast (August).

In the following seven months, the tide of war shifted three times before reaching a stalemate. Following a daring amphibious landing at Inch'ŏn, the UN and Republic of Korea Army forces pushed forward, and the KPA retreated (September 15). In two weeks, the UN forces retook Seoul, after bitter street fighting (September 28), and three days later, the Republic of Korea Army that had been fighting mostly in Kangwŏn crossed the thirty-eighth parallel (October 1). The UN troops did likewise in western central Korea eight days later (October 9), and ten days later, the UN and South Korean forces took P'yŏngyang (October 19). As the UN and South Korean troops approached the Sino–North Korean border, in late October, waves of a million Chinese troops began to push them back; in a little over two months, the communists retook Seoul (January 4, 1951). This time most residents fled the city. Although the bitter winter weather added to the tragic mass exodus of refugees, by then, most Koreans other than leftists or sympathizers had come to fear the people's committees, mass rallies, and "people's trials" that delivered summary justice in the KPA-controlled locales. Pushed back as far as P'yŏngt'aek and Osan in southern Kyŏnggi, the UN and Republic of Korea Army forces again launched a counteroffensive that regained Seoul

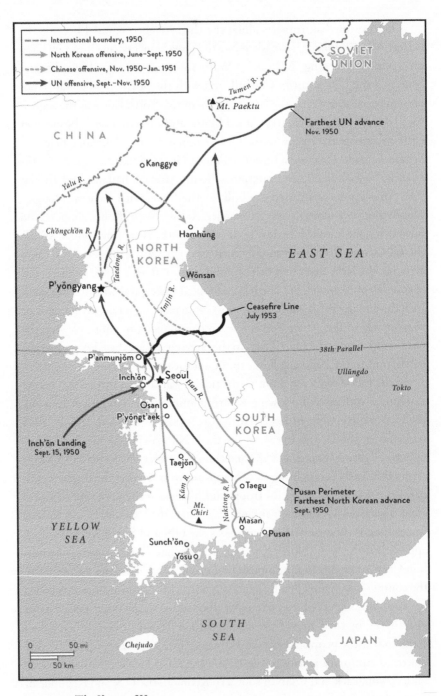

MAP II.I   The Korean War.

(March 14, 1951). By the early summer, the battlefront had stabilized along the present Demilitarized Zone (DMZ).

During the war, both Syngman Rhee and Kim Il-sung further strengthened their positions in their nations' internal politics. In December 1951, in Pusan, then South Korea's temporary capital, Rhee and his supporters formed the Liberal Party (1951–70). For the upcoming presidential election in August 5, 1952, the Liberal Party proposed a constitutional amendment stipulating a direct presidential election. In contrast, the opposition insisted on an amendment to institute a parliamentary system. Subsequently, the regime declared martial law (July). The national assembly passed a compromise amendment, allowing the direct election, and Rhee won his second four-year term—receiving 74.6 percent of the valid popular votes. In North Korea, Kim began to purge rival communist factions from the power structure, first targeting the domestic communists led by Vice Premier and Foreign Minister Pak Hŏnyŏng.

In the interim, representatives of the United Nations, North Korea, and China began negotiations (June 1951), which dragged through two years of stalemate on the battlefield before reaching an armistice agreement. Throughout, Rhee opposed a truce, insisting on conquering the north, but neither the United States nor the Soviet Union wanted the conflict to continue. When MacArthur openly advocated bombing targets inside China, Truman, who did not want to risk a third World War, replaced him with a new UN commander. Due to Rhee's opposition to the ceasefire, ultimately only North Korea, China, and the United Nations, as represented by the United States, participated in the talks before signing an armistice agreement (July 27, 1953). By then, the war's combat casualties numbered roughly one million South Koreans, 510,000 North Koreans, 500,000 Chinese, 40,000 Americans, and 30,000 other UN member troops; civilian casualties numbered about one million South Koreans and 600,000 North Koreans. Combatants on both sides included minors (Figure 11.2). P'yŏngyang, in particular, had suffered intensive American bombing as the UN forces maintained air superiority. To this day, in the absence of a signed peace treaty between its two nations, the Korean Peninsula remains in a state of war, and border clashes of varying scope and intensity have occurred sporadically, as recently as 2010.

In postwar South Korea, the Syngman Rhee regime became increasingly unscrupulous in its efforts to hold on to power. When an attempted

FIGURE 11.2   A captured 12-year-old KPA soldier, Private Song Jong Tae, and a U.S. soldier, Private First Class Desert B. Knight, January 14, 1951. The Americans nicknamed Song "Bugs" for a perceived resemblance to the cartoon character Bugs Bunny. Photograph by Major Angus J. Walker. Source: National Archives and Records Administration.

constitutional amendment to remove the presidential term limit only for Rhee, as the republic's first president, fell one vote shy of the required minimum of a two-thirds majority of the national assembly, the Liberal Party brought in thugs to intimidate the opposition, insisted that the minimum required number of votes, mathematically a fractional figure, be rounded *down*, and declared that the amendment passed (November 1954). Heading into the May 15, 1956, election, the nominee of the new main opposition, the Democratic Party (1955–61), Sin Ikhŭi (1894–1956), enjoyed widespread support, but he died ten days before election day. Rhee won the election, receiving 70 percent of all valid popular votes, and began his third four-year term. However, the Democratic Party nominee for vice president, Chang Myon (Chang Myŏn; 1899–1966), defeated the Liberal Party candidate, Lee Ki-poong (Yi Kibung; 1896–1960).

Surprised by the opposition's strong performance, the regime took further measures to remain in power. To facilitate its suppression of the opposition and other anti-regime forces, the government revised the National Security Act, now to cover a full range of alleged espionage activities by those promoting peaceful reunification (1958), and organized the Anti-Communist Youth Corps (1959). Subsequently, the authorities prosecuted and then executed a popular progressive politician and two-time presidential candidate, Cho Bong-am (Cho Pongam; 1898–1959), charging him with espionage for North Korea, and in the same year shut down a major daily newspaper, *Kyŏnghyang sinmun*, for supporting Chang Myon. In the March 15, 1960, election, Rhee ran for his fourth four-year term, and the Democratic Party fielded a charismatic, American-educated statesman, Chough Pyung-ok (Cho Pyŏngok; 1894–1960). Remarkably, Chough too died just ten days before the election day, and Rhee won 88.7 percent of the votes. The Liberal Party nonetheless resorted to ballot-box stuffing and other fraudulent acts to ensure that Lee Ki-poong, whom Rhee trusted, was elected as vice president. As the ballot count revealed that close to 100 percent of the votes were cast for Lee, the government had to adjust the figure to 79 percent.

Before long, spreading demonstrations against the rigged election sparked the April 19 Revolution. Protests erupted in Seoul, Pusan, Taegu, Masan, and other cities. The public's anger toward the regime peaked when the dumped body of a high school student killed by a direct hit by a police tear-gas canister was found on the seashore. On April 18, Korea University students took to the streets in Seoul, and on the following day, students from other universities and also high schools and ordinary citizens joined them. The avenue in front of Kwanghwa Gate, located 1.5 kilometers south of the president's headquarters, was filled with protesters demanding Rhee's resignation. When some students charged in the direction of the headquarters, the police fired live bullets, and more than 100 protesters died. Moved by these developments, six days later, on April 25, Seoul National University professors joined the protest, marching with a banner that read, "Let us pay back the blood of our students," and the United States, which had been monitoring the situation, pressed Rhee to resign. The next day, Rhee did so and went into exile in Hawaii (April 26), where he had been active as a prominent Korean independence activist for decades before Korea's liberation from the Japanese.

In postwar North Korea, Kim Il-sung pursued dictatorship, claiming that the DPRK had won the war against the American imperialists. The war's immediate consequence for the internal power struggle was Kim's victory over Pak Hŏnyŏng. Kim and the Partisans denounced Pak and other domestic communist leaders' words and deeds as anti-WPK and counter-revolutionary. Going further, Kim accused Pak and other leading domestic communists of espionage for the United States and purged them (1953). Subsequently, Kim made his first known reference to the concept of Juche, during a speech on eradicating blind adherence to Sino-Soviet communist ideas (1955). In doing so, he was targeting both the Yan'an group, consisting of those who had fought during the Chinese Civil War as CPC members, and the Soviet group, comprising ethnic Koreans from Soviet Central Asia. Kim's Juche concept began to evolve into the bedrock of North Korea's guiding ideology, stressing the nation's self-rule (*chaju*), self-sufficiency (*charip*), and self-defence (*chawi*).

Overcoming a strong resistance, Kim purged both the Yan'an and Soviet groups. By the following year, opposition to his economic policy prioritizing heavy industry centered around manufacturing military supplies had become widespread. Denunciation of Stalinism and Stalin's personality cult by the new Soviet leader, Nikita Khrushchev (1894–1971), encouraged both the Soviet and Yan'an groups as they criticized Kim's leadership. Simultaneously, Khrushchev's stance alienated Mao's China, which saw it as revisionism, and Kim capitalized on the Sino-Soviet rift to attack both the Yan'an and Soviet groups. In the name of eradicating factionalism and blind loyalty to China or the Soviet Union, Kim purged such key Yan'an figures as Kim Tubong, and a Soviet group leader, Pak Ch'angok (d. 1958). Kim then launched a two-year campaign to ensure that the entire nation was in line with his ideological stance as articulated through the WPK leadership, especially its vision of postwar reconstruction.

ECONOMIC RECOVERY

The turmoil following the end of the Japanese occupation had crippled the economy. In southern Korea, under the USAMGIK, many companies that used to operate mainly with Japanese capital shut down their factories due to a capital shortage after most Japanese settlers returned home and also due to inadequate natural resources and technology. Since Japan had built much of its colonial industry in the north, the division of Korea and the loss of electrical power from the north devastated the southern economy, which suffered from hyperinflation and acute shortages of daily necessities. Hundreds of thousands of wartime laborers returning home from various parts of the former Japanese empire exacerbated the widespread unemployment. By contrast, the communists in the north took over the industries that the Japanese had created. The northern leadership also did what it could to retain Japanese technicians to continue managing and servicing industrial facilities.

In the south, the Syngman Rhee regime sought to rebuild a capitalist economy by undertaking agricultural land reform and disposing of the Japanese properties taken over by the USAMGIK. Mindful of widespread demand and consensus, the government pursued the reform when the national assembly passed the Agricultural Land Reform Law (June 1949). That legislation allowed the state to acquire land by compensating the owners and redistributing the land among buyers. Designed to give every farming household a plot, the reform ended tenancy and paved the way for a more modern rural economy. The government also sold companies taken over by the USAMGIK, and by the mid-1950s, a considerable number of such corporations had become private businesses, which would constitute South Korea's industrial capital in the long run.

Postwar South Korea was one of the poorest countries in the world. The economy, based primarily on agriculture and light industry, grew annually by 5 to 8 percent from 1953 to 1960, but the per capita gross domestic product (GDP) remained under 100 dollars. Not only did Rhee's government put much effort into reconstruction, the United States also provided 3.1 billion dollars' worth of aid, half of which went to the military. The rest was directed toward agricultural products, raw materials, and intermediary materials for various stages of production. As the aid boosted the flour milling, sugar, and cotton textile industries, food and clothing shortages decreased. Building factories remained difficult as South Korea continued to rely on small thermal power stations, and as of 1960, 82 percent of rural residents and 39 percent of Seoul residents still had no electricity. Because the government and the population alike prioritized economic progress, the Labor Standards Act of 1953, which established minimum conditions for wage laborers regarding wages, work hours, paid vacations, safety and hygiene, and workers compensation, was good only on paper.

Meanwhile, North Korea's socialist economic policy produced some positive results. Half a year after the arrival of the Soviet occupation army, the Provisional People's Committee for North Korea undertook sweeping land reform and nationalized major industries (February 1946). In contrast to the 1949 agricultural land reform in the south, the northern reform outright confiscated private land. It was then redistributed among landless farmers for free—using a formula that considered a household's needs and production capacity. Seven years later, North Korea prohibited the private ownership of land and began implementing socialist collective farms (1953). The government also pursued collectivization for both commerce and handicraft manufacturing, and heavy industry began to grow rapidly. For postwar reconstruction and economic revival, Kim Il-sung and other Partisan leaders replaced the earlier motto, "Let us turn to the Soviet Union and learn," with Juche. As the problem of postwar labor shortage only got worse, the regime launched the first Chollima (Ch'ŏllima; "Flying Horse") Movement (1958–61) to mobilize the workforce and to organize it to increase agricultural and industrial outputs alike. Relying on mass mobilization, the movement incentivized productivity by recognizing worthy workers as "heroes." The Three Great Revolutions Movement that followed advocated replacing "feudal" ways with socialist ideas and actions in thoughts, technology, and culture (1958). Thanks to such efforts, the North Korean economy entered a golden age, growing annually by about 20 percent. By the decade's end, such progress seemed to accelerate the divergence between the two Koreas, both of which were undergoing rapid social change.

SOCIAL TRANSFORMATION

Upon liberation from the Japanese occupation, divided Korea struggled with new challenges that reshaped the society. In 1945, the influence of Confucian *yangban* culture was still strong in rural areas of southern Korea. In contrast, in the north, the more egalitarian Christian ethos was stronger, especially in P'yŏngyang and other urban areas. The northern leadership launched a program to instill socialist values, norms, and ideals in the populace. As mentioned previously, the victims of this program in one way or another, over 600,000 to as many as 1.39 million of them out of some 10 million North Koreans, fled south in the ensuing years. In a single year, South Korea's population increased by 21 percent, from 16.1 million in 1945 to 19.4 million in 1946. The emergence of many northern migrants as prominent figures in the society weakened Confucian *yangban* culture in the south, although genealogical fabrication continued. Also, the millions of Seoul residents who had fled southward as refugees during the Korean War accelerated the spread of more Westernized urban culture. Furthermore, the land reforms in both Koreas accelerated social change.

Besides bringing sheer destruction and physical suffering, the Korean War deepened the North-South divide with mutual antagonism. As the battlefront shifted wildly across the peninsula during the first nine months of the war, even those who were mobilized against their will by an occupation force suffered retaliation and punishment when the other side returned. When the KPA took over a locale, the people's trials it sanctioned meted summary justice as supporters of the occupation force unleashed long-held grudges, and the victims tended to be those of means or influence. When the South Koreans regained the locale, violent retaliation awaited the pro-North Korean residents who somehow could not flee with the KPA. Especially in rural areas, grievances were deep-seated. Besides the Rhee regime's and the USAMGIK's earlier treatment of leftists or leftist sympathizers, socioeconomic conflict among landlords, their agents, tenant farmers, and the colonial government personnel, including the police, dated back generations.

In the aftermath of violence, a remarkable demographic change that was already under way after the liberation accelerated in South Korea, especially in rural areas. During the postwar baby boom, the total fertility rate (TFR; the average number of children born to a woman) increased from 5.05 births in 1950–55 to 6.33 in 1955–60; and during the same period, life expectancy increased from 47.9 to 51.2 years. The total population increased sharply from some 21 million in 1955 to a little over 25 million in 1960. The population as a whole was young, and the majority lived in rural areas, which began to experience rapid social change. Throughout the 1950s, farming villages suffered from overpopulation and chronic household debt. To improve the standard of living and technology and to motivate youth, the Rhee regime expanded Korea's 4-H program. Founded in the United States in 1902 to make public school education more connected to rural life through practical and hands-on learning, 4-H was introduced to southern Korea in 1947. The 4-H program derives its name from its earlier motto, "head, heart, hands, and health."

Eager to get ahead in life, South Korea's growing young population flocked to the public education system introduced by the USAMGIK for six years of primary school, three years of middle school, and three years of high school. The number of secondary or higher educational institutions in particular significantly increased, including Seoul National University, which the USAMGIK established in 1946 by combining Keijō Imperial University and various other institutions of higher learning dating as far back as 1895. As public access to education improved, literacy among those twelve years or older shot up from about 22 percent in 1945 to 59 percent in 1948 to 96 percent in 1958. Even during the Korean War, school-age refugees as a whole were eager to attend classes at make-shift campuses set up by various schools.

After the war, the increase in the population of South Koreans who attained higher education accelerated, as many saw education as the surest way to overcome poverty and achieve success. Those who obtained a university-level education, including the brightest with financial means who pursued higher education in the United States, began to form an elite group of technocrats and business leaders who would spearhead South Korean economic growth in the following decade. Spreading education also contributed significantly to progress in science and technology. Besides the growing number of university-educated scientists and engineers, such government initiatives as the establishment of the nation's first atomic energy research center (1958) added momentum. Drafting and executing a long-term plan for promoting science and technology, the Rhee regime recruited and funded the brightest for overseas education, and they were then assigned to key research positions upon completing their education.

Postwar North Korea too experienced rapid social change, including a demographic shift. The population increased more slowly than in the south, from over 9.3 million in 1953 to 10.8 million in 1960. The TFR increased from 2.7 births in 1950–55 to 3.8 in 1955–60, and life expectancy increased from 37.6 years to 49.9 during the same period. As North Korea began to industrialize and as nuclear families replaced extended families, the population's composition by age brackets changed. Until the end of the 1950s, the population as a whole was young. Also, reflecting the war's human cost, in 1953, the sex ratio recorded was 88.3 males per 100 females. Like South Korea, the north experienced significant urban migration after the war, as urbanization proceeded rapidly between 1953 and 1960 when the urban population grew between 12 and 20 percent annually. In 1953, 17.7 percent of the population lived in urban areas, with an urban settlement defined as at least 20,000 individuals, whereas the southern definition set the minimum number at 50,000.

Increased social control accompanied the demographic changes, with the regime pursuing a more controlled economy. Buying grain privately became illegal (1957). North Koreans obtained food and clothing through either rationing or self-supply. Under the rationing system, the government supplied items according to nine grades of ration, which depended on the recipient's productivity and needs as determined by the state. When the system worked smoothly, most of the citizenry first received ration coupons from the "people's group" (inminban), which was the lowest-level administrative support apparatus. A coupon holder then purchased necessary items at prices set by the government at designated stores. Such major sources of calories in the North Korean diet as rice and corn were available only to those with ration coupons.

Such mechanisms for social control took significant population movements into consideration. After the Korean War, the General Association of Korean Residents in Japan (1955), better known as Chongryon (Ch'ongnyŏn), a pro-North Korean Zainichi organization and the de facto North Korean liaison in Japan, sponsored voluntary migration of ethnic Koreans from Japan to North Korea. The campaign, which would continue until the 1980s, received the Japanese and American governments' tacit support. Both saw the Zainichi as a troublesome minority population, mostly communists and criminals. Also, the Soviet Union sent 27,000 Japanese prisoners of war who were ill to North Korea.

The situation for the ethnic Chinese in Korea was more complicated. Those in the north who had reason to fear persecution fled south, where most maintained their Republic of China citizenship even after the Nationalists lost the Chinese Civil War, although some chose to become naturalized South Korean citizens. The Chinese who remained in the north quickly established their schools and rebuilt their Chinese-language education program with aid from the CPC. The party's Northeast Administrative Committee transferred control of these schools to the North Korean government, which then integrated them into the national education system (April 1949). The government's financial assistance spurred the expansion of Chinese education. For its part, the Republic of China government in Taiwan sought to avenge its defeat in the Chinese Civil War by participating in the Korean War, but the United States, not wanting to risk drawing the PRC into the war, thwarted the plan. Subsequently, however, China's entry into the war gave the Taiwan government the pretext to field psychological warfare personnel. Mostly ethnic Chinese who were teachers and students in Chinese schools in South Korea, their mission was to persuade the PRC troops to defect. At the same time, during the war, Chinese schools in North Korea enjoyed a golden age that would last well into the 1960s—educating some 14,000 ethnic Chinese who had assumed PRC citizenship. As foreign nationals, they were ineligible to join the WPK or advance in the North Korean military or civil bureaucracy.

While Korea's largest ethnic minority negotiated its place in the postwar society, women's legal position in South Korea saw some improvement. Newly won constitutional rights of women in terms of equal rights and opportunities, including suffrage (1948), laid at least the legal foundation for them to pursue education, work, and public life more actively. The educated began to engage in economic activities, teaching, and the arts, as well as engaging with other women in discussions of gender equality. The change was especially noticeable in education, as all the colleges and universities that used to be reserved for men opened up to women. Not only did women assume positions as principals at public schools, but at Seoul National University, where most of the students were men, several women were appointed as faculty members. Also, the notion of a woman's right to choose her marriage partner rather than accepting her family's choice became more popular. Furthermore, the government banned public prostitution. These changes accelerated with the Korean War, which significantly weakened rural agricultural communities with more traditional

social values that had been guarded by local lineages and single-surname villages. Nonetheless, feminism and nationalism clashed as male nationalists leg-
islated patriarchal values. Enactment of Article 809 of the civil code prohibited
any marriage between a man and a woman of the same surname and ancestral
seat while effectively allowing all other unions of relations more distant than
third cousins (1957). Chauvinistic male nationalists defined women's primary
role as being the homemaker mother, whose primary duty was to perpetuate
the patrilineage by giving birth to and raising a son. Accordingly, the inferior
legal status of women in regard to inheritance, property ownership, divorce,
and guardianship of children remained unchanged.

By contrast, in the north, women experienced more radical changes as the
socialist regime self-consciously promoted gender equality. Upon liberation,
the northern leadership immediately abolished the household registration
system, which had generally recognized the oldest male as the household head
(1945). Then the Gender Equality Law awarded women suffrage and equal
rights in inheritance, education, marriage, child support claims, and divorce
while outlawing concubinage, child marriage, and prostitution (1946). In the
same year, a statute on the Labor of Manual and Clerical Workers guaranteed equal pay for equal work. Subsequently, the 1948 People's Constitution
reinforced all of these legal provisions. Political opportunities began to
widen for women, and not just on paper, especially at the lower echelons of
party leadership thanks to such affirmative measures as a quota system. The
most remarkable improvement, though, occurred in the economic arena. In
1958, the government announced a "cabinet decision" that aimed at increasing female participation in all areas of the economy. To promote this goal
and encourage population growth, the government introduced such social
welfare reforms as guaranteed maternity leave and state-sponsored childcare centers. As women's increasing economic participation accelerated the
demise of more patriarchal systems, nuclear families replaced extended kin
groups. Nonetheless, while targeting "feudal relations" between men and
women, the official Marxist rhetoric stressed the importance of the family
as a building block of socialism—with a central role for mothers as self-
sacrificing model citizens. Accordingly, the state advocated the ideal of an
educated, modern mother who embodies both traditional motherhood and
an active role in revolutionary campaigns and nation building. In this spirit,
the North Korean Democratic Women's League (1945; Korean Democratic
Women's League since 1951) spearheaded a mass literacy campaign.

While women's position improved, a milestone event in Korea's transgender history took place. In August 1955 in Seoul, twenty-year-old Cho Kich'ŏl (b. 1935) walked into the hair salon in the Tonghwa Department Store (present-day Shinsegae). Styled in the latest fashion, bobbed hair, Cho stood in front of a mirror with a smile, basking in a barrage of camera flashes. Born a biological male, earlier in the month, Choe had received Korea's first documented sex reassignment surgery. The news media articulated a mixture of awe toward a "twentieth-century miracle" and grave moral concern. A few days later, a newspaper's editorial cartoon depicted a henpecked husband muttering: "Instead of living abused like this, I'd rather be a woman." Sensationalization and mockery of Cho's surgery was only the beginning of the overall LGBT struggle for rights and dignity in Korea's culture wars.

CULTURAL DIVISION IN THE AFTERMATH OF LIBERATION

Liberated Korea's efforts to eradicate colonial legacies faced many challenges. The accommodation and acceptance of Western cultures helped more Koreans better understand Korea's place in the world. As many educated people from Seoul and more northern areas fled south into rural areas during the war, the demise of the more traditional culture shaped by Confucianism accelerated. Also, spreading American popular culture reshaped indigenous forms and fanned a tendency to follow or imitate all things American. By contrast, in the north, nativism became stronger as the Kim Il-sung regime pursued an independent path amidst the post-Stalin Sino-Soviet rift.

In the mid-1950s, scholarship on Korean culture and history began to accumulate. Some scholars in various branches of Korean studies went north before the Korean War, during which the KPA also abducted scholars. Their continuing research established the basic empirical foundations for Korean studies under North Korean government sponsorship, especially research and publications in archeology, history, language, and literature. In the south as well, a scholarly effort to overcome the pernicious legacy of Japanese colonial scholarship gained momentum with the establishment of the National Institute of Korean History (1946) and such professional organizations as the Korean Historical Association (1952) and the Society of Korean Language and Literature (1956). The Korean Language Society (formerly the Society for the Study of Korean) resumed its work and completed the Korean dictionary project that had been banned by the colonial authorities (1947–57).

Besides Korean studies, in the south, religion played an increasingly important role in reshaping contemporary culture in terms of moral values and world views. The majority of South Koreans professed no formal adherence to a religion, but a growing number had turned to one for solace as they suffered in uncertain times. Upon the division of Korea, Chondoists, who were concentrated in the north, stayed put, whereas the majority of northern Christians fled south. Widely perceived in the south as representatives of a faith both powerful and modern, if not synonymous with America as the leader of human progress, Presbyterians, Methodists, and other Protestants enjoyed a rapid growth that would continue until the end of the 1990s. Some American missionaries who returned to Korea after earlier expulsion by the colonial authorities, such as Methodists, who were well represented in the political establishment, and other Protestants as well, served as informal communication channels between the South Korean elite and the U.S. government. All the same, existing Protestant denominations such as Presbyterians, who were the most populous among Korean Protestants, began to split up over a wide range of issues, including participation in colonial Shinto ceremonies and the postliberation left-right divide. Nevertheless, the spread of Christianity, represented by both Protestants and Catholics, accelerated in rural areas where Buddhism and folk spirituality remained influential.

In secular realms, the expanding media shaped the public discourse. After the liberation, not only newspapers and magazines but also radio and television broadcasts made rapid gains in their number of outlets and in the segment of the population with access. The era saw some milestone events, including the first radio broadcast (1947) and the first broadcast by a privately owned radio station (1954). Understanding media's power, the increasingly authoritarian Rhee regime limited press freedom through such time-honored methods as censorship, if not outright intimidation and threats, applied through the police and even hired mobsters.

Broadcast and print media shaped and disseminated various genres of postliberation culture in South Korea. The left-right division and the resulting conflict affected the cultural circles, but each genre increasingly featured a wide range of new trends. Not long after the end of the Korean War, works of "pure literature" that emphasized lyricism appealed to many, but Western literature in translation enjoyed a broader appeal among youth and urbanites. At the same time, the performing arts and fine arts featured a widening range of genres and styles. Both the U.S. occupation and the war accelerated the import and dissemination of American popular culture. In the 1950s, American pop music and dance began to capture the hearts of younger South Koreans and influence indigenous performers, while genres of more traditional popular culture, such as *p'ansori*, continued to lose ground.

In postwar North Korea, the state promoted culture not so much for the pursuit of aesthetic qualities per se as for promoting the spirit of revolution to the masses. Literature fared prominently in the regime's cultural policy. Among various writers, the state promoted the works of Hong Myŏnghŭi (1888–1968), whose daughter became Kim Il-sung's second wife, and other North Korean and foreign authors, all of whom employed socialist realism. Likewise, the WPK sponsored and promoted fine arts and performing arts geared toward inspiring workers, peasants, and "conscionable" intellectuals to build a socialist nation.

From its socialist perspective, the regime upheld the Marxist denounce-ment of religion as "the opium of the people." As of 1945, over 2 million North Koreans, or about 22 percent of the population, professed a religious affiliation, including 1.5 million Chondoists, 375,000 Buddhists, about 200,000 Protestants, and about 57,000 Catholics. Since Christianity had spread earlier and more widely in the north than in the south, the number of churches and overall Christian activists was greater there. Hailing from P'yŏngyang, which earlier Western missionaries, encouraged by its growing Christian population, had dubbed the "Jerusalem of the East," Kim Il-sung had been raised by a church-going Protestant mother. In contrast to the Christians, the majority of whom fled south, Chondoists stayed, as the regime regarded Chondoism as a national religion, owing to its self-identity as a revolution-ary, anti-imperialist, popular movement. Many individuals participated in politics through their membership in the Chondoist Chongu Party, a popular front party founded in 1946 and one of three political parties subordinated under the WPK. At the same time, Kim began to turn himself into the object of worship and adulation as North Korea increasingly constructed its ideol-ogy around the concept of Juche rather than more textbook communism.

While a cultural cold war escalated, many aspects of daily life in the two Koreas remained similar, including clothing. Working men and women abandoned the Japanese imposed *kokumin-fuku* and *monpe*, respectively, return-ing to *hanbok* or Western dress. In the aftermath of the Korean War, when poverty and shortages of all things, including fabric, were commonplace, many women in South Korea turned to blouses made out of durable nylon, and men even donned military uniforms if they were what was available. At the same time, Western fashion spread fast, especially among younger urban women, among whom flared skirts, tight skirts, and drainpipe trousers became popular. Younger urban men generally followed Western fashion trends with dress shirts, pants, jackets, suits, and ties. This was also true for hairstyles for both men and women. By contrast, older adults in rural areas continued to dress not all that differently from their late Chosŏn ancestors. Clothing in North Korea was more or less the same except that the overall Western style remained more conservative, especially for women. The "people's dress" (inminbok), as donned by Kim Il-sung, Mao, and Stalin, quickly became the norm in daily life.

In comparison, the daily diet of most Koreans differed little from that of earlier generations. Acute food shortages persisted with the rapid population increase, the Korean War, and the postwar baby boom. In South Korea, much of the surplus farm produce received as American aid was in the form of wheat flour. To address southern Koreans' traditional bias toward rice, Rhee's government promoted a daily diet that was based more on wheat flour or mixed grains, including barley. During the war, in particular, an increasing number of South Koreans, especially the boys and young men who worked odd jobs at U.S. military bases, got their first taste of various American food commodities such as butter, jam, and Spam.

At the same time, South Korea coped with acute housing shortages, only gradually mitigated by new construction. Most people continued to reside in dwellings ranging in shape and form from thatched-roof houses without running water or electricity—still common in rural areas—to hanok to kaeryang hanok to more Westernized homes. To accommodate a mass influx of Koreans arriving from abroad or northern Korea, the USAMGIK even converted Japanese-owned homes and high-class restaurant buildings (yojŏng) to lodging facilities. Before long, many homeless were ending up in shantytowns and "tent villages" (ch'ŏnmakch'on). After the war, Rhee's government, aided by the UN Korean Reconstruction Agency and other international agencies, built chaegŏn chut'aek ("reconstruction housing") consisting of earthen brick dwellings about 9 p'yŏng (29.8 square meters) in area; and other non-hanok homes, typically with a floor plan of about 15 p'yŏng (49.6 square meters) and featuring a wood-floor living room in the middle, south-facing ondol bedrooms to the east and west of the living room, and the entrance and kitchen in the north. In 1955 in Seoul, the government also built fifty-two attached-home units, each featuring a small front yard; the first floor comprising a south-facing entrance, south-facing *ondol* bedrooms, and a kitchen, bathroom, and stairs, all in the north; and the second floor consisting of a south-facing, wood-floor living room and an *ondol* bedroom in the north. In the late 1950s in the cities, the government built a small number of two-story attached homes, four-story apartment buildings, and four-story buildings that combined businesses (on the first two floors) and residences (on the third and fourth floors), some with a rooftop garden. Typically, the floor space was either 13.3 *p'yŏng* (44 square meters) or 17.3 *p'yŏng* (57.2 square meters), and these constructions employed the same general concept as the new detached single-family homes in terms of the location of various functional spaces.

North Korea at that time worked with a different set of challenges vis-à-vis people's housing and diet. Although spared a mass influx of migrants, the Kim regime had to accommodate many of those returning from abroad, especially China. Also, intense UN air raids had virtually razed cities to the ground. During the postwar reconstruction era, the foreign influence and aid sources were China and the Soviet Union, and collectivization increasingly affected daily life, especially food production and procurement in rural areas. In major cities, the government generally constructed multifamily residences. Before long, North Korea, guided by Juche, would be faced by a South Korea under a new authoritarian leader with a vision that would further sharpen differences between the two Koreas.

CHAPTER 12

Growth and Divergence, 1960–1980

T he developmental paths of the two Koreas diverged. In South Korea, Park Chung-hee (Pak Chŏnghŭi; 1917–79) overthrew the budding democracy with a military coup (1961) and ruled the country for eighteen years. Upon his assassination, Chun Doo-hwan (Chŏn Tuhwan; b. 1931) gained power through a military coup and crushed pro-democracy movements. In North Korea, Kim Il-sung completed a purge of rival communists. He perfected a totalitarian system guided by Juche ideology and groomed his son Kim Jong-il (Kim Chŏngil; 1941–2011) for succession. Meanwhile, the rapidly growing southern economy surpassed the ostensibly self-sufficient northern economy suffering from slowing growth. As industrialization and urbanization accelerated in South Korea, higher education expanded that nation's middle class. In the north, upward mobility was limited, with the elite comprising the WPK leadership and the capital residents. While the Juche ideology shaped all cultural genres in the north, the southern culture privileged material progress over tradition.

THE POLITICS OF AUTHORITARIANISM
VERSUS TOTALITARIANISM

The implementation of democracy in South Korea following Syngman Rhee's resignation encountered numerous challenges. In response to popular demand, Foreign Minister Hŏ Chŏng (1896–1988), who headed the interim government, devised a new constitution, which featured a parliamentary system (June 15, 1960), and the Democratic Party won a landslide victory in the national assembly election (July 29). In turn, the national assembly elected a leading Democrat, Yun Posun (Yun Posŏn; 1897–1990), as president, now a more purely ceremonial office. Yun then appointed Chang Myon as prime minister, the government's de facto leader as stipulated by the constitution, and the Second Republic (1960–61) was born. As the new administration followed democratic principles and tolerated a broad spectrum of political activism, the new freedom unleashed a maelstrom of forces that the Rhee regime had stifled. Among them, a Korean reunification movement and other politically progressive activities spread rapidly. The majority Democratic Party itself became embroiled in the strife between Yun's "old faction" and Chang's "new faction" before Major General Park Chung-hee staged a military coup and gained power (May 16, 1961).

Several developments motivated the coup. Park and the officers supporting him found much to blame in what they saw as the inability of Chang's government to maintain law and order and to revive the economy. Also, the government's downsizing of the military to secure more revenue for the new economic development plan to be executed in 1962 fanned the military's discontent. Furthermore, the inter-Korean student meeting that was to take place in early May 1961, at P'anmunjŏm in the DMZ, was an outrage to the military. As the economy began to stabilize, they decided to act before it was too late. Orchestrated by Lieutenant Colonel Kim Jong-pil (Kim Chongp'il; 1926–2018), who was married to Park's niece, the coup mobilized some 3,750 troops and entered Seoul with tanks, took over the government, and declared martial law.

Park and his colleagues set up a junta, the Supreme Council for National Reconstruction (SCNR), which implemented a series of measures in the revolution's name. Chaired by Park, the SCNR issued the Revolutionary Pledge, in which it vowed to suspend politicians' activities, ferret out procommunists, rectify social mores, and improve the people's living conditions by rebuilding the economy. The junta also indefinitely suspended local autonomy. It prosecuted droves of politicians, progressive intellectuals, and student activists, along with those linked to the rigged March 15, 1960, election and to organized crime. In the same spirit, the SCNR confiscated the assets of those deemed guilty of accumulating wealth unjustly, and it reduced the debts that farmers and fishers had incurred from high-interest loans. To secure more revenue for economic development, the SCNR implemented a currency reform (June 1962). All of these measures, on the whole, were well received by the people, boosting Park's popularity.

The junta implemented such measures, in part, to ease the widespread initial concerns that Park was a leftist or a pro-Japanese collaborator or both, and his checkered career preceding the coup is revealing. After graduating from Taegu Normal School (1937), Park worked as a primary school teacher. Subsequently, with the help of a Japanese colonel who was a drill instructor at Taegu Normal, the ambitious Park enrolled in the Changchun Military Academy of the Manchukuo Imperial Army (1940–42). After graduation, he transferred to the Imperial Japanese Army Academy in Japan and, upon graduation, served as a lieutenant in the Manchukuo Imperial Army (1944). He rose through the ranks when what would eventually become the Republic of Korea Army integrated Park and other officers from Manchukuo upon Korea's liberation. After the leftist Autumn Uprising of October 1, 1946, in Taegu, during which the police killed his brother, an influential advocate of the people's committees, Park escaped punishment and likely execution by presenting a list of military officers involved in the uprising. Subsequently, Park was in no position to do anything that might suggest that he was a communist.

Upon gaining power, Park and his colleagues prepared for wielding power themselves even after restoring procedural democracy. On the day following the coup, Kim Jong-pil organized the Korean Central Intelligence Agency (KCIA) to support the junta. In July, the junta instituted the Anti-Communism Law to prosecute leftist activities. Ostensibly bound by the Revolutionary Pledge, which promised that the SCNR would return political power to civilians, the junta devised a new constitution that featured a presidential system with a unicameral national assembly (December 1962). Park, other junta members, and their allies in the military then established the Democratic Republican Party (DRP; 1963–80). As the party's nominee, Park narrowly defeated his main rival and former president, Yun Posun, 46.6 percent to 45.1 percent, in the presidential election of October 15, 1963. Still, the DRP won a landslide victory in the subsequent national assembly election. Park's inauguration as the new president on December 17 commenced South Korea's Third Republic (1963–72).

As Park Chung-hee prioritized economic growth, his first step, especially as advised by the United States, was to normalize relations with Japan to secure adequate funds. The centerpiece of reestablishing relations was

Japan's economic aid package, comprising a grant of 300 million dollars, a government loan of 200 million dollars, and a package of private commercial loans totaling 100 million dollars. During the negotiations that preceded the Normalization Treaty (June 1965), Japan rejected South Korea's demand for compensation for colonizing Korea. Eventually, the two sides agreed to call the aid package an independence celebration fund for Korea. Also agreeing that any future financial claim by South Korea was to be negotiated through diplomacy, the two governments left many thorny issues unaddressed, including Tokto, the island that South Korea had been administering since the liberation but that was also claimed by Japan. Outraged by Japan's unwillingness to acknowledge responsibility for colonial rule, South Korea's activist university students and others took to the streets to protest, and Park's government had to declare martial law before concluding the treaty. Subsequently, South Korea used the Japanese funds for various significant projects crucial to long-term economic development, including the construction of the Kyŏngbu Expressway to connect the two largest cities, Seoul and Pusan.

Besides the rewards of the Normalization Treaty, South Korea received a significant boost for economic development from the United States after contributing troops to the Vietnam War (1955–75). Upon a request from the United States (1964), Park committed troops to South Vietnam, and in exchange, South Korea secured a loan package and more modern military hardware from America. After the United States itself, which committed over 5 million troops to that war, South Korea was the largest foreign contributor. Some 312,000 Republic of Korea Army troops served combat duty, and about 50,000 at one time were in Vietnam at the peak of South Korea's involvement. During the conflict, South Korea also won lucrative business contracts in South Vietnam, where Korean firms were often the lowest bidders, yet willing to work hard and complete projects on time. Hyundai and other major firms that won contracts made huge profits and gave their workforce experience, expertise, and equipment, all of which the companies would later deploy in the 1970s for major construction projects in the Middle East.

Park capitalized on various developments in and outside the country for his re-election bid. Thanks to some early positive results of economic growth, he again defeated Yun Posun, who represented the New Democratic Party (NDP; 1967–80), this time winning a landslide victory 51.4 percent to 40.9 percent (May 3, 1967). The following year, when tens of

North Korean commandos infiltrated Seoul and Kangwŏn, Park used those incidents and the heightened inter-Korean tension to rationalize a constitutional amendment that would allow him to seek a third term. Bending the legislative procedural rules, the DRP mobilized thugs to intimidate the opposition and push the amendment through the national assembly (September 1969). Park went on to defeat the NDP candidate, Kim Dae-jung (Kim Taejung; 1924–2009) from economically marginalized South Chŏlla, in the presidential election, 53.2 percent to 45.2 percent (April 27, 1971). As student demonstrations with the rallying cry, "Overthrow dictatorship!" subsequently raged into the fall, Park declared martial law for Seoul. In December, he declared a national emergency and implementation of the Special Law for National Security, which further restricted freedom of the press and assembly.

Meanwhile, in North Korea, Kim Il-sung had more or less effected a totalitarian regime. In July 1961, he reaffirmed the support of North Korea's most potent allies by signing a bilateral treaty of friendship, cooperation, and mutual assistance with China and the Soviet Union (Figure 12.1). In the mid-1960s, as discussed, Kim began to emphasize Juche as the guiding ideology to pursue the nation's self-rule, self-sufficiency, and self-defense. Citing Juche, Kim invested heavily in the defense industry and pursued four objectives: (1) ensuring the military preparedness of all citizens; (2) "fortifying" the nation; (3) imbuing all military personnel with an officer's sense of duty and responsibility; and (4) modernizing the KPA. By the end of the decade, his purge of the Kapsan group, the last remaining rival communist faction, including Pak Kŭmch'ŏl (1912–67?), who had prioritized improving the general standard of living, and such members of the military faction as Kim Ch'angbong (b. 1919) over the issue of the aggressive stance toward South Korea, left the political leadership dominated by his group, the Partisans. The apotheosis of Kim as the subject of a leadership cult built on Juche ideology was complete.

Thus as the new decade began, with Kim Il-sung and Park Chung-hee occupying positions as the leader of a totalitarian regime and an authoritarian head of state, respectively, they were confident enough to enter into an inter-Korean dialogue. In August 1971, inter-Korean Red Cross talks began, discussing reuniting families separated by the division between north and south. In the following year, Park secretly dispatched his KCIA director, Yi Hurak (1924–2009), to P'yŏngyang, where Yi and Kim agreed on a joint

FIGURE 12.1   North Korean postage stamps commemorating bilateral alliance treaties with China and the Soviet Union, issued on October 26, 1961. Possessions of the author. Photo © Eugene Y. Park 2021.

statement (July 4, 1972). Issued simultaneously, their statements articulated seven points: (1) both Koreas' collective pursuit of the unity of the Korean people and peaceful reunification of Korea without foreign interference; (2) easing tension and ceasing mutual slander or armed provocation; (3) inter-Korean exchange in various areas; (4) cooperating on Red Cross meetings; (5) setting up a P'yŏngyang-Seoul hotline; (6) forming a North-South Coordinating Committee; and (7) implementation of all terms of the agreement. Red Cross meetings to discuss reuniting separated families followed, first in Seoul, then P'yŏngyang. Subsequently, both Koreas formed the North-South Coordinating Committee, set up the hotline, and agreed to stop slanderous broadcasting (November).

Capitalizing on the South Korean public's warm reception of the ensuing inter-Korean dialogue, Park proceeded to remove any remaining restraint on his power. He declared that the nation must unite for an all-out, efficient effort toward the ongoing talks with North Korea. Park imposed emergency martial law, disbanded the national assembly, and passed the Yusin Constitution (October 17, 1972), which a subsequent national referendum approved (November). The Yusin Constitution turned Park's presidency into a de facto dictatorship, with nearly full control of the executive, legislative, and judicial branches. It instituted the National Congress for Unification (NCU)—headed by the president and comprising delegates elected by eligible voters—for electing the president for a six-year term with no term limit. Also, the president now appointed one-third of the members of the national assembly for a two-year term. Furthermore, the president had the power to take emergency measures and disband the national assembly as he saw fit. Voters elected members of the new NCU (December 15), which then duly elected Park for his new, six-year term as the president (December 23), thus inaugurating the Fourth Republic (1972–81). Park rationalized the Yusin system as "Korean-style democracy."

The opposition, student activists, and intellectuals, as well as much of the general public, saw the Yusin system as the institutionalization of one-person rule, and a pro-democracy movement quickly spread. Leading the anti-dictatorship struggle was a broad coalition of civilian groups, including the National Federation of Democratic Youth and Students; the Tonga Association in Defense of and Struggle for a Free Press, organized by the *Tonga ilbo* newspaper and Tonga Broadcasting System journalists wrongfully laid off by the regime; and the National Congress for the Restoration of Democracy, which anti-government politicians and religious leaders had organized. As the anti-Yusin resistance gained strength, the KCIA abducted an opposition leader and former presidential candidate, Kim Dae-jung, while he was visiting Tokyo (August 8, 1973). Tipped off by a South Korean diplomat in Tokyo, the U.S. government thwarted the KCIA's original plan of throwing Kim into the East Sea, and the KCIA had to settle for bringing him back to Seoul and placing him under house arrest. Not only did this incident likely prompt North Korea to withdraw from inter-Korean talks (August 28), but South Korea's anti-government activists were outraged, and Park responded by laying off or jailing more dissidents (January 1974). Months later, during the National Liberation Day commemoration ceremony, Park survived an assassination attempt by a pro-North Korean Zainichi, but the assassin's bullet killed the first lady (August 15). Regarding the attack as masterminded by the north, Park clamped down, and ruled South Korea with an iron fist.

Park Chung-hee's eighteen-year rule, which had begun with violence, ended in violence. When Park got himself elected to another six-year term, he faced mounting challenges (July 6, 1978). Not only was the regime's abuse of human rights generating criticism abroad, support for Park was eroding even within the ruling DRP. Also, during the worldwide energy crisis of 1979, when crude oil prices more than doubled in twelve months, South Korea's economy fell into a slump, further fanning discontent. And when the regime stripped the NDP leader, Kim Young-sam (Kim Yŏngsam; 1927–2015), of his national assembly membership for openly condemning Park's misrule, mass demonstrations erupted in Pusan, which was Kim's political home base, and nearby Masan (October 16–20, 1979). As protests erupted elsewhere, Park faced a decision on whether to make concessions to the resistance or to suppress it. At that critical juncture, KCIA Director Kim Jae-gyu (Kim Chaegyu; 1926–80) shot and killed Park (October 26). During his subsequent trial, Kim would assert that he had acted to restore democracy.

Park Chung-hee's sudden death created a power vacuum soon filled by new military leadership, which dashed hopes for the restoration of democracy. A month after the assassination, the NCU elected Prime Minister Choi Kyu-hah (Ch'oe Kyuha; 1919–2006) as the new president (December 6). Six days later, however, Major General Chun Doo-hwan, who was the commander of the Defense Security Command; Major General Roh Tae-woo (No T'aeu; b. 1932), who was an infantry division commander; and other officers of the Defense Security Command, staged a coup and took over the government (December 12). Outraged student activists, who had been expecting that a democratic civilian government would be established, began to hold mass demonstrations, the "Spring of Seoul" (May 14, 1980). Chun responded by instituting martial law throughout the country and by banning all political activities (May 17). Shutting down all political parties, he stationed troops on university campuses; arrested such prominent politicians as Kim Dae-jung and Kim Jong-pil, accusing them of illegally accumulating wealth; and placed Kim Young-sam under house arrest.

Chun Doo-hwan's actions sparked the Kwangju Uprising, spearheaded by local university student demonstrations. On May 18, student protesters and airborne troops clashed in front of Chonnam National University. The paratroopers were harsh in the use of force against the demonstrators and any citizen in the way. The next day, the protest intensified as angry citizens joined the students, and the reinforced paratroops used live bullets and bayonets as they pursued demonstrators (May 19). Two days later, para-troopers deployed military helicopters and sharpshooters atop buildings, firing upon protesters indiscriminately and killing four civilians (May 21). Sacking the military ammunition depot, the protesters took up arms, calling themselves the Citizens' Army. By the next day, Kwangju was cut off from the outside world, and the military-controlled media outlets falsely reported to the rest of the country that a radical protest incited by North Korea had erupted in Kwangju (May 22). More citizens joined the uprising before a sudden charge by a paratrooper division killed eight civilians.

The military leadership quashed the uprising with further bloodshed. The protesters and the citizenry, in general, were shifting their attention to law and order by cleaning the city and collecting the weapons when paratroopers fired upon a bus and killed seventeen people (May 23). The next day, friendly fire killed nine soldiers, and as if venting on the uprising, troops raided a village and killed four civilians in execution style (May 24). As the military prepared for a final assault, the Citizens' Army took up its position at the South Chŏlla Province Headquarters and began to send minors and the infirm home. Government troops with columns of tanks entered Kwangju, quickly overcame a resistance in downtown, and stormed the provincial headquarters (May 27). Officially, the uprising and the suppression left at least 165 dead, and there were 376 subsequent deaths due to injuries suffered, 76 missing, and 3,515 injured among the civilians. Among the government personnel, 23 soldiers (including 13 caught by friendly fire) and 4 police officers died. An unofficial estimate of the full number of dead, however, ranged from about 1,000 to 2,000.

After Chung Doo-hwan suppressed the Kwangju Uprising, seemingly nothing stood in his path to power. In many ways reduplicating Park Chung-hee's coup nearly two decades earlier, except shedding far more blood, Chun established a de facto junta, the Special Committee for National Security Measures, with himself as the head (May 31). After forcing the figurehead President Choi to resign (August 16), Chun convened the NCU to get himself duly elected as the new president (September 1). Subsequently, Chun replaced the Yusin Constitution with a new one, which instituted a single term seven-year presidency and replaced the NCU with an Electoral College (October 27).

In North Korea, a far more gradual transition toward a new leader had begun years earlier, when Kim Il-sung moderated the Partisans' hard-line stance, the military-first policy of the 1960s, and began to groom his son for eventual succession. Purging even the Partisans from leadership, Kim promoted more members of his own family and technocrats. Responding to South Korea's Yusin system, Kim replaced the 1948 People's Constitution with the Juche Constitution (December 1972). His position as premier and as the head of the cabinet became the presidency. The new constitution concentrated all power in the president's office by placing directly under it the newly created Central People's Committee. Also, the Juche Constitution changed the nation's official capital from Seoul to P'yŏngyang. Among various family members who occupied key positions, the elder of his two sons, Kim Jong-il, became the heir apparent. He and his cadre of supporters led the Movement of Small Groups for Three Great Revolutions, which covered thought, technology, and culture (September 1973). In the same month, the WPK's Central Committee elected him as the Secretary for Organizational Thought and subsequently elevated him as a Political Committee member (February 1974). The younger Kim further solidified his position as the heir apparent when the Sixth Congress of the WPK (October 1980) elected him as the general secretary of the party, a member of the Presidium of the Politburo, and a member of the WPK's Central Military Commission. The official media vigorously justified and publicized his eventual succession while fine-tuning the Juche ideology. Its central tenet of self-sufficiency, however, was already showing its limits through a slowing economic growth whereas South Korea was writing a success story.

ECONOMIES IN CONTRAST: TAKEOFF VERSUS STAGNATION

In the aftermath of the April 19 Revolution in 1960, South Korea's Second Republic gradually overcame an economic crisis. Initially, the number of unemployed rose to 2.4 million, and 80 percent of the factories were idle. Especially in May and June in the countryside, households suffered from food shortages after exhausting the previous year's fall harvest while barley was still ripening. Prioritizing economic security, in the spring of 1961, the Chang Myon cabinet launched a national land development project that entailed such undertakings as constructing hydroelectric power stations to create jobs. The government also sought to secure revenue for executing a new, long-term economic development plan in the following year. Held back by internal strife within the Democratic Party leadership, Chang could not focus entirely on the effort. By the spring of 1961, however, both high inflation and unemployment were beginning to subside when Park Chung-hee staged the coup.

The Park regime effected South Korea's economic takeoff. Its first five-year economic development plan (1962–66) sustained average annual growth of 44 percent in exports and 8.5 percent in the overall economy. The second five-year economic development plan (1967–71) achieved a yearly average increase of 33.7 percent in exports and 10.7 percent in the economy. During the decade, South Korea also passed such milestones in infrastructure development as completing the nation's first oil refinery in Ulsan (1964), the Masan Free Export Zone (1969), and the Kyŏngbu Expressway (1970). Generating and sustaining this remarkable economic growth were Park's vision, planning, directives, and support for promising business leaders; a relatively young, disciplined population willing to work hard to get ahead in life and for national glory; foreign loans; and South Korea's privileged access to such key markets as the United States and Japan. As South Korea's growing light industry exported such products as textiles and sneakers, the share of manufacturing and mining in the economy increased significantly. To promote exports to lead the overall economic growth, the government kept wages low, in order to produce export goods at a lower cost and keep them competitive overseas. This policy demanded sacrifices on the part of factory workers and farming villages, as throughout the decade, the government kept the price of agricultural produce low as well. This spurred urban migration, in turn increasing the population of urban poor and the unemployed.

In the meantime, North Korea effected a fully controlled economy that prioritized heavy industry and military build-up, and the robust annual economic growth it had experienced since the late 1950s, which at one point was as high as 20 percent, ended by the mid-1960s. Perceiving a security threat from such new developments abroad as the Sino-Soviet rift, the establishment of a military government in South Korea, and a U.S.–Soviet showdown in the form of the Cuban Missile Crisis (1962), Kim Il-sung announced a policy of pursuing both economic development and military build-up (December 1962). Subsequently, the U.S. entry into the Vietnam War (1964), South Korea's normalization of relations with Japan, and the commencement of the Cultural Revolution in China (1966–76) prompted Kim to launch a seven-year plan with those twin goals of economic growth and military build-up. The share of total expenditure spent on defense increased from

3.7 percent in 1959 to 19 percent in 1960; after averaging 19.8 percent between 1961 and 1966, the percentage shot up to 30.4 percent in 1967. By then, private financial transactions had all but ceased, and the state distributed more or less everything of value. Money had little meaning without the requisite ration coupons. The lack of incentives for competitive productivity, the limited inflow of foreign capital and advanced technology, and disproportionately heavy military spending all slowed overall economic growth.

By contrast, South Korea's impressive economic growth continued. The 1973 oil crisis worldwide hurt the South Korean economy as well. Still, during the period of Park's third and fourth five-year economic development plans (1972–76, 1977–81), the economy enjoyed a double-digit annual growth rate and became seven times larger. Also, exports increased annually by about 48 percent during the first period and 21 percent during the second, with industrial products accounting for more than 90 percent of exports. The government's shifting focus from light industry to heavy and chemical industries produced some of the iconic initiatives, such as POSCO (formerly the Pohang Iron and Steel Company; 1973) and the Kori Nuclear Power Plant (1978). Moreover, Hyundai and other construction firms with accumulated experience in Vietnam secured projects in the Middle East's newly wealthy yet technologically limited oil-rich countries. Huge profits generated by the new construction projects in the Middle East helped these companies grow far larger, turning into conglomerates (*chaebŏl*)—groups of companies doing business in a wide range of industries, yet each group owned and controlled by the founder's family. The "Miracle on the Han River," as some dubbed South Korea's economy, became a model for other developing nations.

Simultaneously, the Park regime undertook the New Village Movement (Saemaŭl Undong) to ensure that rural areas did not become a ball and chain on the growing national economy. Launched in 1970, the New Village Movement sought to improve rural living conditions and increase farming household income by promoting better managed, more profitable agriculture. This effort produced positive results. By the mid-1970s, the development of a high-yield variety of rice made South Korea self-sufficient in rice production. Also, farmers began to diversify their income sources through horticulture and livestock farming. Encouraged by success, the government expanded the program's scope to include urban areas, thus turning it into an overall national development strategy. All the same, the income gap between farming villages and cities continued to widen.

North Korea's economic growth continued to slow during the decade, with annual growth limited to 2 percent. Contributing to the slowdown were decreasing foreign aid, minimal technological innovation, and by then chronic energy shortages, including shortages of electricity and oil. Kim Il-sung's insistence on attaining the twin goals of economic development and military build-up reduced overall investment, and extending the seven-year economic plan by three years made little difference. Seeking to capitalize on a détente between the United States on the one hand and the Soviet Union and China on the other, the regime declared its flexibility about expanding exchanges with the West to secure loans (1973); however, North Korea's limited productivity and low credit rating abroad led only to an increase in foreign debt. As Western nations decreased their imports of nonferrous metal due to the 1973 oil crisis, North Korea's export of such materials likewise decreased. Before long, the country was in default and stopped seeking loans (1976). To stimulate growth, Kim launched the so-called Movement to Secure Red Banners for the Three Great Revolutions (1973–74), which resembled China's earlier Cultural Revolution and also implemented a system of independent profit for corporations. Neither effort, though, produced any meaningful results. Coping with increasingly alarming economic challenges, the regime finally began to decrease military spending. After hovering around the 30 percent level until 1971, the share of the GDP going to defense expenditures abruptly fell to 17 percent (1972). The percentage continued to decline for the remainder of the decade. An economy in transition made a powerful social impact in North Korea, as well as in the south.

URBANIZATION, INDUSTRIALIZATION, AND SOCIAL CHANGE

In the 1960s, as South Korea began to industrialize rapidly, a dramatic demographic transformation began. The population increased from some 25 million (1960) to over 32 million (1970) to more than 38 million (1980). Initially, both the TFR and death rates were high, but then the TFR decreased from 5.63 births in 1960–65 to 2.92 in 1975–80, while life expectancy increased from 54.8 to 65 years during that period. The decrease in the TFR reflects the government's launch of family planning, which widely promoted the ideal of a couple with no more than two children and also promoted the use of birth control. The mean age of the population began to increase, and nuclear families increasingly replaced extended families.

Although the population benefited from increased agricultural productivity, living standards in rural communities improved only slowly. By the
mid-1970s, South Korea was producing enough of its staple, rice, to feed the
population. Nonetheless, as the industrializing economy's ability to meet
its own needs for all types of grain continued to decrease—to 65 percent
of those needs as of 1977—imports of such non-staple crops as wheat,
corn, and beans increased. Besides the expansion of the 4-H movement, the
launch of the New Village Movement, which stressed diligence, self-help,
and collaboration, changed the rural landscape. The movement converted
traditional dwellings with thatched roofs into more modern homes, paved
roads, and installed such essential services as running water and electricity.
Such improvements, however, did not stem a mass exodus of younger rural
residents in search of education and jobs in the cities.

During the economic takeoff, educational opportunities continued to
expand in South Korea, and demand too increased. As education remained
the surest path toward success in life, the overall fervor for education was a
significant factor contributing to the country's rapid economic growth. In
the 1960s, those who had obtained bachelor's or postgraduate degrees at elite
universities or in the United States were especially likely to assume leading
roles in various sectors of society. Simultaneously, this fervor also had an
increasingly negative social impact by the late 1970s, when widespread competition to attend the best schools began to fuel extracurricular education
as an industry of its own. While an increasing segment of the population
obtained higher education and white-collar jobs on their way to joining the
expanding middle class, far more people became poor factory workers in
Seoul, Pusan, and the various new industrial cities in the southeast.

Increasing urban concentration exacerbated unemployment, housing
shortages, inadequate transportation systems, overcrowded schools, poverty, and pollution. The Park Chung-hee regime sought to address these
complaints by launching a number of such new policies as constructing
large-scale apartment complexes, building subway train lines, improving
surface road networks, expanding compulsory education, introducing a social
welfare system, and developing new cities. Overconcentration of the nation's
population and resources in Seoul became a grave concern, especially since
the city was within North Korea's field artillery range. Indeed, in the 1970s,
Park initially considered moving the capital farther south. Upon concluding that this was financially unfeasible, he approved the less ambitious plan

of transferring some government offices several kilometers south of Seoul's downtown to Kwach'ŏn, forming an "administrative city." Construction of its infrastructure commenced in 1979.

Including those in Seoul, most of South Korea's urban poor comprised industrial workers in manufacturing and their dependents, and these employees suffered from low wages, long work hours, and deplorable working conditions. Nominal wages continued to increase due to inflation, but real wage increases did not keep up with the rising cost of living. Inflation, land prices, home prices, rent, and key money (*chŏnse*; instead of paying monthly rent, a tenant makes a lump-sum deposit of 50 to 80 percent of the market value of the residence) all contributed to wage laborers' hardship. With the 1953 Labor Standards Act good only on paper, some tragic incidents laid bare the dark side of South Korea's economic takeoff. When the tailor and labor activist Chŏn T'aeil (1948–70) committed suicide by setting himself ablaze in protest at the Ch'ŏnggyech'ŏn P'yŏnghwa Market in Seoul, he shouted: "Abide by the Labor Standards Act!" "We are not machines!" "Let us rest on Sunday!" and "Don't exploit workers!" (November 1970). Not only was his death a wake-up call for many intellectuals and social activists but many workers subsequently pursued movements to secure wage increases and the right to organize labor unions—only to elicit persecution by the Park regime. Years later, when the YH Trading Company owner, a wig manufacturer, discontinued his business, more than 170 former employees, all young women, demanded that the company resume operation and staged a sit-in protest at the NDP headquarters (August 1979). When the police stormed the headquarters and broke up the demonstration, one died, and more than 100 were injured.

Meanwhile, North Korea experienced a demographic transformation of its own, though with patterns different from the south's. In the 1960s, a disproportionately large part of the population was female, but by 1970, the disparity had been reduced, with 95.1 males per 100 females. In the 1960s, the population increased at a high rate of 3.1 percent per year—2.7 percent in 1960 and 3.6 percent in 1970—before falling to 1.9 percent in 1975; the average rate during the 1970s was 1.7 percent per year. The TFR increased from 3.41 births in 1960–65 to a peak of 4.09 in 1965–70. It then decreased to 2.58 in 1975–80, while life expectancy continued to increase from 51.6 years to 57.2 to 65.0 during that entire period. Interrelated contributing factors included relatively late marriage; the government's birth control policy, geared toward mobilizing more women for work; women's increased participation in the labor force while still responsible for housework and childrearing; urbanization; and housing shortages. Over this same period, the urban population increase slowed from 6 percent per year in the 1960s to between 1 and 3 percent per year from 1970 to 1987.

Amidst the demographic transformation of urbanizing, industrializing Korea, both North and South, the largest ethnic minority, the Chinese, lost further ground. In the south, the Park Chung-hee regime implemented currency reform and property restrictions that hurt the Chinese Korean community's business interests and spurred their exodus. In the 1970s, an estimated 15,000 moved to the United States and 10,000 to Taiwan, and others went to Hong Kong and elsewhere; the population of those remaining in the country dwindled to 20,000. Many who immigrated to America settled in areas with large Korean American communities, such as Los Angeles, where they tended to integrate into the Korean American rather than the Chinese American community, which already had a long history of immigration from elsewhere. In the interim, around 1966, North Korea pursued a policy of indigenizing Chinese schools. Also, as the Kim Il-sung regime encouraged those with PRC citizenship to move to China, their number in North Korea decreased sharply, from 14,351 in 1958 to about 6,000 by 1980.

While Chinese Koreans left both Koreas en masse, an increasing number of ethnic Koreans and Japanese moved from Japan to North Korea, either willingly or unwillingly. Between 1959 and 1982, the Chongryon encouraged migration, or "repatriation," of the Zainichi to North Korea, and more than 93,000 did so. Also, by the end of the 1960s, some 6,600 ethnic Japanese had accompanied their Zainichi spouses to North Korea. During that decade, however, the numbers of Japanese and Zainichi moving to North Korea dropped sharply as the poor economic conditions compared to Japan, social discrimination, and political repression faced by the migrants became known in Japan by word of mouth. In the 1970s, North Korea brought in some Japanese nationals for political propaganda purposes, through such measures as granting political asylum to the nine members of the Japanese Communist League–Red Army Faction who had hijacked Japan Airlines Flight 351 (1970). Years later, North Korea kidnapped Japanese citizens to teach Japanese to North Korean intelligence agents. Between 1977 and 1983, at least seventeen and perhaps several hundred Japanese nationals ended up in the country against their will.

While the legal position of ethnic minorities remained insecure in both Koreas, South Korea's industrialization and the economic takeoff facilitated women's participation in the labor force. Women's employment opportunities increased, mostly in the production sector, although gradually more secured clerical, managerial, and professional jobs. The latter trend received a boost from continuing improvement in females' access to education, which led to a rapid decrease in teenage workers and provided more employment opportunities for older married women. Nevertheless, such positive developments did not lead to gender equality in the labor market. Not only did significant wage differences between male and female workers persist, but the majority of employed females remained low-wage factory workers.

By comparison, gender equality saw faster progress in North Korea, thanks to the 1948 People's Constitution, other statutes, and ongoing legislation. While divorce rates remained relatively low, state intervention intensified by way of the court-supervised divorce, which determined whether the marriage in question had lost its meaning for society in general and the partners and children in particular. Also, instituting paid maternity leave both before and after giving birth, the state assumed support for childcare as its responsibility. In 1960, state-managed childcare centers accommodated 65 percent of children under five, and as of 1970, the vast majority of children. Each provincial capital built children's centers to house orphans and other children who could not be looked after by their families. Women with three or more children received such additional benefits as a full working day's pay for reduced work hours. These policies facilitated women's participation in economic activities. In 1965, around 55 percent of the work force was female, and by 1970 the figure reached 70 percent of the workforce in light industry and 60 percent of those employed in the agricultural sector. Female participation in politics too increased, although most women held parliamentary posts that had no real power. In 1972, the Provincial People's Committees had 729 women out of a total of 3,185 members (22.9 percent).

At the same time, patriarchy remained strong as a sociopolitical ideal. The leadership cult around Kim Il-sung and, increasingly, Kim Jong-il, shaped the whole nation in line with traditional family structures. The regime used the analogy of the father and his children consistently to personify the roles of Kim Il-sung and the people, respectively, and the citizenry remained subject to rigid social control. Influenced by Confucianism, the state dominated the private sphere as an extension of the public domain.

In such daily public spaces as work, promotion came to be based on an examination system, according to which most workplaces administered a triennial examination. Promotion and higher pay went to those who passed, and compared to women, a much higher proportion of men took the tests. The culture of a household centered around a married couple with children was such that the father's successful career as the patriarch and the head of the home determined the family's well-being, a pattern also true in South Korea despite cultural divergence between the two Koreas.

CULTURE OF THE COLD WAR

In the 1960s in South Korea, nationalism grew stronger among intellectuals and university students. Academic research in Korean studies, centered around newly founded scholarly organizations, universities, and research institutes, pursued a twin mission of overcoming the colonial legacies and effecting national reunification. The effort intensified, especially after the April 19 Revolution. Many university students also became more nationalistic. They were now exposed to a new inflow of information on the Third World countries that had recently won independence from colonial powers and those still struggling to achieve independence. While Western literature, especially English-language works, was popular among educated youth, nationalistic literature also acquired a following. The more radical among them even advocated an immediate meeting of the students from both Koreas, at P'anmunjŏm, to discuss unification. Upon gaining power, Park Chung-hee and the junta strictly banned such an initiative, and at the same time combined anti-communism and nationalism into a guiding ideology for education. In 1968, in the same spirit, the Park regime issued the National Education Charter. Beginning with the declaration, "We were born on this land with a historic mission of restoring national glory," the charter's 130-word text, which every primary and secondary school textbook included until 1994, asserted that the nation's progress was an individual's progress. At least through the 1980s, students had to memorize and recite the charter.

To meet its demand that every citizen play a part in the pursuit of national glory, the government actively promoted science and technology. Adding momentum to this overall effort, Park established the Korea Institute of Science and Technology (1966) and the Office of Science and Technology to formulate and execute the relevant policies (1967). As developed at the time, South Korea's long-term strategy entailed recruitment and financial support of talented students to pursue higher education abroad, especially in the United States, and assigning them to key research positions upon their return. They assumed leadership roles in both the public and the private sectors during the period of rapid economic growth.

As the number of households with electricity increased, even in rural areas, broadcast media promoted the agendas of the government while providing such entertainment as it approved. The first television broadcast throughout the country (1961) and first FM radio broadcast (1965) heralded a new era of increasingly important outlets through which the regime could shape public opinion and mold a popular culture as approved by the regime. Understanding the power of media, as did Syngman Rhee, Park Chung-hee used his increasingly authoritarian rule to limit the press's freedom through censorship, if not outright intimidation and threats as applied through the regime's henchmen, the Supreme Prosecutors' Office and the police. All the same, the expanding broadcast media, coupled with economic development and improving living standards, accelerated the dissemination of various genres of American and European popular culture that South Korean entertainers quickly made their own. Within the bounds set by the regime's message of austerity, urban consumerism spread with the growing middle class enjoying a broadening range of television and radio programming.

A parallel development was the growth of organized religion, which played an increasingly prominent role in South Koreans' lives. Buddhism and Christianity, in particular, made significant gains. While the vast majority, roughly 88 percent as of 1964, continued to profess no affiliation with a specific religion, that unaffiliated segment continued to decrease. As of 1960, self-identified Buddhists, Protestants, and Catholics accounted for 3 percent, 5 percent, and 2 percent of the population, respectively. By 1970, these figures increased to 15 percent, 7 percent, and 3 percent. Other religions accounted for no more than 2 to 5 percent of the population. The growth of affiliated Christian and Buddhist populations reflects both the indigenization of Western cultures perceived as modern progress and the rediscovery of Korean traditions.

Meanwhile, in North Korea, socialist internationalism, increasingly colored by Juche thought, dominated the cultural landscape. As Kim Il-sung underwent apotheosis as the subject of a leadership cult, he and the Partisans became the central actors in a revisionist account of modern Korean history, and Kim's "instructions" (kyosi) began to inform understandings of history and all other branches of knowledge. The regime turned classical historical materialism, which Marxists present as a scientific method for understanding social development, into a state-promoted instrument for legitimating the political system. The government also formulated and promoted literary theories based on Juche thought. The so-called Leader Representation Literature exaggerated Kim Il-sung's and Kim Jong-il's accomplishments to enhance the younger Kim's stature as the heir apparent and to promote Juche further. At the same time, the regime continued to promote the literary works of Hong Myŏnghŭi, Kim Il-sung's grandson and novelist Hong Sŏkchung (b. 1941), and other writers, Korean and foreign, who employed socialist realism. For disseminating Juche-influenced literature and historical studies, North Korea adopted the Cultured Language (1966) as the standard Korean language. Based on the general dialect of Kyŏnggi, if not Seoul, rather than the speech of P'yŏngyang and vicinity as claimed by the government, the Cultured Language replaced much of the Sino-Korean vocabulary and other loanwords with indigenous words or even newly coined ones. Not confined to written texts, Cultured Language found immediate use in the production and promotion of "revolutionary lyric songs" (hyŏngmyŏng kagok) and "policy songs" (chŏngch'aek kayo), although more purely sentimental songs remained more popular.

More than just an ideological guide for various cultural genres, Juche thought became a de facto religion. In the 1960s, the regime officially articulated a flexible attitude toward religion, declaring that the People's Constitution guaranteed religious freedom. In reality, however, various restrictions drove down the number of active religious practitioners. In place of traditional organized religions, Juche ideology dictated an individual's morality and professional duties regardless of industry or occupation. Also, Juche became increasingly confrontational and militaristic, as it employed such expressions as "agricultural battle," "industrial battle," and "production battle" to inspire virtually all forms of productive labor. Accordingly, military personnel and other government employees alike came to hold military-style ranks and could rise through those ranks, depending on merit.

Although not as all-encompassing or restrictive as Juche thought, in the 1970s in South Korea, the prevailing statism motivated cultural undertakings geared toward promoting national pride. Objectives included debunking colonial historiography, decentering the West in the South Korean weltanschauung, and boosting the nation's self-awareness and self-confidence.

The overall effort inspired the restoration of many historical sites and the National Institute of Korean History's publication of a twenty-five volume *History of Korea* (*Han'guk sa*; 1979), which reflected the latest South Korean scholarship at the time. The government also established the Academy of Korean Studies to facilitate more systematic promotion of interdisciplinary Korean studies (1978). The following year, the academy set about compiling a twenty-seven volume *Encyclopedia of Korean Culture* (*Han'guk minjok munhwa taebaekkwa sajŏn*; 1991).

Nonetheless, South Korea's cultural landscape became more variegated as writers and performers pursued scholarly and creative activities more independently from the state. Among literary circles, nationalist literature remained influential, but the country's literature became more diverse in style and gained a broader base of readership. Reflecting on uncritical acceptance of Western cultures, some intellectuals, artists, and activists spearheaded an effort to revive such traditional genres as masked plays and *samul nori*, a type of music played on four traditional percussion instruments. Performances in these genres gained a following, starting with university students, and the trend gradually turned into an effort to combine Western and indigenous genres into something more uniquely Korean. In such a context, songs, dramas, and comedies broadcast on television quickly became core genres of expanding popular culture. Centered around the urban middle class, the consumer base grew rapidly.

During this decade in South Korea, organized religions too underwent rapid growth. The Park Chung-hee regime strongly discouraged, if not prohibited, shamanism and indigenous folk religious practices as superstition—an attitude widely shared among more Westernized urban elites—and virtually wiped out the traditional shrines (*sadang*). Park himself was not religious, but the policy allowed the three largest groups, Christianity, Buddhism, and Won Buddhism, to win more members. Regardless, many progressive Christian leaders, Catholics and Protestants alike, assumed prominent roles in the growing pro-democracy movement or actively supported labor, farmer, and reunification movements.

In the north, Kim Il-sung continued to marshal Juche thought and nationalism to shape historical studies and literary works in ways that legitimized the regime. The Juche Constitution of 1972 upgraded the status of P'yŏngyang from the DPRK's temporary capital to the official capital, and accordingly, the state began to rewrite national history to put P'yŏngyang at the center.

Published history books narrated early Korean history with a succession of northern states, namely Kojosŏn and Koguryŏ—both of which had their capital in P'yŏngyang—and Parhae, as the mainstream. The Kim regime presented the DPRK as the inheritor of historical legitimacy through Koryŏ and Chosŏn. Such an interpretation was in stark contrast to the South Korean historiography that privileged Silla and labeled the post–Three Kingdoms Silla as "Unified Silla"—never mind Parhae in the north. In literature, North Korean writers employed Juche literary theory in turning theatrical performances that praised class revolution, such as *The Sea of Blood* (*Pi pada*; 1971) and *The Flower Girl* (*Kkot p'anŭn ch'ŏnyŏ*; 1972), into novels.

North Korea likewise made use of various performance genres guided by Juche thought to legitimate the regime as the vanguard for the Korean communist revolution. In particular, cinema enjoyed the special attention of the regime, which regarded movies as a medium of political propaganda more effective than any other in instilling revolutionary fervor into the masses. Groomed as the heir apparent leading the new generation, Kim Jong-il himself not only put much effort into producing movies to such ends but reportedly even authored a treatise, *On the Art of the Cinema* (*Yŏnghwa yesul ron*; 1973). North Korea also developed and promoted its own unique style for such group presentation genres as mass games, card section performances, and circuses.

In part shaped by the state, the culture of everyday life in both Koreas underwent increasingly rapid changes, including in clothing. In the south, when Park gained power, the junta conducted an austerity campaign, promoting working clothes, or "reconstruction dress" (*chaegŏnbok*), for men and "new casual dress" (*sin saenghwalbok*) for women. Simultaneously, Western-style dress, especially American fashion, became the standard outfit, and younger urban women were the trendsetters. Appearing first in the 1960s, during the 1970s, miniskirts and pantaloons became even more popular while maxi skirts and hot pants debuted as new trends. By then, among younger South Koreans, jeans and long hair had become widely popular as the fashion of youth culture—symbolized by acoustic guitars and pop music. During the decade, women's dress transitioned from mostly custom-made clothes to mass-produced, ready-made garments. Western influence grew stronger also in North Korea, except the state strictly prohibited any fashion it deemed decadent, including long hair, jeans, and high skirt hems. And the people's dress (*inminbok*) largely replaced Western suits for public events, especially those infused with the spirit of Juche.

While both North and South Koreans followed increasingly uniform fashion in clothing in their respective countries, a transformation of their food cultures continued. In the 1960s, the southern government focused on ending food shortages through increasing rice production and also increasing the variety of a daily diet that traditionally privileged a bowl of steamed rice. In part spurred by the government's promotion of a more wheat-based diet, including flour and white bread, more South Koreans found things American appealing. Still, a meal comprising steamed grain, soup, kimchi, and other side dishes—mostly a varying combination of vegetables and marine products—remained the norm. In the 1970s, acute food shortages were becoming a thing of the past, thanks to the economic takeoff. Continuing industrialization exposed more people, especially the growing urban middle class, to such processed food as ramen (Ko. ramyŏn), white bread, butter, jam, ham, sausages, canned fish and fruits, milk, and carbonated drinks. The middle class also ate out, patronizing venues with Korean-style cooking (hansik), Koreanized Chinese cooking (chunghwa yori), Japanese cooking, and "light Western-style" cooking (kyŏngyangsik), which featured soups, salads, tea sandwiches, Japanese-style curry, and omuraisŭ (Ja. omu-raisu), fried rice covered with a thin layer of egg. Struggling to keep up with the middle-class demand was a thriving black market in surplus processed American food and drinks from the U.S. military bases. In North Korea, an overall shift from a daily diet based on plant and marine products to greater consumption of processed food was underway but not to the extent seen in the south. Especially among elites and urbanites, Soviet and Eastern European food and drink continued to wield some influence, albeit not to the degree true of anything American in South Korea. Upon completing economic collectivization, North Korea's more or less fully state-controlled food production and distribution increasingly struggled to meet the population's minimum dietary needs as the country's economic growth slowed.

Meanwhile, an overall change in South Korea's housing situation accelerated, especially in Seoul and its vicinity. The government-owned Korea Housing Corporation (KHC; 1962–2007) launched a series of large projects, beginning in 1962 with a 450-unit complex of six six-story apartment buildings in Map'o, located north of the Han River in southwestern central Seoul. Between 1966 and 1971, KHC constructed a complex of five-story apartment buildings along the Han River, comprising 3,260 units, including 700 middle-class family apartments that featured boiler heating. Simultaneously, downtown redevelopment got underway with new apartment buildings that had shops on the first floor. Focusing on middle-income families, KHC delegated low-income family housing projects to local governments. Between 1972 and 1976, in central Seoul just south of the river in Panp'o, KHC constructed a greater variety of apartment complexes, with units ranging from 22 to 64 *p'yŏng* (72.7 to 211.6 square meters), housed in five- or six-story buildings. In 1974, when Seoul began to build a large apartment complex to the east of Panp'o in Chamsil for 100,000 residents, the project replaced the older concept of south-facing units in a single row with a square layout to secure more space for common green areas, parks, and playgrounds. Between 1977 and 1981, farther outside the old city, KHC oversaw the construction of 1.1 million new units, 620,000 of which were privately funded. Rapidly running out of land, in 1979, the government began to develop a new city bordering southern Seoul, Kwach'ŏn. The next year, a new law facilitated the construction of large residential complexes on the capital's periphery, including in Kwangmyŏng bordering southwestern Seoul.

The mass housing projects of the two Koreas in this era stood in stark contrast to each other. Far more modest in scale and limited in variety, North Korea's projects remained focused on providing minimal-standard housing to its population as collectivization saw completion. As urbanization continued, residence in multistory apartment buildings became common among an increasing segment of the population. In South Korea, the main beneficiaries of the mass housing projects were the capital's middle-class citizens, while the poor struggled. Certainly, in the 1970s, housing in rural communities began to improve, with more paved roads, running water, and electricity while an increasing number of *kaeryang hanok* and Korean-style Western homes replaced thatched roof dwellings and *hanok*. Regardless, a mass migration of job-seekers from rural areas to Seoul and other cities that began in the 1960s soon gave rise to *taltongne*, or shantytowns, of urban poor, whose lives were a far cry from the lives led by their families back home or by the growing middle class moving into new apartment units. Housing culture was one among an increasing number of areas where the two Koreas would become increasingly different from each other even as overall inter-Korean tension decreased in the following decades.

CHAPTER 13

Toward Détente, 1980–2000

T oward the end of the twentieth century, inter-Korean relations stabilized, mostly unaffected by occasional incidents. In South Korea, the June Struggle (1987) ended authoritarian rule and heralded a vibrant democracy. As the country gained ground in the global political economy, North Korea's further isolation upon the collapse of the Eastern Bloc (1991) spurred Kim Il-sung to pursue nuclear weapon and ballistic missile programs for strategic leverage vis-à-vis South Korea and the United States Continuing the effort, his successor, Kim Jong-il, prioritized the military. Overburdened, the stagnant economy collapsed, under massive flooding, ruined harvests, and widespread famine. A desperate North Korea responded favorably to the engagement policy of South Korea as an emerging economic powerhouse with high tech. The internet and mobile communication devices facilitated both the spread and the ghettoization of information. In the north, the gap between the party line and the population's cynicism widened as the new technology made surveillance more difficult.

THE POLITICS OF GLOBALIZATION VERSUS ISOLATION

In the 1980s in South Korea, Chun Doo-hwan took further steps to consolidate his power. After launching the Democratic Justice Party (1981–90) as his political organization, Chun convened the Electoral College, which re-elected him as president (February 25, 1981) and thus inaugurated the Fifth

Republic (1981–88), based on a new constitution. Drawing lessons from Park Chung-hee's successes and failures, Chun implemented a mixture of repressive policies and concessions. Among the concessions were repealing the Anti-Communism Law, making it a part of the National Security Act (1980), and abolishing the Student Corps for National Defense while allowing autonomous student organizations on university campuses (1984). Repressive measures, though, were more dominant. The Fifth Republic continued to bar Kim Dae-jung, Kim Young-sam, Kim Jong-pil, and many other prominent political figures. The regime even convicted Kim Dae-jung of conspiracy and sentenced him to death (January 1981), only to suspend the sentence upon a barrage of criticism from abroad (December 1982). Also, the government deployed police on university campuses to forestall student demonstrations, the intensity of which did not decrease. Further, the Chun regime made media outlets lay off journalists who were critical of the regime.

In the meantime, inter-Korean relations underwent a rollercoaster ride. Preparing for Kim Jong-il's eventual succession, North Korea's ongoing effort to fine-tune Juche thought as an all-encompassing national ideology culminated with the publication of *On the Juche Idea* (*Chuch'e sasang e taehayŏ*; 1982). Attributed to Kim Jong-il, the ostensibly authoritative treatise legitimized the heir apparent as the sole, bona fide interpreter of the ideology. The younger Kim nonetheless was under pressure to demonstrate revolutionary credentials worthy of the successor of his father as an anti-Japanese resistance fighter, and that likely contributed to two high-profile terrorist incidents. During Chun Doo-hwan's state visit to Burma (present Myanmar), exploding bombs at the Martyrs Mausoleum in Yangon killed seventeen members of his delegation and injured fourteen (October 1983). The subsequent investigation by the Burmese authorities blamed North Korean agents. Four years later, a Korean Air passenger plane exploded in mid-air over the Indian Ocean (November 1987), and again North Korean agents were deemed responsible. Hawks within the regime reportedly staged both incidents, probably with the younger Kim's tacit approval. Nonetheless, the two Koreas agreed on an unprecedented reunion of families separated by the division of Korea. Out of more than 10 million believed to have been so separated, the agreement brought together a delegation of fifty from each side for three days (September 20–23, 1985). During the televised reunion, viewers found it difficult to hold back tears, not to mention the emotions felt by the briefly reunited family members themselves.

During the decade, tension arose in South Korea-Japan relations, although both governments remained committed to close contact as sealed by the 1965 Normalization Treaty, with the United States as its de facto sponsor. When the Japanese government began to sanction textbooks that justified colonialism and downplayed Japan's war crimes, South Korean public sentiment turned hostile toward Japan (1982). While still maintaining good relations with the Japanese political leadership, Chun's government launched a national fundraising campaign in 1983 to build a national shrine, the Independence Hall in Ch'ŏnan, at the epicenter of the March First Movement. The Independence Hall opened in 1987.

Chun's politics of nationalism did little to stem the tide of the pro-democracy struggle which ultimately prevailed. The movement gained further momentum with two tragic incidents. During police interrogation, a Seoul National University student, Pak Chongch'ŏl (1964–87), died from water torture (January 14, 1987). Months later, Yonsei University student Yi Hanyŏl (1966–87) was hit by a police tear-gas canister (June 9), dying twenty-six days later. Weeks of student demonstrations not only spread throughout the country but even brought ordinary citizens out to the street, with an estimated one million participating nationally in what became known as the June Struggle (Figure 13.1). On June 26 in Seoul, clashes between demonstrators and riot police continued throughout the night. Three days later, concluding that suppressing the demonstrations was not feasible without risking bloodshed and also warned against doing so by the United States, Chun had Roh Tae-woo, who by then was the leader of the Democratic Justice Party and Chun's designated successor, issue a statement making concessions to the pro-democracy movement (June 29). Four months later, stipulating direct election of the president for a single five-year term, a new constitution passed a national referendum (October 27). Failing to unify the liberal opposition, both Kim Young-sam and Kim Dae-jung ran in the December 16 presidential election, joined also by Kim Jong-pil, and Roh won 36.6 percent of the valid votes, ahead of the three Kims (28.0 percent, 27.0 percent, and 8.1 percent). Roh's inauguration (March 1988) marked the beginning of the current Sixth Republic.

During Roh Tae-woo's presidency (1988–93), South Korea implemented various features of democracy and improved relations with socialist countries. In the summer of 1988, the government successfully hosted the Summer Olympic Games in Seoul, featuring the largest number of countries ever to

FIGURE 13.1   A massive crowd gathered in front of Seoul city hall on July 9, 1987, following the funeral procession for Yi Hanyŏl, who had died four days earlier. Source: Seoul Photo Archives.

attend up to that time, and it subsequently established formal diplomatic relations with the Soviet Union, China, and other socialist countries that had sent athletes to the Seoul Olympics. Shortly after, communist governments of Eastern Bloc nations fell one after another, West Germany absorbed East Germany (October 1990), and the Soviet Union broke up into Russia and other successor states (December 1991)—signaling the total collapse of the Eastern Bloc. Internally in South Korea, the opposition parties won the majority of seats in the national assembly, which then initiated hearings on the Fifth Republic to investigate Chun's and his colleagues' military coup and their suppression of the Kwangju Uprising, as well as allegations of corruption among Chun and his family members. As the opposition-dominated national assembly flexed its muscle, Roh formed a giant new ruling party, the Democratic Liberal Party (1990–95), by merging his Democratic Justice Party with the parties of Kim Young-sam and Kim Jong-pil while excluding Kim Dae-jung (January 1990). A key part of the deal was that Kim Young-sam would be the new ruling party's nominee in the next presidential election. While effecting a major political realignment at the national level, the Roh administration also began to restore local autonomy, beginning with city, county, and city ward (ku) council elections (March 1991), followed by provincial assembly elections (July).

For its part, North Korea struggled to cope with the collapse of the Eastern Bloc and China's transition toward a market economy. Increasingly isolated thanks to the end of the Cold War, the regime promoted a more nationalistic ideology and vested more power in Kim Jong-il as the heir apparent. The first session of the ninth Supreme People's Assembly (SPA; 1990–98) ratified various power structure changes. The newly created National Defense Commission (NDC), which epitomized the military-first policy, functioned as the state's highest decision-making body and an emergency deliberative council combined into one (May 1990).

Encouraged by the end of the Cold War elsewhere and the successful hosting of the Seoul Olympics, Roh extended conciliatory gestures toward North Korea, and relations improved. When discussing fielding a joint team for the 1990 Beijing Asian Games, the two Koreas agreed on the Korean Unification Flag (Figure 13.2). Although the combined team did not materialize, both Koreas' cheerleading squads waved the new flag during the Beijing Asian Games. A series of talks at the prime ministerial level followed, alternating between Seoul and P'yŏngyang (September 1990), and a

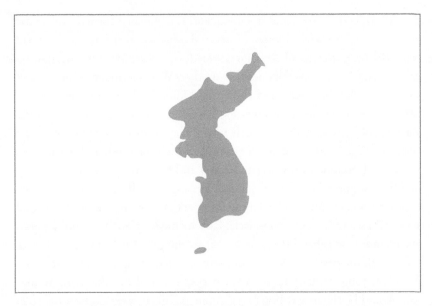

FIGURE 13.2   Korean Unification Flag, the original version of 1990. Source: Ksiom via Wikimedia Commons.

year later, both Koreas simultaneously joined the United Nations (September 1991). Subsequent high-level talks resulted in adopting a basic agreement on mutual nonaggression, reconciliation, exchanges, and cooperation (December 13), and produced a joint statement on keeping the Korean Peninsula nuclear weapons free (December 31). This joint statement was not only a meaningful step forward in implementing the July 4, 1972, joint statement but also facilitated subsequent inter-Korean economic cooperation.

A year later, South Korea's democracy elected a president with a civilian background for the first time since 1960. In the election of December 18, 1992, Kim Young-sam ran as the nominee of the ruling Democratic Liberal Party and won 42.0 percent of the valid votes, defeating Kim Dae-jung (33.8 percent) and a third-party candidate, Chung Ju-yung (Chŏng Chuyŏng; 1915–2001), founder and former chairman of the Hyundai Group (16.3 percent). Upon his inauguration (February 25, 1993), Kim Young-sam required all government officials of the fourth rank (*kŭp*) or higher (out of nine) and all members of the national assembly to report their assets; those found guilty of corruption had to resign or else be prosecuted. Kim then set about reforming the military leadership by discharging the generals belonging to

Hanahoe ("Group of One"), which had been the power base for Chun's December 12, 1979, coup (1994). Purging the ruling party of such figures, aside from Kim Jong-pil and his supporters, Kim Young-sam recruited former pro-democracy movement leaders from outside the political establishment and experts in various areas, and renamed the party the New Korea Party (1995–97). The recruits entered politics at multiple levels, including the newly instituted mayoral and gubernatorial elections that completed restoration of local autonomy (June 1995). Continuing the political reforms, the Supreme Prosecutors' Office arrested Roh Tae-woo for accumulating a slush fund (November) and Chun Doo-hwan for the December 12, 1979, coup, for suppressing the Kwangju Uprising, and for bribery (December). Subsequent trials found them guilty, sentencing Chun to death and Roh to twenty-two years and six months in prison (August 1996), but a second trial commuted their sentences to life and seventeen years in prison, respectively (April 1997). Deeming that he had made his point, Kim pardoned both (December).

During Kim Young-sam's presidency, both South Korea's global standing and inter-Korean relations continued to improve. Besides dispatching an engineering battalion, the Sangnoksu Unit of 252 troops, as a peacekeeping force to Somalia (1993) and making other contributions to multinational collaborative efforts, South Korea confidently approached economically struggling North Korea, still pursuing the twin goals of economic growth and military buildup under heir apparent Kim Jong-il's leadership. The younger Kim had assumed a series of additional positions in preparation for succeeding his father—including becoming supreme commander of the KPA (December 1991) and NDC chairman (April 1993). Despite initial tension stemming from North Korea's continuing quest for nuclear weapons, the two Koreas agreed to hold an unprecedented inter-Korean summit (June 28, 1994), but then Kim Il-sung died suddenly (July 8). Nonetheless, the DPRK–U.S. Agreed Framework (October 21, 1994) froze the program at North Korea's Yŏngbyŏn Nuclear Scientific Research Center, which the United States, South Korea, and other concerned nations regarded as a proto–nuclear weapons program, stipulating North Korea's peaceful use of nuclear technology. Subsequently, South Korea, the United States, and Japan established the Korean Peninsula Energy Development Organization (KEDO; March 15, 1995) to implement the framework with the construction of light-water nuclear reactors for North Korea, funded by the three countries and a number of others.

While inter-Korean cooperation expanded, the power transition unfolded in North Korea. Although Kim Il-sung died suddenly, Kim Jong-il was able to assume power without difficulty, thanks to some twenty years of preparation. Out of respect for his father as the founding North Korean leader, Kim Jong-il took up neither the post of president nor the post of general secretary of the central committee of the WPK—instead ruling the nation as the NDC chairman and the supreme commander of the KPA. Upon the end of an official three-year mourning period, the party elevated him to the post of general secretary, although he never assumed the presidency (October 1997).

In the same year, a leadership transition was under way in South Korea as well. By November, its economy was reeling from the Asian Financial Crisis resulting from some Asian countries' currency devaluations, and the long-sustained popularity of the New Korea Party decreased. In the December 18, 1997, presidential election, the ruling party candidate, former prime minister Lee Hoi-chang (Yi Hoech'ang; b. 1935) lost, 38.7 percent to 40.3 percent, to the long-time opposition leader Kim Dae-jung, who represented the National Congress for New Politics (1995–2000). Thus for the first time, an opposition party nominee became the president through a direct vote of the electorate.

After its inauguration (February 25, 1998), the Kim Dae-jung administration successfully enhanced South Korea's global standing. The herculean task at hand was economic recovery, with financial reforms mandated by the International Monetary Fund (IMF) as a condition for its bailout loan. South Korea achieved recovery by 2001—in fact paying off the loan early. South Korea's contribution of the Sangnoksu Unit of 419 troops to East Timor as a peacekeeping force (October 1999) was one of the many actions taken by the Kim administration to expand the nation's role in multinational collaborative efforts. As a long-time pro-democracy movement leader, Kim's international reputation further enhanced South Korea's stature in the world.

Kim Dae-jung's crowning achievement was his "Sunshine Policy," which dramatically improved inter-Korean relations. Encouraged by Kim's desire to engage with North Korea, Chung Ju-yung, the honorary chairman of the Hyundai Group, twice visited that country with a procession of trucks loaded with cows, 1,001 in all, as a donation (June and October 1998). Kim Jong-il responded favorably, especially once all was in order politically: in September, a constitutional amendment during the first session of the tenth SPA (1998–2003) had officially completed the power transition by upgrading the post of NDC chairman to the nation's highest position, now with an expanded role and authority. As the nation's unquestioned supreme leader, Kim allowed Hyundai to develop Mount Kŭmgang for South Korean tourists, who soon began to visit the scenic site (November 18). A maritime clash on June 15, 1999, on the Yellow Sea off Yŏnp'yŏngdo, did not hurt the warming relations, even though the DPRK navy suffered significant casualties (seventeen to thirty troops killed, up to seventy wounded, one ship sunk, and five damaged). South Korea's losses were relatively light (nine wounded and two ships damaged).

The inter-Korean rapprochement culminated with a historic inter-Korean summit when the two Kims met in P'yŏngyang (June 13, 2000), followed by further encouraging developments thereafter. Their joint statement of June 15 articulated five main points: (1) achieving reunification through both Koreas' own efforts; (2) recognition of common ground between South Korea's confederation model and North Korea's federation model for a unified Korea; (3) reunion of separated families and an effort to resolve the issue of pro-North Korean loyalists imprisoned in South Korea for refusing to renounce Juche thought; (4) more balanced economic development for the Korean Peninsula as a whole through inter-Korean economic cooperation and the promotion of non-governmental collaboration and exchanges in such areas as culture, sports, public health, and the environment; and (5) holding working-level talks to implement the terms of the agreement. A series of ministerial-level meetings followed to address implementation. The long overdue first reunion (August 15–18, 2000), since 1985, of families separated by the division of Korea would turn out to be the first of six in the remainder of Kim Dae-jung's presidency. A month later, the two Koreas held a groundbreaking ceremony launching the project to reconnect the Seoul-Ŭiju railway across the DMZ (September 18).

Domestically, Kim Dae-jung's presidency was fraught with bitter political strife. In contrast to the past political battles about prioritizing economic growth over democracy, this era pitted conservatives against liberals, each with its own base in terms of region and age group. A recurring theme was the exposure of a political adversary's corruption and wrongdoing. The national assembly, preoccupied with such scandals, was unable to formulate adequate legislation for the electorate's benefit. As disappointed voters increasingly tuned out of politics, voter turnout for the April 13, 2000, national assembly election was the lowest it had ever been, at 57.2 percent. The election results reflected lingering regionalism: both the liberal ruling Millennium Democratic Party (MDP; 2000–05) and the conservative opposition Grand National Party (GNP; 1997–2012) won a landslide victory, in the southwest and southeast, respectively. Also, a majority of the prominent politicians failed in their re-election bids. In contrast, thirteen first-time national assemblymen were members of the so-called 386 Generation: those in their thirties who entered university in the 1980s and were born in the 1960s and had been politically active as young adults and instrumental in the pro-democracy movement of the 1980s. Contributing to the election results was the emergence of non-governmental organizations (NGOs) as a significant political force that problematized statism for prioritizing economic growth over individual citizens' rights and well-being.

ENGAGEMENT VERSUS WITHDRAWAL VIS-À-VIS THE GLOBAL ECONOMY

Earlier, during Chun Doo-hwan's presidency, South Korea's economy had remained on an impressive upward trajectory. While capitalizing on drops in crude oil prices, the value of the dollar, and interest rates, the government pursued a tight fiscal policy entailing scaling back on excessive investment in heavy and chemical industries and disposing of financially struggling corporations while moving toward deregulating the financial sector. The policy was successful: the chronically high inflation rate fell below 10 percent, exports continued to increase, and industries requiring more advanced technology such as automobile, electronics, and semiconductor manufacturing grew rapidly. South Korea began to export Hyundai automobiles to the United States (1986). Boosted by export growth, the GDP (real) enjoyed a remarkably high average annual growth of 10.1 percent from 1981 to 1987. All the same, the conglomerates' overall share of the economy increased, and the gap between rich and poor citizens widened. A continuing increase in the number of industrial workers stimulated labor movements, which, in conjunction with the Kwangju Uprising, intensified student activism against the Chun regime.

By stark contrast, in the 1980s, North Korea's economy began to flounder as the rapid mass mobilization that the state fundamentally relied on in the 1970s reached its limit. To overcome the economic downturn following the decade's highest annual growth of 2.7 percent (1985), the regime began to institute more pragmatic economic policies, although nowhere near the scope of post-Mao China's economic reform since 1978. As the heir apparent,

Kim Jong-il gave more attention to light industry in an effort to reduce the imbalance among various sectors of production. Also, he adopted some features of China's economic reform, of which he had previously been critical. For instance, North Korea instituted a law to allow joint management with foreign businesses (September 1984). Nonetheless, the economy remained stagnant while chronic energy and raw material shortages, difficulties with transportation, ballooning foreign debt, and inadequate infrastructure and technology only got worse. The government even officially acknowledged that its economic policy was failing to achieve its growth targets.

By the end of the 1980s, a democratized South Korea coped with slowing growth as the country transitioned from a developmental state to a more liberalized, market-driven condition. Labor movements, which the authoritarian regimes had suppressed for decades in collaboration with big business, quickly gained strength, and unionization spread not just among wage laborers in manufacturing but also among schoolteachers and part-time university lecturers. Within two years after the spread of pro-democracy demonstrations in June 1987, the number of labor unions had nearly tripled, from 2,742 to 7,861. The number of union members almost doubled from some one million to about 1.9 million. Unlike his authoritarian predecessors, Roh Tae-woo committed South Korea in earnest to international labor standards with the country's membership in the International Labour Organization (1991). Frequent strikes, unionization, and improving working conditions significantly contributed to increased production and product costs and a higher cost of living, and decreased the competitive advantage of exports relying on low production costs.

While South Korea transitioned from a developmental state to a more liberalized economy in the 1990s, the stagnant North Korean economy began to contract. The collapse of the Eastern Bloc and the consequent drastic reduction in the supply of cheap oil and other imports further hurt the economy. Available annual growth rates were all negative— −3.7 percent (1990), −5.2 percent (1991), −7.6 percent (1992), −4.3 percent (1993), −1.7 percent (1994), −4.5 percent (1995)—before the era of the Arduous March (as it was dubbed by the regime; 1994–98), when the centrally planned system began to crumble, and the economy shrank by 6.5 percent in 1997. In the early 1990s, the government took such measures as establishing the Rajin-Sonbong Economic Special Zone (renamed Rason Special Economic Zone in 2000) in the northeast, near the Sino–North Korean and Russo–North

Korean borders, to promote economic growth through foreign investment (1992?); instituting a law to allow joint ventures (October 1993); and revising the existing joint management law to increase profitability for foreign investors (January 1994). These efforts as a whole failed to secure enough foreign capital to turn the economy around. With exports declining by 38.5 percent in 1998 alone, the government sought to earn foreign currency by opening restaurants in various countries, including China, which accounted for more than 90 percent of such restaurants.

North Korea's centrally planned economic system had virtually collapsed by the end of the decade. The rate of operation for factories dropped to just 20 to 30 percent, and factory employees were not only without work but also unable to live on their wages. With the end of the rationing system for all except the privileged elite, who continued to receive rationed food (1995), and massive flooding leading to crop destruction and harvest failures (1995–96), starvation began spreading. Also, ordinary North Koreans had to obtain food, clothing, and other daily necessities mostly from the spreading farmers' markets, local markets, and black markets, collectively known as *jangmadang* (*changmadang*; "market squares"), where an enterprising participant's income could be tens of times higher than the wages from factory or collective farm work. During the Arduous March, unofficial sectors of the economy became as large as 77 percent of the official GDP.

In stark contrast, South Korea's economy during Kim Young-sam's presidency made some noteworthy successful adjustments. His government instituted the Real-Name Financial System, which prohibited a bank account holder from using someone else's name, as was common at the time (August 12, 1993). The change did much to promote transparency and ultimately improve economic justice. In response to increasing demands by the United States and other advanced economies, in December, toward the end of the Uruguay Round (1986–93), South Korea signed the General Agreement on Tariffs and Trade, which required signatories to open up all sectors of their markets to foreign capital. Nonetheless, for South Korea, its advances in science and technology sustained increases in foreign trade volume. Indeed, the export-driven economy enjoyed robust growth of around 8 percent each year, and the standard of living continued to improve. Befitting its position in the global economy, South Korea joined the Organisation for Economic Co-operation and Development (OECD), long dominated by Western nations (September 1996).

Before long, however, the Asian Financial Crisis proved that South Korea's seemingly robust economy was still vulnerable, although the nation ultimately overcame the crisis. Toward the end of Kim Young-sam's presidency, the government, which was unable to repay its foreign creditors a debt amounting to 150 billion dollars, had to seek a bailout loan of 20 billion dollars from the IMF (November 1997). South Korea's global credit rating plummeted. The loan came with a list of conditions that demanded financial restructuring—overall amounting to curtailing or ending until-then rampant corporate practices associated with overexpansion and lax financial management. The following year, the real GDP shrank by 5.5 percent, and the per capita GDP (purchasing power parity, PPP) dropped by 5.1 percent (1998). During the IMF-mandated restructuring, as executed by the succeeding Kim Dae-jung administration, ten out of the top thirty conglomerates folded. Those who survived had to reduce their number of affiliated companies. Sixty financial institutions closed, and the rest underwent merger and acquisition processes. Among public corporations, one hundred and eight were subjected to merger or acquisition, and some were privatized. South Koreans nationwide dealt with significant financial hardship, especially mass layoffs. Still, many contributed what they could to the nation's debt repayment campaigns, rather than pushing back on the IMF-mandated reforms. On its end, the Kim Dae-jung administration formed a tripartite commission of labor, management, and government to deal with unemployment and labor disputes, besides putting much effort into securing foreign capital investments. Before long, the economy recovered, and both foreign currency reserves and foreign investment increased rapidly. At the end of 1999, the GDP (PPP) was the fifteenth largest globally, South Korea's highest ranking ever. Reflecting the sector's growing importance, the contribution of information and communication technology (ICT) to GDP growth increased from 33 percent in 1999 to 47 percent in 2000.

Around the same time, North Korea's failed economy experienced a modest recovery, driven mainly by increasing private economic activity. Declaring that the Arduous March was over, in December 1998, the Kim Jong-il regime announced building a "strong and prosperous nation" (kangsŏng taeguk) through the "Military First" policy as its vision for the nation's future development. In implementing the idea, the government pursued a conservative economic policy of restrictive measures on jangmadang and farmers markets and ordered workers to return to their officially assigned workplaces. The underground economy, however, continued to grow as the centrally planned economy could no longer support the lives of the population.

THE LAST PHASE OF SOCIAL MOBILITY

As South Korea experienced demographic changes typical of advanced economies in the final two decades of the twentieth century, the country coped with the overconcentration of the population in Seoul and the associated problems. The TFR continued to decrease, from 2.23 births in 1980–85 to 1.51 in 1995–2000, while life expectancy continued to increase, from 67.4 years to 75.0 years during the same period. The increasing average age of women at marriage, changing attitudes toward having children, and the rising cost of children's education all contributed to these changes. Decades of an exodus of younger rural residents to urban areas as they sought jobs and education had left behind an aging rural population. To distribute the nation's population more evenly, the government moved several ministries from Seoul to Kwach'ŏn, where newly constructed residential districts housed the employees. Although Kwach'ŏn had been officially designated a city (1986), much of its workforce commuted from Seoul, where family members stayed put for advantages unmatched elsewhere in the country, especially the quality of education.

Competition for education grew fierce at the pre-collegiate levels, as most South Koreans saw the end goal of education as attending a prestigious university to land a good white-collar job. In the 1980s, the number of families turning to extracurricular programs for children in order to gain a competitive advantage in the university entrance examinations increased rapidly. Accordingly, the Chun Doo-hwan regime sought to improve access to education by abolishing entrance examinations for primary and secondary schools, accrediting more colleges and universities, and increasing university admission quotas (1984). To keep university students more focused on graduating on time, the government enforced a more rigid academic standard by capping the number of graduates for each year (1984). Not only were campus facilities inadequate for accommodating the suddenly increased number of students, the overall quality of education suffered, and the scale of student demonstrations increased. The government soon abolished the admission-graduation quota system (1986).

With democratization, South Korea's education system gained greater autonomy and enjoyed a decade of rapid growth. As the education fervor fueled corruption in private schools' ownership and management, many kindergarten, elementary school, and middle school teachers responded by forming the Korean Teachers and Education Workers Union to promote quality education (1989). From the outset, the public's opinion of the union's objectives and strategies was polarized, with conservatives regarding them as leftist. By comparison, public reactions were on the whole favorable when the Roh Tae-woo administration abolished periodic government review of each university faculty member's continuing employment and began to allow universities to elect their presidents (1989). After their rapid growth, the IMF-mandated reform following the 1997 Asian Financial Crisis forced universities to expand each academic program's student recruitment pool and curriculum content while merging or closing overly specialized academic units. Universities also introduced a new admission review system, which weighed—in addition to grades and examination scores—each applicant's unique skills, volunteer activities, and recommendation letter from his or her high school principal.

While educators embraced overall encouraging changes, farmers became more active in defending and promoting their interests as South Korea gradually opened its markets to more imports. In the 1980s, when the Chun Doo-hwan regime began to allow the import of a greater variety of foreign goods for sale at retail outlets, consumers welcomed the change as they no longer had to depend mostly on the black market. Still, imported grain and ingredients for processed food hurt rural villages. In the 1990s, rice imports further hurt farmers, and although the government offered subsidies and other types of support, their situation did not improve. As the farmers became vocal in demanding more financial assistance for mounting farming household debts, an increasing number participated in organized mass protests against produce imports.

Not only did various occupation groups become more assertive in defending their interests, an increasing number of NGOs promoted their own agendas. In addition to South Korea's democratization, decreasing left-right ideological confrontation, continuing expansion of the middle class, increasing social diversity, and spreading ecological and environmental problems inspired the citizens' groups. In the 1990s, an increasing number of NGOs addressed a widening range of issues related to socioeconomic justice and the quality of life. Often working in solidarity with their counterparts abroad, NGOs monitored and promoted greater awareness of government corruption, abuse of power by agents of the state, lack of transparency in corporate management, and acts of environmental destruction by the government and businesses. NGOs also became more active in defending and promoting the poor, foreign migrant workers, women, and LGBT rights.

Rather than equity, survival became the critical issue in North Korea, as the failing economy produced dire consequences. Annual population growth decreased from 1.6 percent in the 1980s to 1.02 percent in the 1990s and thereafter. The drop reflects the official continuation of the birth control policy in place until the 1980s to ensure that labor shortages affecting for the 1960s socialist industrialization efforts could be addressed with female workers. Also, the government began to allow abortion (1983). In the 1990s, however, starvation and infant mortality increased due to acute food shortages and inadequate medical facilities. The TFR continued to decrease from 2.93 births in 1980–85 to 2.40 in 1990–85 to 2.20 in 1995–2000; average life expectancy increased from 67.1 years in 1980–85 to a peak of 70.0 in 1990–95, then dropped to 63.5 in 1995–2000. North Korea responded with a policy of securing a greater labor supply by offering incentives to women giving birth and to their children (1996).

Amidst the country's economic woes, in the late 1990s, the trickle of North Koreans fleeing south began to swell. Between 1950 and 1993, a total of 641 North Koreans are known to have defected to the south. Most did so for political reasons, including foot soldiers and air force pilots who crossed the DMZ, and the South Korean government gave each a hero's welcome and huge publicity. Upon the advent of massive natural disasters, crop failures, famine, and acute food shortages, in 1994, the number of escapees began to increase, and the total number settling in the south increased to 947 in 1998 and to 1,405 in 2000. Rather than cross the heavily guarded, thoroughly mined DMZ, most escapees crossed the Sino–North Korean border into the Yanbian Korean Autonomous Prefecture of China by evading or bribing border patrol troops. As China valued its relations with North Korea and sent those caught back rather than treating them as refugees, the escapees maintained a tenuous existence in China while seeking to escape to another country, if not entering such extraterritorial edifices in China as foreign embassies and schools. Many female escapees were sold and resold as farmhands, restaurant workers, servants of elderly Chinese, brides of bachelor farmers, or even sex workers. Among the escapees sent back to North Korea, first-time offenders underwent rigorous re-education and performed hard labor, if not being executed, depending on the grounds for their offense.

Although better off than North Korean escapees in China, the legal position of ethnic minorities in North Korea varied. Until 1983, the Kim Il-sung regime continued to abduct Japanese nationals, and their legal status in the country remained tenuous. By then, between seventy and eighty were being held. As of 1997, North Korea refused to confirm the names of surviving Japanese in the country and had only permitted a few small groups of ten to fifteen to visit Japan. By contrast, the overall position of the ethnic Chinese minority improved. Around 1980, North Korea began to allow them to travel abroad and even participate in significant, profitable export-import business ventures. As of the late 1990s, North Korea had four Chinese middle schools, all of which followed the PRC curriculum.

At that time in South Korea, the overall position of the Chinese minority improved even more. In the 1990s, China's economic liberalization and normalized relations with South Korea encouraged some Chinese Koreans to move to the PRC to pursue business opportunities or return to their ancestral homes. At the same time, a new wave of Chinese migrants arrived in South Korea. The 1997 Asian Financial Crisis also spurred some Chinese Koreans to move to the PRC or elsewhere. All the same, during the decade, many Chinese Koreans who had left South Korea earlier began to return as the country implemented policies more favorable to foreign nationals. Among those returning were earlier immigrants to the United States or Taiwan who had had difficulty adapting to their new life. In the 1990s, Christianity began to make inroads among Chinese Koreans. The establishment of a Chinese-language Protestant church by a pastor from Taiwan was a milestone event, though Catholics continued to attend Korean-language masses.

During the decade, the Chinese Korean share of South Korea's ethnic minority population began to decrease rapidly as the population of residents born abroad and the nationals with at least one foreign-born parent increased. South Korean businesses eager to keep production costs low increasingly brought in foreign workers from Southeast Asia and South Asia and Korean Chinese (Ch. Chaoxianzu; Ko. Chosŏnjok) from Yanbian and elsewhere. Also, as the rapidly aging population of rural South Korea suffered from a gender imbalance, male farmers, who were having difficulty finding spouses, turned to introduction agencies to help them marry wives from

Southeast Asia, especially Vietnam. Furthermore, South Korea acceded to the Convention Relating to the Status of Refugees (1992) and subsequently began to accept refugee applications (1994).

While South Korea's ethnic and racial diversity increased, the women's rights movement made some gains. The female presence in the workforce grew from 43.6 percent as of 1988 to 47.6 percent as of 1995. As women assumed a larger role in economic activity, their educational level increased, thus driving professionalization, and the percentage of females among working professionals steadily increased. Nonetheless, the majority of South Korean women continued to believe that they should be good housewives and mothers. Not only did professionally trained women often lack employment opportunities, those employed also tended to hold poorly paid, dead-end positions and worked only until they married or had families. South Korea's democratization did not significantly increase female candidacy for political office. The transition, however, did enable more women to join anti-government groups and to force gender-specific issues onto the public agenda. Increased numbers of women's organizations turned their grievances into a capacity to act collectively in a political environment that was now more conducive to women's associations. A public discussion of women's rights culminated with the national assembly addressing some of their concerns by enacting the Sexual Equality Employment Act (1987) and the Act on Equal Employment and Reconciliation of Work and Family (1989). Effective January 1, 1991, child custody no longer went automatically to the father in divorce cases. Also, all surviving children became legally entitled to an equal share of the inheritance. And although the household headship system remained, some of the head's duties and responsibilities came to be shared with other family members.

In comparison, the position of North Korean women only deteriorated in the 1980s and 1990s. Not only did the gender wage gap persist, the wage difference continued to reflect the higher concentration of women in occupations that paid less. Thus, the husband remained the primary income earner in a typical household. In 1986, the government introduced extended paid maternity leave, but in the late 1980s, the number of women leaving the workforce after marriage to assume more purely domestic roles began to increase. At the same time, official pronouncements started to emphasize the traditional role of women. By the mid-1990s, the economic crisis was taking a toll on families. Economic opportunities for women decreased, and employers tended to lay off first those who were married. Some married women left jobs voluntarily, as they could generate income by participating in sideline production teams while staying at home. Still, cases of family break-up increased, as members separated to search for food or ways to earn money. Unsurprisingly, many women began to prefer having only one child. The Korean Democratic Women's League could do little about women's deteriorating position, as the organization's influence declined. Indeed, women's presence in the political leadership remained weak. Although women occupied about one-third of the representative positions in the lower echelons of power, they were vastly underrepresented in the upper levels— except in the SPA, but it was not a real decision-making center. Neither did Kim Jong-il's Military First policy help, as women were virtually absent in the military leadership.

In terms of gender equality, little is known about the status of members of the LGBT community in North Korea in this period when active LGBT movements in South Korea were seeking to improve LGBT rights. In the 1980s, the growing awareness of AIDS among the general public, which more or less ascribed queer sexuality only to gays, and a misperception that gays were the cause of AIDS, further intensified the debate on gay and lesbian sexuality. By then, gays had formed their own communities and subcultures in Chongno and It'aewŏn in Seoul. Centered around gay clubs and bars, such communities enjoyed some clout in the local economy. By comparison, the visibility of lesbians was more limited, as they sought to assert their identity and rights primarily through feminist discourse and movements. Eventually, gays and lesbians jointly formed their first rights group, Chodonghoe (Ch'odonghoe; 1993), but in the following year, the organization divided into Chingusai (Ch'in'gu sai; "Between Friends") for gays and Kkiri kkiri (Lesbian Counseling Center; since 2005) for lesbians. As more gay and lesbian groups arose, especially with the advent of the internet, Chingusai activists organized local chapters at universities (1995). Also, lesbian coming-out became more common in the late 1990s. As the ongoing LGBT movement gained momentum, activists organized the first Seoul Queer Film Festival and a mass queer rally and launched the University Students' LGBT Human Rights Association (1997). In the following year, the association expanded its scope, turning itself into Solidarity for LGBT Human Rights of Korea. Not only did the first-ever Queer Culture Festival follow (2000), an actor and television personality, Hong Seok-cheon (Hong Sŏkch'ŏn; b. 1971), came out as gay (2000). Fired from network programs and advertisements amidst the public uproar, Hong remained active in other entertainment industry genres. He was becoming a prominent, openly gay celebrity as the culture wars raged. But the public's support for LGBT rights was on the upswing.

CULTURES OF GLOBALIZATION AND ISOLATION

While struggling with cultural diversity, South Korea continued to pass milestones in science and technology. In the 1980s, the country began to manufacture more of its own military hardware and to export self-propelled artillery, air-burst rifles, guided-missile frigates, fleet tankers, amphibious assault ships, and trainer aircraft, mostly to non-Western nations. By the 1990s, moving into aerospace technology, South Korea began to manufacture and launch multipurpose satellites, starting with Koreasat 1 (Mugunghwa 1) (1995). During this decade, South Korea became a leader in other areas such as semiconductors, especially as spearheaded by Samsung Electronics. Whenever Samsung developed a new product, especially for flash memory, it was more or less the world's first. The Kim Dae-jung administration launched the large, government-funded BK 21 project (1999), which especially boosted support for the biotechnology and ICT sectors, to sustain the momentum.

While achieving advances in science and technology, the dynamics of South Korea's religions, old and new, continued to undergo a transformation. By the 1980s, many dissidents and intellectuals were rediscovering shamanism, not only as what they deemed a genuinely indigenous Korean form of spirituality but also as a vehicle for expressing popular discontent toward authoritarian rule. In the 1990s, the Catholic population increased faster than the Protestants, as the Korean Catholic church gained visibility as a moral authority during South Korea's transition to democracy. The Catholic church also appealed to many for its perceived moral superiority over the wealthy, politically conservative Protestant megachurches of Kangnam when it came to issues of social justice and reunification. By the end of the decade, however, the increase in the percentage of the population claiming a religious affiliation more or less stopped at around 50 percent. Also, as more mainstream religious groups participated in a wide range of citizens' movements, many began to turn away from divisive or polarizing issues in favor of reaching out to those who needed help. All the same, some evangelical Protestants began to gain publicity as outliers, especially when targeting

Buddhism, Daejongism, and other non-Christian religions. On the rise were reported incidents of arson and vandalism such as cutting off the heads of Buddha, bodhisattva, and Tan'gun statutes, and painting Christian crosses on symbols or property of non-Christian groups.

Such behaviors, though, remained fringe activities, as a statist obsession with progress gave way to an awareness that developed Western nations boast globally recognized cultural heritages rather than skyscrapers. Beginning within intellectual circles in the 1980s, the nationalist literature movement grew in depth and breadth in sync with South Korea's progress toward democracy. The public's interest in traditional Korean music grew, and the visibility of university-trained performers in particular increased both in and outside the country. As issues regarding workers, farmers, and reunification attracted more attention, *minjung* artists' increasing activism searched for and drew from indigenous Korean culture, real and imagined. Also, people's interest in genealogy and tombstone inscriptions written in Literary Sinitic grew, especially among the nouveau riche from culturally more conservative regions. By the end of the 1990s, nearly half of South Koreans could find themselves or close relatives in a published genealogy, but far less than half of them belonged there.

Much of the South Korean public remained more in tune with the continuing growth and expansion of popular culture for leisure consumption. In the 1980s, as the Chun Doo-hwan regime sought to shift the people's attention away from politics, its cultural liberalization policy entailed many relevant measures, including commencing color television broadcasting (1980); allowing ordinary citizens to travel abroad, except to socialist countries and apartheid South Africa (1980); lifting midnight curfews (1982); launching a professional baseball league (1982); and doing away with required middle school and high school uniforms (1983). At the same time, the government built some significant cultural edifices for the public's consumption. The opening of the National Museum of Modern and Contemporary Art in Kwach'ŏn (1986) and the Seoul Arts Center (1993) immediately served the growing middle-class demand for "high culture."

An expanding consumer base also allowed popular culture to achieve greater autonomy from the state and corporate control. Performers and entertainers remained vulnerable to the demands of politicians and representatives of conglomerates meddling in artistic content, seeking performances for political events, and even making sexual advances. Nonetheless, the efforts of intellectuals and activists who sought democratization and socioeconomic justice began to make a positive impact on various genres. Also, freedom of the press increased after the June Struggle. The appearance of cable broadcast networks and the internet in the 1990s rapidly increased the number of information content providers, thus weakening the state monopoly on news and other types of information. Moreover, some intellectuals and activists were becoming more critical of the media outlets' commercialism and content selection and demanding greater social responsibility. Demand for more material that was pure entertainment was also increasing, and popular music, television dramas, and films became more diverse in genre and style. The film industry, in particular, began to produce works with more distinctly Korean characteristics that started to beat Hollywood blockbusters as domestic box-office hits and to compete successfully in international film festivals. Thus, in 1998, when the Kim Dae-jung administration began to open the domestic market for Japanese popular culture products, the impact was minimal—contrary to the initial fear that South Korean analogs would be hurt.

Meanwhile, sports and performing arts increasingly helped to bridge the divide between the two Koreas. North Korea continued to promote domestically produced music, and most popular songs extolled the WPK, Kim Il-sung, and Kim Jong-il. Excluding such materials and those that the northern regime deemed decadent, an inter-Korean cultural exchange that commenced in the 1980s featured content amenable to both sides—including performances by groups of singers, instrumental musicians, and Taekwondo (T'aekwŏndo) practitioners. In 1990, the North-South Unification Soccer games featured matches in P'yŏngyang and Seoul. In the next year, the two Koreas fielded a joint team—under the Korean Unification Flag—for the 1991 World Table Tennis Championships, held in Chiba, Japan, and won the championship. For the first time in the history of the Olympics, North and South Korean athletes walked together, holding the Korean Unification Flag, during the opening ceremony of the 2000 Summer Olympic Games in Sydney. Athletes and performing artists involved in inter-Korean cultural exchanges had little difficulty communicating, even though each side's Korean language had been changing independently of the other in the decades since the Korean War.

Considerably later than South Korea, North Korea effectively completed its linguistic standardization with the *Dictionary of the Korean Language* (*Chosŏn mal taesajŏn*; 1992). Among the 330,000 featured words were newly created Cultured Language words, including Sino-Korean, Western scientific, and sports-related vocabulary that the compilation team had turned into more purely Korean words; uniquely North Korean political terms; modifications of words that the Japanese occupation had influenced; and local dialect words. North Korea's standardized vocabulary and expressions continued to be used in official broadcast and print media and in works of literature that extolled Kim Il-sung and Kim Jong-il. Nonetheless, literary works not so explicit about the state agenda also appeared, including *Ode to Youth* (*Ch'ŏngch'un songga*; 1987), an epic novel on the theme of romantic love.

Likewise, the North Korean state-regulated religion was imbued with a blend of Juche thought and nationalism while maintaining the appearance of freedom of religion. Chondoism, in particular, remained a logical choice for state sponsorship, given its nationalistic grass-roots credentials from history. In the 1980s, the Kim Il-sung regime put forth a more nationalistic interpretation of Korean history and claimed the discovery of royal tombs of mythical ancient rulers. Subsequently, the Central Guidance Committee of the Korean Chondoist Association organized an impressive ceremony at the newly constructed Mausoleum of Tan'gun near P'yŏngyang (1994). To a lesser extent, Buddhism too enjoyed the state's support for its prominent place in traditional culture. In comparison, Christianity remained a more complex issue. Mindful of his Protestant roots through his mother, Kim Il-sung understood Christianity's potential, and the regime maintained strict control rather than suppression. Accordingly, the government established the Korean Catholic Association and built the country's only Catholic edifice, Changch'ung Church, in P'yŏngyang, which can accommodate 250 worshippers (1988). Although not under the ecclesiastical jurisdiction of the Vatican, the association published a catechism and a prayer book (1991). Eager for a new ally in the post–Eastern Bloc era, after the 2000 inter-Korean summit, Kim Jong-il took up a suggestion from Kim Dae-jung, a devout Catholic, and sought to invite Pope John Paul II (1920–2005) to North Korea, but the visit never materialized. Reportedly, when the North Korean authorities searched for practicing Catholics in preparation for a possible papal visit and found one, she acknowledged her faith only after persistent questioning: declaring that once God enters a person's heart, He never leaves. Kim decided not to invite the pope.

While the role of inward religious belief in the culture of daily life differed markedly between the two Koreas, in the 1980s and 1990s, outward fashion experienced significant changes with more similarities. As the North Korean state sought to increase the working segment of the adult female population, suits, skirts, and permed hair became more common. At the same time, overalls and a modernized, distinctly North Korean-style of *hanbok* also remained common among workers and women, respectively. In South Korea, ready-made clothes became more common than custom-made garments among men as well, replicating the same transition made earlier among women. Thanks in part to color broadcasting, overall fashion became more diverse. For example, casual wear became widely popular, especially as more consumers sought to find time for sports and other leisure activities.

At the same time, Korea's food culture underwent a profound change. In the 1980s in South Korea, the consumption of food that was more flour-based, processed, or animal-based, including fast food, increased rapidly. Nevertheless, each day, most South Koreans ate at least one or two meals featuring *pap*, that is, steamed rice with or without other grains, a soup, *kimchi*, and at least one or two other side dishes. Besides the traditional vegetables that served as ingredients for soup and side dishes, people were eating more relatively new vegetables and fruits, such as cabbage, bell peppers, bananas, oranges, grapefruit, lemons, melon, and pineapple. Also, certain types of seafood that used to be unique to particular regions, including raw seafood (*hoe*), became readily available more or less throughout the country. An even more dramatic change, though, was the increasing consumption of such processed foods as ramen, other types of instant noodles, bread, ham, sausages, cheese, canned tuna, ketchup, mayonnaise, chocolates, cookies, crackers, and chips. Such American fast-food chains as Burger King, KFC, McDonald's, and Pizza Hut, that had been making inroads since the 1980s, became so popular, especially among teenagers and young adults, that the overall demand for rice decreased. At the same time, overconsumption of animal protein and fat contributed to the increasing prevalence of such lifestyle diseases as obesity, stroke, diabetes, and cancer—among which breast cancer and colon cancer began to replace stomach cancer as the more common types. Besides reflecting on their overreliance on animal products, in the 1990s, the public, increasingly aware of processed food's dangers, showed a growing interest in organic food. In North Korea too, similar trends were underway although on a far more limited scale and with less variety, confined to the residents of P'yŏngyang, and certainly without American fast-food chains. By the 1990s, the rest of the DPRK population was struggling to survive amidst crop failure, food shortages, and famine. As mentioned, the government began to operate restaurants in and outside the country as a revenue source, but the customer base inside the country was mainly confined to P'yŏngyang residents and government personnel.

In South Korea, compared to the changes in diet and clothing, the changes in housing were even more dramatic, as more than half the population was now living in apartments. In the 1980s, the construction of larger apartment complexes continued in Seoul and spread to its satellites and the smaller provincial cities. The price of land and homes rose sharply—turning many among those who had bought the new apartments into members of the upper-middle class. Also, the redevelopment of *taltongne* and shantytowns produced more apartment complexes. Nonetheless, an acute shortage continued, exacerbated by a continuing influx of population into the capital region. The Roh Tae-woo government launched an ambitious project of constructing 2 million apartment units, mainly through five new satellite cities, including Ilsan, Pundang, and P'yŏngh'on. The total number of new housing units increased rapidly from 244,301 in 1987 to 316,570 in 1988 to 462,159 in 1989 to 750,378 in 1990. A new policy of returning profits from land development to the community established local government corporations in Seoul and Taegu. Each local government also set up publicly managed development groups. In 1993, the Kim Young-sam government eased restrictions on redeveloping old apartment buildings, and by July 1994, in Seoul alone, 237 redevelopment cooperatives, joint public-private collaborations, had formed. The number of floors in high-rise apartment buildings in the capital increased from fifteen in the early 1980s to twenty to thirty by the mid-1990s. By then, some constructions, new and redeveloped alike, were suffering from various problems due to poor workmanship.

Meanwhile in North Korea, the gap in the quality of housing for the elite on the one hand and for the rest of the population on the other widened. Except for the elite, including the overall privileged P'yŏngyang population, whose housing arrangements were comparable or superior to those of South Korea's middle class, many North Koreans used firewood to warm their houses, as they were without other heating options. For many in the late 1990s, housing conditions began to deteriorate as the authorities banned firewood sales; the measure was an effort to stem deforestation and in the long term prevent mudslides and flooding that contributed to crop failures. Those who needed firewood suffered hardship, and many reportedly died from lack of heating. In contrast, those most privileged lived in P'yŏngyang, where residence itself was possible only with the government's approval, and construction of higher-story apartment buildings continued. As such, the capital did not experience the phenomenon of the urban poor as industrializing capitalist nations historically have. Privileging the party's upper echelons and its loyal base would become even more pronounced in the new millennium as North Korea increasingly struggled with economic survival while pursuing nuclear armament.

CHAPTER 14

Recent Developments

P rospects for a lasting peace have improved further in the new millennium. Inter-Korean relations deteriorated during South Korea's two consecutive conservative administrations (2008–17), when the state fell back on authoritarian tendencies before mass protests, impeachment, and conviction ousted the leader. In the north, Kim Jong-il's successor, Kim Jong-un (Kim Chŏngŭn; b. 1984), further expanded nuclear weapon and ballistic missile programs before reciprocating the peace gestures of the new South Korean president, Moon Jae-in (Mun Chaein; b. 1953). Inter-Korean relations warmed before reaching the current roadblock, as the U.S.-led international sanctions against North Korea have prevented South Korea from full engagement as an economic powerhouse. Internally in the south, multiculturalism has gained strength as the foreign-born population, their Korean-born children, and the LGBT community continue to grow, while such exports as K-pop are enhancing the country's "soft power." In the north, most are struggling to survive, with the country's economy crippled by sanctions. Its youth flock to the ever-expanding black market.

INTER-KOREAN RELATIONS: PROGRESS AND SETBACKS

The improvement in inter-Korean relations following the June 15, 2000, summit gradually lost its momentum. In his New Year's address of 2001, Kim Jong-il articulated an intention to pursue pragmatism that entailed reform and open-door policies. Subsequently, when he visited Shanghai, he was deeply impressed by China's economic progress, but new developments abroad held him back from taking bold measures. In early February, the United States and Britain jointly conducted an air raid in the outskirts of Bagdad, Iraq. Also, America began to apply pressure on various "axis of evil" nations—including North Korea—as publicly labeled by President George W. Bush (b. 1946). The developments hindered further improvement in inter-Korean relations and hardened the North Korean stance toward the United States

America's hard-line stance had further repercussions. On September 11, 2001, a militant Islamic fundamentalist, Osama bin Laden (1957–2011), masterminded simultaneous terrorist attacks against the United States, using hijacked commercial airliners to bring down the World Trade Center building in New York City and to attack the Pentagon, the U.S. military headquarters in Arlington, Virginia. In October, the United States retaliated by attacking terrorist bases in Afghanistan; securing surrender from the country's militant Islamic fundamentalist group, the Taliban, in early December. Responding to America's request but mindful that half of South Koreans disapproved of U.S. airstrikes in Afghanistan, the Kim Dae-jung administration committed non-combatant troops, stationed in Afghanistan in 2002 and 2003. Then on March 20, 2003, the United States set off the Iraq War (2003–11). In addition, increasing concern about North Korea's nuclear weapons and long-range ballistic missile programs made the United States insist on strict inspections and increased pressure on North Korea in other ways. Kim Dae-jung's Sunshine Policy was floundering.

At the time, the Japanese government, under Prime Minister Junichiro Koizumi (b. 1942), pursued policies that aroused public resentment in both Koreas and in other countries that had suffered from Japanese militarism. It had been five years since any Japanese minister had visited the Yasukuni Shrine when Koizumi paid his respects at this memorial (August 13, 2001), which honors several Class A war criminals. Also, his cabinet stood firm on Japanese history textbooks that downplayed or denied Imperial Japan's wrongdoings. Likewise, Japan pursued a hard-line policy toward North Korea by playing up and generating much publicity around the issue of Japanese abductees. And in November, Japan dispatched its Self-Defense Force warships to the Middle East to support the aggressive U.S. policy toward that region actively. While welcomed by America, the move was disturbing to other Asian countries, as the increasingly conservative Japanese leadership showed little remorse for Japan's past militarism and wartime atrocities.

For some time in the remaining years of Kim Dae-jung's presidency, inter-Korean dialogue, exchanges, and even cooperation continued. North Korea unilaterally canceled talks when the South Korean authorities arrested some South Koreans for violating the National Security Act by participating in the National Unification Festival on August 15, 2001, in P'yŏngyang, and when South Korea put its military on alert after the September 11 terrorist attack. Nonetheless, North Korea advocated "national cooperation" as its strategy for dealing with America's and Japan's pressures. While South Korea and Japan were co-hosting the FIFA World Cup (May–June 2002), a surprise attack by a North Korean patrol craft sparked another clash on the Yellow Sea near Yeonpyeongdo (Yŏnp'yŏngdo), resulting in South Korean casualties of at least six dead, eighteen injured, and one patrol craft sunk. Evidently, this was caused not so much by any Kim Jong-il directive as by the DPRK navy, which had provoked the incident to avenge what it saw as the humiliation of the previous clash with South Korea in June 1999. When North Korea conveyed its regrets, South Korea accepted them as a de facto apology. Thereafter, when North Korea expressed its intention to participate in the upcoming Busan (Pusan) Asian Games (September–October), South Korea invited and hosted the North Korean national soccer team for a friendly match in Seoul (September 7), and North Korean athletes subsequently competed in the Asian Games. In the interim, the two Koreas held a ground-breaking ceremony for a project to reconnect the Seoul-Ŭiju railway (September 18), followed by a North Korean delegation's tour of South Korean industrial facilities (October 26).

Before long, inter-Korean relations soured again. South Korea increasingly supported America's hard-line stance vis-à-vis North Korean nuclear weapons development. South Korea's accommodation of North Korean defectors and articulation of concerns about South Koreans abducted by the north further strained relations. Ministerial-level talks ended with the eighth such meeting, on October 19, 2002, in P'yŏngyang. Then on January 10, 2003, North Korea withdrew from the international Nuclear Non-Proliferation Treaty. North Korea nonetheless continued profit-sharing joint ventures with the south, and on February 14, the land route tour of Mount Kŭmgang for South Korean tourists commenced. Since the Bush administration did not welcome inter-Korean economic exchanges without North Korea first ending its nuclear weapons development program, Kim Dae-Jung found it difficult to continue pursuing his Sunshine Policy.

Domestically, the Kim administration continued the democratic reform of its predecessors since 1988. Such measures as changing the Ministry of Education to the Ministry of Education and Human Resources Development, upgrading its minister's position to cabinet vice minister, and upgrading the minister of planning and budget to cabinet vice minister as well generated no controversy. Other measures, however, were highly politicized. In February 2001, the government launched a press reform that prosecuted conservative media outlets, in effect blaming them for the GNP's strong showing in the national assembly election of April 2000. Finding them guilty of tax evasion worth over 500 billion won, the government imposed fines and arrested the major shareholders of the *Donga Ilbo (Tonga ilbo)*, the *Kukmin Ilbo (Kungmin ilbo)*, and the *Chosun Ilbo (Chosŏn ilbo)*.

As the presidential election of 2002 drew near, the public's support for Kim Dae-jung continued to erode. A series of corruption scandals involving some members of the ruling MDP leadership and the president's own relatives severely weakened the legitimacy of Kim's reform effort. The MDP's junior national assembly members launched a movement to reform the party, and in January 2001, they successfully pressured core members of the party leadership to resign from key positions, accusing them of enjoying ethically questionable privileges. In November, the reformists succeeded in pressuring Kim to step down as party leader, and in May 2002, he officially left the party. In June, his son's arrest for corruption prematurely turned Kim into a lame duck leader. In the presidential election on December 19, the MDP candidate, Roh Moo-hyun (No Muhyŏn; 1946–2009), formerly a human rights lawyer and the minister of oceans and fisheries, defeated Lee Hoi-chang of the GNP, 48.9 percent to 46.6 percent. Roh won an election that, in many ways, pitted the younger against the older generation.

Inaugurated on February 25, 2003, the Roh Moo-hyun administration found that one of its most pressing challenges was foreign policy. When the United States started the Iraq War (2003–11) and toppled Saddam Hussein's (1937–2006) regime in three weeks (April 2003), continuing local resistance, mostly by militant Sunni Muslims, inflicted considerable casualties on occupation forces. South Korea's public opinion was divided on America's request for troops, but it was difficult for the Roh administration to deny it. Upon securing the national assembly's consent, South Korea dispatched a contingent of 600 military medics and engineers to Iraq in the same month. Upon America's request for additional soldiers (September), South Korea sent a division of 2,200 troops, mostly engineers, by September 2004, and subsequent deployments of reinforcements brought the troop strength up to 3,600. South Korea would keep its forces in Iraq until December 2008. Its contribution hardly noted by the Western media, South Korea finally won attention when Roh's government lobbied successfully for former foreign minister Ban Ki-moon (Pan Kimun; b. 1944) to be elected UN secretary general (October 2006).

Domestically, members of the 386 Generation formed the core of Roh's political base. Roh placed the 386ers among his supporters at the forefront of politics, especially those who had been student activists in the 1980s. He also recruited prominent progressives outside the political establishment. Feeling the momentum, Roh's staunchest supporters launched aggressive attacks against those they deemed corrupt members of the establishment— thus further polarizing politics by exacerbating generational and ideological conflict. To get away from the shadow of Kim Dae-jung and his supporters, on November 11, 2003, Roh and his supporters broke from the MDP and launched their own Uri Party (2003–07). The new ruling party, though, could claim just 47 members of the national assembly, compared to the combined total of the more than 190 GNP and MDP members constituting the majority.

On March 12, 2004, the two opposition parties impeached Roh Moohyun, an unprecedented initiative against the executive branch, only to see their tactic backfire. The impeachment motion accused Roh of failing to maintain neutrality during the national assembly election campaign as required by the law; accepting illegal political contributions during his presidential election campaign; accumulating tens of billions of won through illegal fundraising by the president's in-laws during his campaigns for the MDP primaries and the presidential election; and misgovernment leading to economic failure. The motion passed 193 to 2 after security guards removed the 47 Uri Party members for trying to block the vote physically, and Prime Minister Goh Kun (Ko Kŏn; b. 1938) performed the president's duties while the constitutional court reviewed the grounds for impeachment. Roh's approval rating dropped during the first year of his presidency due to corruption scandals involving his inner circle and widespread worry about the economic downturn. All the same, the general public consensus was that the impeachment motion initiated by the GNP, which had previously suffered embarrassment from some notorious corruption scandals, was unreasonable if not also hypocritical. Riding on such sentiments, the Uri Party won the national assembly election of April 15, becoming the new majority party with 152 seats. The rest of the votes were split among the GNP (121), the nearly wiped-out MDP (9), and others. And on May 14, the constitutional court overturned the impeachment, allowing Roh to resume his duties as president.

Buoyed by the dramatic turnaround, Roh pushed ahead with his reform agenda. He and the Uri Party sought to move the national capital to the Yeongi-Gongju (Yŏn'gi-Kongju) region in South Chungcheong (Ch'ungch'ŏng); repeal the National Security Act long abused by authoritarian regimes to persecute their critics; revise the Private Educational Institutions Law, which allowed much room for corruption in the management of such institutions; set the record straight on pro-Japanese collaborators; actively engage with North Korea; and reform the conservative media. Among these goals, the effort to repeal the National Security Act encountered stiff opposition. Arguing that the law was out of line with inter-Korean reconciliation and cooperation, the government sought to abolish it, ultimately thwarted by the GNP and other conservative forces. A widespread perception that Roh was passive about North Korea's nuclear weapons development program and that during the June 2004 military officials' talk on preventing future clashes in the Yellow Sea he was willing to compromise on the Northern Limit Line (NLL), which is the de facto postwar maritime boundary disputed by North Korea, elicited further criticism from conservatives.

While North Korea's ongoing development of nuclear weapons strained inter-Korean relations, the Roh Moo-hyun administration persisted with efforts to improve relations. Beginning with the seventh reunion of separated families (June 27–July 2, 2003), the two Koreas effected ten more reunions and seven video calls, starting on August 15, 2005. Also, ten minister-level talks fine-tuned various aspects of economic cooperation, especially profit-sharing joint ventures. South Korea constructed the North Korean Kaesŏng Industrial Region (June 2003–December 2004), followed by completing the project to reconnect the Seoul-Ŭiju railway (March 2006). And one-day package tours of Kaesŏng commenced (December 2007). Simultaneously, the volume of cultural exchange also increased. The men's and women's basketball teams of the Hyundai Group played friendly games with their

North Korean counterparts on the opening day of the P'yŏngyang Arena (Ryugyong Chung Ju-yung Gymnasium; October 2003), which the Hyundai Asan Corporation had designed and primarily funded. An affiliate of the Hyundai Group, Hyundai Asan, became a significant investor in North Korea, mostly by running the Mount Kŭmgang tours for South Koreans. Later in the month, a delegation of North Korean athletes participated in the National Peace Festival held in Jeju (Cheju) City. Then on August 15, 2005, when Seoul hosted an inter-Korean soccer match and the Grand National Festival on the sixtieth anniversary of national liberation, the North Korean delegation leader paid respects at the Seoul National Cemetery and visited President Roh. Later in the year, when the UN General Assembly voted on a resolution concerning North Korean human rights, South Korea abstained in consideration of inter-Korean relations (November).

The continuing cultural and economic exchanges culminated with a second inter-Korean summit. On October 2, 2007, Roh Moo-hyun became the first South Korean president to walk across the DMZ, visiting P'yŏngyang by car. Two days later, he and Kim Jong-il issued a joint statement that articulated eight main points: (1) achieving reunification through both Koreas' joint efforts; (2) upgrading and strengthening the inter-Korean relationship to one of mutual respect and trust; (3) ending military confrontation; (4) coming to a shared understanding of securing a lasting peace regime on the peninsula; (5) expanding economic cooperation; (6) increasing social and cultural exchange and cooperation; (7) actively pursuing humanitarian collaborative projects; and (8) increasing cooperation on promoting rights and benefits for diasporic Koreans. In South Korea, the overall public reaction to the joint statement was positive. Still, with a presidential election two months away, many saw it as Roh's election campaign ploy and complained that it ignored widespread starvation in North Korea. Due to the continuing economic crisis, the number of North Koreans fleeing to South Korea via China surpassed 10,000 in May 2007, and the figure had climbed to about 30,000 by 2013.

South Korea's conservatives saw Roh's engagement with North Korea as abetting that nation's nuclear weapons program. Having withdrawn itself from the Non-Proliferation Treaty, in April 2003, North Korea declared that it already possessed nuclear weapons and demanded replacing the armistice agreement with a treaty of mutual non-aggression, formally ending the Korean War. For dealing with the nuclear weapons program, the Six Party Talks (August 2003–September 2007) brought together both Koreas, China,

Japan, Russia, and the United States through a series of six meetings. Not compromising its bargaining position, North Korea successfully detonated a nuclear bomb underground (October 9, 2006), but the talks produced a breakthrough (February 13, 2007). On the condition that North Korea dismantle its nuclear facilities and register all aspects of its program, both America and Japan promised to improve relations with the country, and all five negotiating nations promised to supply North Korea with heavy fuel oil as emergency energy assistance. For implementing the agreement, the sixth meeting adopted a deal centered around America's promise to lift, in March, a freeze on North Korea's account with a bank in Macau and to remove, in September, the country from the U.S. government's list of nations sponsoring terrorism. The agreement, however, ultimately did not materialize, as America insisted that North Korea dispose of its nuclear weapons first, and North Korea wanted the delivery of the aid package first.

Meanwhile, election-year politics were well under way in South Korea. As the approval ratings of both Roh Moo-hyun and the ruling Uri Party continued to fall, Roh left the party (February 2007). In August, the Uri Party joined with those who had left other liberal parties or the GNP, and with some civic engagement groups, to form the United New Democratic Party (2007–08). In the December 19 presidential election, the GNP candidate, Lee Myung-bak (Yi Myŏngbak; b. 1941), a former CEO of Hyundai Construction and former mayor of Seoul, easily defeated both the United New Democratic Party candidate Chung Dong-young (Chŏng Tongyŏng; b. 1953), who was a former minister of unification, and Lee Hoi-chang, who ran as an independent—with 48.7 percent, 26.1 percent, and 15.1 of the valid votes, respectively. Lee Myung-bak won the election by winning the support of conservatives and appealing to those who believed that he, as a former CEO, could revive the economy.

Inaugurated on February 25, 2008, the Lee Myung-bak administration got off to a rocky start. While his adoption of overall business-friendly policies and pursuit of deregulation raised hopes for economic recovery, the fact that many newly appointed officials possessed real estate wealth in Gangnam (Kangnam), attended Somang Church (a megachurch that Lee himself attended), or hailed from his home region, North Gyeongsang (Kyŏngsang) elicited public criticism. Before long, massive candlelight demonstrations erupted upon the government's agreement with the United States (April 18) to import American beef. Spurred by media reports that the import of

American beef contaminated with bovine spongiform encephalopathy, or mad cow disease, seriously threatened public health, evening candlelight demonstrations by protesters spread nationwide, raging on for weeks. On June 10, a protest in front of Seoul City Hall reportedly brought out a million people, the largest turnout of anti-government protesters since June 1987. Both the frequency and scale of the demonstrations began to decline only when the public became more aware that earlier media reports had exaggerated the health risks and that anti-government, liberal political forces were behind such reporting.

The next year, a government investigation of the former president, and his subsequent suicide, gave the liberal opposition and its base a martyr. The Supreme Prosecutors' Office had launched an investigation of bribery allegations against Roh Moo-hyun in April 2009, the main charge being that during his presidency, Roh had received 1.3 billion won from a businessman who was close to him and who had delivered the fund to Roh's wife through a presidential secretary. The opposition pointed out that in contrast to the likes of Chun Doo-hwan and Roh Tae-woo, who had amassed slush funds hundreds of times greater to finance election campaigns and enrich their families, Roh's family had used what was in effect borrowed money from a friend to cover their children's living expenses during their studies in the United States. The ruling GNP did not hold back, and during the prosecution's continuing investigation, Roh committed suicide (May 23). His death not only shocked many but helped pro-Roh figures within the opposition rally and gain ground politically. A former human rights lawyer and Roh's former chief presidential secretary, Moon Jae-in, emerged as a leading figure and became president of the Roh Moo-hyun Foundation.

Another major issue that further polarized South Korean politics was Lee Myung-bak's Four Major Rivers Project (2009–12). During his presidential election campaign, Lee had pledged to construct a grand canal. Still, the critics' concerns about its feasibility, environmental impact, and effect on cultural artifacts and sites forced the administration to launch the Four Major Rivers Project as a redevelopment of the basins of the nation's four longest rivers instead (January 2009). Costing about 22.2 trillion won and disregarding various environmental issues raised by some concerned government agencies, the project entailed dredging, constructing weirs and dams to increase the overall volume of water in storage for each river, water quality improvement, flood control enhancement, and ecological restoration. The overall workmanship was shoddy, and the results were mixed. Upon completion (April 2012), the project allowed safer management of all four rivers, especially summer flood alleviation along the lower banks of the Nakdong (Naktong) and Yeongsan (Yŏngsan) Rivers, but immediately evident were such problems as excessive dredging of the deposited riverbed soil, a serious risk of water quality deterioration, and questions about the safety of the drinking water supply.

While internal political controversies continued, inter-Korean relations took a nose dive. Earlier, North Korea had ended the cargo train service between Kaesŏng and South Korea's Munsan and drastically reduced the number of resident South Korean personnel allowed in the Kaesŏng Industrial Region (November 2008). Six months later, when North Korea conducted its second nuclear bomb test (May 25, 2009), all fifteen members of the UN Security Council, including China and Russia, voted unanimously in favor of a resolution that imposed further economic sanctions on North Korea and encouraged UN member states to search North Korean cargo. A defiant North Korea announced a plan to weaponize all its plutonium and start uranium enrichment, adding that any attempt at a blockade would be considered an act of war. As South Korean conservatives were convinced that Kim Dae-jung's and Roh Moo-hyun's policy of engagement and providing economic aid had funded the North Korean nuclear weapon and ballistic missile programs, the Lee Myung-bak administration stopped the Mount Kŭmgang and Kaesŏng tours. Also, inter-Korean trade volume rapidly decreased. As Kim Jong-il's health declined, the regime sought to strengthen internal control by taking a hard-line stance. When a South Korean navy corvette, the *Cheonan* (*Ch'ŏnan*), sank in the Yellow Sea from a torpedo attack and forty-six crewmen died (May 2010), Lee's government blamed it on the north and worked with other countries in trying to increase sanctions on North Korea. In December, North Korea used the South Korean navy's live-fire exercise near the disputed NLL as a pretext to shell the nearby South Korean island of Yeonpyeongdo, killing two soldiers and two civilians. As inter-Korean relations deteriorated, reunions of separated families took place just twice during Lee's presidency.

While becoming more confrontational, North Korea underwent a leadership transition. Sometime earlier, Kim Jong-il had designated as the heir apparent his third son, Kim Jong-un, who had spent his adolescent years at a school in Switzerland. In September 2010, this son assumed the position of general of the KPA, followed by his becoming vice chairman of the Central Military Commission and a member of the Central Committee of the WPK. Upon Kim Jong-il's death (December 17, 2011), the twenty-seven-year-old Kim Jong-un became the supreme leader, though his father's sister, Kim Kyong-hui (Kim Kyŏnghŭi; b. 1946), and her husband, Chang Song-thaek (Chang Sŏngt'aek; 1946–2013), also wielded influence. Nonetheless, after the end of the official period of mourning, the 4th Conference of the WPK (April 11, 2012) and the SPA (April 13) elevated Kim to be first secretary of the WPK, a member of the Presidium of the Politburo of the WPK, and the first chairman of the NDC—thus concluding the power transition. Notably, a constitutional amendment on the same day stated that the country was a nuclear power. Subsequently, Kim assumed the position of marshal of the KPA (July 18). On December 12, North Korea launched a ballistic missile with a satellite that entered into orbit, followed by a third nuclear weapon test (February 12, 2013) to project the new leader's resolve. North Korea also began boasting that now it possessed intercontinental ballistic missiles with nuclear warheads capable of striking the United States. Kim not only transferred effective military command from the old-guard generals to the party leadership but also, on December 8, the authorities arrested Chang Song-thaek, accusing him of conspiring to mount a coup, and executed him just four days later.

By then in South Korea, a new conservative administration had been inaugurated. In the previous year, the ruling GNP had changed its name to the Saenuri Party (2012–17), rebranding itself as a reformist conservative party in preparation for the December 19, 2012, election. The Saenuri Party nominee, Park Geun-hye (Pak Kŭnhye; b. 1952), a daughter of Park Chung-hee, defeated the Democratic United Party (2011–13) nominee, Moon Jae-in, 51.6 percent to 48 percent, and thus became the republic's first female president. Inaugurated on February 25, 2013, Park Geun-hye announced the "Trust Building Process on the Korean Peninsula," which proposed providing generous aid to North Korea in exchange for the latter giving up nuclear weapons.

Nonetheless, the proposal did little to improve strained inter-Korean relations. Tensions ran high between February and June 2013, when North Korea issued a series of statements that it would not refrain from war. This aggressive stance invited tougher UN sanctions led by the United States, and it increasingly upset the new Chinese government, headed by President

Xi Jinping (b. 1953), albeit without fundamentally jeopardizing the Sino–North Korean alliance. For their parts, the United States and South Korea put on a display of force by conducting large-scale military drills on the Yellow Sea, even mobilizing nuclear submarines. Unfazed, North Korea announced the resumption of the full operation of its Yŏngbyŏn Nuclear Scientific Research Center (April 2). The next day, reacting to what it viewed as a grave insult to Kim by South Korea's defense minister, who had earlier promised a pinpoint strike against the top northern leadership if necessary, North Korea suddenly banned all 123 South Korean companies that had invested in the Kaesŏng Industrial Region and subsequently withdrew all 50,000 North Korean employees. In response, South Korea cut off electricity to the complex and recalled its management personnel and supplies. When the south expressed its willingness to shut down the complex and proposed talks, the north took up the offer. A round of talks produced an agreement to jointly manage and to internationalize the Kaesŏng Industrial Region and to improve the management of transportation, communication, and customs clearance for the complex. Regular operations in the region resumed in September.

Domestically in South Korea, various issues and incidents fueled political turmoil. Initially, the political establishment wrangled over President Park Geun-hye's key personnel appointments; manipulation of public opinion by the National Intelligence Service before the December 2012 presidential election; former president Roh Moo-hyun's alleged, off-the-record statement during the 2007 inter-Korean summit that the NLL was negotiable; and Park's scaling back the social welfare policy she had promised during her election campaign. Then on April 16, 2014, when the tourist ferry *Sewol* (*Sewŏl*) sank, and 299 out of 476 passengers died, the government came under fire for poor handling of the accident during the initial critical hours. From May to July 2015, an outbreak of the Middle East Respiratory Syndrome (MERS) coronavirus prompted the government to quarantine at least 6,508 individuals. The Ministry of Health and Welfare was slow in disclosing relevant information to hospitals, municipal governments, and the public, thus inviting criticism. The virus infected at least 186, among whom 36 died.

The next year, inter-Korean relations deteriorated further while Kim Jong-un tightened his grip on power. On January 12, 2016, North Korea conducted its fourth nuclear bomb test. The next month, Park's government complained about North Korea's earlier rocket launch, describing it as a disguised ballistic missile test, and announced that it would for the first time halt its operations in the Kaesŏng Industrial Region, ostensibly to stop North Korea from using South Korean investments to fund nuclear and missile development (February 10). The next day, North Korea announced that it would expel all 280 South Korean workers and freeze South Korean assets and equipment. Continuing the hard-line policy, Kim became WPK chairman, replacing his position as the WPK first secretary (May 9). When the thirteenth SPA (2014–19) replaced the NDC with the State Affairs Commission, Kim became its chairman, a new position (June 29). Two months later, North Korea conducted a fifth nuclear bomb test (September 9).

Around that time in South Korea, a political scandal led to a relatively sudden power transition from Park Geun-hye to Moon Jae-in. Earlier, the opposition Democratic Party (2013–14; formerly the Democratic United Party) had won the national assembly election of April 2016. The number of its seats increased from 102 to 123, whereas the Saenuri Party's representation decreased from 146 to 122. In mid-2016, the public began to learn of Choi Soon-sil (Ch'oe Sunsil; b. 1956), who had come to mastermind Park's policies although holding no government position. Media reports that Choi's daughter had gotten into a prestigious university through illicit means crashed Park's approval rating to single-digits and sparked nation-wide candlelight demonstrations that raged on for months. Heeding the public's outrage, the national assembly impeached Park (December 9), and Prime Minister Hwang Kyo-ahn (Hwang Kyoan; b. 1957) assumed the president's duties. After reviewing the case, the constitutional court ruled unanimously in convicting Park, thus removing her from office (March 10, 2017). In the subsequent presidential election on May 9, Moon Jae-in of the newly constituted Democratic Party (formerly New Politics Alliance for Democracy; renamed in 2015) handily defeated the candidate of the ruling Liberty Korea Party (formerly the Saenuri Party; renamed in 2017), Hong Jun-pyo (Hong Chunp'yo; b. 1954), a former governor of South Gyeong-sang, and the centrist third-party candidate, Ahn Cheol-soo (An Ch'ŏlsu; b. 1962), a physician and former software entrepreneur—the three receiving 41.1 percent, 24 percent, and 21.4 percent of the valid votes, respectively. Inaugurated the next day, Moon enjoyed a high approval rating for much of the remainder of 2017. Riding on his popularity, Moon sought to resume Roh Moo-hyun's engagement policy vis-à-vis North Korea, despite that nation's sixth nuclear bomb test (September 3).

Moon was determined to secure an irreversible framework for inter-Korean relations, and his efforts paid off in 2018, ushering in détente and brokering a dialogue between North Korea and the United States In his New Year's address, Kim Jong-un expressed both openness to talk with the south and willingness to send athletes to the upcoming Winter Olympics hosted by Pyeongchang (P'yŏngch'ang), South Korea. Alongside tighter UN sanctions, North Korea's development of ballistic missiles capable of hitting the continental United States persuaded Kim that his country now had meaningful leverage vis-à-vis the United States despite the enormous difference in military power otherwise between the two nations (Table 14.1). Seeking to achieve his regime's long-term security by officially ending the Korean War, Kim decided to rebuild the economy by improving relations with the United States and South Korea. In February, North Korea took part in the Olympics and sent a high-level delegation headed by Kim's younger sister, Kim Yo-jong (Kim Yŏjŏng; b. 1987), as a special envoy. Two months later, Moon and Kim held a summit meeting in the southern part of the DMZ (April 27), followed by another the next month, this time in the northern part (May 26). While promoting mutual trust, Moon also persuaded U.S. president Donald Trump (b. 1946) to engage with North Korea. The resulting dialogue led to an unprecedented DPRK–U.S. summit when Kim and Trump met in Singapore (June 12). In general terms, the two leaders agreed on a shared commitment to improving relations and achieving the Korean Peninsula's denuclearization.

Subsequently, tortuous DPRK–U.S. negotiations continued while inter-Korean relations warmed. The United States insisted that North Korea denuclearize first, whereas the latter demanded the end of sanctions first. Some mutual good-will gestures were accomplished, however. North Korea turned over fifty-five sets of remains of American soldiers killed during the Korean War and shut down some nuclear weapon and ballistic missile facilities; for its part, the United States canceled two joint military exercises with South Korea. Since then, however, the two sides have locked horns over which should take the first big step. Meanwhile, improving inter-Korean relations passed some milestones. Not only did Moon and Kim meet for a third time (September 18–20, 2018; P'yŏngyang), the two Koreas established a liaison office in Kaesŏng, began arms reduction in border areas, and launched cooperation on upgrading and expanding North Korean rail lines in preparation for connecting them with South Korea's lines. Kim and

TABLE 14.1   Estimated 2020 defense spending by country, top ten. Ranking seventy-fourth, North Korea's figure was about 1.6 billion dollars (about 8.9 percent of its estimated 2019 nominal GDP).

GLOBAL RANK	COUNTRY	SPENDING (US$, IN BILLIONS)	% OF GDP
1	United States	750.0	3.6
2	China	237.0	1.6
3	Saudi Arabia	67.6	9.9
4	India	61.0	2.4
5	United Kingdom	55.1	2.1
6	Germany	50.0	1.3
7	Japan	49.0	1.0
8	Russia	48.0	3.3
9	South Korea	44.0	2.8
10	France	41.5	1.6

SOURCES   Global Firepower 2020 (https://www.globalfirepower.com/); International Monetary Fund (https://www.imf.org/external/index.htm); Trading Economics (https://tradingeconomics.com).

Trump met in Hanoi for their second summit (February 27–28, 2019), cut short by Trump, without an agreement. Four months later, though, during Trump's visit to South Korea, he and Kim met in the DMZ, expressing hope for peace, before joining Moon for a brief chat (June 30).

By then, Moon's role as a facilitator had reached its limit, with no further meaningful progress in either the DPRK–U.S. or inter-Korean dialogue. In September 2019, Trump replaced his national security advisor, who had been suggesting applying the "Libyan model" and making North Korea first give up its nuclear weapons for incentives. Still, subsequent DPRK–U.S. talks in Stockholm produced no result (October 5–6). On the second anniversary of the summit, the DPRK minister of foreign affairs released a press statement denouncing the Trump administration's efforts (June 12, 2020). In part reacting to a row with South Korea over North Korean defectors' plans to send anti-P'yŏngyang propaganda leaflets from the south across the DMZ, North Korea subsequently cut communications with South Korea, demolished the joint liaison office in Kaesŏng (June 17), and ceased efforts toward diplomatic relations with the United States. Nonetheless, Kim Jong-un has maintained a moratorium on nuclear weapons and ballistic missile testing. In September, he issued a rare, official apology after North Korean soldiers shot dead a South Korean government employee who had drifted across the maritime inter-Korean border, either by accident or to defect.

Internally, Kim Jong-un effectively completed a generational change in the WPK leadership and effectively raised his sister Kim Yo-jong to the second-in-command. The older leadership, who had served under Kim Jong-il, may have harbored doubts about the younger Kim's ability, and in their place, his sister has emerged as the key figure. While holding the position of the party's First Deputy Director of the Propaganda and Agitation Department for five years (2014–19), she was elected to the fourteenth SPA (since April 2019). Not only was she an important part of her brother's delegation to every summit with Trump, her involvement in foreign affairs has continued. Kim Yo-jong has assumed the responsibility of issuing the strongest hard-line statements on relations with South Korea or the United States, while her brother kept his communication channel with Trump open.

Since early 2020, North Korea, like most countries, has been coping with coronavirus disease 2019 (COVID-19), taking drastic measures to prevent an outbreak and spare its fragile health infrastructure. In late January, the country officially closed its borders with both China and Russia. Also, the government has quarantined tens of thousands of citizens deemed "suspected" cases. Denying that the country has had any COVID cases, in early December North Korean officials declared that the country was facing multiple crises, including the pandemic and a series of natural disasters in the summer. In P'yŏngyang, the government imposed such measures as the closure of public places and restrictions on people's movements in and out of the capital. Kim Yo-jong articulated a sharp, verbal attack on South Korea's foreign minister for disputing North Korea's claim that it had no COVID cases and accused her of damaging already strained inter-Korea relations.

In the same year, in South Korea, the national assembly's majority support for Moon Jae-in increased. In February 2020, the conservative opposition, the Liberty Korea Party, merged with two small conservative parties, producing the People Power Party, in preparation for the April 2020 national assembly election. Buoyed at the time by the progress in inter-Korean relations, the ruling Democratic Party (and a minor alliance party that was later absorbed) secured 180 out of 300 seats (60 percent), and the People Power Party (and a small alliance party also later absorbed) won 103 (34.3 percent)—with the 17 remaining seats split among three minor parties and five independents. With its victory, the Democratic Party secured enough seats to propose a constitutional change but still not enough to effect a change unilaterally.

Despite the ruling party's comfortable majority in the national assembly, Moon made no headway with one of his manifest priorities, reforming the Supreme Prosecutors' Office. In many ways reviving Roh Moo-hyun's effort, the reform as pursued by the Moon administration entailed democratic oversight of the office's ability to conduct transparent investigations independent from influence by a particular individual or regime. Moon's initial effort with Cho Kuk (b. 1965), a law professor, as the minister of justice was unsuccessful. Appointed in September 2019, Cho vowed a sweeping reform, only to resign just thirty-five days later due to various allegations against him and his family, including plagiarism, tax evasion, and illicit business activities. Appointed as Cho's successor in January 2020, Choo Mi-ae (Ch'u Miae; b. 1958), a former judge and a long-time high-profile politician in the Democratic Party and its predecessors, fought a war of nerves over personnel matters with Prosecutor General Yoon Seok-youl (Yun Sŏgyŏl; b. 1960), who had investigated allegations against Cho. Then in July, the conflict escalated, with Choo enforcing oversight on the Supreme Prosecutors' Office as it investigated an allegation that a prosecutor had colluded with a media outlet in attacking the president of the Roh Moo-hyun Foundation. The showdown climaxed when Choo ordered an investigation of various allegations against other prosecutors (October 16). The next month, she announced disciplinary action against Yoon and suspended him for ethical violations, abuse of power, and interference in investigations of his associates and family members (November 24). Not backing down, Yoon secured a court injunction against the suspension, and a week later, he was able to resume his duty (December 1). Subsequently, though, the Ministry of Justice's disciplinary committee on prosecutors approved a two-month suspension (December 16). Choo and Moon approved the recommendation, but Yoon again obtained a court injunction against the suspension. Throughout the controversy, Choo and Yoon clashed over how much authority the justice minister has over the prosecutor general. South Korea's chronic problem of a powerful Supreme Prosecutors' Office investigating and prosecuting cases according to the ebb and flow of national politics has yet to show any meaningful sign of change.

Throughout 2020, just about the only issue making the South Korean headlines more often than the conflict between the justice minister and the prosecutor general has been COVID-19. Although among the first countries hit by the virus, South Korea initially managed to avoid lockdown measures, thanks mainly to aggressive testing and sophisticated contact-tracing techniques. By April, the World Health Organization and other global agencies praised the country as a model for containing the outbreak effectively. Moon Jae-in even launched a "coronavirus diplomacy" effort with countries struggling with much bigger outbreaks and death tolls. By the fall, however, the citizenry let its guard down after months of widespread mask wearing and social distancing and periods of individual isolation facilitated by contact tracing. The authorities identified new clusters among groups that failed to practice social distancing, including such offenders as evangelical Protestant churches, businesses dependent on the nightlife economy, and large gatherings of family and friends. Also, the government's decision in October to ease restrictions seems to have been premature. As of December, South Korea was confronting the prospect of an unstoppable wave of infections caused by new outbreaks, with Seoul and its vicinity rapidly running out of hospital beds, although the overall situation was still much better than that in the United States and Europe. The Moon government warned that failure to contain the resurgence could force it to raise restrictions to the highest level thus far—a soft lockdown for the first time since the start of the pandemic, which has so far not impacted the national economy in South Korea as much as it has the economies of other advanced nations.

ECONOMIES IN TRANSITION

In the final years of Kim Dae-jung's presidency, South Korea's economy moved well beyond the 1997 Asian Financial Crisis. In August 2001, the country paid off the IMF loan of 19.5 billion dollars early and still possessed more than 102 billion dollars of foreign currency. Exports were booming, especially in automobiles, household electronics, mobile phones, and semi-conductor memory chips, including Samsung's products as that company emerged as a world leader. Within South Korea, mobile phones spread rapidly, to the level of a device for every two persons. In 2002, the economy grew by 7.2 percent. In terms of GDP (PPP) per capita, a rough indicator of a country's standard of living, the economy was back on a growth track (Figure 14.1).

During Roh Moo-hyun's presidency, South Korea sustained relatively robust growth of 4 to 5 percent per year, even while the average workweek began to decrease. In 2004, the government initiated the decrease in the workweek, from six days to five days by 2011, in phases, depending on the firm's size. Exports continued to lead economic growth, and to sustain export growth, the country began to secure one free trade agreement (FTA) after another, starting with Chile. When the 2002 South Korea–Chile FTA took effect (April 2004), it facilitated the export of manufactured goods to Chile and the latter's export of agricultural products to South Korea. Negotiation of an FTA with a far bigger trading partner, the United States, consumed more than four years (May 2006–December 2010), mainly due to American concerns about the effect of Hyundais and Kias on the U.S. automobile industry and South Korean concerns about the impact of American agricultural produce and beef. Export growth continued to depend on South Korea's internationally competitive manufacturers in shipbuilding, automobiles, information, and communications. Hyundai Heavy Industries, Samsung Heavy Industries, Daewoo Shipbuilding, Samsung Electronics, LG Electronics, and the Hyundai Motor Company all became global leaders in their respective business sectors. The ICT sector remained critically important, accounting for 41.9 percent of total economic growth in 2003.

Under the Roh administration, South Korea also passed a transportation milestone with a high-speed rail system service. Operation of both the Gyeongbu (Kyŏngbu) KTX line, which connected Seoul and Busan, and the Honam KTX line, which extended the service to Mokpo (Mokp'o), commenced simultaneously (April 2004). The two lines considerably shortened travel times between the capital and the nation's southeastern and south-western regions. The train traveled at a maximum operating speed of about 305 kilometers per hour. KTX services also accelerated the overconcentration of the country's resources in Seoul. They made it easier for provincial

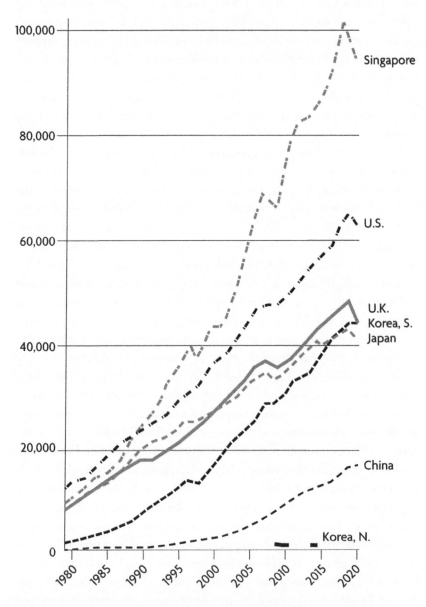

FIGURE 14.1   South Korea's and North Korea's GDP (PPP) per capita compared to select countries, 1980–2020. Sources: International Monetary Fund; Central Intelligence Agency, The World Fact Book 2020.

residents to visit the capital to engage in commercial transactions or use the nation's best hospitals.

The domestic transportation of people and goods was significantly facilitated within South Korea, and inter-Korean economic cooperation also increased during Roh's presidency. Hyundai Asan completed construction of the Kaesŏng Industrial Region (December 2004). Three months later, South Korea began to supply electricity directly to the factories for which North Korea provided labor (March 2005). Two years later, the reconnected Seoul-Ŭiju railway commenced cargo train service between Kaesŏng and Munsan, close to the southern edge of the DMZ, thus enabling the daily commute of the South Korean management staff (December 2007). This joint venture capitalizing on disciplined yet low-wage North Korean labor was a win-win for both Koreas as they shared the profits.

The succeeding Lee Myung-bak administration had to cope with an economic downturn for two years. In September 2008, a financial crisis originating in the United States had a domino effect, and a recession descended on the rest of the world. The value of the South Korean won declined sharply, investments in foreign funds nearly evaporated, exports were sluggish, and domestic demand decreased. The economy shrank by 0.6 percent in 2008, although it grew by 1.6 percent in the following year. Also, per capita GDP (PPP) continued to grow incrementally from 2007 to 2009.

By 2011, South Korea's economy was back on an upward trajectory. In that year, the economy grew by 6.3 percent, the total volume of trade ranked ninth in the world, and the balance of trade improved. In fact, from then on, not only both export and per capita GDP (PPP) but also the trade surplus would continue to grow one year after another. Facilitated by currency swap agreements with China, Japan, and the United States, South Korea's foreign currency reserve increased to more than 316 billion dollars in 2012—the eighth largest in the world. To sustain export-led growth, Lee's government secured additional FTAs. Effecting one with the European Union went relatively smoothly, and it was signed in October 2010 and went into effect in July 2011. By contrast, the negotiation with the United States, which the Roh Moo-hyun administration had initiated, was intense. Despite the liberal opposition's resistance, the national assembly ratified the KORUS FTA (November 2011), and months later, the agreement went into effect (March 2012). South Korea also signed FTAs with such major emerging economies as India (August 2009). The economy's strong performance depended heavily on a small number of conglomerates that produced successful exports, including Samsung's mobile devices, semiconductors, and household electronics; Hyundai's automobiles and shipbuilding; and LG's household electronics.

During Park Geun-hye's presidency, economic growth slowed to a rate more typical among other advanced economies, such as the United States—2 to 3 percent per year. Among the contributing factors were sluggish domestic consumption, a drop in foreign demand for exports, greater competition from China and Japan, and declining investment. Nonetheless, current accounts achieved a record surplus at the end of 2013, up 47 percent from 2012, despite the uncertainties of global economic turmoil. In 2014, South Korea was the world's seventh largest exporter and seventh largest importer, signing even more FTAs, with such significant economies as Canada (March), Australia (April), and China (June 2015). Technology products accounted for much of the export rate, including the products of the auto industry, which was the fifth largest in the world as of 2015. By 2016, the economy struggled to balance a heavy reliance on exports and domestic restructuring efforts in the shipbuilding industry.

After the political turmoil of the final months of Park's presidency, Moon Jae-in's election brought a surge in consumer confidence essential for economic vitality. The Moon administration was successful with its effort to increase wages and government spending. Also, an uptick in export growth drove real GDP growth in 2017 to more than 3 percent, despite disruptions in the South Korea–China trade due to the latter's retaliatory measures taken over Park's decision to deploy a U.S. missile defense system, to which China vigorously objected. In that year, South Korea's GDP (PPP) was the fourteenth largest in the world—roughly one-tenth the size of China's or America's and about fifty times greater than North Korea's—and the country continued to contend with gradually slowing economic growth hovering in the 2 to 3 percent range. Even more significantly, the GDP (PPP) per capita surpassed Japan's in 2017. Japan's retaliation against a South Korean supreme court ruling (October 2018) ordering a Japanese company to compensate surviving Korean victims for forced wartime labor cut the nation's supply of essential Japanese parts for high-tech products, but by 2020 the Moon administration turned the crisis around by successfully weaning the industry off the imported parts through domestic production. All the same, an ongoing effort to boost growth also required addressing challenges arising from the nation's rapidly aging population, inflexible labor market, continuing conglomerate dominance, and heavy reliance on exports rather than domestic consumption. As the economy had become tightly integrated into the global value chain, and given its vulnerability in the event of any Sino-American trade war, South Korea persisted in its efforts to secure additional FTAs and to improve the existing ones. The economy also continued to grapple with rising inequality, poverty among the elderly, high youth unemployment, still long working hours, low worker productivity, and corruption. In 2018, Moon's approval rating steadily declined with the general public's growing discontent over the economy. Nonetheless, committed to a liberal agenda, he increased green subsidies and expanded subsidies for electric vehicles the next year.

As of December 2020, South Korea enjoys a secure standing as a significant player in the global economy. The country is the fourteenth largest economy (2.3 trillion dollars) with an estimated GDP (PPP) per capita of 44,292 dollars, thus surpassing the GDP (PPP) figures of such economies as Britain and Japan. Ever dependent on international trade, South Korea's total exports and imports of goods and services amount to 83 percent of its GDP. Rightfully concerned that complicated regulations are becoming outmoded, Moon's government has sought businesses' input regarding new and existing regulations. The market, rated highly in the international Index of Economic Freedom, has become more open than ever before. The financial sector continues to undergo consolidation, with still-improving transparency and efficiency.

In stark contrast to South Korea's robust economy with an ever-increasing standard of living, North Korea's ruined economy has shown little sign of recovery in the past two decades. A balance of power has prevailed between the regime, on the one hand, and, on the other, those who constitute a distinct economic force capitalizing on the growth of an unofficial market economy since the late 1990s. With the demise of the planned economy, the population has sought various means of survival. Alarmed by the market economy intrusion, the government initially tried in vain to suppress it with measures ranging from currency reform to public executions of those who violated the law. The currency reform of 2009 and the resulting drop in the value of the North Korean won, however, strengthened the unofficial market economy in a way that made returning to an entirely planned economic system increasingly unfeasible. The top political leadership began to divide up and distribute shares of the growing market to members of the leadership and bureaucracy, in effect redistributing the country's economic assets. Simultaneously, between 2004 and 2014, military expenditure remained a significant burden on the economy—with about 23.3 percent of the GDP (PPP) devoted to defense even as the regime began to promote both light industry and agriculture. Nonetheless, the overall economic policy remained centered around the heavy industry, emphasizing the defense sector as the government continued to invest in nuclear weapons and ballistic missiles.

Upon succeeding his father, Kim Jong-un has pursued twin goals of developing nuclear weapons and achieving economic growth through securing more foreign investment in special economic zones. Accordingly, North Korea has increased its number of special economic zones more than five-fold to twenty-seven. It has expanded its light industry by constructing sock and textile factories to improve its capacity to self-supply consumer products. Also, Kim has shown keen interest in attracting foreign tourists by completing such ambitious projects as the Masikryong (Masingnyŏng) Ski Resort (December 2013), a part of the Wŏnsan Special Tourist Zone, a massive seashore resort district.

Widening UN sanctions, however, continued to choke the DPRK economy, which, in 2017, contracted at its sharpest rate in two decades. International trade, industrial production, which accounted for about a third of the nation's output, and the overall economy suffered the steepest decline since 1998 due to restricted imports of oil and other energy resources. The biggest trading partner, China, stopped coal purchases, thus denying North Korea its main source of export revenue. China's suspension of fuel sales to North Korea raised diesel and gasoline prices, which then began to stabilize thanks in part to increased smuggling. Aggravating the situation was the worst drought in sixteen years, although late summer rains helped prevent acute food shortages. As of 2017, *jangmadang* accounted for about 60 percent of the economy, wherein more people were on their own than ever before.

In 2018, sanctions continued to choke North Korea's economy. In April, immediately after his first summit with Moon Jae-in, Kim Jong-un vowed to shift the strategic focus from nuclear arsenal development to jump-starting the economy. Kim continually articulated his intention to stimulate growth through domestic consumption and accommodation of foreign tourists, building such significant facilities as the P'yŏngyang's Taedonggang Seafood Restaurant, fitted with a huge aquarium (July). Drops in fuel prices (June–July), stable prices for rice, corn, and other staples, and increasing

use of appliances powered by solar panels were helpful. Still, the continuing international sanction against the profitable export of minerals blocked
any possibility of economic recovery. Overall, suffering increased among the
population, especially in South Hamgyŏng, where some died of hunger. Due
to sanctions, even foreign humanitarian aid groups had difficulty accessing
international banks and delivering goods into North Korea.

In 2019, North Korea's economy actually grew 0.4 percent, the first upswing in three years, mostly thanks to construction activity and increased
agricultural output. Still, the overall economy certainly was not on a recovery
trajectory. Construction grew by 2.9 percent, as Kim Jong-un continued to
spur the development of tourist resorts, homes, and power plants, and also
farming and fishing output rose by 1.4 percent. All the same, manufacturing fell by 1.1 percent, and mining, a key cash generator, decreased by 0.7
percent, decreasing for the third consecutive year. Even though estimates
do not reflect the underground economy, including *jangmadang*, the general
picture was undeniably bleak.

As of December 2020, North Korea's economy remains repressed and
stagnant. Figures more recent than the estimated GDP of 40 billion dollars
and a GDP (PPP) per capita of around 1,700 dollars as of 2015 are unknown,
though GDP growth is estimated to have been negative in 2018, after four
years of minimal growth. Indeed, Kim Jong-un continues to pursue limited
development of markets and private entrepreneurship to boost government
revenue. Also, such black markets as *jangmadang* continue to grow despite
the state's attempted crackdown. Overall, though, the regime fully controls the currency, owns almost all property, commands and dictates nearly
all aspects of the economy, and directs all significant economic activities.
State-owned industries with government-set production targets account for
virtually the entire GDP, including the disproportionately large military
expenditure. The stricter enforcement of UN sanctions has indeed had a
detrimental impact on North Korea's trade. China remains the main trading partner and provides extensive energy and food subsidies. The WPK,
the KPA, and the cabinet run companies that earn foreign exchange. The
closed, state-controlled financial sector allows limited foreign investment
in special economic zones.

Combined with international sanctions and some natural disasters over the
summer, COVID-19 has also done its part to cripple North Korea's economy.
In late January 2020, North Korea's official closure of the border with China

brought Sino–North Korean trade down to record lows. Enforcing border control and a domestic lockdown, the authorities executed an official for violating import restrictions (August) and a money changer in P'yŏngyang—which the government has been restricting movements into and out of—after being blamed for falling exchange rates (October). North Korea desperately needs economic aid but has nowhere to turn. Usually, international aid organizations can operate in the country despite constraints, but the pandemic has halted their activities. The United Nations secured 3.5 million dollars in COVID aid for North Korea, which is only about 9 percent of the desired amount and is the lowest funding rate among Asia Pacific countries. And the funds contributed by the members of the UN Office for the Coordination of Humanitarian Affairs are less than one-third of the required amount. More than ever before, the question of the long-term social impact of North Korea's crippled economy on the population looms large.

SOCIAL CHANGE: FROM CLASS MOBILITY TO MULTICULTURALISM

In the new century's first decade, South Korea became similar to many advanced Western economies and Japan in terms of demographic trends regarding children. The TFR decreased from 1.22 births in 2000–05 to 1.05 in 2017, while life expectancy rose from 77.2 years in 2000–05 to 82.6 in 2017. Couples without children continued to increase in number, but university entrance remained intensely competitive. Despite the continuing improvement in the standard of living since the economic takeoff, pressure for academic performance accounts in large part for the self-reported low degree of happiness among South Korean children—ranking the lowest among twenty-two OECD countries studied in 2016. Society no longer considers higher education the sole vehicle for upward social mobility, but attending a four-year university remains the goal for most high school students and their guardians.

The Kim Dae-jung administration's efforts to rationalize the university admission review system produced mixed results. In 2002, the government instituted a new system that made the review for each student consider not only academic performance at school but also special talents, volunteer activities, and a principal's recommendation letter, in order to reduce the relative weight of standardized test scores and school grades on the students' opportunities and to encourage an overall more balanced learning experience.

The new system also changed the university admission review unit from the individual academic department to a larger undergraduate division, thus not binding every entering student to a specific major. When the government announced the reform, however, universities defended their existing academic department–based admission review systems. High schools complained that the new system would lower the students' overall academic performance and make ranking the students for college admission difficult for teachers. In response, the government allowed each university to add its own method of further evaluating an applicant, such as an essay test.

Continuing the overall education system reform, in 2005, the Roh Moo-hyun administration sought to further rationalize the management of private schools, a policy that fueled partisan debate. The government devised a law to end corrupt management practices and conflict between a school's admin-istration and its teaching staff by improving the transparency of manage-ment and finances and requiring at least one-fourth of the board of trustees to be external personnel. The law elicited stiff opposition from private school founders, foundations, and the opposition GNP. Complaining of infringement on the autonomy of private education, the opponents argued that the law's stipulated appointment of Korean Teachers and Education Workers Union members as mediation committee members would make the curriculum leftist. Nonetheless, the ruling Uri Party pushed ahead with passing the legislation.

Another polarizing issue was Roh Moo-hyun's attempt to create a new administrative capital as he sought to address the overconcentration of assets, resources, and opportunities in Seoul and its vicinity. When the govern-ment announced a plan to build the administrative capital in the Yeongi-Gongju region (July 2004), it elicited a strong pushback, especially from the conservative GNP and its base, which had a vested interest in the status quo that entailed, among other issues, high-value real estate in Gangnam, Seoul. Before long, some citizen movement groups sued the government. The constitutional court ruled that depriving Seoul of its status as the nation's capital in any way violated the "customary constitution." Subsequently, the government changed the plan, calling instead for a "comprehensive admin-istrative city" (March 2005), which the GNP ultimately accepted. The new plan materialized during Lee Myung-bak's presidency as the Sejong Spe-cial Autonomous City (July 2012). The government began to relocate some major agencies to this area, and as was the case with Gwacheon (Kwach'ŏn), government employees working in Sejong tended to commute while their family members stayed put in Seoul for all the advantages it enjoyed over the rest of the country in terms of resources and opportunities.

While the competition for such privileges as are popularly perceived has grown fierce, South Korea has also become an increasingly multicultural society. With the country's stature within the global political economy attracting more foreign workers, the number of non-national legal residents doubled from some 1.1 million in 2009 to over 2 million in 2016. Including an estimated 210,000 undocumented migrants, foreigners accounted for around 4 percent of the total population of about 51 million. Public schools had been propagating the modern myth of Korean racial purity until 2007, when the United Nations urged the government to stop promoting such a notion. As the number of South Korean male–Southeast Asian female marriages and their South Korean–born children increased, the government began to educate the public about tolerance, diversity, and multiculturalism.

At the same time, South Korea's growing Chinese minority population became more diverse in origins and citizenship. As of 2010, this population numbered about 50,000, including an increasing number of people who had earlier left and then returned. The majority retained Taiwanese citizenship, although many had become naturalized South Korean citizens. Around the same time, new migration from China to South Korea increased. By 2009, almost 700,000 PRC nationals had moved to South Korea, mostly in pursuit of economic opportunities, and they constituted 55.1 percent of the some 1.1 million foreign nationals in residence at that time. Among them were over 488,000 Korean Chinese (70 percent of PRC citizens in South Korea and 40 percent of the total number of foreign nationals), and 208,761 were of other nationalities. Most of the new arrivals from China lived in Seoul and its vicinity. As of 2016, the number of Chinese migrants who were not South Korean nationals numbered 1,643,611, mostly PRC citizens.

Joining the Chinese were a growing number of refugees from other parts of the world. In 2013, Park Geun-hye's government enacted the Refugee Act, becoming the first Asian country to pass legislation admitting refugees with sufficient grounds for fear of persecution in their home countries due to their race, nationality, social group, religion, or political views to seek asylum. The South Korean government had begun to accept refugee applications in 1994, and by June 2018, more than 40,000 had applied for asylum. Still, only 2.5 percent had received asylum—not counting North Koreans. Among those admitted were 839 people who had fled the Yemeni Civil War (ongoing since 2014) and arrived in Jeju (Cheju) Province, a visa-free zone for tourists from most countries.

While South Korea was transitioning to a more multicultural society, a declining birth rate was among the factors that spurred it to address gender inequality more aggressively. In 2001, the Kim Dae-jung administration created the Ministry of Gender Equality (Ministry of Gender Equality and Family since 2005) and allocated a position quota for women. In 2004, Roh Moo-hyun's government began providing loans or subsidies for businesses to build childcare facilities, provide more than thirty days of childcare leave a year, allow full-time female employees with qualifying family responsibilities to work less than full time, and re-employ women returning from maternity leave. Such policies increased the accessibility of early childhood education and helped both parents to work if they so wished. However, the number of mothers regularly using these benefits still constituted a minority of qualifying women. Then in 2005, the national assembly revised the civil law by effectively repealing not only Article 809, which prohibited same surname–same ancestral seat marriage, but also the concept of family centered around a male household head. Thanks to these and other government measures, gender equality at workplaces and institutionalized support for working women with children have improved. More than ever before, South Korean women achieve high levels of education and actively participate in a wide variety of fields. The Me Too movement gained traction in South Korea when a female public prosecutor exposed sexual assault as rampant among officials (January 2018). Subsequently, the number of women bringing complaints against prominent figures to public attention has increased.

Nonetheless, South Korea still lagged behind other OECD nations as significant gender gaps in earnings, labor market participation, and representation in the government persisted. In 2017, the OECD, using the latest data available, reported that South Korea's gender gap was the highest among the member nations, as working women earned only 63 percent of what their male counterparts earned. Moreover, 56.2 percent of employed women had left their jobs due to family commitments, some giving up even mid-career or senior-level jobs. The still dominant attitude, particularly among the college-educated middle class, was that the husband is the primary source of economic support, whereas the wife manages the household, including its finances. The most critical responsibility of mothers is their children's education, ultimately geared toward admission into a prestigious university. Thus, college-educated women were tending to invest more time and capital in raising their children than mothers without a degree did. Even after the children reached adulthood, most mothers found it difficult to return to well-paid regular employment.

Meanwhile, the South Korean LGBT community's continuing struggle against discrimination won some notable victories. The Kim Dae-jung administration passed the First National Human Rights Commission Act, which introduced the term "sexual orientation" (2001). In the same year, Harisu (b. 1975) became South Korea's first transgender entertainer to gain public attention, after appearing in a successful commercial for cosmetics and subsequently branching out into other genres. The next year, Harisu became the second South Korean to change their sex legally, from male to female. The succeeding Roh Moo-hyun administration implemented a series of revised statutes to protect better gay rights. The first revision removed homophobic language from the Youth Protection Act (2005). Subsequently, the supreme court ruled in favor of recognizing transgender sex change (2006), and activists launched a movement to pass a comprehensive Anti-Discrimination Act, which would prohibit discrimination based on sexual orientation (2007). LGBT awareness attracted more public attention when a television series drama, *Life Is Beautiful* (*Insaeng ŭn arŭmdawŏ*), which aired for two months on Saturday and Sunday evenings, featured a sensitive portrayal of a loving, openly gay couple and scored high ratings (2010). And changing one's self-identified sex without gender reassignment surgery became legal under Park Geun-hye's government (2013).

The growing public awareness of the rights of LGBT individuals and of women, ethnic minorities, and refugees also elicited blatant expressions of bigotry in words and deeds. Not only did some online platforms become sites for refugee-bashing but also a powerful evangelical Protestant lobby and its conservative political allies fueled Islamophobia. As of 2013, refugees constituted 0.02 percent of the South Korean population, while the figure in Germany—one of the most popular destinations for refugees—was 0.24 percent. As of June 2018, 39 percent of South Koreans supported accepting Yemeni refugees, whereas 49 percent were opposed. Bowing to a growing public demand for stemming the tide, the Moon Jae-in administration announced that it had removed Yemen from the list of visa-exempt countries in that same month. While many evangelical Protestant groups remained active in attacking LGBT rights, even Moon, a Catholic and former human rights lawyer, stated that he opposed same-sex love during a presidential debate before winning the election. And open expressions of misogyny took an upturn as the Me Too movement gained strength. Due to opposition centered among evangelical Protestants, the national assembly has yet to pass the comprehensive Anti-Discrimination Act introduced in 2007.

In North Korea, the economic crisis and the food shortage have produced powerful demographic repercussions. With the peak of the crisis having passed, the total population has increased from about 23 million in 2001 to 24.2 million in 2009 to 25.5 million in 2017—an average annual increase of about 1 percent during the period. The TFR remained relatively stable, decreasing from 2.05 births in 2000–05 to 1.95 in 2017, while life expectancy rebounded, increasing from 68.1 years in 2000–05 to 71.0 in 2017. As of 2006, most marriages were taking place between people in the same rural cooperative or urban enterprise. Regardless, a nuclear family remained the norm—with a still widespread preference for sons over daughters as couples continued to expect sons to provide for their parents in old age. In 2002, 61 percent of the DPRK population resided in cities, thus making labor shortages in farming villages more acute in the aftermath of the massive flooding and famine of the 1990s. The population remained concentrated mostly in the northwestern plains, including P'yŏngyang, and along the eastern shoreline with such major cities as Wŏnsan. Food shortages also fueled widespread population movements, including many who even crossed the Sino–North Korean border, leaving and then coming back. Some never returned.

In the absence of any sustained, sizable influx of foreign migrants, the Chinese have constituted the only sizable ethnic minority in North Korea. As of 2008–09, roughly 4,000 to 10,000 were in the country, including 100 international students as of 2008. Most resided in P'yŏngyang or the areas near the Sino–North Korean border. In 2002, Yanbian University, in the Yanbian Korean Autonomous Prefecture of China, began to offer training programs for Chinese schools in North Korea. Some graduates of such schools attended universities in China, but after China supported the UN Security Council resolution of June 2009, which imposed further sanctions, North Korean surveillance and repression of Chinese residents increased; one such resident was charged with espionage. Many refrained from making trips out of the country in order to avoid scrutiny.

North Korea's economic crisis and food shortage offered both challenges and opportunities for women as well. Equality in the workplace remained elusive, and significant occupational segregation between the sexes persisted, as women were concentrated in low-skilled labor or unpopular work. Also, with the lingering, more traditional division of labor at home, women remained the leading performers of domestic tasks. At the same time, for many families, the end of the rationing system and the inability of many men to provide for their families expanded women's role in producing, procuring, and selling food and goods through an expanding network of local markets. As such entrepreneurism enhanced women's economic independence, those married to abusive or unfaithful husbands left them. Separation and divorce rates increased, although getting a divorce remained difficult due to expensive court fees and the court's general reluctance to accept lawsuits. Unsurprisingly, more women became reluctant to marry or have children. About 85 percent of North Korean refugees abroad were women.

Including women, the annual outflow of refugees had sharply increased at the beginning of the new millennium. South Korea's population of North Korean settlers shot up from 1,991 in 2001 to 20,400 in 2010 and 31,339 by the beginning of 2018. The total number of North Korean escapees in 2001 was 586, the highest figure up to that point, and the annual total peaked at 2,914 in 2009, followed by a steady decrease since 2011 from 2,706 to 1,047 in 2019. The percentage of escapees who were female surpassed 50 percent for the first time in 2002 and has increased further since then to about 71 percent as of December 2017. At the time, those in their twenties or thirties accounted for 57.5 percent of all North Koreans arriving in the south. Among the escapees, 70 percent were high school graduates, and 16.5 percent had at least two years of post-secondary education in terms of the highest level of education attained. Most had been either unemployed (47 percent) or wage laborers (38.5 percent) before leaving North Korea. Upon arriving in the south, many struggled to adjust. As of 2007, their crime rate (9.1 percent) was more than twice that of the South Korean average (4.3 percent). Conversely, 23 percent of the settlers became crime victims. South Korea was not the only destination: as of 2011, globally, 1,110 North Koreans had secured refugee status, and 1,027 were awaiting review in various countries. The highest number of North Koreans recognized as refugees resided in Britain, Canada, Germany, and the United States—with 158 living in the United States as of May 2012. Estimated hundreds of thousands maintain a tenuous existence in China and Southeast Asia, including 50,000 to 200,000 in China alone. North Koreans caught trying to escape have joined a sizable population of those who live in horrid conditions with even the most basic rights curtailed.

As the new millennium arrived, North Korea's violations of human rights were receiving much attention worldwide. The regime had come to maintain internment camps for political prisoners at six locations. By the 2010s, the six prison camps kept some 154,000 incarcerated, of formerly high and low social status alike, accounting for 0.85 percent of the country's population. As of 2017, prison camps dedicated to those accused of political crimes held an estimated 200,000 subjected to forced labor, physical abuse, and execution. The government has been sending political prisoners and their family members to these camps with a summary trial at most, and the detainees receive inhumanely low rations. Such atrocities as rape, torture, forced labor, lack of medical service, forced abortion, human biological experiments, and executions by cruel and unusual methods continue. Also, children have suffered from abuses rare elsewhere in the world. North Korea has acknowledged the possibility of mobilizing children as soldiers if required by circumstances.

In 2020, North Korea's isolation made the adverse impact of COVID-19 on the population even worse, including human rights abuses in the name of the fight against the pandemic. Strict controls on movement in and around the capital have increased the number of executions. Considering North Korea's socioeconomic ties to China before sealing off the border in January, outside experts dispute the government's continuing refusal to confirm any cases. More than likely, as has been true for citizens of other countries, North Koreans have died of the virus, especially since the country's health care system is woefully inadequate. In November, Kim imposed lockdowns in P'yŏngyang and ordered the execution of at least two violators, while South Korea has managed to avoid lockdowns.

CONTEMPORARY CULTURE

Entering the new millennium, South Korea has continued to construct new venues for celebrating its cultural heritage. Especially noteworthy was the opening of the National Museum of Korea at its new location in Yongsan, Seoul (October 2005). Seven years later, the National Museum of Korean Contemporary History opened (December 2012). Given the subjects covered by the latter, its government-appointed directors and its exhibits have reflected the viewpoints of the president in office toward such issues as the assessment of the place of Syngman Rhee and Park Chung-hee in history.

Far from being contained within museums and archives, the issue of pro-Japanese collaboration during the colonial years generated a storm. Introduced by the ruling liberal Uri Party, the Special Law on Investigation of Pro-Japanese Collaboration entailed setting the historical record straight by identifying many prominent figures in modern Korean history as pro-Japanese collaborators, and the national assembly passed this legislation (March 2004). The law created the Committee on Investigation of Pro-Japanese Collaboration, which moved forward with investigations based on historians' research. Subsequently, from December 2006 to November 2009, the committee released three lists of those it deemed guilty of anti-national, pro-Japanese actions between 1904 and 1945, ultimately 1,006 individuals in total. While the committee made progress with its task, the Uri Party and the conservative GNP busily investigated the colonial-era ancestors of each other's prominent members and sensationalized various findings through the media. Such an exposé was highly divisive in a nation where most knew relatively little about their ancestors' lives and careers before 1945—yet the education system and the dominant public discourse had been narrating colonial Korean history with a binary of collaboration versus resistance.

While the acrimony over the past raged on, South Korea continued to invest in the future through science and technology. The country emerged as a leading producer of automobiles, semiconductors, mobile phones, and higher-end appliances for consumers throughout the world. Continuing investment in research has not only allowed South Korea to assemble imported American military aircraft parts for its own use but also to design and produce the country's own light aircraft and supersonic trainer combat aircraft. In ICT and biotechnology, South Korea joined the ranks of the global leaders.

The advances in science and technology have also highlighted weak areas and raised ethical concerns. Becoming one of the most wired nations globally, South Korea has put out successful products in many sectors of high-tech hardware manufacturing, with competition growing fierce between Samsung and Apple. All the same, software development remains a conspicuous area of relative stagnation, and in this field, the country continues to rely on products from such ubiquitous American giants as Microsoft. More fundamentally, the relative neglect of the government and the corporate sectors in supporting academic research in basic science during the previous decades of rapid economic growth was such that well into the new millennium, South Korea still lags behind the West and Japan. At the same time, such emerging ethical issues as cloning in the field of genetic engineering captured the public's attention. Also, far from futuristic or theoretical in concern are the consequences of the rise of the internet as the alternative to print and broadcast media and the primary information source. The availability of an increasingly broad spectrum of media outlets and other information content providers online has made South Koreans more likely to focus on particular content and viewpoints. Moreover, the anonymity felt by users of the growing plethora of online discussion fora and displayed in their comment postings has facilitated not only the disappearance of even a modicum of decorum but also the spread of misinformation, deliberate or otherwise.

At the same time, the internet has played a significant role in disseminating South Korea's popular culture globally. This" Korean Wave" has centered around movies, dramas, and pop music (K-pop). By the beginning of the new millennium, South Korean popular culture had not only grown in depth and breadth but was also securing sizable fan bases in the rest of East Asia, starting with Japan and followed by Southeast Asia, the Middle East, Latin America, Europe, and North America. In Japan, first, South Korean movies became box office hits. In 2003, the multipart television drama *Winter Sonata* captured the hearts of many, especially middle-aged women, before the nation as a whole embraced the Korean Wave. Among various genres, the international fan base of K-pop, in particular, has grown rapidly. In December 2012, a mega-hit by Psy (b. 1977), "Gangnam Style," became the first YouTube video to reach one billion views. From the global perspective, Psy was a one-hit-wonder, but various "girl bands" and, somewhat later, such "boy bands" as BTS (active since 2013) have won over a growing number of fans throughout the world. In November 2020, the BTS single "Life Goes On" debuted at the top of the Billboard Hot 100 chart—the band's third consecutive chart-topper in three months (matching the feat by The Beatles in 1964), and the first song mostly in Korean to debut in the top spot. The achievement made BTS the first group in chart history with two number one Hot 100 debuts. Including K-pop, which has driven up enrollment in

Korean language classes worldwide, the Korean Wave has not only generated significant income but has also enhanced the nation's soft power—for long the monopoly of the West and Japan in the modern era. Earlier, in February 2019, the black comedy thriller *Parasite*, a film directed by Bong Joon-ho (Pong Chunho; b. 1969), won four Academy Awards, becoming the first non–English language film in Academy Awards history to win Best Picture.

In the meantime, South Korea's attitudes toward more spiritual realms have continued to evolve in the first two decades of the twenty-first century. First of all, the population segment not professing a religion has increased from 46 percent in 2005 to 56 percent in 2015, a new high for the period since 1985 (when the number was 57 percent). A 2012 Gallup International poll reported that the country had the fifth largest population of atheists globally, including the 15 percent of the people who were "convinced atheists." In 2005, the two largest religious groups, Christians and Buddhists, accounted for 28 percent (20 percent Protestants and 8 percent Catholics) and 23 percent of the population, respectively, but the figures had changed to 31 percent Christians (18 percent Protestants and 13 percent Catholics) and 16 percent Buddhists as of 2020. Secondly, religious pluralism within a family or a household, which used to be the norm, has become less common. Those wherein members uniformly practice Protestantism, typically in a more evangelical form, have increased. Compared to others, such South Koreans tended to expect the same religion in their marriage partners. Thirdly, while Catholics and Buddhists remain mutually respectful toward each other's beliefs, a growing rift between Buddhists and many evangelical Protestants has assumed a political dimension. The latter tend to be conservative apologists for authoritarian leaders of the past.

In North Korea, the religious sphere remains conspicuous for the state's self-conscious effort to maintain a semblance of cultural diversity. As of 2005, the four largest religious groups reportedly accounted for about 36 percent of the population: namely, shamanism (16 percent), Chondoism (13.5 percent), Buddhism (4.5 percent), and Christianity (1.7 percent). As the largest organized religion, as of 2007, Chondoism was maintaining about 800 churches. The rest of the registered religious edifices in the country included 60 Buddhist monasteries, not so much venues for worship as historical sites, and 5 Christian churches: 3 Protestant, one Catholic, and one Russian Orthodox, all in P'yŏngyang. Among worshippers, Catholics numbered between 800 and 3,000. Including foreign diplomats, journalists, and tourists, 70 to 80 attended Sunday worship, and about 200 gathered on significant feast days at

Changch'ung Church. Since North Korea has no ordained priest recognized by the Vatican, even an ordinary Sunday worship is a lay fellowship rather than a mass. However, a steady stream of baptisms has taken place—since Christian tradition does not dictate that only the clergy can perform the ritual. In 2014 at Mount Kŭmgang, North Korea hosted, as an inter-Korean meeting, the Korea Conference of Religions for Peace. The government's continuing interest in demonstrating religious freedom has even produced some unintended consequences: a considerable number of Protestant church personnel, such as ministry staff and choir members appointed and managed by the state, reportedly have become devout Christians.

The degree to which most North Koreans find solace in organized religion is uncertain, but far more turn to worldly enjoyments, increasingly in the form of South Korean cultural products, even to the extent of risking their lives. Along with South Korean and Japanese electronics, such items as South Korean cosmetics for women enjoy considerable popularity and are sold in black markets of one form or another. Enjoying an even greater demand are recordings of South Korean movies, soap operas, and music, including K-pop. Considering them decadent materials of capitalism, officials from time to time crack down on the consumers. Citizens found guilty face prison, labor camp, or death sentences. In March 2018, the court sentenced six teenagers for dancing to about fifty K-pop songs and distributing them to others on a flash drive. Four were found guilty of "anti-national" conspiracy and received a year of labor, and the sentences for the other two are unknown.

Besides popular culture that is autonomous rather than state produced, fashion consciousness is stronger than ever before in daily life in both Koreas. South Korea has begun to produce unique styles, winning recognition globally for expressiveness and individualism. Also, such factors as individuals' generation, income, and education and also the media (including the internet) have contributed to the greater diversity of fashion. All the same, a social bandwagon effect persists, as South Koreans tend to follow the latest trends as publicized by the mainstream media. Thus any notion of a classic fashion is relatively weak. Albeit to a lesser extent, such tendencies have also become pronounced among North Korea's elites. Simultaneously, the everyday style of more ordinary North Koreans donning Western dress of any kind remains a more conservative, if not older, version of South Korea's styles.

Culinary culture in South Korea too has become more variegated in the past two decades. The domestic market's gradual opening to imported agricultural produce and other food types has affected the daily diet. While posing a massive challenge to farming households' continuing struggle to maintain their competitiveness vis-à-vis imports, the availability of a greater variety of imports has enriched South Korea's culinary culture. Among other developments, the 2002 South Korea–Chile FTA quickly made wine consumption more affordable and popular. The price of a commonly sold 750-milliliter bottle of table wine dropped from tens of thousands of won to twenty thousand won or less, and wine bars began to appear in neighborhoods throughout the country. All the same, although the initial fear of imported American beef subsided fast, the public has developed a growing appreciation for the *hanu* ("Korean cow"), a breed of small cattle native to Korea and formerly used as draft animals but now raised mainly for meat. As prices per kilogram remain significantly higher for beef than for pork, chicken, or fish, a wine and steak dinner remains out of reach for most. Still, such other types of food as pasta, wieners, pho, pad thai, and Indian curry (as distinct from the Korean-style curry that had been popular for decades) have become more widely available through the newer restaurants.

As of December 2020, the daily diet in North Korea is deteriorating, with the government's strict COVID-19 containing measures taking a further toll on an economy already crippled by sanctions. Lockdowns and reduced trade with China have exacerbated the food shortage. Large quantities of vegetables that were expected to be available after Ch'usŏk did not arrive, including napa cabbage. In November, when many Korean families traditionally prepare *kimchi* for the winter months (though far less do so in South Korea now, as most no longer live in homes with yards), the low supply of cabbage was such that its price had risen by at least 25 percent compared to 2019. Anticipating worsening food shortages, those well off reportedly have been hoarding food. Even before COVID, the overall diet was already inadequate for more than 40 percent of the population, and the people do not see any light at the end of this tunnel. The current stretch of food shortages may turn out to be as disastrous as the famine in the 1990s, if not worse.

FURTHER READINGS

This is a selective listing of books in English for general readers. Excluded are academic monographs for specialists and primary sources that are mainly literary, philosophical, or religious in scope. For a comprehensive database of English-language publications in Korean history, see *Korean History: A Bibliography* (http://www.hawaii.edu/korea/biblio/BiblioOpen.html).

PRIMARY SOURCES

Allen, Horace N. *Information for the Benefit of American Residents in Korea*. Hansŏng: U.S. Legation and Consulate General, 1899.

Best, Jonathan W., trans. *A History of the Early Korean Kingdom of Paekche: Together with an annotated translation of the Paekche Annals of the Samguk sagi*. Cambridge, MA: Harvard University Asia Center, 2006.

Bishop, Isabella Bird. *Korea and Her Neighbours: A Narrative of Travel, with an Account of the Recent Vicissitudes and Present Position of the Country*. New York: Revell, 1897.

Brother Anthony, ed. *Discovering Korea at the Start of the Twentieth Century*. Seongnam: Academy of Korean Studies Press, 2011.

——— of Taizé and Robert D. Neff, eds. *Brief Encounters: Early Reports of Korea by Westerners*. Irvine: Seoul Selection, 2016.

Cha, Hacksun, Yoonjeong Shim, Leif Olsen, Edward Park, and Timothy Atkinson, trans. *The Veritable Records of King Sejong*. Vol. 1, *1418 (Month 8)–1419 (Month 2)*. Gwacheon: National Institute of Korean History, 2016.

Ch'oe, Yŏng-ho, Peter H. Lee, and Wm. Theodore de Bary, eds. *Sources of Korean Tradition*. Vol. 2, *From the Sixteenth to the Twentieth Centuries*. New York: Columbia University Press, 2000.

Choi, Byonghyon, trans. *The Book of Corrections: Reflections on the National Crisis during the Japanese Invasion of Korea, 1592–1598*. Berkeley: Institute of East Asian Studies, University of California, Berkeley, 2002.

———, trans. *The Annals of King T'aejo: Founder of Korea's Chosŏn Dynasty*. Cambridge, MA: Harvard University Press, 2014.

————, Seung B. Kye, and Timothy V. Atkinson, trans. *A Korean Scholar's Rude Awakening in Qing China: Pak Chega's Discourse on Northern Learning.* Honolulu: University of Hawai'i Press, 2019.

Eun Ki-Soo, Moon Hyuna, and Minja Kim Choe, eds. *Modern Korean Family: A Sourcebook.* Seongnam: Academy of Korean Studies Press, 2015.

Finch, Michael, trans. *Min Yŏnghwan: The Selected Writings of a Late Chosŏn Diplomat.* Berkeley: Institute of East Asian Studies, University of California, Berkeley, 2008.

Ha Tae-hung, trans. *Nanjung Ilgi: War Diary of Admiral Yi Sun-sin.* Seoul: Yonsei University Press, 1977.

————, trans. *Imjin changch'o: Admiral Yi Sun-sin's Memorials to Court.* Edited by Lee Chong-young. Seoul: Yonsei University Press, 1981.

———— and Grafton K. Mintz, trans. *Samguk Yusa: Legends and History of the Three Kingdoms of Ancient Korea.* Seoul: Yonsei University Press, 1986.

Haboush, JaHyun Kim, ed. *Epistolary Korea: Letters in the Communicative Space of the Chosŏn, 1392–1910.* New York: Columbia University Press, 2009.

————, trans. *The Memoirs of Lady Hyegyŏng: The Autobiographical Writings of a Crown Princess of Eighteenth-Century Korea.* Berkeley: University of California Press, 2013.

————, and Kenneth R. Robinson, trans. *A Korean War Captive in Japan, 1597–1600: The Writings of Kang Hang.* New York: Columbia University Press, 2013.

Han, Jieun, and Franklin Rausch, trans. *An Chunggŭn: His Life and Thought in His Own Words,* Leiden: Brill, 2020.

Hanscom, Christopher P., Walter K. Lew, and Youngju Ryu, eds. *Imperatives of Culture: Selected Essays on Korean History, Literature, and Society from the Japanese Colonial Era.* Honolulu: University of Hawai'i Press, 2013.

Hulbert, Homer B. *The Passing of Korea.* New York: Doubleday, Page & Company, 1906.

Hwang, Yun Mi, and Stephen Epstein, eds. *The Korean Wave: A Sourcebook.* Seongnam: Academy of Korean Studies Press, 2016.

Jaisohn, Philip. *My Days in Korea and Other Essays.* Edited by Sun-pyo Hong. Seoul: Institute for Modern Korean Studies, Yonsei University, 1999.

Kallander, George, trans. *The Diary of 1636: The Second Manchu Invasion of Korea.* By Na Man'gap. New York: Columbia University Press, 2020.

Kim Keong-il, Choi Hyaeweol, and Shin Kyung-ah, eds. *Korean Women: A Sourcebook.* Seongnam: Academy of Korean Studies Press, 2017.

Kim, Sun Joo, and Jungwon Kim, trans. *Wrongful Deaths: Selected Inquest Records from Nineteenth-Century Korea.* Seattle: University of Washington Press, 2014.

Lee, Jongsoo, trans. *Paekpŏm ilchi: The Autobiography of Kim Ku.* Lanham: University Press of America, 2000.

Lee, Namhee, and Kim Won, eds. *The South Korean Democratization Movement: A Sourcebook.* Seongnam: Academy of Korean Studies Press, 2016.

Lee, Peter H., trans. *Lives of Eminent Korean Monks: The Haedong kosŭng chŏn.* Cambridge, MA: Harvard University Press, 1969.

———, and Wm. Theodore de Bary, eds. *Sources of Korean Tradition.* Vol. 1, *From Early Times through the Sixteenth Century.* New York: Columbia University Press, 1997.

McKenzie, F. A. *The Colonial Policy of Japan in Korea.* London: Central Asian Society, 1906.

———. *Korea's Fight for Freedom.* New York: Fleming H. Revell, 1920.

Neff, Robert, ed. *Letters from Joseon: 19th-Century Korea through the Eyes of an American Ambassador's Wife.* Irvine: Seoul Selection, 2012.

Robinson, David M., trans. *Seeking Order in a Tumultuous Age: The Writings of Chŏng Tojŏn, a Korean Neo-Confucian.* Honolulu: University of Hawai'i Press, 2016.

Shultz, Edward J., and Hugh H. W. Kang, eds. *The Koguryŏ Annals of the Samguk Sagi.* By Kim Pusik. Second edition. Translated by Kenneth H. J. Gardiner, Daniel C. Kane, Hugh H. W. Kang, and Edward J. Shultz. Seongnam: Academy of Korean Studies Press, 2012.

———, trans. *The Silla Annals of the Samguk Sagi.* By Kim Pusik. Seongnam: Academy of Korean Studies Press, 2012.

———, trans. *Koryŏsa chŏryo II: Essentials of Koryŏ History.* Seoul: Jimoondang Publishing Company, 2014.

Suh, Dae-Sook, Wan Bom Lee, and Seung Hyun Lee, eds. *North Korean Modern History: A Sourcebook.* 2 vols. Seongnam: Academy of Korean Studies Press, 2018.

Underwood, Horace G. *The Call of Korea: Political, Social, Religious.* New York: Fleming H. Revell, 1908.

Underwood, L. H. *Fifteen Years among the Top-Knots: or, Life in Korea.* Boston: American Tract Society, 1904.

Vermeersch, Sem, trans. *A Chinese Traveler in Medieval Korea: Xu Jing's Illustrated Account of the Xuanhe Embassy to Koryŏ.* Honolulu: University of Hawai'i Press, 2016.

———, trans. *Koryŏsa chŏryo Ia: Essentials of Koryŏ History.* Seoul: Yonsei University Press, 2021.

Yoon, In-Jin, and Young-Hun Jeong, eds. *The Korean Diaspora: A Sourcebook.* Seongnam: Academy of Korean Studies Press, 2017.

Yoon, Inshil Choe, trans. *A Place to Live: A New Translation of Yi Chung-hwan's T'aengniji, the Korean Classic for Choosing Settlements.* Honolulu: University of Hawai'i Press, 2018.

SECONDARY SOURCES

Baker, Don. *Korean Spirituality.* Honolulu: University of Hawai'i Press, 2008.

Center for International Affairs. *Cultural Landscapes of Korea.* Seongnam: Academy of Korean Studies Press, 2010.

Chung, Edward Y. J. *Korean Confucianism: Tradition and Modernity.* Seongnam: Academy of Korean Studies Press, 2015.

Deuchler, Martina. *Pictorial Memoir: Korea Fifty Years Ago.* Seoul: Seoul Selection, 2020.

Hwang, Kyung Moon. *Past Forward: Essays in Korean History.* London: Anthem Press, 2019.

Jeon BongHee. *A Cultural History of the Korean House.* Seongnam: Academy of Korean Studies, 2016.

Jeon Sang-woon. *A History of Korean Science and Technology.* Translated by Robert Carrubba and Lee Sung Kyu. Singapore: National University of Singapore Press, 2011.

Jungmann, Burglind. *Pathways to Korean Culture: Paintings of the Joseon Dynasty, 1392–1910.* London: Reaktion Books, 2014.

Kawashima, Fujiya. *What Is Yangban? A Legacy for Modern Korea.* Seoul: Institute for Modern Korean Studies, Yonsei University, 2002.

Kim, Kyung Hyun. *Hegemonic Mimicry: Korean Popular Culture of the Twenty-First Century.* Durham: Duke University Press, 2021.

Kwon Sangcheol, Kim Jonghyuk, Lee Eui-Han, and Jung Chi-Young. *Geography of Korea.* Seongnam: Academy of Korean Studies, 2016.

Lee, Peter H., ed. *A History of Korean Literature.* Cambridge: Cambridge University Press, 2009.

The National Trust of Korea. *Korean Villages and Their Cultures.* Seongnam: Academy of Korean Studies Press, 2013.

Noh Taedon. *Korea's Ancient Koguryŏ Kingdom: A Socio-Political History.* Translated by John Huston. Leiden: Global Oriental, 2014.

Northeast Asian History Foundation. *A New History of Parhae.* Translated by John Duncan. Leiden: Global Oriental, 2012.

The Organization of Korean Historians. *Everyday Life in Joseon-Era Korea: Economy and Society.* Edited by Michael D. Shin. Leiden: Brill, 2014.

Palais, James B. *Views on Korean Social History.* Seoul: Institute for Modern Korean Studies, Yonsei University, 1998.

Park, Moonho. *Seoul.* Seongnam: Academy of Korean Studies Press, 2015.

Park, Yongjin. *Modern Korean Economy, 1948–2008.* Translated by Seongbak (Jamie) Jin. Seongnam: Academy of Korean Studies Press, 2018.

Peterson, Mark. *Korea's Religious Places.* Seongnam: Academy of Korean Studies Press, 2016.

Pettid, Michael J. *Korean Cuisine: An Illustrated History.* London: Reaktion Books, 2008.

Pratt, Keith, and James Hoare. *Korea: A Historical and Cultural Dictionary.* London: Routledge, 1999.

Reich, David. *Who We Are and How We Got Here: Ancient DNA and the New Science of the Human Past.* Oxford: Oxford University Press, 2018.

Shin, Michael D., ed. *Korean History through Maps: From Prehistory to the Twenty-First Century.* Cambridge: Cambridge University Press, 2014.

Totman, Conrad. *Pre-Industrial Korea and Japan in Environmental Perspective.* Brill: Leiden, 2004.

INDEX

Puyŏ, 26; in Silla, 77–78; in stupas, 82; in Three Kingdoms, 37–38, 56, 57; tomb mural paintings, 52, 56, 57, 58; Tomb of the General, 41 (fig.)
Bush, George W., 342, 343–344
Business leaders: economic nationalism, 252; under Japanese occupation, 252
Butchers, discrimination against, 255

Calendars: Chinese, 77, 109, 130, 188; Gregorian, 223; Shoushi, 130
Calligraphy, 54, 77, 110, 131, 166, 212
Capital Gazette (Hwangsŏng sinmun), 238
Cartography, *see* Maps
Censorate, 94, 135, 139, 142. *See also* Remonstrance
Ceramics: blue-and-white, 212–213; celadon porcelain, 109–110, 111 (fig.), 131; in Parhae, 79–80; *punch'ŏng*, 165–166; white porcelain, 165–166, 212. *See also* Pottery
Chaebŏl, *see* Conglomerates
Ch'ae Yongsin, 194 (fig.), 199 (fig.)
Chang Chiyŏn, 238
Chang Chiyŏng, 261
Chang Inhwan, 227
Ch'ang, King, 119
Chang Myon (Chang Myŏn), 277, 292, 300
Chang Pogo, 65, 71, 74
Chang Song-thaek (Chang Sŏngt'aek), 351
Chang Sŭngŏp, 239
Chang Yŏngsil, 164
Changmadang, see *Jangmadang*
Changsu, King, 41, 57
Ch'anyang Association, 232
Chejudo, 14, 29, 139, 188, 191. *See also* T'amna
Chejudo Uprising, 271, 272

Cheju language, 14, 15
Chi Sŏgyŏng, 237
Chiang Kai-shek, 249, 250, 272
Chijŭng, King, 43–44
Children: childcare, 307, 369; health care, 208. *See also* Education; Families
Ch'imnyu, King, 32
Chin, 19, 26, 27 (map), 28. *See also* Samhan
China: agriculture, 121; anti-Japanese resistance groups, 248–249; cultural influence, 1–2; era names, 41; Five Dynasties, 88; foods, 112; Han dynasty, 24, 25–26, 28; high culture, 37; historiography, 2–3; Japanese invasion (1937), 247, 248–249; Jin dynasty (265–420), 26, 110; Northern and Southern Dynasties, 41, 50, 57; Qin dynasty, 25; Red Turbans, 118; Sui dynasty, 47–48; trade, 50–51, 71; Warring States, 25; Wei dynasty, 30; Yuan dynasty, 116, 118, 119, 120, 123, 128, 130–131, 132; Zhou dynasty, 24, 161. *See also* Confucianism; Daoism; Ming China; People's Republic of China; Qing China; Song China; Tang China
China-Korea Treaty of 1882, 229
Chindan Academic Society, 262
Chinese Civil War, 272, 278, 284
Chinese Koreans, 235, 284, 306, 331, 368
Chinese Nationalist Party, 248–249, 272, 284
Chinggis Khan, 115, 116
Chingusai (Ch'in'gu sai), 333
Chinhan, 28–30, 39. See also Samhan; Saro; Silla
Chinhŭng, King, 45, 53, 54, 58
Chinsŏng, Queen, 68, 75

Pyŏnhan, 28, 29, 31, 39. *See also* Kaya confederacy; Samhan

Qing China: calendar, 188; culture, 175; dynasty, 174; economic interests in Korea, 234–235; emigration to Korea, 234; Evidential Learning, 186; expansion, 175; First Sino-Japanese War, 217, 222, 223, 229, 241; Jesuit missionaries, 188, 208; Korea as tributary state, 220–221; merchants, 241; Northern Learning and, 205, 206; relations with Chosŏn, 175; trade, 180; treaties with Korea, 229; treaties with Western powers, 218
Qingshanli (Ko. Ch'ŏngsan-ri), Battle of, 247

Radio, 260, 287, 309
Railroads: construction, 229, 230, 235–236; high-speed trains, 359–361; in Manchuria, 226; between South and North Korea, 323, 343, 346, 350, 354, 361
Record of Chŏng Kam (Chŏng Kam rok), 202
Red Cross, 295, 296
Red Turbans, 118
Refugees: in Korean War, 281, 282; from North Korea, 372–373; in South Korea, 368–369, 370
Religions: Chondoism (Ch'ŏndogyo), 238, 239, 261, 287, 288, 337, 376; Daejongism (Taejonggyo), 239, 260, 261; Daoism, 56, 108, 163, 185, 186; early, 9–10, 22–23, 24, 34, 35; festivals, 108; under Japanese occupation, 260, 261–262, 264; Maitreya worship, 202; in North Korea, 287, 288, 310, 337, 376–377; popular beliefs in prophecies, 201–202; ritual

artifacts, 22; Shinto, 38, 264, 287; in South Korea, 287, 309, 311, 334–335, 376; Tonghak, 202–203, 221–222, 231, 232, 238, 239. *See also* Buddhism; Christianity; Shamanism
Remonstrance, 94, 138, 139, 143, 144, 170, 174, 195. *See also* Censorate
Republic of China, 249, 284. *See also* Taiwan
Republic of Korea, *see* South Korea
Republic of Korea Army, 294
Restaurants: Chinese, 241; North Korean, 326, 339; in South Korea, 313
Reunification movement, 292, 308, 323, 335. *See also* Inter-Korean dialogue; Korean unification flag
Rhee, Syngman (Yi Sŭngman), 244, 268, 269, 271, 275–278
Rhee regime: April 19 Revolution, 268, 277–278, 300, 308; autocratic policies, 275–277, 287, 309; downfall, 278; economy, 272, 279–280; education policies, 282; housing construction, 289–290; land reform, 272, 279; laws, 272; martial law, 275; political parties, 275, 277. *See also* Korean War
Ricci, Matteo, 208
Rice: consumption, 266, 313, 338; exports, 228, 229, 251, 252, 253; high-yield variety, 302; imports, 329; self-sufficiency of South Korea, 302, 304. *See also* Agriculture; Foods
Righteous armies (*ŭibyŏng*), 171, 173–174, 223, 226, 231–232, 233–234
Righteous Government, 247
Rites Controversy, 174, 185
Rock carvings, 22
Roh Moo-hyun (No Muhyŏn): impeachment, 345–346; North Korea